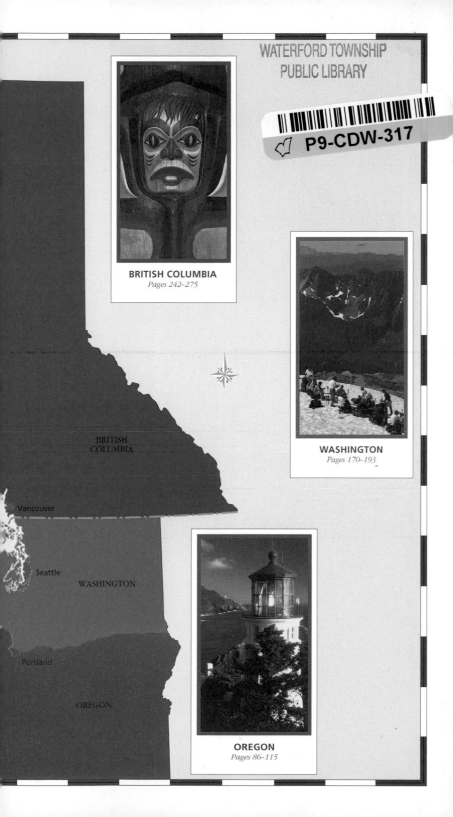

BRITISH COLUMBIA
Pages 242–275

WASHINGTON
Pages 170–193

OREGON
Pages 86–115

BRITISH
COLUMBIA

Vancouver

Seattle

WASHINGTON

Portland

OREGON

EYEWITNESS TRAVEL

PACIFIC
NORTHWEST

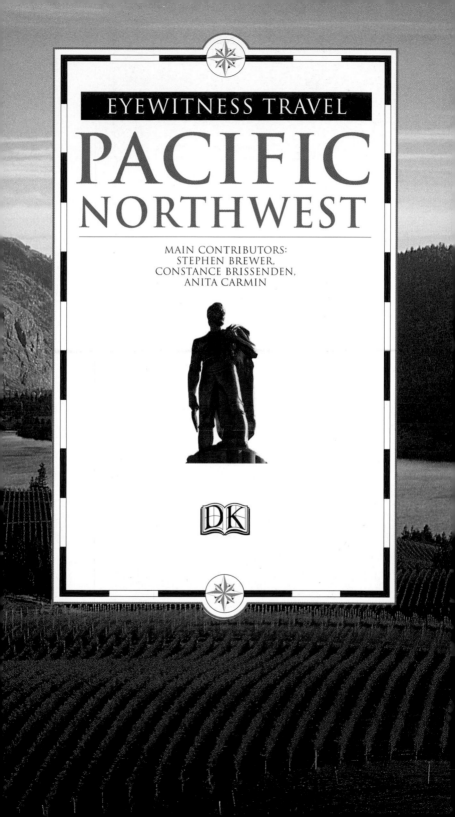

EYEWITNESS TRAVEL

PACIFIC
NORTHWEST

MAIN CONTRIBUTORS:
STEPHEN BREWER,
CONSTANCE BRISSENDEN,
ANITA CARMIN

LONDON, NEW YORK, MELBOURNE, MUNICH AND DELHI
www.dk.com

PRODUCED BY International Book Productions Inc.,
Toronto, Ontario, Canada

PROJECT EDITOR Barbara Hopkinson
ART EDITORS James David Ellis, Barbara Hopkinson
EDITORS Judy Phillips, Sheila Hall, Debbie Koenig, Tara Tovell
DTP DESIGNERS Dietmar Kokemohr, Nicola Lyon
PICTURE RESEARCH AND PERMISSIONS Diana Bahr

MAIN CONTRIBUTORS
Stephen Brewer, Constance Brissenden, Anita Carmin

PHOTOGRAPHERS
Bruce Forster, Gunter Marx, Scott Pitts

ILLUSTRATOR
William Band

PRODUCTION CONTROLLER
Shane Higgins

Printed in China by L Rex Printing Co Ltd

First American Edition, 2003
13 14 15 10 9 8 7 6 5 4 3 2

Published in the United States by DK Publishing, 345 Hudson Street
New York, New York, 10014

Reprinted with revisions 2006, 2008, 2010, 2012

Copyright 2003, 2012 © Dorling Kindersley Limited, London
A Penguin Company

A CATALOG RECORD FOR THIS BOOK IS AVAILABLE
FROM THE LIBRARY OF CONGRESS.

ISSN 1542-1554
ISBN 978-0-7566-8577-5

Front cover main image: Mount Rainier National Park, Washington

MIX
Paper from
responsible sources
FSC
www.fsc.org   FSC™ C018179

**The information in this
DK Eyewitness Travel Guide is checked regularly.**
Every effort has been made to ensure that this book is as up-to-date
as possible at the time of going to press. Some details, however, such
as telephone numbers, opening hours, prices, gallery
hanging arrangements and travel information are liable to change.
The publishers cannot accept responsibility for any consequences
arising from the use of this book, nor for any material on third party
websites, and cannot guarantee that any website address in this book
will be a suitable source of travel information. We value the views
and suggestions of our readers very highly. Please write to: Publisher,
DK Eyewitness Travel Guides, Dorling Kindersley, 80 Strand,
London WC2R 0RL, UK, or email: travelguides@dk.com.

◁ **Beautiful vineyards in the Okanagan Valley, British Columbia**

Windsurfers and kayaks, Vancouver

CONTENTS

INTRODUCING THE PACIFIC NORTHWEST

**Emmons Glacier, Mount Rainier
National Park, Washington**

Freshly caught crab

Sea kayaks at Snug Harbor,
San Juan Island, Washington

Guitar from the collection at the
EMP Museum, Seattle

Illustrated view of
the Seattle Center

Victorian home in Portland's
neighborhood of Nob Hill

HOW TO USE THIS GUIDE

This guide helps you to get the most from your visit to the Pacific Northwest. It provides detailed information and expert recommendations. Introducing the Pacific Northwest maps the region and sets it in its historical and cultural context. Features cover topics from wildlife to geology. The three area sections, as well as the three city sections, describe important sights, using maps, photographs, and illustrations. Restaurant and hotel listings can be found in *Travelers' Needs*. The *Survival Guide* offers tips on everything from public transport to using the telephone system.

PORTLAND, SEATTLE, AND VANCOUVER

The center of each of these cities is divided into several sightseeing areas, each with its own chapter. A last chapter, *Farther Afield*, describes sights beyond the central areas. All sights are numbered and plotted on the chapter's area map. Information on each sight is presented in numerical order, making it easy to locate within the chapter.

Sights at a Glance lists the chapter's sights by category, such as Museums and Galleries; Historic Buildings and Churches; Parks and Squares; Gardens and Viewpoints; and Shops.

2 **Street-by-Street map**
This gives a bird's-eye view of the heart of each sightseeing area.

A star indicates a sight that no visitor should miss.

All pages about Portland have orange thumb tabs. Seattle's are purple, and Vancouver's are green.

A locator map shows where you are in relation to other areas of the city center.

1 **Area map**
For easy reference, sights are numbered and located on a map. City center sights are also marked on Street Finders: Portland (pp80–85); Seattle (pp164–9); Vancouver (pp236–41).

A suggested route for a walk is shown in red.

3 **Detailed information**
The sights in the three main cities are described individually. The address, telephone number, opening hours, and information on admission charge, tours, wheelchair access, and public transport are provided. The key to the symbols is on the back flap.

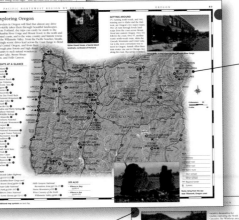

1 Introduction
The landscape, history, and character of each state or province is outlined here, showing how the area has developed over the centuries and what it has to offer to the visitor today.

PACIFIC NORTHWEST AREA BY AREA
In this book, the Pacific Northwest has been divided into the two states and one province, each of which has its own chapter. Portland, Seattle, and Vancouver are dealt with in separate chapters. Interesting sights to visit are numbered on a regional map.

2 Regional map
This shows the road network and gives an illustrated overview of the region. Interesting places to visit are numbered, and there are also useful tips on getting to, and around, the region by car and public transport.

Each area of the Pacific Northwest can be quickly identified by its color coding, shown on the inside front flap.

3 Detailed information
Noteworthy towns, cities, and other places to visit are described individually. They are listed in order, following the numbering on the regional map. Within each sight there is detailed information on interesting buildings and other attractions.

A visitors' checklist provides all the practical information needed to plan your visit.

4 Top sights
These are given two or more pages. The most interesting town or city centers are shown with sights picked out and described; parks have maps showing facilities, major exhibits, and the main roads and trails.

INTRODUCING THE PACIFIC NORTHWEST

DISCOVERING THE PACIFIC NORTHWEST

The Pacific Northwest may be only a small section of the North American continent, but it contains an astonishing diversity of natural and man-made attractions. Cosmopolitan cities, rugged coastline, well-preserved wilderness, and an excellent tourism infrastructure combine

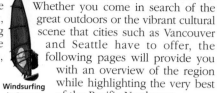

Windsurfing in Oregon

to create a fantastic travel destination. Whether you come in search of the great outdoors or the vibrant cultural scene that cities such as Vancouver and Seattle have to offer, the following pages will provide you with an overview of the region while highlighting the very best of the Pacific Northwest.

An elephant with her newly born calf at Washington Park

PORTLAND

- **Walkable historic precinct**
- **Endearing streetcars**
- **Washington Park**

The well-planned metropolis of Portland blends historic attractions and plentiful green space. The original namesake port is known as **Old Town** *(see pp51–5)*, where the influence of early Asian residents can be seen at the **Chinese Garden** *(see p54)*, and the city's nautical links can be explored at the **Oregon Maritime Center and Museum** *(see p54)*. Old Town is busiest on weekends, when the **Portland Saturday Market** *(see p53)* fills with visitors seeking local handicrafts. **Streetcars** *(see p63)* link the Old Town to **Downtown** *(see pp57–65)* where the **Portland Art Museum** *(see p62)* and popular gathering spot of **Pioneer Courthouse Square** *(see p60)* are hidden

amid the highrises. Portland's parks include the tiny **Mill Ends** *(see p65)* and sprawling **Washington Park** *(see pp70–73)*, home to a zoo and one of the country's largest rose test gardens.

OREGON

- **Windsurfing capital of the world**
- **Unspoilt coastline**
- **Intriguing Crater Lake**

Leaving Portland behind, Oregon's natural wonders quickly become apparent. **Columbia River Gorge** *(see pp90–91)* boasts waterfalls, orchards, and quaint towns, but for outdoor enthusiasts the focus is on **Hood River**, windsurfing capital of the world. The Oregon coastline offers a string of inviting beach towns, such as **Cannon Beach** *(see p92)*, the rugged **Three Capes Scenic Route** *(see p93)*, and the expansive **Oregon Dunes National Recreation Area** *(see p96)*.

Those who drag themselves away from the ocean will experience the "other" Oregon. The state capital of **Salem** *(see pp100–101)* is home to museums and historic parks, while wineries are the attraction in the nearby **North Willamette Valley** *(see pp98–9)*. One of the world's deepest lakes, created by a volcanic explosion, is protected by **Crater Lake National Park** *(see pp106–7)*. Oregon is also known for the rugged scenery of **Steens Mountain** *(see p109)* and **Hells Canyon National Recreation Area** *(see pp114–15)*.

SEATTLE

- **Iconic Space Needle**
- **Bustling Pike Place Market**
- **EMP Museum**

Washington's principal metropolis, Seattle, sprawls along sparkling Puget Sound. Most of the city's major attractions are within striking distance of downtown. The

Stunning view of Cannon Beach, Ecola State Park, Oregon

◁ Watercolor painting of a logger's camp on Vancouver Island, British Columbia, c.1890

Seattle's landmark Space Needle dominates the city's skyline

top of the **Space Needle** *(see pp144–5)* is the best place to get a feel for the layout of the city, but **Pike Place Market** *(see pp132–5)* is at the top of most visitors' itineraries. The **Seattle Aquarium** *(see p136)* and **Washington State Ferries** *(see p136)* are other popular waterfront attractions. Meanwhile, history buffs gravitate to **Pioneer Square** *(see pp122–3)*, families to **Woodland Park Zoo** *(see pp156–7)*, music lovers to the **EMP Museum** *(see pp146–7)*, and baseball fans to the state-of-the-art **Safeco Field** *(see p152)*, where the Seattle Mariners play.

The city is home to the original **Starbucks** *(see p132)* and specialty seafood restaurants along the waterfront.

WASHINGTON

- **Rugged Olympic Peninsula**
- **Idyllic San Juan Islands**
- **Mount Rainier National Park**

Beyond Seattle, Washington thrives on its reputation for wilderness wonders and many visitors focus their time on the Pacific Coast. Here, the snowcapped peaks of **Olympic National Park** rise dramatically from the forest-cloaked **Olympic Peninsula** *(see pp174–5)*, while the idyllic **San Juan Islands** *(see pp178–9)* provide the perfect venue for boating and kay-aking. Reaching the summit of the volcano at the heart of

Mount Rainier National Park *(see pp184–5)* is popular with mountain climbers, while the less adventurous explore the surrounding glaciers, waterfalls, and meadows. Glaciers also abound within **North Cascades National Park** *(see pp188–9)*, a rugged, forested wilderness with abundant wildlife. Also popular is the **Grand Coulee Dam** *(see p190)*, an impressive engineering feat, while a tour of the **Walla Walla Valley** wineries *(see pp192–3)* will tempt you with the finer things in life.

VANCOUVER

- **Bustling harborfront**
- **Captivating cultural scene**
- **Museum of Anthropology**

Inextricably linked to the ocean, Vancouver is a modern, vibrant city filled with all manner of attractions and cultural interludes. Along the harborfront, the billowing architecture of **Canada Place** *(see p202)* is difficult to miss, while **Gastown** *(see pp200–201)* is home to many historic buildings. The **Downtown** precinct *(see pp207–13)* is dotted with notable buildings, including **Christ Church Cathedral** *(see p210)* and **Fairmont Hotel Vancouver** *(see p210)*. Locals descend on **Granville Island** *(see pp216–19)* for its daily market, and there are also artisan studios, the acclaimed **Emily Carr University of Art & Design**

Indian Totem Pole at the Museum of Anthropology, Vancouver

(see p218), and a market for children. Learn about local history at the Vancouver Museum in **Vanier Park** *(see pp220–21)*, then leave the city for **Stanley Park** *(see pp226–7)*. If you only have time for one museum make it the **Museum of Anthropology** *(see pp230–31)*, which tells the story of Northwest Coast natives and their artwork.

Skiing in the popular resort of Whistler, British Columbia

BRITISH COLUMBIA

- **Provincial capital of Victoria**
- **Winter sports**
- **Outdoor recreation**
- **Mountain wilderness**

The vast province of British Columbia has much to offer the visitor. Across Georgia Strait from Vancouver is Vancouver Island, home to **Victoria** *(see p246–51)*. This small, vibrant provincial capital with its Inner Harbour and surrounding attractions draws most visitors. Vancouver Island's wild side is represented by **Pacific Rim National Park** *(see pp254–5)*, protecting long sandy beaches and coastal rainforest. North of Vancouver is the resort town of **Whistler** *(see pp256–7)*, known for winter sports.

The **Okanagan Valley** *(see p259)* attracts wine lovers to its wineries and families to its warm lakes and resort towns. British Columbia's mountainous wilderness is on show in the **Kootenays** *(see pp260–63)* and protected areas such as **Yoho National Park** *(see pp266–7)*. The islands of **Haida Gwaii** *(see pp272–3)* are one of the province's most remote yet intriguing sights.

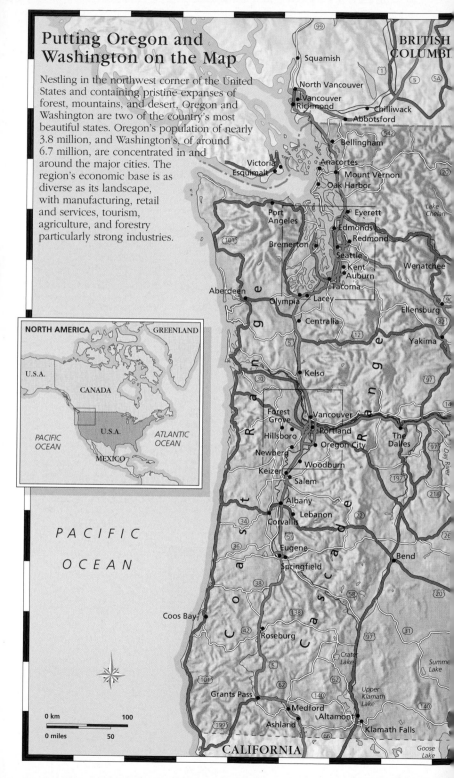

Putting Oregon and Washington on the Map

Nestling in the northwest corner of the United States and containing pristine expanses of forest, mountains, and desert, Oregon and Washington are two of the country's most beautiful states. Oregon's population of nearly 3.8 million, and Washington's, of around 6.7 million, are concentrated in and around the major cities. The region's economic base is as diverse as its landscape, with manufacturing, retail and services, tourism, agriculture, and forestry particularly strong industries.

BRITISH COLUMBIA

Squamish

North Vancouver

Vancouver

Richmond

Chilliwack

Abbotsford

Bellingham

Victoria

Esquimalt

Anacortes

Mount Vernon

Oak Harbor

Lake Chelan

Port Angeles

Everett

Edmonds

Redmond

Bremerton

Seattle

Kent

Auburn

Wenatchee

Aberdeen

Tacoma

Olympia

Lacey

Ellensburg

Centralia

Yakima

Kelso

Vancouver

Forest Grove

Hillsboro

Portland

Oregon City

The Dalles

Day River

Newberg

Keizer

Woodburn

Salem

Albany

Lebanon

Corvallis

Eugene

Springfield

Bend

Coos Bay

Roseburg

Crater Lake

Summer Lake

Grants Pass

Medford

Altamont

Klamath Falls

Ashland

Upper Klamath Lake

Goose Lake

CALIFORNIA

PACIFIC OCEAN

Coast Range

Cascade Range

NORTH AMERICA

GREENLAND

U.S.A.

CANADA

U.S.A.

PACIFIC OCEAN

ATLANTIC OCEAN

MEXICO

0 km   100

0 miles   50

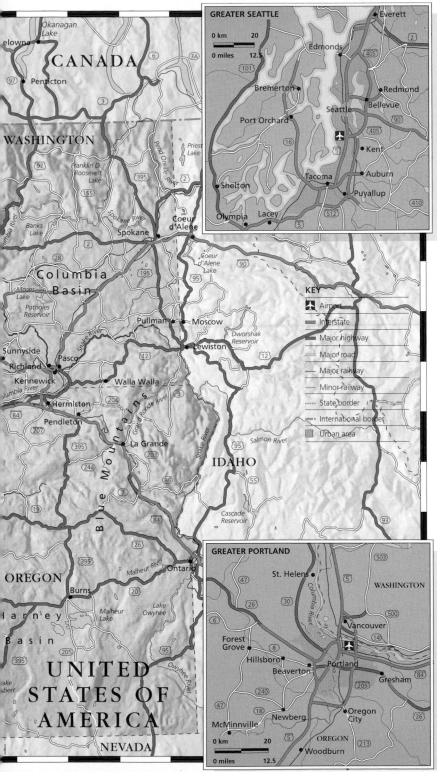

GREATER SEATTLE

0 km 20
0 miles 12.5

Everett
Edmonds
Bremerton
Redmond
Seattle
Bellevue
Port Orchard
Kent
Shelton
Tacoma
Auburn
Puyallup
Olympia Lacey

CANADA

Okanagan Lake
elowna
Penticton

WASHINGTON

Priest Lake
Franklin D. Roosevelt Lake
Pend Oreille River
Banks Lake

Columbia River
Spokane River
Spokane
Coeur d'Alene

Columbia Basin

Coeur d'Alene Lake

Moses Lake
Potholes Reservoir

Sunnyside
Pullman
Moscow
Richland
Pasco
Dworshak Reservoir
Kennewick
Lewiston
Walla Walla
Columbia River
Hermiston
Snake River
Grande Ronde River
Pendleton
La Grande
Salmon River
Snake River

KEY

✈ Airport
━━ Interstate
━━ Major highway
━━ Major road
━━ Major railway
┄┄ Minor railway
┈┈ State border
━ ━ International border
▪ Urban area

IDAHO

Blue Mountains

Cascade Reservoir

OREGON
Burns

Malheur River
Lake Owyhee
Malheur Lake

arney Basin

Ontario

UNITED
STATES OF
AMERICA

Owyhee River

NEVADA

GREATER PORTLAND

St. Helens
WASHINGTON
Columbia River
Vancouver
Forest Grove
Hillsboro
Beaverton
Portland
Gresham
McMinnville
Newberg
Oregon City
Woodburn
OREGON

0 km 20
0 miles 12.5

Putting British Columbia on the Map

British Columbia, Canada's westernmost province and the country's gateway to the Asia-Pacific region, is home to over 4.5 million people. Traditionally strong industries such as forestry, mining, and fishing remain vital to the province's economy, though recent years have seen a boom in the high-tech, film, and eco-tourism areas. Hydroelectricity and natural gas are other important resources. The beauty of the British Columbian wilderness – from the rugged coastline to the commanding mountain ranges – is preserved in the province's 830 parks and protected areas.

YUKON

Pelly Mountains

R O C K Y

Cassia Y

BRITISH COLUMBIA

Teslin
Liard
Atlin Lake
Juneau
Stikine

ALASKA (U.S.A.)

C o a s t

Terrace
Prince Rupert
Skeena
Kitimat

PACIFIC OCEAN

Haida Gwaii (Queen Charlotte Islands)

Vancouver Island

0 km 150
0 miles 100

GREATER VANCOUVER

BRITISH COLUMBIA

North Vancouver
Burnaby
Port Moody
Vancouver
Port Coquitlam
Richmond
Surrey
Mission
Langley
White Rock
Abbotsford
Lynden
WASHINGTON

0 km 15
0 miles 10

KEY

✈ Airport

━ Major highway

━ Highway

━ Major road

─ Major railway

─ Minor railway

---- Provincial border

-·- International border

▮ Urban area

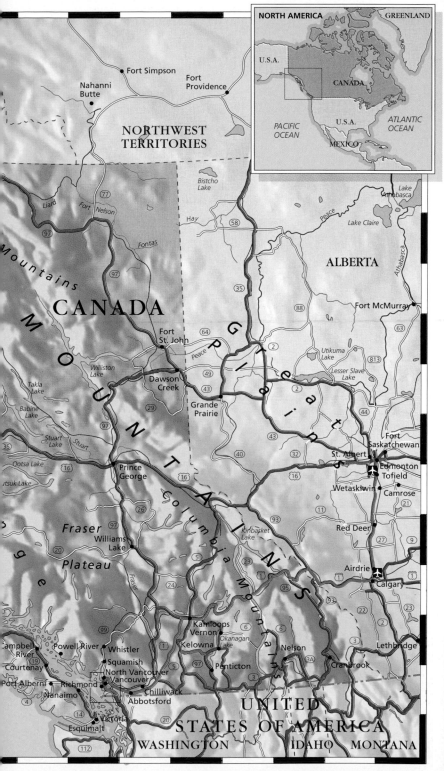

NORTH AMERICA · GREENLAND
U.S.A. · CANADA
PACIFIC OCEAN · U.S.A. · ATLANTIC OCEAN
MEXICO

Fort Simpson
Nahanni Butte
Fort Providence

NORTHWEST TERRITORIES

Bistcho Lake
Hay
Liard
Fort Nelson
Fontas
Peace
Lake Claire
Lake Athabasca

ALBERTA

Fort McMurray
Utikuma Lake
Lesser Slave Lake

CANADA

M O U N T A I N S

Mountains

Williston Lake
Takla Lake
Babine Lake
Stuart Lake
Stuart
Qotsa Lake
tsuk Lake

Fort St. John
Peace
Dawson Creek
Grande Prairie

G r e a t   P l a i n s

St. Albert
Fort Saskatchewan
Edmonton
Tofield
Wetaskiwin
Camrose
Red Deer

Prince George

C o l u m b i a   M o u n t a i n s

Fraser
Williams Lake
Plateau

Kinbasket Lake

Airdrie
Calgary

g e

Fraser

Kamloops
Vernon
Kelowna
Okanagan Lake
Penticton

Nelson
Cranbrook
Lethbridge

Campbell River
Powell River
Whistler
Squamish
North Vancouver
Vancouver
Richmond
Chilliwack
Abbotsford
Courtenay
Port Alberni
Nanaimo
Esquimalt
Victoria

UNITED STATES OF AMERICA

WASHINGTON · IDAHO · MONTANA

A PORTRAIT OF
THE PACIFIC NORTHWEST

*S*ome of North America's most rugged and spectacular terrain unfolds across the Pacific Northwest. Settled by Europeans barely 150 years ago, the region has cradled Native cultures for thousands. The region is now also home to three of the continent's most sophisticated cities – Portland, Seattle, and Vancouver – surrounded by soaring mountains, dense forests, and sparkling water.

The Pacific Northwest, comprising Oregon, Washington, and British Columbia, is richly varied – with its desert, mountain, and seashore landscapes, its mild and extreme climates, and a cosmopolitan mix of cultures and ethnicities. The region straddles two nations – the US and Canada – and comprises 526,000 sq miles (1,362,240 sq km), making it larger than France, Germany, and Italy combined. The one quality that characterizes all of the Pacific Northwest is its natural beauty, the result of eons of geological activity that has left the region with lofty mountains, deep gorges, rocky shorelines, and mighty rivers.

One of Washington's prized apples

all had a negative impact on this great wilderness, enough of its many natural wonders – such as 800-year-old Sitka spruce in the coastal rainforests – remains intact to offer a welcome escape from the stresses of the 21st century.

Another characteristic of the Pacific Northwest is its infamous weather. It can indeed rain for days on end here, but the weather varies as much as the topography does. Whereas west of the mountains the north Pacific Ocean currents ensure wet and mild winters and pleasant summers, an entirely different climate prevails east of the mountains. On the eastern plateaus and steppes, temperatures dip to well below freezing in the winter, often accompanied by heavy snow, and soar in the summer. In the central mountain region, inland deserts experience harsh winters – resulting in frequent road closures – and dry hot summers.

NATURAL WONDERS
The call of the wild is the draw for many travelers to the Pacific Northwest. Although highways, suburban sprawl, large-scale ranching, logging, dams, and other encroachments have

Sailboats in a regatta held on the waters of Burrard Inlet, British Columbia

◁ The striking landscape of the John Day fossil beds in central Oregon

Local hikers on a trail near Bellingham, Washington

OUTDOOR ACTIVITIES

Pacific Northwesterners claim to enjoy their cloudy skies and drizzly days. In defiance of the elements, many residents adopt the "grunge" look (hiking boots and heavy socks, khaki shorts, and flannel shirt) year-round and enthusiastically embrace the outdoors. The region offers some of the world's best white-water rafting, kayaking, hiking, skiing, fishing, scuba diving, windsurfing, and rockclimbing. For those who prefer more placid pursuits, such as sitting beside a still mountain lake or a rushing stream, or strolling along a remote surf-pounded beach, the opportunities here are seemingly endless.

CITY LIFE

All this natural beauty provides a backdrop for the urban sophistication of the Pacific Northwest's three major cities, Portland, Seattle, and Vancouver. Here

Portlanders relaxing at a local café and wine bar

residents have worked together to preserve the scenic virtues and old quarters of their cities while accommodating new growth. Portland has converted much of its downtown riverfront into parkland and laid the tracks of an efficient rapid transit system. Due to the efforts of residents, Seattle has restored its historic Pike Place Market, the colorful and quirky heart of the city, and Vancouver has incorporated striking new architecture into a landscape dominated by mountains and inlets.

Of course, the residents of each city tend to claim that theirs is the most beautiful and livable in the Pacific Northwest, if not in all of North America. Each has its own unique virtues. Portland takes first place for careful urban planning, for containing urban sprawl, and for preserving a charming small-town atmosphere. Seattle, with its imposing skyline, is the largest of the three cities. Well known for its high-tech industries, it also offers a vibrant music and theater scene. Cosmopolitan Vancouver, nestled between the Strait of Georgia and the Coast Mountains, arguably enjoys the best setting.

ART AND CULTURE

Long gone are the days when the Pacific Northwest was considered a poor country cousin in terms of the arts. Highly regarded and wide-ranging collections of art now hang in many museums throughout the region, and excellent concert halls and other venues play host to world-renowned orchestras and performing artists, and to stellar home-grown talent. Unforgettable experiences such as a classical concert beneath a canopy of ponderosa pines at the annual Britt Festivals in Jacksonville, Oregon; an evening of jazz with a sunset backdrop of Seattle's Elliott Bay; or a Shakespeare play at a waterfront park in Vancouver, bring artistic flair to some of the most spectacular settings in the world.

Tourists at the top of Seattle's Space Needle

ECONOMY AND INDUSTRY

While the economies of the major cities are healthy, the interior regions are suffering from high unemployment as traditional industries such as mining and logging decline and the economy shifts to one based largely on services and technology. In coastal areas, the fishing industry too has seen increasingly hard times. Fruit cultivation remains a major Pacific Northwest industry, its orchards yielding some of the most prized fruit in the world.

The emergence of high-tech companies in the region (some 3,000 software and e-commerce businesses are in the Seattle area alone) began with the rise in the 1980s of Microsoft, now employing 40,000 Washingtonians. In 1995, entrepreneur Jeff Bezos opened the doors to the online shopping business, founding Amazon.com in his Seattle home. Aerospace giant Boeing operates several plants in western Washington. Manufacturing facilities for computer industry giants Intel, Epson, and Hewlett-Packard are located in Oregon's Willamette Valley; sportswear chain Nike is also based in Oregon.

Vancouver has benefited from its incarnation as Hollywood North: movie companies inject $3 billion annually into the local economy.

The increase in white-collar jobs has led to an influx of professionals into the three cities, not only expanding the urban areas but also raising the standard (and the cost) of living within them.

Amid this economic transformation, the tourist industry has consistently thrived. Increasing numbers of tourists come to enjoy what locals have long considered their greatest resource: the Pacific Northwest's natural beauty.

PEOPLE AND POLITICS

Some 13 million people call the Pacific Northwest home. Portland, Seattle, and Vancouver are among the fastest-growing cities in North America. After a US-wide spike in growth in the 1990s, the Hispanic population is today Oregon's largest ethnic group, representing nearly 12 percent of that state's population. And Hispanics now represent 11 percent of Washington's population. Vancouver has swelled in size and prosperity since the 1980s with the arrival of Asian immigrants, particularly from mainland China, Hong Kong, India, Philippines, and South Korea. The First Nations and bands of the Pacific Northwest, many continuing to live in traditional communities, are recovering from a decline in population that occurred after European settlement.

Portland, Seattle, and Vancouver tend to be liberal in their politics, other areas of the region, conservative. Even so, a unique political climate emerges in the Pacific Northwest. Oregonians are the first in the US to have approved assisted suicide for the terminally ill; Washingtonians elected the US's first Asian-American governor; and British Columbians have bounced between right- and left-leaning parties, often bucking the national trend.

A lunchtime concert at Pioneer Courthouse Square, Portland

Geology of the Pacific Northwest

No small amount of geological activity has shaped the present-day Pacific Northwest. One hundred and fifty million years ago, much of the western part of the region was at the bottom of the sea. Over the eons, the North American continental landmass crept westward and collided with the landmass moving eastward across the Pacific Ocean, forcing the Earth's crust upward and creating the coastline of the Pacific Northwest as we know it today. Meanwhile, the eruption of volcanoes thrust up mountain peaks, and glaciers and ice sheets advanced and retreated, carving out deep gorges and canyons. As recent volcanic eruptions and earthquakes in the area attest, the Pacific Northwest is still a geologically active region, and its topography will continue to change as a result.

Washington's Mount Rainier – the most active volcano of the Cascades

Fossil records *are found throughout the Pacific Northwest, with its sedimentary rock bearing traces of plant, marine, and animal life from as long ago as 136 million years. The world-renowned John Day Fossil Beds National Monument in Kimberly, Oregon, and the fossil beds at Burgess Shale near Field, British Columbia, are both extensive repositories of this ancient past.*

SEDIMENTARY ROCK

As the Pacific plate periodically lurched eastward, sedimentary rock from older coastal mountains was uplifted to form the peaks of the Rocky and Cascade mountain ranges. Layers of the sedimentary rock, such as sandstone and shale, that were formed about 15 to 20 million years ago can be seen when visiting the ranges.

Volcanoes *such as Mount St. Helens are formed when a plate descends (subducts) beneath another plate and it begins to melt. The molten rock rises to the surface to form a volcano. In the Pacific Northwest, volcanoes began erupting about 55 million years ago. The Cascade Mountains in Oregon and Washington, the Blue Mountains in Oregon, and the Olympic Mountains in Washington are in the Ring of Fire, a zone of volcanic activity that partially encircles the Pacific Ocean.*

Glaciers *are masses of ice that advance and retreat, scooping out deep gorges and sculpting jagged mountain peaks. Continent-sized glaciers are known as ice sheets. About 15,000 years ago, the Cordilleran ice sheet covered much of Washington and British Columbia; it was 4,000 ft (1,219 m) thick in places. When it melted, the raised water levels of the Pacific Ocean filled two of the deepest gouges, creating Puget Sound and the Strait of Juan de Fuca.*

PLATE TECTONICS

Three main forces are responsible for the formation of mountain ranges such as the Rockies or the Cascades. First, large areas of the Earth's crust (known as tectonic plates), constantly moving together and apart, created uplift. Second, the North American plate, subducted by the Pacific plate, caused a chain of volcanoes to form from the molten rock of the oceanic crust. Third, erosion caused by ice ages deposited sedimentary rocks on the North American plate, which was then folded by more plate movement between 50 and 25 million years ago.

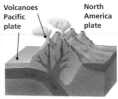

Volcanoes
Pacific
plate

North
America
plate

1 Some 150 million years ago, the Pacific plate moved east, adding to the molten rock from great depths of the North American plate. This then rose up to form the Western Cordillera Mountains.

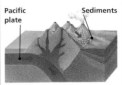

Pacific
plate

Sediments

2 The Cordilleras were eroded over millions of years and during various ice ages. This led to sediments being deposited in the sagging, wedge-shaped crust east of the mountain range.

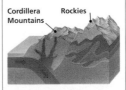

Cordillera
Mountains

Rockies

3 Around 50 million years ago, the Pacific plate continued to push east, forcing the Cordillera range eastward, compressing sedimentary rocks, folding and uplifting them to form the Rockies.

Gorges *were formed at the end of the last ice age, when massive floods were triggered periodically by melting glaciers. These floods etched out deep narrow chasms such as the one shown here, or much wider ones such as the Columbia River Gorge, which forms the boundary between Washington and Oregon.*

Wildlife of the Pacific Northwest

The landscapes of the Pacific Northwest are the most varied in North America. The cold waters of the Pacific Ocean fill sheltered bays and wash onto great lengths of sandy beach, dense old-growth forests carpet the Coast and Cascade Mountains, and arid plateaus and high deserts spread across the eastern parts of the region. Over the past 150 years, settlers have created new landscapes, including the fertile farmland of Oregon's Willamette Valley and the expanses of orchards and wheatfields in eastern Washington and British Columbia. These landscapes – lush river valleys and harsh deserts alike – provide rich habitats for a great diversity of wildlife, and viewing these animals is a rewarding part of a visit to the Pacific Northwest.

Sea lions *make their homes on rocky outcroppings along the Pacific shore.*

Pacific salmon *migrate from cold ocean waters, where they feed until maturity, into the inland streams, rivers, and lakes of their birth where they spawn, then die. Once they have reached fresh water, they stop feeding and live on their stored body fats. The fish often make journeys of more than 1,000 miles (1,600 km), swimming up rapids and bypassing dams. Each of the five species of Pacific salmon – sockeye, pink, chum, coho, and chinook – has a distinct appearance and life cycle. The pinks, for example, live up to two years and weigh little more than 5 lbs (2.3 kg), while the chinook can reach 120 lbs (54 kg) in weight and live up to seven years.*

ELK

Elk reside in the subalpine forests of the Rockies and eastern Oregon mountains. During the mating season in the fall, males become aggressive and fight for herd domination. The nasal, whining sound they emit, known as "bugling," should be taken by humans as a warning.

Sea otters *were rendered almost extinct in the 19th century by trappers who obtained enormous prices for their pelts but are now making a comeback along the Pacific Northwest coast. These creatures eat the equivalent of a third of their weight a day, providing quite a show as they feed. A sea otter lies on its back and, using its paws, smashes crabs, mussels, and other shellfish against a rock it has placed on its chest. Otters are easily spotted, lolling on rocks or floating asleep on the water, their bodies entwined in kelp to keep them from drifting.*

Whales *belonging to over 20 species pass Vancouver Island, the Olympic Peninsula, and the Oregon coast as they travel between the Arctic and their breeding grounds off southern California and Mexico. It is estimated that 20,000 gray whales and 2,000 orcas make the 5,500-mile (8,850-km) trip each year. The whales migrate south from December to early February and return north from March through May.*

Bald eagles, *once common throughout North America, are now mainly found in the Pacific Northwest, in coastal areas or near large inland lakes. The bald eagle is regarded as a symbol of strength and independence, and was designated as the national bird of the US in 1782. Contrary to what its name implies, this eagle is not actually bald; the term comes from the Old English word "balde," meaning white.*

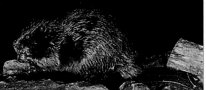

Beavers *are very industrious, using their sharp upper teeth to fell small trees, which they then float to a chosen dam site. The lodges they build within the dam can be as wide as 16 ft (5 m).*

Moose, *distinguishable by their magnificient spreading antlers, are often spotted grazing by streams, ponds, and other marshy areas.*

Grizzly bears, *weighing up to 800 lbs (350 kg) and standing as tall as 8.8 ft (2.68 m), roam remote parts of the northern Cascades and the Rockies. Far more common is the black bear, smaller than the grizzly but imposing nonetheless.*

Flora of the Pacific Northwest

Deep forests, wildflower-filled alpine meadows, and grass-covered steppes are all typical of the Pacific Northwest. Although vastly different, these landscapes are often found in close proximity to one another. The moist, temperate climate of the region's coastal areas fosters an abundance of plant life, including the towering trees, mosses, and shrubs that thrive in centuries-old forests, such as the rainforest in British Columbia's Pacific Rim National Park Reserve. In Washington's Skagit Valley, tulips covering thousands of acres bloom each spring. In the Cascade and Rocky Mountains, and in the deserts and steppes east of the mountains, the terrain is less hospitable and only the hardiest plants survive. But even here, alpine meadows and stands of juniper that scent the high desert attest to the rich diversity of the region's flora.

Wildflowers
The moist climate of the coastal forests and high-country meadows provide perfect growing conditions for colorful wildflowers, such as wood lilies, asters, Jacob's ladder, and purple mountain saxifrage.

Lichens
Hardy lichens – along with mosses, liverworts, ferns, skunk cabbage, and orchids – flourish in the dampness of rainforests that grow along the coast of the Pacific Ocean.

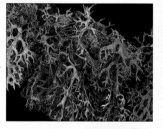

Sagebrush
The arid environment of the Columbia River basin and the high plateaus of Oregon and Washington support only vegetation that can survive with little moisture, such as sagebrush.

MOUNTAIN FORESTS
Many of the trees in the rugged mountain forests are several centuries old. Douglas firs can live as long as 1,200 years and grow to be 260 ft (79 m) tall. Fallen logs foster young trees which, if they survive 200 years, will earn "old-growth" status.

Deciduous Forests
Deciduous trees grow in river valleys in the Pacific Northwest. In the fall, these trees provide a brilliant show of color, all the more dramatic because the multihued leaves are usually set against a backdrop of evergreen trees.

Ferns
Lady's fern and deer fern are among the many species that grow in the region. In the Hoh Rainforest, ferns grow taller than the hikers.

Pines and Junipers
Ponderosa pines, lodgepole pines, and junipers have long roots that tap subterranean water tables. With flat needles that retain moisture, junipers can survive on just 8 inches (20.5 cm) of precipitation a year.

Rainforests
Rainforests carpet much of the Pacific Northwest, on British Columbia's Vancouver Island and Haida Gwaii archipelago, and along the Pacific coast. These lush green forests of Sitka spruce, Douglas fir, red cedar, Pacific silver fir, western hemlock, and yew can receive more than 150 inches (381 cm) of rain per year.

Native Peoples of the Pacific Northwest

For the Native peoples of the Pacific Northwest, 15,000 years of a bountiful life and rich cultural tradition were abruptly upset when European traders and settlers began arriving in the late 18th century. Diseases introduced by these newcomers all but obliterated many First Nations. Those who survived were forced to surrender their lands and ways of life, and move to government-designated reservations. Today, although indigenous people continue to fight against racism and for their self-determination, Native traditions are increasingly recognized as a vital part of the region's rich heritage. Native cultures and history can be explored in such places as the Royal British Columbia

A stone inukshuk, sign of friendship

Museum, in Victoria *(see pp252–3)*; Whatcom Museum of History and Art, in Bellingham, Washington *(see p180)*; and Oregon's Museum at Warm Springs *(see p102)*.

Totem poles *are among the best-known artifacts created by the Native peoples of the Pacific Northwest. Each pole depicts a legend; magical birds and beasts mix with semi-human figures to tell a story in carved panels arranged in sequence up the pole. Other elaborate carvings, such as those on masks, ornaments, and utensils, often also represent real and supernatural beings.*

ARTISANS AND BUILDERS

The trunks of cedar trees were used by Pacific Northwest Natives to make masks, cooking utensils, wooden chests, elaborate dwellings up to 500 ft (150 m) long and aptly called long-houses, and magnificent dugout canoes, used for transportation, hunting, and fishing.

Respect for the land

underpins the spirituality and way of life of Native peoples of the Pacific Northwest. Nature provides all, so long as nature's balance is not disturbed. Chief Seattle once said: "We are part of the Earth and it is part of us. The perfumed flowers are our sisters; the deer, the horse, the great eagle, these are our brothers. The rocky crests, the juices in the meadows, the body heat of the pony, and man – all belong to the same family."

Canoes *made of birch bark or dug out of massive cedar logs provided an essential mode of transportation on the many rivers which formed a network of trade routes throughout the Pacific Northwest. Canoes ranged in size from small vessels for personal use to large and elaborately decorated ceremonial canoes.*

Wigwams *were built as dwellings by tribes living in the interior, such as the Nez Perce, Yakama, Cayuse, Shoshone, and Modoc. More permanent longhouses were preferred by many of the tribes that settled along the Pacific Northwest coast from southern Alaska down to Oregon. They include the Tlingit, the Tsimshian, the Haida, the Kwagiutl, the West Coast, and the Coast Salish.*

NOTEWORTHY CHIEFS

Chief Seattle (1786–1866), *leader of the Duwamish and Squamish tribes, was just six years old when he witnessed the arrival of Captain Vancouver in Puget Sound. He frequently petitioned American and British authorities for Indian rights and urged peaceful co-existence with settlers.*

Chief Joseph (1840–1904) *was the renowned leader of the Nez Perce tribe. In 1877, his tribe was forced out of its beloved Wallowa Valley in Oregon. The tribe fled, fighting, and Chief Joseph showed great skill leading his warriors in battle against the American troops until his defeat the same year.*

Chief Joe Capilano (1850–1910) *was born on what is now Vancouver's North Shore. An esteemed Squamish chief, he and his wife Mary, known as the "Indian Princess of Peace," visited King Edward VII in Great Britain in 1906 to present a petition for Indian rights.*

Landscapes of the Pacific Northwest

The Pacific Northwest is blessed with an abundance of dramatically different landscapes. Seashores give way to coastal mountains, which drop into the Fraser Plateau in British Columbia, into Puget Sound in Washington, and into the Willamette Valley in Oregon. The peaks of the Cascade Mountains bisect both Oregon and Washington, and the majestic Rockies rise in eastern British Columbia. Other distinct landscapes are the Columbia Plateau's layers of ancient lava that spread across eastern Oregon and Washington, and the high deserts of central and southern Oregon.

Sea Stacks
Portions of wave-eroded headlands that remain as offshore mounds rise majestically from the surf of the Pacific Ocean. The stacks are most numerous along the southern Oregon coast near Cape Blanco and off Washington's Olympic Peninsula.

Coasts
In Oregon and southern Washington, sandy beaches and rocky headlands extend for more than 450 miles (725 km) along the coast. The Strait of Juan de Fuca etches Washington's northern coastline with a succession of bays and inlets, while in British Columbia, 10,340 miles (16,640 km) of shoreline wrap around inlets, fjords, and islands.

MOUNTAIN RANGES
The Coast and Cascade ranges form a spine of mountains that rises almost continuously from southern Oregon to northern British Columbia. Much of the lower slopes of the mountains is carpeted with forests that give way to alpine meadows, then to glaciers.

The Canadian Rockies
With their dominating peaks and vast ice fields, the Rocky Mountains cover a large part of British Columbia. Thirty mountains of this immense range are more than 10,000 ft (3,048 m) high.

Gorges
Gorges reveal the dramatic geological history of the region. Over the course of thousands of years, rushing rivers have carved away rock and earth, leaving behind huge gorges as well as long and narrow chasms, such as Oregon's Oneonta Gorge in the Columbia River Gorge National Scenic Area.

Mountain Areas
The mountains in the Pacific Northwest form a barrier that traps great amounts of moisture, which in winter can cause heavy snowfall on peaks such as Oregon's Diamond Peak.

Waterfalls
The spectacular Lower Kentucky Falls in Oregon's Siuslaw National Forest is one of thousands of waterfalls in the Pacific Northwest. The Kentucky Creek runs through old-growth forest before spilling over a cliff, plummeting 75 ft (23 m), then an additional 25 ft (8 m), to the rocky slopes below.

Dry Lands and Desert Country
East of the mountains, the terrain tends to be flat, and precipitation can average as little as 12 inches (30.5 cm) a year. As a result, the landscape here is vastly different from that found in the mountain and coastal regions. In eastern Oregon, steppes and deserts are covered with juniper and sagebrush. Rocky outcroppings, usually composed of volcanic basalt, are also common here, and vegetation is often sparse.

THE PACIFIC NORTHWEST THROUGH THE YEAR

The image of the Pacific Northwest's weather as consistently wet is rooted as much in myth as in fact. Rain is a distinctive presence in only half of the Pacific Northwest – the part west of the mountains that divide the region. The weather in this western, coastal section remains mild throughout the year, and snow is rare in all but the higher elevations. In the mountains, winter snowfall is heavy, much to the delight of skiers. East of the

Hot air balloon, Oregon

mountains, where cold and heat reach extreme levels, winter snowfall can be heavy but summers can be bone dry. In spite of the variable weather throughout the Pacific Northwest, the unique rewards of living and traveling in the region are many. Even in the damp and most heavily populated western sections, rain doesn't prevent residents and visitors alike from heading outdoors to enjoy a large variety of entertaining festivals and events.

SPRING

March and April bring the signs of spring to the lower elevations of the Pacific Northwest. A number of festivities celebrate the region's lush gardens as they come into bloom in an array of glorious colors.

MARCH

Playhouse International Wine Festival *(Feb or Mar)*, Vancouver, BC. A week of wine tastings held at Canada Place *(p202)* and other locales.
Oregon Cheese Festival *(mid-Mar)*, Central Point, OR. Artisan cheesemakers from Oregon and Northern California dairies show their wares, along with local wines.

Blossoming fruit trees in April, the Hood River Valley, Oregon

Sandhill Crane Festival *(late Mar)*, Othello, WA. Witness the sounds and rituals of 25,000 migrating cranes.
Victorian Festival *(late Mar)*, Port Townsend, WA *(pp176–7)*. All things Victorian are celebrated in this historic seaport.

APRIL

Skagit Valley Tulip Festival *(Apr)*, Skagit Valley, WA. A month-long festival of arts and crafts fairs, barbecues, and walking tours amid 1,000 acres (405 ha) of tulips.
Hood River Valley Blossom Festival *(third weekend)*, Hood River Valley, OR. Arts and crafts fairs and tours of orchards and wineries in towns along the Hood River.
Washington State Apple Blossom Festival *(late Apr–early May)*, Wenatchee, WA. Parades, a carnival, and concerts to usher in spring.

MAY

Seagull Calling Festival *(first Sat)*, Port Orchard, WA. This waterfront festival is centered on a seagull-calling contest.
Bloomsday Run *(first Sun)*, Spokane, WA. Every year, this 7.5-mile (12-km) race through downtown attracts more than 50,000 runners.

A perfect rose on show at the Portland Rose Festival in June

Cinco de Mayo Festival *(early May)*, Portland, OR. Four days of Mexican food, art, music, and dance on the Portland waterfront.
Annual Rhododendron Festival *(third weekend)*, Florence, OR. A parade and carnival to celebrate the rhododendron blossoms.
Northwest Folklife Festival *(Memorial Day weekend)*, Seattle, WA. Enjoy dance, exhibits, and workshops at one of the largest free events in the US.
Brookings Azalea Festival *(Memorial Day weekend)*, Brookings, OR. Blossoms and food in a coastal town famous for its azaleas.
Blessing of the Fleet *(late May)*, Westport, WA. A parade and a blessing of the town's famous fishing fleet.
Vancouver International Children's Festival *(late May)*, Vancouver, BC. Local, national, and international performing artists present theater and music for children.

SUMMER

Summer in much of the Pacific Northwest is not assuredly sunny. But locals do not hesitate to venture outdoors for a variety of activities and events, including wine festivals, rodeos, plays, and concerts under the stars.

JUNE

Portland Rose Festival *(Jun)*, Portland, OR. Parades, concerts, races, and a carnival in honor of the rose.

Bard on the Beach Shakespeare Festival *(Jun–Sep)*, Vancouver, BC. Lively plays at Vanier Park *(pp220–21)*.

Sisters Rodeo *(mid-Jun)*, Sisters, OR *(p102)*. Rodeo held every year since 1940.

Britt Festivals *(mid-Jun–early Sep)*, Jacksonville, OR *(p108)*. Music concerts from classical to pop under the ponderosa pines and stars.

JazzFest International *(late Jun)*, Victoria, BC. Jazz and blues concerts at venues all over town.

Pi-Ume-Sha Treaty Days *(late Jun)*, Warm Springs, OR *(p102)*. A powwow, parade, and rodeo mark the treaty that formed the Confederated Tribes of Warm Springs.

Oregon Bach Festival *(late Jun–mid-Jul)*, Eugene, OR *(p101)*. A series of concerts honoring J.S. Bach.

Summer Nights at South Lake Union *(late Jun–Aug)*, Seattle, WA. Concert series at South Lake Union Park with beautiful views.

Costumed dancer, Caribbean Days Festival, North Vancouver, July

Hoopfest *(last weekend)*, Spokane, WA. The largest three-on-three basketball tournament in the US.

JULY

Seafair *(Jul–Aug)*, Seattle, WA. This month-long festival, including a torchlight parade, hydroplane races, and an air show, takes place in several spectacular venues around the city.

International Folk Music Festival *(Jul)*, Vancouver, BC. An annual folk festival, in Jericho Beach Park.

Ripe peaches in the Okanagan Valley, BC

Canada Day *(Jul 1)*, across British Columbia. Parades, live music, and evening fireworks are held.

Willams Lake Stampede *(Jul 1 weekend)*, Williams Lake, BC. Rodeo fun at one of North America's largest stampedes.

Waterfront Blues Festival *(early Jul)*, Portland, OR. Five days of blues from local and nationally acclaimed artists.

Washington Mutual Family Fourth *(Jul 4)*, Seattle, WA. Over 5,000 fireworks over Gas Works Park *(p155)*.

Bite of Seattle *(mid-Jul)*, Seattle, WA. A popular two-day event with food from more than 60 restaurants.

Oregon Coast Music Festival *(mid–late Jul)*, Charleston, Coos Bay, and North Bend, OR. Classical music and jazz performed next to the ocean.

Caribbean Days Festival *(late Jul)*, North Vancouver, BC. A celebration of all things Caribbean.

International Pinot Noir Celebration *(late Jul)*, McMinnville, OR *(p100)*. Pinot noirs coupled with food from noted local chefs.

Celebration of Lights *(late Jul–early Aug)*, Vancouver, BC. Fireworks competition at English Bay.

AUGUST

Penticton Peach Festival *(early Aug)*, Penticton, BC. A charming festival celebrating the local peach harvest.

Mount Hood Jazz Festival *(early Aug)*, Gresham, OR. Two days of jazz, food, and local wines.

ExtravaGAYza! Parade and Festival *(early Aug)*, Vancouver, BC. Fun and fanciful events for Gay Pride Week.

First Peoples Festival *(early Aug)*, Victoria, BC. Three days of art, food, and performances by First Nations peoples.

Omak Stampede and World Famous Suicide Race *(mid-Aug)*, Omak, WA. A rodeo, stampede, and daredevil horse race.

Oregon State Fair *(late Aug–early Sep)*, Salem, OR *(p100)*. Twelve days of Oregon produce and livestock, rides, concerts, and food.

Evergreen State Fair *(late Aug–early Sep)*, Monroe, WA. Arts and crafts, rides, races, and rodeo events.

Steer roping at the Sisters Rodeo, held mid-June in Sisters, Oregon

Ride at the September Pacific National Exhibition, Vancouver, BC

FALL

Fall foliage can be quite spectacular in the Pacific Northwest, as brilliant reds and yellows stand out against evergreens. Colorful landscapes are the backdrop for events celebrating the harvest of cranberries, oysters, and other regional specialties.

SEPTEMBER

Pacific National Exhibition *(late Aug–early Sep)*, Vancouver, BC. Big-ticket entertainment, rides, pavilions, and agricultural exhibits.
Great Canadian Beer Festival *(Sep)*, Victoria, BC. Forty craft breweries from Canada and the Pacific Northwest take part and offer beer samples.

Bumbershoot *(Labor Day weekend)*, Seattle, WA. A mix of music and film at the Seattle Center *(pp142–3)*.
Classic Boat Festival *(early Sep)*, Victoria, BC. Racing of classic sailboats and power-boats in the Inner Harbour.
Puyallup Fair *(early Sep)*, Puyallup, WA. A 17-day state fair with rides, exhibits, a rodeo, and live music.
Oktoberfest *(mid-Sep)*, Mount Angel, OR. Bavarian food and plenty of beer.
Pendleton Round-Up *(mid-Sep)*, Pendleton, OR *(p111)*. A rodeo featuring calf-roping, bull-riding, and a town full of real cowboys.
Depoe Bay Salmon Bake *(third Sat in Sep)*, Depoe Bay, OR. Fresh salmon cooked Indian-style over an open fire beside the town's tiny harbor.

OCTOBER

Okanagan Wine Festival *(early Oct)*, Okanagan Valley, BC. Vineyard tours and wine tastings at harvest time.
OysterFest *(early Oct)*, Shelton, WA. A weekend of oyster shucking, wine tastings, and cooking contests.
Annual Cranberrian Fair *(mid-Oct)*, Ilwaco, WA. Cranberry tastings, music, and dancing to celebrate the local harvest.
Vancouver International Writers Festival *(third week)*, Vancouver, BC. Readings by Canadian and international writers.
Earshot Jazz Festival *(mid-Oct–early Nov)*, Seattle, WA. This celebrated jazz festival draws big names at various venues around the city.

NOVEMBER

Cornucopia *(mid-Nov)*, Whistler, BC *(pp256–7)*. A festival featuring fine dining, wine tastings, and seminars.
Christkindlmarkt *(weekend after Thanksgiving)*, Leavenworth, WA *(p186)*. An open-air market selling German treats, such as bratwurst.
Seattle Marathon *(Sun after Thanksgiving)*, Seattle, WA. More than 10,000 participants run off Thanksgiving excesses.

Climate

Climate varies widely across the Pacific Northwest. Coastal areas, such as Portland, Seattle, and Vancouver, are mild and wet, while inland deserts, such as the areas around Spokane and Kamloops, have seasonal extremes. Climates of mountain ranges in the Pacific Northwest, represented here by the Cascade Mountains, have divergent microclimates.

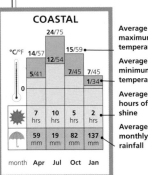

COASTAL

month	Apr	Jul	Oct	Jan
°C/°F	14/57	24/75	15/59	7/45
	5/41	12/54	7/45	1/34
☀	7 hrs	10 hrs	5 hrs	2 hrs
☂	59 mm	19 mm	82 mm	137 mm

Average daily maximum temperature

Average daily minimum temperature

Average daily hours of sunshine

Average monthly rainfall

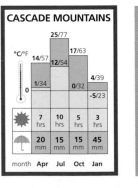

CASCADE MOUNTAINS

month	Apr	Jul	Oct	Jan
°C/°F	14/57	25/77	17/63	4/39
	1/34	12/54	0/32	-5/23
☀	7 hrs	10 hrs	5 hrs	3 hrs
☂	20 mm	15 mm	15 mm	45 mm

INLAND DESERT

month	Apr	Jul	Oct	Jan
°C/°F	16/61	30/86	14/57	0/32
	3/37	13/55	3/37	-7/19
☀	7 hrs	10 hrs	5 hrs	3 hrs
☂	15 mm	28 mm	14 mm	26 mm

In December, a cheering Christmas Lighting Festival in Bavarian-themed Leavenworth

WINTER

When snow covers the region's mountains, many Pacific Northwesterners take to downhill ski slopes or cross-country trails. In mild coastal areas, where winter days are short and rainy, unique Christmas celebrations provide a cheerful glow.

DECEMBER

Portland Parade of Christmas Ships *(Dec)*, Portland, OR. Gaily decorated boats sail down the Willamette River.
VanDusen Botanical Gardens' Festival of Lights *(Dec)*, Vancouver, BC. Thousands of lights glitter throughout 55 acres (22 ha) of lush plantings in this botanical garden during the month before Christmas.

One of many ski competitions held in the region during winter

Christmas Lighting Festival *(first three weekends in Dec)*, Leavenworth, WA. Visitors enjoy roasted chestnuts, bratwurst, strolling carolers, and twinkling lights against the snow-capped Cascade Mountains in a Bavarian-style town.
Christmas Carol Ships Parade of Lights *(three weeks before Christmas)*, Vancouver, BC. Beautifully decorated vessels light up local waters.

JANUARY

Eagle Festival and Count *(early Jan)*, Brackendale, BC. Festival centered on a competition to count the number of bald eagles settling for the winter on the Squamish River.
Chinese New Year *(late Jan or early Feb)*, Vancouver, BC. Almost two weeks of colorful festivities, including dance, music, and a parade celebrate the new lunar year.

FEBRUARY

Northwest Flower and Garden Show *(third week of Feb)*, Seattle, WA. Full-scale landscaped garden displays and a flower show featuring creative designs attract flower-lovers to this event.
Oregon Shakespeare Festival *(mid-Feb–Oct)*, Ashland, OR *(p108)*. Classic and contemporary plays draw actors and spectators from around the world to this highly acclaimed drama festival.

PUBLIC HOLIDAYS

UNITED STATES

New Year's Day
(Jan 1)
Martin Luther King Day
(3rd Mon in Jan)
Presidents' Day
(mid-Feb)
Memorial Day
(last Mon in May)
Independence Day
(Jul 4)
Labor Day
(1st Mon in Sep)
Columbus Day
(2nd Mon in Oct)
Veterans' Day
(Nov 11)
Thanksgiving Day
(4th Thu in Nov)
Christmas Day
(Dec 25)

CANADA

New Year's Day
(Jan 1)
Good Friday
(late Mar or mid-Apr)
Victoria Day
(Mon before May 25)
Canada Day
(Jul 1)
Civic holiday (BC Day)
(1st Mon in Aug)
Labor Day
(1st Mon in Sep)
Thanksgiving Day
(2nd Mon in Oct)
Remembrance Day
(Nov 11)
Christmas Day
(Dec 25)
Boxing Day
(Dec 26)

THE HISTORY OF
THE PACIFIC NORTHWEST

he vast landscapes of the Pacific Northwest bear the imprint of the geological forces that carved deep gorges and thrust up soaring mountain peaks. The imprint left by Native peoples who lived in harmony with the land for thousands of years is less visible. In the early 19th century, after explorers had opened up the territory, settlers began to arrive and the modern Pacific Northwest was born.

Enough is known about the early inhabitants of the region to suggest that many enjoyed a good life among the natural riches. The earliest inhabitants were likely nomadic hunters who, 15,000 to 25,000 years ago, crossed a land bridge across the then-dry Bering Strait from Russia to North America.

**British explorer
Captain James Cook**

These early societies left various traces of their presence. Among intriguing finds is a 14,000-year-old spear point left embedded in fossilized mastodon bones. Sagebrush sandals, on display at the University of Oregon Museum of Natural History, are possibly the world's oldest shoes, revealing that 9,000 years ago the art of shoemaking was practiced. Other signs that the region was long settled can be found in oral traditions, rife with tales of the eruption of Mount Mazama, some 8,000 years ago. Rock carvings and

paintings in Petroglyph Provincial Park, near Nanaimo, BC, are thought to be at least 3,000 years old.

EARLY LIFE

Food and other resources were abundant for tribes living in the forests west of the Cascade Mountains and along the Pacific coast. Many tribes lived in well-established settlements, fished the rivers for salmon, and, in long dugouts, set out to sea in search of whales. They also cut timber for longhouses – massive dwellings that could house as many as 50 to 60 people. Tribes living in the harsher landscapes east of the mountains had fewer resources at hand and migrated across high-desert hunting grounds in search of bison, deer, and other game. In spring and summer, they moved up mountain slopes to pick berries and dig roots. By the 19th century, tribes

<◁ **A contemporary illustration of Captain George Vancouver's ship, HMS *Discovery***

A Shoshone hunting elk with bow and arrow

living in the high deserts had acquired horses and rode them east to the Great Plains to hunt bison, which had become extinct farther west.

For many tribes, life was so bountiful that a tradition of potlatch evolved. At these elaborate ceremonies, which marked important occasions and which were centered around a feast, the host chief would offer gifts with the expectation that the recipients would eventually repay the gesture with loyalty and gifts at a subsequent potlatch.

Captain George Vancouver

ARRIVAL OF EXPLORERS

Native peoples thrived in the Pacific Northwest until the 18th century, disturbed only by occasional incursions by explorers and traders. In the 16th century, the first Europeans began exploring the coastline in search of the Northwest Passage, a sea route that would provide a passage between Europe and the Far East.

The first European to sight the Pacific Northwest was Spanish explorer Juan Rodriguez Cabrillo, who sailed with his crew from Mexico to southern Oregon in 1543. Once the Spanish had gained a stronghold in the New

World, the British, too, wanted a share of the riches. The mission of Sir Francis Drake (1540–96), financed by Queen Elizabeth I, was to sail up the west coast of North America, plundering gold from Spanish galleons. After claiming the land around San Francisco Bay for Britain, Drake sailed up the Oregon coast, as far north as the Strait of Juan de Fuca, first navigated by Juan de Fuca in 1592. Drake then traveled across the Pacific Ocean back to England.

In the 1770s, Captains George Vancouver (1758–98) and Peter Puget (1765–1822) accompanied Captain James Cook (1728–79) on a voyage along the Pacific Northwest coast in search of the fabled Northwest Passage. The explorers sailed up the coasts of Oregon, Washington, and British Columbia. In 1791, Vancouver and Puget also charted what are now Puget Sound (Washington) and Vancouver (British Columbia).

Ship caught in the ice along the northern Pacific coast

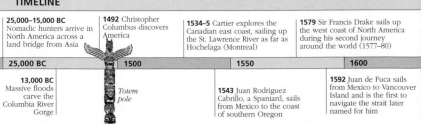

TIMELINE

25,000–15,000 BC Nomadic hunters arrive in North America across a land bridge from Asia	**1492** Christopher Columbus discovers America	**1534–5** Cartier explores the Canadian east coast, sailing up the St. Lawrence River as far as Hochelaga (Montreal)	**1579** Sir Francis Drake sails up the west coast of North America during his second journey around the world (1577–80)
25,000 BC	**1500**	**1550**	**1600**
13,000 BC Massive floods carve the Columbia River Gorge	*Totem pole*	**1543** Juan Rodriguez Cabrillo, a Spaniard, sails from Mexico to the coast of southern Oregon	**1592** Juan de Fuca sails from Mexico to Vancouver Island and is the first to navigate the strait later named for him

Simon Fraser and companions on the Fraser River

However, they did not notice the Columbia River, discovered the following year by Captain Robert Gray, an American fur trader from the East Coast, who named the river after his ship, *The Columbia Rediviva*. Other American vessels soon arrived in search of animal pelts and other bounty. The Spanish, who had been attempting to establish strongholds along the Pacific coast for centuries, retreated to their claims in California.

In 1793, Scotsman and Montreal fur trader Alexander Mackenzie crossed Canada to British Columbia, proving that an overland trade route was feasible. Mackenzie was also the first European to navigate the Peace River, the only river in British Columbia that drains into the Arctic Ocean.

From 1805 to 1808, Simon Fraser (1776–1862), a partner in the fur-trading North West Company, was charged with extending the company's trading activities west of the Rocky Mountains to the Pacific Ocean, and exploring a river thought to be the Columbia. In this capacity, Fraser established Fort McCleod, Fort St. James, Fort Fraser, and Fort George, all in British Columbia.

Fraser's major accomplishment though, was to be the first to navigate the longest river in British Columbia, now known as the Fraser River, which courses through the rugged BC interior to the Pacific Ocean.

LEWIS AND CLARK

US President Thomas Jefferson called on his former secretary, Meriwether Lewis, and Lewis's friend, William Clark, to find an overland route to the Pacific Ocean. The pair and an entourage of 33 set out from St. Louis, Missouri, in May 1804 and walked, rode horseback, and canoed to the Oregon coast, which they reached a year and a half later, in November 1805. The only female member of the expedition was Sacagawea, a young Shoshone woman who proved to be an invaluable guide and translator. The famed expedition set the stage for the rapid settlement of the Pacific Northwest. The expedition members not only plotted the first overland route across the US, mapping unexplored territory and collecting data on Native peoples and wildlife, but they also published journals that sparked a wave of migration from the east.

William Clark, explorer

Pioneer log cabin, Champoeg State Park, Oregon

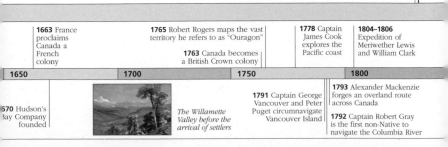

	1663 France proclaims Canada a French colony	1765 Robert Rogers maps the vast territory he refers to as "Ouragon"		1778 Captain James Cook explores the Pacific coast	1804–1806 Expedition of Meriwether Lewis and William Clark
		1763 Canada becomes a British Crown colony			
1650		1700	1750		1800
1670 Hudson's Bay Company founded		*The Willamette Valley before the arrival of settlers*	1791 Captain George Vancouver and Peter Puget circumnavigate Vancouver Island	1793 Alexander Mackenzie forges an overland route across Canada	
				1792 Captain Robert Gray is the first non-Native to navigate the Columbia River	

A BATTLE FOR THE SPOILS

The battle to control the Pacific Northwest was waged by the British and the Americans not with gunfire but through trade. The expedition of Lewis and Clark opened up the region to US fur traders. They could now compete with the British, who dominated the lucrative pelt trade. In 1811, the American John Jacob Astor established a fur-trading post, Astoria, at the mouth of the Columbia River. Although US President Jefferson had hoped that Lewis and Clark's expedition would displace the British, the British-owned Hudson's Bay Company effectively continued to rule the Pacific Northwest until the middle of the 19th century. The company controlled both the growing population of settlers and much of the trade activity. Company headquarters at Fort Vancouver, overlooking the confluence of the Columbia and Willamette Rivers, and at Fort Victoria, on Vancouver Island in British Columbia, were the region's major settlements. Hudson's Bay Company trading posts became such common sights in the wilderness that it was quipped that the initials "HBC" stood for "Here Before Christ."

Territorial tensions between Britain and the US erupted in the War of 1812. Although neither side "won" this war, the dominance of the British was later undermined when thousands of American farmers migrated westward along the Oregon Trail. Britain and America divided the spoils of the Pacific Northwest in 1846, using the 49th parallel as the

Sir James Douglas of the Hudson's Bay

new boundary, with the land to the north (British Columbia) being claimed by Britain, and that to the south (Oregon) by the US. Oregon, which included the present-day states of Oregon, Washington, and Idaho, became a US territory in 1848. The Oregon Territory was itself divided in 1852, with lands north of the Columbia River forming the new Washington Territory. Oregon gained statehood in 1859, Washington in 1889. British Columbia and Vancouver Island joined to become one colony in 1866, and joined the Dominion of Canada in 1871.

Those who profited least from the division of spoils were the Native peoples. Already decimated by diseases introduced by settlers, such as smallpox, measles, and influenza, they were forcibly removed from the lands they had inhabited for millennia and resettled on reservations.

THE GREAT MIGRATIONS

Between 1843 and 1860, more than 60,000 settlers embarked on a 6-month, 2,000-mile (3,218-km) trek from Independence, Missouri, across the US along the Oregon Trail mapped by Lewis and Clark in 1804–1805. Many settlers left the trail

Astoria, founded by John Jacob Astor in 1811

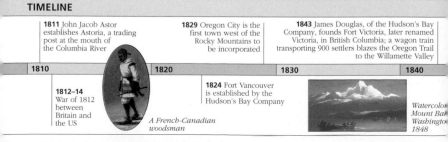

TIMELINE

1811 John Jacob Astor establishes Astoria, a trading post at the mouth of the Columbia River

1829 Oregon City is the first town west of the Rocky Mountains to be incorporated

1843 James Douglas, of the Hudson's Bay Company, founds Fort Victoria, later renamed Victoria, in British Columbia; a wagon train transporting 900 settlers blazes the Oregon Trail to the Willamette Valley

1810	1820	1830	1840

1812–14 War of 1812 between Britain and the US

A French-Canadian woodsman

1824 Fort Vancouver is established by the Hudson's Bay Company

Watercolor Mount Bak Washingto 1848

Fort Vancouver, a strategically located trading post, in 1848

Willamette Rivers, Portland became the region's major port and most important city.

By the 1870s, transcontinental railroads were steaming across the US and Canada, making the Pacific Northwest accessible to hundreds of thousands more settlers. Trains began crossing Canada between Montreal and Vancouver in 1886, opening up British Columbia to mass settlement.

In the US the arrival of the railroad was especially beneficial to the tiny settlement of Alki-New York in Washington, which soon burgeoned into Seattle, and eventually outstripped Portland as the Pacific Northwest's major port and center of trade.

in Idaho and headed south to California. Most of those who continued west to Oregon followed the Snake River to the Columbia River, where they put their wagons on rafts. The downstream trip across dangerous rapids led to the mouth of the Willamette River and, just upstream, the trail's end at Oregon City. Rather than pay the exorbitant fee of $50 to float a wagon down the river, some settlers opted for the treacherous climb across Barlow Pass on the flanks of Mount Hood, one of the peaks of the Cascade Mountains.

The reward for those who made the arduous trek to Oregon's fertile Willamette Valley was a land grant of 350 acres (140 ha). Many settlers staked their claims in Oregon, while others made their way farther north and settled in Washington. With its strategic location at the confluence of the Columbia and

GOLD RUSHES

Gold fever gripped the Pacific Northwest in 1848, when gold was discovered in California's Sierra Nevada mountains. Many of the new settlers who had staked land claims in Oregon headed south, lured by the hope of making their fortune.

Romantic vision of the westward trek, painted c.1904

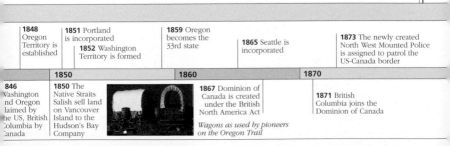

| **1848** Oregon Territory is established | **1851** Portland is incorporated | | **1859** Oregon becomes the 33rd state | | **1865** Seattle is incorporated | **1873** The newly created North West Mounted Police is assigned to patrol the US-Canada border |
| | | **1852** Washington Territory is formed | | | | |

1850		**1860**		**1870**

| **846** Washington nd Oregon laimed by he US, British Columbia by Canada | **1850** The Native Straits Salish sell land on Vancouver Island to the Hudson's Bay Company | | **1867** Dominion of Canada is created under the British North America Act | **1871** British Columbia joins the Dominion of Canada |

Wagons as used by pioneers on the Oregon Trail

Government House, New Westminster, BC, in 1870

In fact, two-thirds of the male population of Oregon followed the lure of gold. Many returned soon afterward with gold nuggets in their pockets. The Gold Rush moved north in 1851, when prospectors found gold in southern Oregon, and farther north again, to British Columbia's Fraser River, in 1858. Canadian prospectors also struck it big in 1860 in the Cariboo Mountains, in the BC Interior.

The Klondike, in Canada's Yukon Territory, was the stage for the next frenzy of gold fever. Once prospectors stepped off ships in Seattle and San Francisco, in 1896, with gold they had found along Bonanza Creek, the word was out. More than 100,000 prospectors flooded into the Klondike gold fields, and Vancouver and Seattle prospered by supplying and housing the miners and banking their finds.

Portland, City of Roses

MODERN TIMES

By the early 20th century, the Pacific Northwest was celebrating its prosperity. Portland hosted the Lewis and Clark Exposition in 1905, honoring the pair's voyage 100 years earlier. The

city put up new buildings downtown, planted thousands of roses, and laid out new parks for the event. Many of the thousands of exposition visitors stayed in the newly dubbed "City of Roses," and the population doubled to more than 250,000 by 1910. Seattle, having quickly rebounded from an 1889 fire that leveled all of downtown, followed suit in 1909 with the Alaska-Yukon-Pacific Exposition.

These expositions set the stage for the region's growth throughout the 20th century. The Boeing Airplane Company, founded in Seattle in 1916 and rivaling the state's timber industry in economic importance, created tens of thousands of jobs through its military and commercial aircraft contracts. During World War II (1939–45), factories in the Pacific Northwest produced aircraft, weapons, and warships for the Allies' war effort. When Seattle-based Microsoft took off in the 1980s, this ushered in a wave of high-tech business.

Vancouver became the focus of world attention when 21 million visitors attended festivities at Expo '86 to celebrate Canada's 100th anniversary. In the years immediately following, there was a huge surge in population growth, business development, and cultural diversification.

Historic cannery along the British Columbia coast

TIMELINE

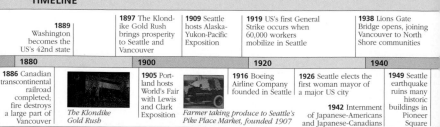

1889 Washington becomes the US's 42nd state	**1897** The Klondike Gold Rush brings prosperity to Seattle and Vancouver	**1909** Seattle hosts Alaska-Yukon-Pacific Exposition	**1919** US's first General Strike occurs when 60,000 workers mobilize in Seattle		**1938** Lions Gate Bridge opens, joining Vancouver to North Shore communities
1880		**1900**		**1920**	**1940**
1886 Canadian transcontinental railroad completed; fire destroys a large part of Vancouver	*The Klondike Gold Rush*	**1905** Portland hosts World's Fair with Lewis and Clark Exposition	*Farmer taking produce to Seattle's Pike Place Market, founded 1907*	**1916** Boeing Airline Company founded in Seattle	**1926** Seattle elects the first woman mayor of a major US city	**1942** Internment of Japanese-Americans and Japanese-Canadians	**1949** Seattle earthquake ruins many historic buildings in Pioneer Square

Mount St. Helens before its cataclysmic explosion

In the late 1990s, trade liberalization and the globalization of goods manufacturing increasingly became topics for public debate. On the streets of Seattle, in December 1999, more than 30,000 protested against the World Trade Organization and its policies on multinational corporations, environmental and labor laws, and subsidies for developing countries.

The Pacific Northwest has also had its share of natural disasters in modern times. Washington's Mount St. Helens *(see pp192–3)* erupted violently in 1980; an earthquake triggered the largest avalanche in recorded history, killing 57 people as well as millions of birds, deer, elk, and fish. Floods and avalanches devastated parts of Oregon and Washington in February 1996, as a result of heavy rains and melting snow caused by unusually mild temperatures; the swelling of the Willamette River and its tributaries forced the evacuation of residents in low-lying areas, stranded hundreds of drivers, and resulted in at least one fatality. On the evening of February 28, 2001, Seattle was rocked by a Mardi Gras riot and then a 6.8-magnitude earthquake. The façades of many of the

Snowy owl, endangered species

historic red-brick buildings in Pioneer Square were destroyed by a combination of the rioters' violence and the effects of the quake.

For the Native peoples of the Pacific Northwest, the 20th century brought gains as well as losses. Fishing rights were restored, but the construction of dams along many rivers destroyed some traditional fishing grounds and greatly diminished salmon runs. The casinos on Native lands brought economic benefits to some tribes but not to others. With the Nisga'a Treaty, drawn up in 2000, the Canadian and BC governments acknowledged that 744 sq miles (1,927 sq km) of crown land in northern British Columbia belongs to the Nisga'a Nation.

Keeping the landscape pristine in the Pacific Northwest continues to be both a source of pride and an ongoing bone of contention. Conservationists fight to curtail lumbering operations and limit growth, while loggers and ranchers often resist government intervention in their affairs. This conflict between the need to protect the environment and interests in capitalizing on the region's natural resources shows no sign of slowing.

Airplanes on the Boeing assembly line, Seattle

THE PACIFIC
NORTHWEST
REGION BY REGION

The Pacific Northwest at a Glance

An area of many contrasts, the Pacific Northwest has much to offer visitors. From Portland, Seattle, and Vancouver, its vibrant and attractive cities, many of the region's impressive natural wonders are only a short excursion away. Imposing mountain ranges, vast stretches of deserts, deep, wild canyons, crystal-clear lakes, and a magnificent coastline ensure that there is a sight or activity to suit every taste. While in summer wildflowers carpet alpine meadows, in winter, visitors and locals take advantage of the snow-covered slopes to enjoy winter sports. On the West Coast, whale-watching enchants visitors year-round.

Alta Lake, *in Whistler, British Columbia, offers many summer activities in a town which, in winter, is one of the world's most popular ski destinations* (see pp256–7).

Cannon Beach *is just one of the many beautiful stops along the Oregon coast offering breathtaking vistas of sand, sky, and sea-stacks that rise out of the ocean* (see p92).

Deepwood Estate *(1894), one of Salem's many historic buildings, is now a museum showcasing period pieces that offer a glimpse of what life was once like in this city, Oregon's capital since 1851* (see pp100–1).

| 0 kilometers | 150 |
| 0 miles | 100 |

◁ **Coaling station in Nanaimo, Vancouver Island, British Columbia (1859)**

Sinclair Pass, *located on the parkway that cuts through British Columbia's Kootenay National Park, is surrounded by the high walls of Sinclair Canyon, a red limestone gorge. It is just one of many natural wonders that attracts visitors to this national park, which covers 543 sq miles (1,406 sq km) of diverse terrain* (see p265).

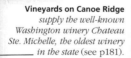

Fort Steele Heritage Town *is a re-created BC mining town. The original town of Fort Steele was established in 1864 after gold was discovered nearby. When its fortunes faded, it became a ghost town – until reconstruction began in 1961* (see p264).

Whatcom Museum of History and Art, *in Bellingham, Washington, houses many excellent exhibits on the Native peoples of the Pacific Northwest coast* (see p180).

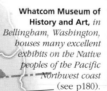

Vineyards on Canoe Ridge *supply the well-known Washington winery Chateau Ste. Michelle, the oldest winery in the state* (see p181).

Granite, *in Oregon, once a thriving Gold Rush town, is now a ghost town* (see p112).

PORTLAND

Portland's Best

Portland enhances its beautiful natural surroundings with a healthy dose of urban vitality and a relaxed yet sophisticated lifestyle. Spectacular parks and gardens flourish throughout the City of Roses. Historic landmarks and neighborhoods show off the city's commitment to preserving its rich past, while Pioneer Courthouse Square, a bustling pedestrian-only space in the heart of what is now the city center, reflects the effective urban planning that makes Portland so pleasant. Meanwhile, the city continues to enhance its many charms with locales such as the Pearl District, a neighborhood that has emerged out of an old industrial area.

One of Portland's many roses

Pearl District
Portland has reclaimed this former industrial district as its neighborhood for art galleries, boutiques, restaurants, and sophisticated urban living (see pp54–5).

Portland Streetcar
Modern, low-slung trams link Nob Hill, the Pearl District, and downtown Portland. Not only is a ride a handy way to get around town, but it's free within the city center (see p63).

Governor Hotel
Early 20th-century grandeur prevails at the Governor Hotel. Murals in the ground-floor Jake's Grill honor an earlier chapter of local history – the Lewis and Clark Expedition (see p60).

Portland Art Museum
The holdings of the oldest art museum in the Pacific Northwest include European paintings, Asian ceramics, and Native American basketry (see p62).

South Park Blocks
A farmers' market is held here every Saturday (Mar–Dec) in this area of elm-shaded lawns laid out in 1852 (see p62).

| 0 meters | 200 |
| 0 yards | 200 |

◁ Downtown Portland's skyline at twilight

Powell's City of Books
The largest independent bookstore in the world houses more than a million volumes (maps of the store are provided) and is one of Portland's most popular spots (see p55).

Classical Chinese Garden
This Ming Dynasty-style walled garden, with its tile-roofed pavilions, embodies traditional Chinese concepts of harmony and tranquility (see p54).

Pioneer Court-house Square
At the city center is a welcoming expanse of brick paving where Portlanders gather, come rain or shine (see p60).

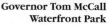

Governor Tom McCall Waterfront Park
Portland has reclaimed this 1.5-mile- (2.5-km-) long stretch of Willamette River waterfront as a park, waterside promenade, and locale for the Rose Festival and other public celebrations (see pp64–5).

Keller Auditorium
Keller Auditorium hosts operas and Broadway shows; the adjacent Ira Keller Memorial Fountain suggests the waterfalls of the Cascade Mountains (see p65).

OLD TOWN
AND THE PEARL DISTRICT

Portland grew up along the west bank of the Willamette River. Following its establishment in 1843, it became a major port, and docks in the riverfront quarter now known as Old Town were often lined with schooners that sailed across the Pacific Ocean to China and around Cape Horn to the east coast of the US. Old Town was the city's commercial center and home to many Asian immigrants who came to work at the port. The city center moved inland in the late 19th century, when the arrival of the railroad reduced river trade. Declared a National Historic Landmark in 1975, Old Town is now once again a popular part of the city. Many 19th-century buildings have been restored, and a Chinese-American community still lives here. The Pearl District, an early 20th-century industrial area west of Old Town, has also been transformed into a trendy neighborhood.

Glass art at the Saturday Market

SIGHTS AT A GLANCE

Gardens and Districts
Classical Chinese Garden ❷
Pearl District ❸

Museums
Oregon Maritime Center
and Museum ❶

Portland Institute for
Contemporary Art ❹

Shops
Powell's City of Books ❺

NW MARSHALL STREET
NW LOVEJOY STREET
NW KEARNEY ST
NW JOHNSON STREET
NW IRVING ST
NORTHWEST 11TH AVENUE
NORTHWEST 10TH AVENUE
NW 9TH AVENUE
NW PARK AVENUE
NORTHWEST BROADWAY

Union Station
Greyhound Bus Terminal
Union Station/ NW 6th & Hoyt
NORTHWEST HOYT STREET
Union Station/ NW 5th & Glisan
NW GLISAN STREET
NORTHWEST FLANDERS STREET
NORTHWEST EVERETT STREET
NORTH PARK BLOCKS
NW 14TH AVENUE
NORTHWEST 13TH AVENUE
NORTHWEST 12TH AVENUE
NW 8TH AVENUE
NW 6TH AVENUE
NW 5TH AVENUE
NW 4TH AVENUE

Old Town/ Chinatown
NORTHWEST DAVIS STREET
NW 6th & Davis
NW 5th & Couch
NORTHWEST COUCH STREET
WEST BURNSIDE STREET
SW OAK STREET
SW 6th & Pine
SW 5th & Oak
SW PINE STREET
SW ASH STREET
SOUTHWEST ANKENY STREET
Skidmore Fountain

Willamette River
Broadway Bridge
NORTHWEST NAITO PARKWAY
Steel Bridge
SOUTHWEST NAITO PARKWAY
GOVERNOR TOM McCALL WATERFRONT PARK
Burnside Bridge

0 meters 200
0 yards 200

KEY

▮ Street-by-Street map
See pp52–3

🚉 MAX station

🚉 Train station

🚉 Long-distance bus station

🚋 Streetcar stop

☒ Post office

GETTING THERE

Metro Area Express (MAX) red, blue, green, and yellow lines pass through Old Town. Portland Streetcar serves the Pearl District; Old Town and most of the Pearl District stops are in the Fareless Square zone.

◁ The main gateway leading to Portland's Saturday Market, held both days of the weekend in Old Town

Street-by-Street: Old Town

Metal pennant at Portland's Saturday Market

Elegant brick façades and quiet streets belie Old Town's raucous, 19th-century frontier-town past, when the district hummed with traders, dockworkers, shipbuilders, and sailors from around the world. While the saloons and bordellos that once did a brisk business are long gone, Old Town is still known for harboring some of the city's wilder night life. The street life here can be colorful, too, especially on weekends, when the Saturday Market takes over several blocks, as well as during the many festivals held year-round on the nearby waterfront.

Chinatown Gate
This multicolored, five-tiered, dragon-festooned gate is the official entryway to Chinatown, home to many immigrants from Asia for more than 135 years.

The New Market Block
This group of Italianate buildings is typical of the cast-iron and brick structures built after fire destroyed much of Portland in the 1870s.

STAR SIGHTS

★ Classical Chinese Garden

★ Oregon Maritime Center and Museum

★ Portland Saturday Market

Skidmore Fountain
Built in 1888 as a place for citizens and horses to quench their thirst, this elegant fountain and the adjacent plaza are at the center of Old Town.

0 meters	100
0 yards	100

LOCATOR MAP
See Street Finder Map 2

★ **Classical Chinese Garden**
*In this one-block-square walled
enclave, stone paths wind through a
beautiful landscape of water, stone,
plantings, and Chinese pavilions* ❷

★ **Portland
Saturday Market**
*On Saturdays and
Sundays, over 300
vendors gather here
for America's largest
handicrafts market.*

**Governor Tom McCall
Waterfront Park Walkway**
*This path extends along the west side
of the river from Burnside Bridge to
RiverPlace Marina (see p65).*

★ **Oregon Maritime Center
and Museum**
*One of the best things about this inform-
ative little maritime museum is where
it's housed – aboard the tugboat Portland, which is docked in the Willamette
River alongside the waterfront* ❶

Oregon Maritime Center and Museum ❶

113 SW Naito Pkwy. **Map** 2 E5.
Tel (503) 224-7724. 🚋 Skidmore
Fountain (red, blue lines).
⬜ 11am–4pm Wed–Sat, 12:30–
4:30pm Sun. ⬤ major hols. 📷
www.oregonmaritimemuseum.org

This small but colorful museum is housed aboard the *Portland*, a stern-wheel, steam-powered tugboat – the last to be in operation in the US when it was decommissioned in 1982. The ship is now permanently moored alongside Governor Tom McCall Waterfront Park *(see pp64–5)* where docks once bustled with seafaring trade.

Visits include a climb up to the captain's quarters and the wheelhouse, which provides a captivating view of the river, the downtown waterfront, and the bridges that span the Willamette River. Visitors can also descend into the huge below-decks engine room.

In the main cabin, photographs, paintings, models of ships, navigation instruments, and other marine memorabilia record the pre-railroad days when Portland, with its key position at the confluence of the Willamette and Columbia Rivers, flourished as a major seaport. Visitors also get a glimpse of maritime life in Portland throughout the 20th century, during which the city was an important shipping center and its shipyards were some of the largest in the world. Portland continues to be a major port today.

Ship's wheel on board the Oregon Maritime Center and Museum

An intricately carved pavilion at the Classical Chinese Garden

Classical Chinese Garden ❷

NW 3rd Ave & NW Everett St.
Map 2 D3. **Tel** (503) 228-8131.
🚌 1, 4, 5, 8, 10, 16, 33, 40, 77.
🚋 Old Town/Chinatown (red, blue
lines), Union Station/NW Glisan St
(green, yellow lines). ⬜ Apr–Oct:
10am–6pm daily; Nov–Mar: 10am–
5pm daily. ⬤ Jan 1, Thanksgiving,
Dec 25. 📷 ♿ partial. 📷 📷 📷
www.portlandchinesegarden.org

Artisans and architects from Suzhou, Portland's sister city in China, built this walled garden in the late 1990s. The gardens, which cover one entire city block, or 40,000 sq ft (4,000 sq m), are located in Portland's Chinatown.

The landscape of pavilions, waterfalls, lily pads, bamboo, a bridged lake, and stone paths, is classic 15th-century Ming Dynasty style and provides a tranquil glimpse of nature amid urban surroundings. Hundreds of plants grow in the garden, many of which are indigenous to Southeast China. Artfully placed rocks mimic mountain peaks, below which water flows through lily ponds and gurgles across rock gardens. Mosaic-patterned footpaths winding through stands of bamboo and across bridges lead to nine pavilions, intended to be places for rest and contemplation. One of the ornate pavilions contains a teahouse that serves tea and *dim sum*.

Throughout the garden, poems and literary allusions are inscribed on rocks, entryways, plaques, and above doors and windows.

Pearl District ❸

W Burnside to the Willamette River
(N), from NW 8th to NW 15th Aves.
Map 1 B3. 🚋 to NW Glisan St.

Portland's "newest" neighborhood occupies an old industrial district on the north side of Burnside Street, between Chinatown to the east and Nob Hill *(see p68)* to the west. Galleries, shops, design studios, breweries, cafés, restaurants, and clubs – especially hip and trendy ones – occupy former warehouses, factories, and garages. Meanwhile, buildings are being renovated as condos and apartments, and modern residential blocks are going up all the time. Visitors may notice many similarities to urban renewal projects in other cities such as Boston, New York, and London, but the Pearl District is still relatively free of large-scale commercialism. Some big-name stores, such as REI and North Face, have moved in; a sign that the neighborhood is changing.

One of the most enjoyable times to visit the Pearl District neighborhood is during a First Thursday event (the first Thursday of every month), when the many art galleries in the area remain open late to show the latest pieces. The collections feature a broad range of contemporary art and artists. The gallery receptions are open to the public and are free of charge.

Art galleries have played such an important role in the development of the Pearl

The Pearl District's First Thursday, showcasing the work of local artists

District that Jamison Square Park is named after William Jamison, the first art dealer to set up shop in the area. Jamison Square, the first of three new parks built in the area, includes a water feature that fills and recedes over a central plaza. When the fountain is not in use, the plaza is used as an amphitheater for small performances. The park also features a wooden boardwalk, lawns, and colorful public art. It is an excellent place to begin a walk around the area, taking in the contemporary and historical buildings, and the district's ongoing regeneration.

The name of the district itself is said to have been coined by a local gallery owner, Thomas Augustine. He suggested that the buildings in the Warehouse District were like gray, dull oysters, and that the galleries within were like pearls.

Portland Institute for Contemporary Art ❹

224 NW 13th Ave. **Map** 1 B3. *Tel (503) 242-1419.* 🚃 *to NW Everett St.* ⬤ *10am–5pm Mon–Fri.* ⬤ *major hols.* ♿ www.pica.org

Portland's venue for the latest trends in art does not have a permanent collection but hosts a variety of exhibitions, lectures, and residencies culminating in the annual Time-Based Art (TBA) festival every July and August. The institute also provides a stage for performing artists from around the world, and has sponsored appearances of new-music composer Philip Glass and the experimental performance-art troupe, Dumb Type.

Powell's City of Books ❺

1005 W Burnside St. **Map** 1 B4. *Tel (503) 228-4651.* 🚃 *20.* ⬤ *9am–11pm daily.* ♿ *See Shopping in Portland p76.* www.powells.com

The largest independent bookstore in the world houses more than one million volumes on a wealth of subjects. The store welcomes 6,000 shoppers each day, and has become one of Portland's most beloved cultural institutions.

Despite its size, Powell's is easy to browse in: the 3,500 sections are divided into nine color-coded and well-marked-rooms, and knowledgeable staff at the information desks possess the remarkable ability to lay their hands on any book in the store. The in-store coffee shop allows browsers to linger for hours, making Powell's a popular hangout any day of the year. Indeed, it's open all 365 of them.

Entrance to Powell's City of Books, a mecca for book lovers

CITY OF BRIDGES

Portland, the City of Roses, is also called the City of Bridges because the east and west banks of the Willamette River are linked by eight bridges. The first to be built was the Morrison, in 1887, though the original wooden crossing has long since been replaced. Pedestrian walkways on many of the bridges connect the Eastbank Esplanade on the east side of the river with Governor Tom McCall Waterfront Park on the west side. The Steel Bridge affords the most dramatic crossing: a pedestrian path on the lower railroad deck seems to be almost at water level; when a ship needs to pass, the entire deck is lifted into the bottom of the roadway above.

St. Johns Bridge, built in 1931

One of the many specialty shops in the Pearl District

DOWNTOWN

With the decline of river traffic in the late 19th century, Portland's center moved inland to the blocks around the intersection of Morrison Street and Broadway. The 1905 Lewis and Clark Exposition brought new prosperity and new residents to the city: downtown became a boomtown. Steel-frame buildings with façades of glazed, white terra-cotta tiles (Macy's department store is a fine example) began to rise; they

Allow Me sculpture by Seward Johnson

continue to give the downtown a bright, distinctive look. Since the 1970s, urban planning efforts have earned Portland's downtown a reputation as one of the most successful city centers in the US. The area around Pioneer Courthouse Square is the city's commercial and cultural hub, while many government offices are housed in innovative new buildings to the east, near historic Chapman and Lownsdale Squares.

SIGHTS AT A GLANCE

Buildings, Churches, and Museums

Governor Hotel ❸
Keller Auditorium ⓰
KOIN Center ⓯
Mark O. Hatfield
 US Courthouse ⓭
Multnomah County Library ❹
Old Church ❽
Oregon Historical Society ❻
Pioneer Courthouse ❷
Portland Art Museum ❼
Portland Building ⓫
Portland Center for the
 Performing Arts ❺

Parks and Squares

Chapman and Lownsdale
 Squares ⓬
Governor Tom McCall
 Waterfront Park ⓮
Pioneer
 Courthouse
 Square ❶
RiverPlace
 Marina ⓱
South Park
 Blocks ❾

Other Attractions

Portland
 Streetcar ❿

KEY

▢	Street-by-Street map *See pp58–9*
🚇	MAX station
🚋	Streetcar stop
ℹ️	Information
🚓	Police station

0 meters   300
0 yards   300

GETTING THERE

Buses on most major routes share the transit malls on SW 5th Ave. (northbound) and SW 6th Ave. (southbound) with the MAX green and yellow lines. MAX red and blue lines run east on SW Taylor St., west on SW Morrison. The Portland Streetcar runs north on SW 10th Ave., south on SW 11th Ave.

◁ Light-filled atrium at the Pioneer Place shopping mall near Pioneer Courthouse Square

Street-by-Street: Downtown

The top of the Weather Machine

One of the most appealing characteristics of Portland is the way the city combines cosmopolitan sophistication with a relaxed, low-key ambience. Nowhere is this more in evidence than on the attractive downtown blocks that surround Pioneer Courthouse Square. Broadway and the streets that cross it here are lined with department stores and boutiques, office complexes, hotels, restaurants, theaters, and museums, many occupying well-restored century-old buildings. Busy and vital as these downtown blocks are, sidewalks are shaded, parks are plentiful, and glimpses of the hills and mountains that encircle the city are easy to come by.

★ Portland Art Museum
The holdings of the oldest art museum in the Pacific Northwest range from Monet paintings to Native American crafts 7

Oregon Historical Society
Huge murals on the façades of this complex depict scenes from the Lewis and Clark expedition and other great moments in Oregon history. Inside is a wealth of memorabilia from the early days of the state 6

★ South Park Blocks
Daniel Lownsdale laid out these city blocks as parkland in 1848. A local farmer's market is held here Saturdays in spring through fall 9

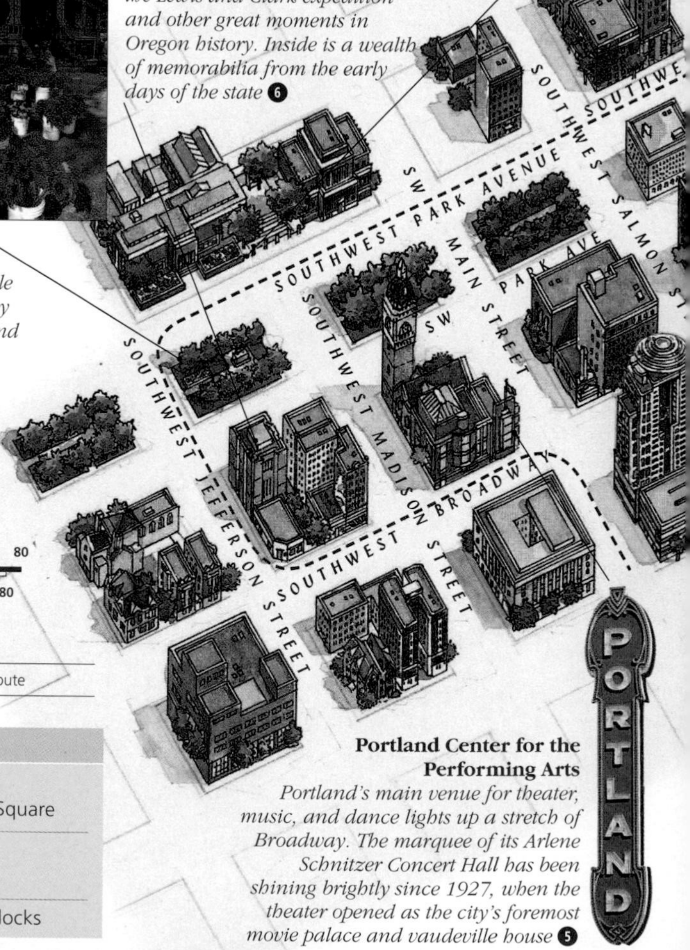

0 meters 80
0 yards 80

KEY

- - - Suggested route

Portland Center for the Performing Arts
Portland's main venue for theater, music, and dance lights up a stretch of Broadway. The marquee of its Arlene Schnitzer Concert Hall has been shining brightly since 1927, when the theater opened as the city's foremost movie palace and vaudeville house 5

STAR SIGHTS

★ Pioneer Courthouse Square

★ Portland Art Museum

★ South Park Blocks

Weather Machine
A whimsical, 25-ft- (8-m-) tall sculpture comes to life every day at noon, when figures emerge from its top to announce the weather for the next 24 hours.

Jackson Tower, built by the Reid brothers in 1912 for a newspaper magnate, features glazed terra-cotta as a decorative element for its steel frame.

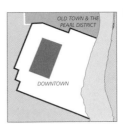

LOCATOR MAP
See Street Finder map 1

American Bank Building
This classical building, finished in 1914, features Corinthian columns at its base and is decorated with terra-cotta eagles and griffins.

★ **Pioneer Courthouse Square**
This one-block-square open space is the heart of Portland, where fountains splash and Portlanders gather for free lunchtime concerts, flower shows, and other events, or simply for a chance to sit and enjoy their city ❶

Pioneer Courthouse
The octagonal tower of the first federal building in the Pacific Northwest has been a fixture of the Portland skyline since 1873 ❷

Pioneer Courthouse Square, a popular public gathering place

Pioneer Courthouse Square ❶

SW Broadway & Yamhill St. **Map** 1 C5. **Tel** (503) 223-1613. 🚆 Pioneer Square (red, blue, green, yellow lines). & **www**.pioneercourthouse square.org

Pioneer Courthouse Square resembles the large central plazas of many European cities, which was the intent of the city planners who designed this brick-paved pedestrian-only square in the mid-1980s. Despite its recent vintage, the square stands on hallowed Portland ground: the city's first schoolhouse was erected on this site in 1858, and the much-admired Portland Hotel stood here from 1890 to 1951, when it was demolished to make way for a parking lot.

According to plan, Pioneer Courthouse Square has become the center of the city, a friendly space where Portlanders gather to enjoy a brown-bag lunch or free outdoor concert. Architectural flourishes include a graceful, amphitheater-like bank of seats, a fountain that resembles a waterfall, and a row of 12 columns crowned with gilt roses.

Underground spaces adjoining the square accommodate offices and businesses, including the Portland Visitors Association Information Center, a coffee shop, and a 75-seat theater featuring films on the history and highlights of Portland. The most compelling aspect of the square, though, is the lively presence of the many residents who use the space.

Pioneer Courthouse ❷

700 SW 6th Ave. **Map** 1 C5. **Tel** (503) 833-5311. 🚆 Pioneer Square (red, blue, green, yellow lines). ⭘ 9am–4pm Mon–Fri. ⬤ Sat, Sun & major hols. &

Completed in 1873 and re-stored in 2005, Pioneer Courthouse was the first federal building to be constructed in the Pacific Northwest and is the second oldest federal building west of the Mississippi River. The trees planted here at that time are still standing. The Italianate structure, faced with freestone and topped by a domed cupola, houses the US Court of Appeals. There are panoramic views of Portland from the cupola and historic photographs next to each window show how the same view looked in the city's early years.

Governor Hotel ❸

614 SW 11th Ave. **Map** 1 B5. **Tel** (503) 224-3400. 🚆 Galleria/SW 10th Ave (red, blue lines). 🚎 to SW Alder St. & See **Where to Stay** p282. **www**.governorhotel.com

The hotel opened as the Seward Hotel in 1909 and, after sitting empty in disrepair for years, as the Governor Hotel in 1991. The expedition of Meriwether Lewis and William Clark (see p37), whose 1804–1806 journey across the US and down the Columbia River put Oregon on the map, figures promi-nently in the Governor Hotel.

A sepia-colored, four-section mural in the former lobby, now part of the restaurant, shows a map of the Lewis and Clark expedition and depicts scenes from the explorers' journey: Native Americans fishing at Celilo Falls on the Columbia River, Meriwether Lewis trading with members of the Nez Percé tribe in present-day Idaho, and the guide Sacagawea (see p37) surveying the Pacific Ocean. Even the lampshades pay tribute to the pair – they are decorated with excerpts from the explorers' journals.

The hotel incorporates the ornate former headquarters of the Elks Lodge as its west wing, built in the luxuriant style of the pre-Depression early 1920s to resemble the Palazzo Farnese, in Rome. Mahogany detailing, leather chairs, fireplaces, and warm tones create an atmosphere of old-fashioned opulence.

Façade of the stately Governor Hotel

The light-filled stairwell of the Multnomah County Library

Multnomah County Library ❹

801 SW 10th Ave. **Map** 1 B5.
Tel (503) 988-5123. 🚇 Library/SW
9th Ave (red, blue lines). 🚌 to SW
Taylor St. ⬜ 10am–6pm Mon &
Thu–Sat, 10am–8pm Tue & Wed,
noon–5pm Sun. 🗓 major hols.
♿ 📷 www.multcolib.org

Alfred E. Doyle, the architect whose work in Portland includes such landmarks as the Meier and Frank department store and the drinking fountains that grace downtown streets, chose limestone and brick for this distinctive Georgian structure. The building, completed in 1913, is the headquarters of the county library system, established in 1864 and the oldest library system west of the Mississippi.

Construction cost $475,000 and was marred by accusations that materials were being diverted to private hands. Renovations, completed in 1997, amounted to $25 million. Notable holdings

of the collection, which is valued at $1.9 million, include one of the two known copies of the original Portland charter, housed in the John Wilson Rare Book Room.

Portland Center for the Performing Arts ❺

1111 SW Broadway. **Map** 3 B1.
Tel (503) 248-4335. 🚌 to SW
Broadway. ♿ 📷 www.pcpa.com

Since the mid-1980s, the Portland Center for the Performing Arts has been the city's major venue for theater, music, and dance. The complex consists of the Arlene Schnitzer Concert Hall and the New Theatre Building, on Broadway, and the Keller Auditorium, a few blocks east at Southwest 3rd Avenue and Clay Street (see p65). In the New Theatre Building, the 916-seat Newmark Theatre and the 292-seat Dolores Winningstad Theatre open off a dramatic, five-story, cherry-paneled rotunda capped by a dome designed by glass-artist James Carpenter.

The Arlene Schnitzer Concert Hall occupies a former vaudeville house and movie palace built in 1927. Its ornate, Italian Rococo Revival interior has been restored, and it is now the home of the Oregon Symphony. The marquee continues to illuminate Broadway with 6,000 lights, and it now props up a 65-ft-(20-m-) high sign that screams "Portland" in blue neon.

Oregon Historical Society ❻

1200 SW Park Ave. **Map** 3 B1.
Tel (503) 222-1741. 🚇 Library/
SW 9th Ave (red, blue lines). 🚌 to
Jefferson St. **Museum** ⬜ 10am–
5pm Tue–Sat, noon–5pm Sun.
Library ⬜ 1–5pm Tue, 10am–5pm
Wed–Sat. 📷 ♿ 📷 www.ohs.org

Eight-story murals by Richard Haas on the west and south façades of the Oregon Historical Society depict the Lewis and Clark expedition (see p37), fur trading, and other important events that have shaped the history of Oregon. On display in the galleries, which extend through three buildings, are some of the 85,000 objects that make this museum the largest repository of Oregon historical artifacts. The exhibits, which include maps, paintings, photographs, and historical documents, change frequently since space does not allow for the display of the entire collection at once.

The permanent collection includes the exhibit "Oregon My Oregon". This remarkable exhibition includes 50 separate displays that recount the history of the state. There are 12 distinct sections depicting Oregon's rich past, including Native American languages and culture, memorabilia tracing the state's maritime history, and the region's varied geography. Journals of pioneers can also be viewed in the society's research library.

The New Theatre in the Portland Center for the Performing Arts

Decorative murals on the façade of the Oregon Historical Society

Portland Art Museum's gallery of late 19th-century European art

Portland
Art Museum ❼

1219 SW Park Ave. **Map** 3 B1.
Tel (503) 226-2811. 🚇 Library/SW
9th Ave (red, blue lines). 🚌 to Jefferson St. ⬜ 10am–5pm Tue, Wed &
Sat, 10am–8pm Thu & Fri, noon–5pm
Sun. ⬤ major hols. 📷 ♿ 🖥 🏛
www.portlandartmuseum.org

The oldest art museum
in the Pacific Northwest
opened in 1892, introducing
the citizenry to classical art
with a collection of plaster
casts of Greek and Roman
sculpture. Today, the 42,000-
piece-strong collection, which
places the museum among
the 25 largest in the country,
is housed in a building
designed by modernist architect Pietro Belluschi. In 2005,
the North Building was extensively renovated in order to
house the Center for Modern
and Contemporary Art.

A sizable collection of
European paintings, including
works by Van Gogh, Picasso,
Italian Renaissance masters,
and French Impressionists,
hang in the galleries. Works
by Rodin and Brancusi fill
the sculpture court; further
galleries house works by Frank
Stella and Willem de Kooning;
and there is a wing devoted to
historical and contemporary
photographs, prints, sculptures, and drawings by artists
from the region. The Grand
Ronde Center for Native
American Art displays masks,
jewelry, totem poles, and
works by artists from 200 North
American indigenous groups.

The museum is an important
stop for traveling exhibitions.

Old Church ❽

1422 SW 11th Ave. **Map** 3 A1.
Tel (503) 222-2031. 🚌 to SW Clay
St. ⬜ 11am–3pm Mon–Fri. 🚶 self-
guided. www.oldchurch.org

Completed in 1883, this church
reflects a Victorian Gothic
Revival style, also known as
Stick or Carpenter Gothic style,
with exaggerated arches, a tall
steeple, and sleek windows.

The rough-hewn wood
exterior lends it a
distinctly Pacific Northwestern flavor. On
Wednesdays at noon,
the Hook and Hastings Tracker organ
is put into service
for free concerts.

The Gothic Revival–style Old
Church with its decorative arches

South Park Blocks ❾

Bounded by SW Salmon St & I-405,
SW Park & SW 9th Aves. **Map** 3 B1.
🚌 to stops between SW Salmon &
SW Mill Sts.

In 1852, frontier business
man and legislator Daniel
Lownsdale set aside the
blocks between Park and 9th
Avenues as parkland. After
the city council authorized
the landscaping of these

blocks, landscape designer
Louis G. Pfunder planted 104
Lombardy poplars and elms
between Salmon and Hall.
The so-called South Park
Blocks continue to form a
12-block ribbon of tree-shaded
lawns through the central city,
running past the Portland Art
Museum and the Portland
Center for the Performing Arts
(see p61) and into the campus
of Portland State University.
In this city forested by so
many evergreens, the blocks
of deciduous trees are
refreshingly pleasant in the
fall, when the foliage turns
vibrant colors. Particularly
vivid is the area around
Madison Street, where the
First Congregational Church
rises above the trees.

Notable statuary along the
blocks includes, between
Madison and Main Streets,
a dour-looking US president
Abraham Lincoln (1861–5) by
George Fite Waters, who was
a student of Rodin. One block
south is the 18-ft- (5.5-m-) tall
bronze equestrian *Rough
Rider*, a statue of President
Theodore Roosevelt (1901–
1909), by his friend and hunting partner Phimister Proctor.

Among the most distinctive
ornaments are the Benson
drinking fountains. In 1917,
lumber baron Samuel Benson
commissioned prominent
architect A.E. Doyle to design
these graceful, four-bowled
fountains. He placed 20 of
them throughout the South
Park Blocks and the rest of
downtown to quench the thirst
of Portland residents who
might otherwise be tempted
to frequent saloons. Since
then, 20 more fountains
have been added.

Offerings at the Saturday farmers'
market, South Park Blocks

Portland Streetcar ⑩

East- & southbound on NW Lovejoy St & 11th Ave, north- & westbound on 10th Ave & NW Northrup St. **Map** 1 A2–3 B2. ☐ *5:30am–11:30pm Mon–Fri, 7:15am–11:30pm Sat, 7:15am–10:30pm Sun.*

Horse-drawn streetcars began running in the 1870s. By the early 20th century, electric streetcars were rumbling all across downtown, bringing downtown within reach of newly established residential neighborhoods. Cars had put the streetcars out of service by the 1950s, but in the late 1990s, city planners turned to streetcars again as part of a scheme intended to reduce congestion and ensure the vitality of the central business district.

The Czech-built streetcars travel a route that links the Nob Hill neighborhood, the Pearl District, the western edge of downtown, the campus of Portland State University, and the south waterfront, where they connect with the Aerial tram to Oregon Health and Science University. A ride on the streetcar and transfer to MAX lines *(see p78)* are free within the city's Fareless Square zone.

Portland Building ⑪

1120 SW 5th Ave. **Map** 3 C1. *Gallery* **Tel** *(503) 823-5252.* 🚋 *Transit Mall.* ☐ *6am–6pm Mon–Fri.* ⚫ *major hols.*

The Portland Building, designed by New Jersey architect Michael Graves, has been featured on the covers of both *Time* and *Newsweek* and was called Portland's "Eiffel Tower" by the city's former mayor Frank Ivancie. The building has been controversial ever since it was completed in 1982. Displaying an experimental combination of architectural styles, this first large-scale postmodern office building in the US has been hailed as a major innovation in contemporary urban design and a credit to forward-thinking Portland. It has also been denounced as just plain ugly. The use of muted colors and ornamental swags and pilasters lends a certain playfulness to the exterior, while the 15-story building's relatively modest height and multiple rows of small square windows suggest practicality and a lack

Portlandia **watching from the Portland Building**

The landmark Portland Building, home to City of Portland offices

of pretension, as befits the home of government offices.

More ostentatious is *Portlandia*, a 36-ft- (11-m-) tall statue fashioned from 6.5 tons of copper that emerges from a second-floor balcony above the main doors. The figure crouches, with one hand extended and the other brandishing a giant trident. Completed by sculptor Raymond Kaskey in 1985, *Portlandia* is modeled on Lady Commerce, the symbolic figure that appears on the city seal and that supposedly welcomed traders into the city's port. After New York City's Statue of Liberty, *Portlandia* is the largest copper statue in the US.

A small gallery on the second floor of the building displays public art of the region. There are also plans and models related to the design and construction of the building and the *Portlandia* statue.

PORTLAND THE GREEN

Justifiably, Portland's abundant parks and gardens are often described in superlatives. The city can make claim to one of the largest forested city parks in the US, 5,000-acre (2,025-ha) Forest Park, and the smallest park in the world, 452-sq-inch (0.3-sq-m) Mill Ends Park *(see p65)*. The city boasts some of the nation's largest and most extensive rose test gardens *(see p72)*, one of the world's most renowned rhododendron gardens *(see p74)*, one of the finest Japanese gardens outside Japan *(see p72)*, and the largest classical Chinese garden outside China *(see p54)*. Many of the other parks and gardens included in the city's 36,000 acres (14,600 ha) of greenspace have no such claims attached, but they are nonetheless pleasant places in which to enjoy the great outdoors.

Mill Ends Park, the world's tiniest park

Czech-built Portland streetcars, environmentally sound transit

Chapman and Lownsdale Squares ⑫

Bounded by SW Salmon & SW Madison Sts, SW 3rd & SW 4th Aves. **Map** 3 C1. 🚊 *Mall/SW 4th Ave (red, blue lines), City Hall/SW Jefferson St (green, yellow lines).*

It is only fitting that Daniel Lownsdale should have a one-block-square park named for him. The tanner who became one of Oregon's early legislators had the foresight to set aside a parcel of downtown for the South Park Blocks *(see p62)*, and he did much to encourage trade on the nearby waterfront by building a wood-plank road into the countryside so that lumber and other goods could be transported to the Portland docks.

Judge William Chapman, for whom the adjoining square is named, was one of the founders of the *Oregonian* newspaper. Along with Terry Schrunk Plaza – a third, adjacent park-like block – the squares provide a soothing stretch of greenery in Portland's quiet courthouse and government-building district. The neighborhood was not always so sedate though: anti-Chinese riots broke out here in the 1880s, and the area was raucous enough in the 1920s that Chapman Square was declared off-limits to men so that women could enjoy the space in safety.

Portland's popular Elk Fountain, built in 1852, near the courthouse

The limestone, aluminum, and glass Mark O. Hatfield US Courthouse

Mark O. Hatfield US Courthouse ⑬

1000 SW 3rd Ave. **Map** 3 C1. **Tel** *(503) 326-8000.* 🚊 *Transit Mall.* ⏰ *7am–5pm Mon–Fri.* ⬤ *major hols.* ♿

Named for a popular Oregon governor and senator, the Mark O. Hatfield US Courthouse defies any preconceived notion that a government building is by definition unimaginative. Designed by the New York firm of Kohn Pedersen Fox and completed in 1997, the courthouse presents a hand-some and bold façade of glass, aluminum, and limestone. A ninth-floor sculpture garden provides excellent views of both the river and one of Portland's most beloved pieces of statuary, the **Elk Fountain**, which stands across the street.

Erected in 1852 on land where elk once roamed freely, for many years the Elk Fountain provided citizens' horses with a place to drink. When automobile traffic began to increase in the early 20th century, the fountain stood in the path of a proposed extension of Main Street. Angry citizens protested plans to move the fountain; it now stands in the middle of the street.

Governor Tom McCall Waterfront Park ⑭

Bounded by SW Harrison & NW Glisan Sts, SW Naito Pkwy & Willamette River. **Map** 4 D1. 🚊 *Skidmore Fountain, Morrison/SW 3rd Ave, Yamhill District (red, blue lines).*

This 1.5-mile- (2.5-km-) long park on the west bank of the Willamette River covers 23 acres (9 ha) of land that once bustled with activity on the Portland docks and which, from the 1940s to the 1970s, was buried beneath an expressway. The city converted the land to a park as part of an urban renewal scheme and named it for the environmentally minded Tom McCall, Oregon's governor, 1967–75.

The park is a much-used riverside promenade and the locale for many festivals. One of its most popular attractions is **Salmon Street Springs**, a fountain whose 100 jets splash water directly onto the pavement, providing easily accessible relief on a hot day. The foot of nearby Southwest Salmon Street was once the roughest part of town. Here, drunken revelers were routinely knocked unconscious and then taken aboard ships as involuntary crew members.

The Battleship Oregon Memorial, Gov. Tom McCall Waterfront Park

A block away, at the foot of Southwest Taylor Street, is **Mill Ends Park**, measuring only 452 sq inches (0.3 sq m). The park is the former site of a telephone pole, removed in the late 1940s. Local journalist Dick Fagan began planting flowers on the patch of earth and writing articles about what he dubbed the "World's Smallest Park," which it officially became when the City of Portland adopted it as part of the park system in 1976.

The **Battleship Oregon Memorial**, built in 1956, honors an 1893 US Navy ship. A time capsule sealed in its base in 1976 is due to be opened in 2076.

The multifunctional KOIN Center, rising 29 stories above Portland

KOIN Center ⓯

222 SW Columbia St. **Map** *3 C2.* Transit Mall.

Like the Portland Building *(see p63)*, the KOIN Center is designed in the postmodern style, which incorporates a plurality of architectural styles in one structure. However, this 29-story blond-brick tower capped by a pyramidal blue steel roof has elicited none of the controversy that the Portland Building has. Instead, the KOIN Center, designed by the Portland firm of Zimmer Gunsul Frasca and completed in 1984, is considered a model urban complex. The building houses residences, offices – including those of the television station for which it is named – and shops, as well as a popular steakhouse.

Keller Auditorium, part of the Portland Center for the Performing Arts

Keller Auditorium ⓰

222 SW Clay St. **Map** 3 C2. **Tel** *(503) 248-4335.* Transit Mall. ♿

When a Broadway roadshow or other big production comes to Portland, the 3,000-seat Keller Auditorium often plays host. Built in 1917 on the former site of an exhibition hall and sports arena known as the Mechanics' Pavilion, the auditorium was completely remodeled in the late 1960s, gaining clean sightlines as well as excellent acoustics. The auditorium is part of the Portland Center for the Performing Arts *(see p61)* and is home to the Portland Opera, the Oregon Ballet, and the Oregon Children's Theatre.

Across the street is the **Ira Keller Memorial Fountain**, a waterfall cascading over 18-ft (5.5-m) concrete cliffs into a pool crisscrossed with platforms laid out like stepping stones. The fountain, enclosed by a delightful garden, successfully presents a typical Pacific Northwest experience – that of emerging from the shade of trees to the sight, sound, and spray of a plunging torrent. Completed in 1970, the fountain was designed by Angela Danadjieva. Originally called the Forecourt Fountain, it was renamed in 1978 to honor civic leader Ira C. Keller.

RiverPlace Marina ⓱

SW Clay St & Willamette River. **Map** 4 D3. *95X, 96.* RiverPlace. 🍴 🛍

RiverPlace Marina is located on the west bank of the Willamette River, situated at the southwest end of Governor Tom McCall Waterfront Park.

Among the amenities here are upscale shops, several restaurants, including Portland's only floating restaurant, and one of the city's higher-end hotels, RiverPlace Hotel. The complex also has sloping lawns, riverside walks, and a large marina. Sea kayaks are available for rental, providing an alternative way to view the river and city.

Ira Keller Memorial Fountain, across from Keller Auditorium

FARTHER AFIELD

By the late 19th century, Portland was fast growing from a small riverfront settlement surrounded by forests into an important port city. It expanded westward into Nob Hill, where wealthy merchants settled, and eastward across the Willamette River. In 1871, the City created Washington Park, now Portland's favorite green retreat. Crystal Springs Rhododendron Garden, to the south, is another tranquil spot. Numerous important events in Oregon's history transpired just south of Portland. Oregon City, at the end of the Oregon Trail, was the site of the first meeting of the territory's provisional legislature, in 1843. At Aurora a Utopian society once thrived, and at nearby Champoeg State Heritage Area pioneers voted to break from Britain.

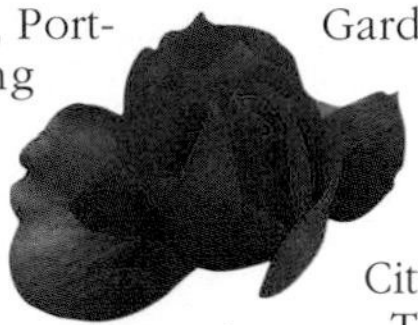

A rose in Washington Park

SIGHTS AT A GLANCE

Towns and Neighborhoods
Aurora 14
Hawthorne District 8
Nob Hill 4
Oregon City 13
Rose Quarter 5
Sellwood District 9

Institutions
Reed College 11

Museums
Oregon Museum of Science and Industry 7

Historic Buildings
Pittock Mansion 3

Historic Sites
End of the Oregon Trail Interpretive Center 12

Parks, Gardens, and Natural Areas
Crystal Springs Rhododendron Garden 10
Eastbank Esplanade 6
Sauvie Island 1
Washington Park pp70–73 2

KEY
Central Portland
Urban area
Major highway
Highway
Minor road
Airport

5 miles = 8 km

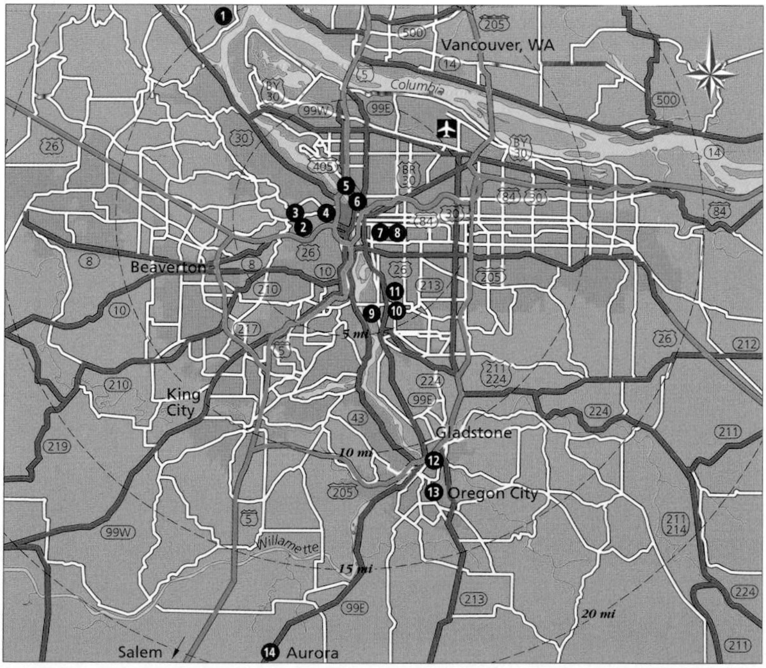

◁ **View of downtown Portland as seen from the International Rose Test Garden in Washington Park**

One of several beaches along Sauvie Island's Columbia River side

Sauvie Island ❶

🛈 18330 NW Sauvie Island Rd, (503) 621-3488. 🚌 17 NW 21st Ave/ St Helens Rd. **Sauvie Island Wildlife Area** ◯ mid-Apr–Sep: 4am–10pm daily.

Sauvie Island comprises 26,000 acres (10,500 ha) of low-lying land at the confluence of the Willamette and Columbia Rivers, just 10 miles (16 km) from downtown Portland. With rich soil that supports many berry farms and orchards, the southern half of the island is primarily agricultural. The northern half is set aside as the **Sauvie Island Wildlife Area**, managed by the Oregon Department of Fish and Wildlife. Birdwatchers come to see some of the estimated three million birds – including swans, ducks, and cranes – that stop here on their spring and fall migrations.

During the summer, swimmers and sunbathers enjoy beaches on the island's Columbia River side, and anglers fish for sturgeon and salmon in nearby channels.

The island's **Bybee-Howell House**, a Greek Revival-style house built in 1858 by James Y. Bybee, is surrounded by orchards with flourishing fruit trees, brought by pioneers on the Oregon Trail. An adjoining barn houses antique farm equipment.

🏛 **Bybee-Howell House**
Howell Territorial Park. **Tel** (503) 222-1741. ◯ until further notice.

Washington Park ❷

See pp70–73.

Pittock Mansion ❸

3229 NW Pittock Dr. **Tel** (503) 823-3623. 🚌 77. ◯ Feb–Jun & Sep–Dec: 11am–4pm daily; Jul–Aug: 10am–5pm daily. ◯ Jan, Thanksgiving weekend, late Nov & major hols. 🎫 ♿ (partial; call 48 hrs ahead). 🌐 📷 www.pittockmansion.org

Henry Pittock, who came west on the Oregon Trail as a young man and founded the *Oregonian* newspaper, commissioned this mansion in 1909. Designed by San Francisco architect Edward T. Foulkes, the house is still the grandest residence in Portland. Perched on a 1,000-ft (305-m) summit in the West Hills, it commands superb views of the city and snow-capped mountain peaks. The mansion's gardens are a good picnic spot.

Guided tours show off the mansion's remarkable embellishments. Among them are a marble staircase, elliptical drawing room, and circular Turkish-style smoking room. Family artifacts decorate the home. The furnishings, though not original to the house, reflect the finest tastes of Pittock's time.

The sweeping entrance of the imposing Pittock Mansion

A Nob Hill mansion, typical of those in the fashionable district

Nob Hill ❹

W Burnside to NW Pettigrove Sts, from NW 17th to NW 24th Sts. 🚋 to NW 23rd St.

Also known as Northwest 23rd in reference to its main business street, Nob Hill is a gracious, late 19th-century neighborhood of shady streets, large wooden houses, and apartment buildings. With its proximity to downtown and its inherent charms, Nob Hill has become one of the city's most popular commercial and residential neighborhoods. A slightly bohemian atmosphere, together with upscale shops and restaurants, make Nob Hill a pleasant place to stroll.

A turn-of-the-19th-century house in Nob Hill

Northwest 23rd Street from West Burnside to Northwest Lovejoy Streets is the neighborhood's commercial core. The side streets are lined with lovely old houses. The 1892 Victorian gingerbread **Pettigrove House** (2287 Northwest Pettigrove Street) was the home of Francis Pettigrove, the city founder who flipped a coin with fellow founder Asa Lovejoy to determine the city's name. Pettigrove won and choose the name of a city in his native Maine (Lovejoy preferred "Boston"). Northwest Johnson Street between Northwest 22nd and 23rd Streets is lined with many fine houses from the 1880s, when Nob Hill first became fashionable.

Rose Quarter ❺

1 Center Ct. 🚇 *Rose Quarter (red, blue lines). See **Entertainment in Portland** p77.*
www.rosequarter.com

Portland's major venues for sports, big-ticket entertainment events, and conventions are clustered in the Rose Quarter, a commercial riverside area on the east bank of the Willamette River. Portlanders come in droves to the otherwise quiet neighborhood to attend Portland Trail Blazer basketball games, Portland Winter Hawks ice hockey games, and major pop and rock concerts by the likes of Paul McCartney and Bruce Springsteen at the **Rose Garden Arena**. Designed by the Kansas City firm of Ellerbe Becket, the arena was completed in 1996. It features a unique "acoustical cloud" made up of 160 rotating acoustic panels which can be tailored to the needs of the specific event.

The smaller, nearby **Memorial Coliseum** (300 Winning Way) once hosted these events. Its glass-fronted hall, designed by New York firm Skidmore, Owens and Merrill and completed in 1960, is now used for conventions and trade shows.

The **Lloyd Center**, just east of the Rose Quarter, is recognized as the US's first covered shopping center. Although such malls are now ubiquitous, the Lloyd Center retains an old-fashioned charm, with more than 200 shops and restaurants lining handsome, well-planted walkways that radiate from a skating rink.

Portland's cityscape, the Eastbank Esplanade in the foreground

Eastbank Esplanade ❻

Bounded by Willamette River & I-5, Steel & Hawthorne Bridges. 🚇 *Rose Quarter (red, blue lines).* 🚌 *4, 5, 6, 8, 10, 14.*

This pedestrian and bicycle path following the east bank of the Willamette River between the Hawthorne and Steel Bridges was part of a massive riverfront redevelopment. While the esplanade's unobstructed views of downtown Portland and the opportunity it provides to enjoy the river are compelling reasons to visit, the walkway is an attraction in its own right. A 1,200-ft (365-m) section floats on the water, and another cantilevered portion is suspended above one of the city's original commercial piers.

The esplanade provides access to four of the city's major downtown bridges, linking the walkway to Governor Tom McCall Waterfront Park *(see pp64–5)* on the west bank of the river. The most dramatic crossing is via the Steel Bridge Riverwalk, perched just 30 ft (9 m) above the water.

Oregon Museum of Science and Industry ❼

1945 SE Water Ave. **Tel** *(503) 797-4000.* 🚌 *83, 14.* 🕐 *mid-Jun–Labor Day: 9:30am–7pm daily; Labor Day–mid-Jun: 9:30am–5:30pm Tue–Sun.* 🔴 *major hols.* 🎟 🚹 *(partial).* 🎟 *of submarine.* 🖥 🚻 **www**.omsi.edu

Commonly referred to as OMSI, the Oregon Museum of Science and Industry is one of the top science museums in the US. The multiple exhibition halls and science labs of this world-class tourist attraction house hundreds of interactive exhibits. Visitors may enjoy hands-on experiences in subjects such as physics, chemistry, space exploration, computers, and mathematics. A favorite is the earthquake simulator, in which visitors are shaken and rattled while learning about the tectonic plates that continue to shift beneath Portland.

The Kendall Planetarium, a state-of-the-art facility, places OMSI at the forefront of astronomical education, and an Omnimax theater with a five-story screen takes audiences on exciting adventures. For kids under nine, the Science Playground is a wonderland with interactive zones.

Moored alongside the museum is the USS *Blueback*, first launched in 1959 and the last diesel submarine to be used by the US Navy. Guided tours provide a chance to look at downtown through a periscope and to experience the claustrophobic conditions in which 85 submariners lived.

An interactive exhibit at the Oregon Museum of Science and Industry

Washington Park ❷

Though a park first took shape in the western hills of downtown Portland in 1871, it was not until 1903 that Washington Park acquired much of its present appearance. This was the year Boston landscape architect John Olmsted came to Portland to help plan the Lewis and Clark Exposition and lay out a parks plan for the young city. Reflecting Olmsted's suggestions, Washington Park has developed, over the years, to encompass gardens, open spaces, great groves of evergreens, a zoo, and recreational facilities. Today, the park is one of Portland's most popular outdoor playgrounds.

Sign at Washington Park's Oregon Zoo

★ Hoyt Arboretum
More than 8,000 trees and shrubs from around the world grow in this arboretum; they can be appreciated along the 12 miles (19 km) of well-marked hiking trails.

Vietnam Veterans of Oregon Memorial, a ring of dramatic black granite blocks, honors Oregonians who served in the Vietnam War.

World Forestry Center
This renowned center includes a discovery lab and a museum, with its "talking" 70-ft (21-m) Douglas fir that explains how trees grow and excellent exhibits on rain- and old-growth forests.

Portland Children's Museum is an exciting interactive museum designed for children from ages six months to ten years.

PEARL DISTRICT

West Burnside Street

Wildwood Trail

Kingston Drive

Southwest Canyon Road

P

P

STAR SIGHTS

★ Hoyt Arboretum

★ International Rose Test Garden

★ Japanese Garden

★ Oregon Zoo

★ Oregon Zoo
Oregon's most-visited attraction, famous for its elephants, is a noted research institute, harboring over 50 threatened and endangered species on 64 acres (25.5 ha) of forested hillside.

★ **Japanese Garden**
Plants, stones, and water are arranged to reflect the essence of nature in five distinct traditional Japanese gardens.

VISITORS' CHECKLIST

SW Park Pl. **Tel** *(503) 823-2525.*
🚃 *Washington Park (blue line).*
🚌 *63.* ⬜ *5am–10pm daily (not all sights).* 💰 *to some exhibits.*
🖥 *www.portlandonline.com*

KEY

🏕	Picnic area
🍴	Restaurant
– –	Trail
🅿	Parking
Ⓜ	MAX station
⊬	Train route
ℹ	Information
☽	Viewpoint

0 meters 400

0 yards 500

★ **International Rose Test Garden**
Award-winning roses from around the world, a grass amphitheater, and a walkway honoring every queen of the city's annual Rose Festival since 1907 are among the treasures of this 4-acre (1.5-ha) garden, the oldest public garden of its kind in the US.

Wildwood Trail, a 30-mile (48-km) portion of the 40-Mile Loop, runs the length of Washington Park and into Forest Park to the north, winding past Douglas firs and wildflowers.

Washington Park and Zoo Railway
Three trains – the old-style Steamer, the sleek 1958 Zooliner, and a circus train known as the Oregon Express – meander through the park's lush landscape, offering great views of downtown Portland, Mounts Hood and St. Helens, and the zoo.

Exploring Washington Park

Elephant in the Oregon Zoo

Hiking on a forest trail beneath a canopy of old-growth pine trees or coming upon a meadow filled with wildflowers, visitors may find it hard to believe that 320-acre (130-ha) Washington Park is surrounded by the city. Wild as the hilly terrain is in places, however, the park also contains some of the city's best-tended gardens and the always busy zoo, as well as large expanses of manicured lawn. Scenic roadways, an extensive trail system, and even a miniature railway make it easy to explore the park and enjoy its diverse experiences.

Roses in full bloom in the International Rose Test Garden

International Rose Test Garden

400 SW Kingston Dr. **Tel** (503) 823-3664. 🕖 7:30am–9pm daily. 🚻 🛈
A magnificent treat for all those who love flowers, this garden is the oldest continuously operated rose test garden in the US. It can trace its beginnings to a summer day in 1888, when Georgianna Pittock, wife of pioneer publisher Henry Pittock (see p68), invited her friends to display their prize roses in a tent on the lawn of her mansion. The enthusiasts formed the Portland Rose Society in 1888, planted roses along city streets, and dubbed Portland the "City of Roses." In 1917, the society established the rose garden in Washington Park, on a terraced hillside commanding memorable views of the city and Mount Hood. Today, the garden's 8,000 bushes and 525 species come into bloom in a spectacle of color every June, in time for the annual Portland Rose Festival (see p31).

In the All-American Rose Test Garden, new varieties of roses are carefully observed for two years, as a panel of judges evaluates them for color, form, fragrance, and other criteria. The evaluations are then combined with those of judges at 23 other test gardens around the country to determine the best roses. The City of Portland also chooses its own favorites; these annual winners are on display in the Gold Medal Garden.

Only at the Shakespeare Garden do roses not take center stage – this pleasant bower is planted with flowers mentioned in the bard's plays.

The Rose Society also maintains gardens in Peninsula Park, in north Portland, and in the neighborhood of Ladd's Addition (see p74), in southeast Portland.

Japanese Garden

611 SW Kingston Dr. **Tel** (503) 223-1321. 🚌 63. 🕖 Apr–Sep: noon–7pm Mon, 10am–7pm Tue–Sun; Oct–Mar: noon–4pm Mon, 10am–4pm Tue–Sun. 🔒 Jan 1, Thanksgiving, Dec 25. 🎦 Apr–Oct: 10:45am, 1pm & 2:30pm daily. 🛈 www.japanesegarden.com
This lovely, manicured landscape, spread across hilly terrain next to the International Rose Test Garden, is said to be one of the most authentic Japanese gardens outside of Japan and is certainly one of the most tranquil spots in Portland. Within the garden, designed by noted Japanese landscape architect Takuma Tono, meticulously tended plantings surround ponds, streams, and pavilions.

Paths wind through five distinct landscapes: the Flat Garden, a typical urban garden design; the Tea Garden, built around a ceremonial tea house; the Strolling Pond Garden, where zigzagging bridges cross carp-filled pools and iris beds; the Natural Garden, where shrubs, ferns, and mosses grow in their natural state alongside ponds, streams, and waterfalls; and the Sand and Stone Gardens, in which raked gravel simulates the sea and plantings depict a sake cup and gourd to wish the visitor happiness.

Stone pagoda in the Japanese Garden

The wood, tile-roofed entrance gate can be reached by a short uphill climb on a woodland path or via a shuttle bus departing every 25 minutes from the parking lot below.

The authentic and tranquil Japanese Garden, designed by Takuma Tono

Stately conifers in the plantings of the Hoyt Arboretum

Hoyt Arboretum

4000 SW Fairview Blvd. *Tel (503) 865-8733.* ◯ *6am–10pm daily.* 🖼 *Jun–Sep: 10am first Sat each month.* **www**.hoytarboretum.org

In the groves and meadows of this 187-acre (76-ha) arboretum grow 218 species of conifers (which is the world's largest such collection), dozens of species of wildflowers indigenous to the Pacific Northwest, and other trees and plants gathered from around the world.

The visitors' center – the departure point for tours – also provides maps of the many trails that crisscross the arboretum and detailed lists of the trees and plants to be found along the way.

At the south end of the Hoyt Arboretum, the **Vietnam Veterans of Oregon Memorial** – a subdued assemblage of lawns, gardens, and six granite slabs inscribed with the names of veterans – commemorates those Oregonians who were killed or reported missing during the Vietnam War.

Oregon Zoo

4001 SW Canyon Rd. *Tel (503) 226-1561.* 🚉 *Washington Park (blue line).* 🚌 *63.* ◯ *Jan & Feb: 10am–4pm daily; Mar–May & Sep–Dec: 9am–4pm daily; Jun–Aug: 9am–6pm daily.* ● *Dec 25.* 🖼 ♿ 🖥 🍴 **www**.oregonzoo.org

In 1887, pharmacist Richard B. Knight donated a grizzly bear and a brown bear to the city. A zoo has been located in Washington Park ever since, moving to its present location on the hillsides and ravines of the south side of the park in 1959. More than 1,000 birds, mammals, reptiles, and invertebrates – representing 200 species – live in the zoo, many in spacious, naturalistic habitats. The zoo, home to the largest breeding herd of elephants in captivity, is noted for its efforts to perpetuate some 21 endangered and 33 threatened species.

Among the zoo's most popular denizens are the Humboldt penguins from Peru that live in the Penguinarium; the sea lions and sea otters in Steller Cove; the impalas and giraffes that graze in the zoo's African Savanna exhibit; and the wolves and grizzly bears of the Alaskan Tundra exhibit. The Cascade exhibit provides a look at the goats, otters, elk, and other animals that roam the Pacific Northwest wilds.

World Forestry Center Discovery Museum

4033 SW Canyon Rd. *Tel (503) 228-1367.* ◯ *10am–5pm daily.* ● *Thanksgiving, Dec 25.* 🖼 ♿ 🍴 **www**.worldforestry.org

Trees steal the show at this museum devoted to the world's forests. On the main floor of the stylishly designed timber building is a grove of trees native to the area. There is also an outstanding collection of petrified wood – wood that has been buried for thousands of years and transformed into mineral deposits.

Upstairs, photographs and text panels explore the importance of old-growth forests and tropical rainforests. The Forest Discovery Lab provides hands-on exhibits for kids.

The interactive Global Forest exhibit, featuring the sights, sounds, and smells of each different world forest, is definitely worth a visit.

The timbered exterior of the World Forestry Center Discovery Museum

Portland Children's Museum

4015 SW Canyon Rd. *Tel (503) 223-6500.* 🚉 *Washington Park (blue line).* 🚌 *63.* ◯ *9am–5pm Mon–Sat, 11am–5pm Sun.* 🖼 🖥 🍴 **www**.portlandcm.org

When it was established in 1949, the Portland Children's Museum was one of the first of its kind in the US. Today the museum attracts some 250,000 visitors yearly and offers a wide range of exhibits geared to kids under the age of 10.

"Play" is the operative word at the museum, as youngsters turn cranks and operate valves to send water cascading through Water Works, use giant rain sticks to make music in the Zounds! exhibit, perform medical operations in the Kids' Clinic, and in other creative ways explore the world around them.

One sea lion draped over another in Stellar Cove at the Oregon Zoo

Street shopping in Portland's funky Hawthorne District

Hawthorne District **❽**

NE Hawthorne Blvd, from SE 17th to SE 39th Sts.

An east-side residential and business area somewhat reminiscent of parts of Berkeley, California, the Hawthorne District is hip, funky, and bustling with young people, many of whom attend nearby Reed College. Hawthorne Boulevard is lined with coffeehouses, clothing boutiques, bookstores, bakeries, delis, and restaurants, several serving ethnic foods, including Vietnamese, Indian, Lebanese, and Ethiopian. Buskers add their sounds to the area's vibrant street scene.

The district's surrounding residential neighborhoods, dating from the early 20th century, were among Portland's first so-called "streetcar suburbs." Of these, Ladd's Addition is one of the oldest planned communities in the western US. Built in a circular grid of streets that surround five rose gardens, the plan was considered radical when it was laid out in 1939. Today, the area boasts many styles of 20th-century architecture: bungalow, craftsman, mission, colonial revival, and Tudor.

To the east, Hawthorne Boulevard ascends the slopes of Mount Tabor, an extinct volcano whose crater is now surrounded by a lovely forested park, popular with picnickers. Walking trails are to be found throughout the park.

Sellwood District **❾**

SE 13th to SE 17th Aves, from SE Tacoma St to SE Bybee Blvd.

Sellwood, a quiet residential neighborhood on a bluff above the Willamette River in the southeast corner of the city, has become the antiques center of Portland. Long gone are the days when Sellwood was a bargain-hunter's paradise, but shoppers continue to descend upon Sellwood's 30 or so antique shops – many of which occupy old Victorian houses along Southeast 13th Avenue, known as **Antique Row**. They may then enjoy a meal in one of the area's many restaurants or in the adjoining Westmoreland neighborhood.

The riverbank just below the Sellwood bluff is made festive by the presence of the Ferris wheel, roller coaster, roller-skating rink, and other attractions of **Oaks Park**, a shady amusement park that opened during the 1905 Lewis and Clark Exposition (*see p40*).

Chairs for sale in front of shops in Sellwood's Antique Row

Crystal Springs Rhododendron Garden **❿**

SE 28th Ave & SE Woodstock Blvd. **Tel** (503) 771-8386. 🚌 19. ◯ Apr–Sep: 6am–10pm daily; Oct–Mar: 6am–6pm daily. 📷 ♿

This 9.5-acre (3.8-ha) garden is laced with trails that cross streams, pass beneath misty cascades, and circle a springfed lake attracting ducks, geese, herons, and other waterfowl.

The garden erupts into a breathtaking blaze of color from March through June, when hundreds of species of rare rhododendrons and azaleas – one of the world's leading collections of these woodland plants – are in bloom.

The serene lake at Crystal Springs Rhododendron Garden

Reed College **⓫**

3203 SE Woodstock Blvd. **Tel** (503) 771-1112. 🚌 19. **Grounds** ◯ dawn–dusk daily. **www**.reed.edu

Established in 1908 with a bequest from Oregon pioneers Simeon and Amanda Reed, Reed College occupies a wooded, 100-acre (40-ha) campus at the edge of Eastmoreland, one of Portland's most beautiful residential neighborhoods. Brick Tudor Gothic buildings, along with others designed in traditional Northwest timber style, are set amid rolling lawns surrounding the "canyon," a wooded wetland; shade is provided by 125 species of maples, cedars, and other trees. This setting seems to have a beneficial effect on the college's 1,400 students – Reed has produced the second highest number of Rhodes scholars of all US liberal arts colleges.

One of the several brick Tudor buildings on Reed College campus

Artifacts of early pioneers, End of the Oregon Trail Interpretive Center

End of the Oregon Trail Interpretive Center ⓬

1726 Washington St, Oregon City. *Tel* (503) 657-9336. ☐ Mar–Sep: 9:30am–5pm Mon–Sat, 10:30am–5pm Sun; Oct–Feb: 11am–4pm Tue–Sat, noon–4pm Sun. ⬤ Jan 1, Thanksgiving, Dec 25. 🖼 ♿ 🏠 www.historicoregoncity.org

Although many of the pioneers who crossed the country on the Oregon Trail went their separate ways once they reached eastern Oregon, for those who continued west across the Cascade Mountains, Abernethy Green near Oregon City was the end of the trail. Here they stocked up on provisions and set up farmsteads in the fertile Willamette Valley.

The End of the Oregon Trail Interpretive Center tells the story of life on the trail in three oversized, 50-ft- (15-m-) high covered wagons that encircle Abernethy Green. Exhibits of heirlooms, hands-on experiences in which visitors choose supplies and pack a wagon, and mixed-media shows bring the hardships to life.

Oregon City ⓭

Road map 1 A3. 🚶 29,500. 🛈 1201 Washington St, (503) 656-1619.

Terminus of the Oregon Trail and capital of the Oregon territory from 1849 to 1852, Oregon City's past prominence is largely due to its location beside the 40-ft (12-m) Willamette Falls, which powered flour and paper mills. The mills brought prosperity to the city, which was the site of the first meeting of the territory's provisional legislature, in 1843.

Museum of the Oregon Territory traces this history from the days when John McLoughlin, an Englishman sympathetic to the cause of bringing Oregon into the US, settled the town in 1829. In 1846, the "Father of Oregon" built the then grandest home in Oregon, now the **McLoughlin House**, a unit of Fort Vancouver National Historic Site. Stairs and an elevator connect this historic area, located on a bluff, to the stores below.

🏛 **Museum of the Oregon Territory**
211 Tumwater Dr. *Tel* (503) 655-5574. ☐ 11am–4pm Wed & 1st and 3rd Sat of month. ⬤ major hols. 🖼

🏚 **McLoughlin House**
713 Center St. *Tel* (503) 656-5146. ☐ 10am–4pm Wed–Sat. ⬤ mid-Dec–Jan & major hols. 🖼

The stately McLoughlin House (1846) in Oregon City

Aurora ⓮

Road map 1 A3. 🚶 650. 🛈 (503) 939-0312.

The town of Aurora traces its roots to the Aurora Colony, a Utopian community founded by Prussian immigrant William Keil in 1852. Similar to Shaker communities in the east, it was a collective society based on the principles of Christian fundamentalism and shared property. The colony thrived for more than a decade, until it was decimated by a smallpox

epidemic. Exhibits tracing the colony's history fill the **Old Aurora Colony Museum**'s handsome white-frame buildings. Many of Aurora's other historic buildings now house antique shops.

Nearby **Champoeg State Heritage Area** is the site of an 1843 convention at which settlers voted to break from Britain and establish a provisional American government in Oregon. By that time, Champoeg was a thriving trading post on the banks of the Willamette River, having been established by the Hudson's Bay Company in 1813. The town that grew up around the trading post was abandoned as a result of devastating floods in 1861 and 1890; the park now comprises 650 acres (265 ha) of meadows and stately stands of oaks and evergreens.

Displays in the visitor center pay tribute to the Calapooya Indians, who once lived here on the banks of the river, and to the traders and pioneers who came in the wake of the Hudson's Bay settlement. Its historic buildings include a jail, a schoolhouse, a barn, and several early dwellings.

🏛 **Old Aurora Colony Museum**
15018 2nd St NE. *Tel* (503) 678-5754. ☐ Feb–Dec: 11am–4pm Tue–Sat, noon–4pm Sun. ⬤ Jan; major hols. 🖼 www.auroracolony.org

🌿 **Champoeg State Heritage Area**
Rte 99 W, 12 miles (7.5 km) west of Aurora. *Tel* (503) 678-1251. ☐ dawn–dusk daily. 🖼 🏠

Picturesque cottages in Aurora's National Historic District

Shopping in Portland

One of the many pleasures of shopping in Portland is the fact that no state sales tax is levied. Another is the convenient location of the city's commercial areas in or near downtown. Portland has its share of nationally known department stores and chains, but it also has many specialty shops, often selling locally manufactured goods.

SHOPPING DISTRICTS

Downtown, near Pioneer Courthouse Square, is the city's main shopping district. Major department stores are here, as are jewelry and clothing stores, and other specialty shops. In Nob Hill, Northwest 23rd Avenue west of Burnside is lined with an eclectic mix of chic and trendy shops specializing in home furnishings, clothing, gifts, and gourmet foods. The Pearl District (see pp54–5) has a concentration of commercial galleries, along with shops offering designer furniture and wares.

In Sellwood (see p74), antique stores line Southeast 13th Avenue. A funky counterculture holds sway on nearby Southeast Hawthorne Boulevard (see p74), with book, music, and vintage clothing shops. At Portland Saturday Market (see p53), over 300 artisans gather on weekends to sell their work.

DEPARTMENT STORES AND SHOPPING CENTERS

Founded in 1857, Meier & Frank is these days known as **Macy's**, an upscale store selling everything from beauty products to housewares. **Nordstrom**, established in Seattle in 1901 as a shoe store,

Sign atop one of the unique Made in Oregon stores

is well known for its quality clothing for men, women, and children and superb service, while **Bridgeport Village** has about 90 shops and restaurants, as well as a cinema. More than 70 upscale retailers are housed in the three-level **Pioneer Place**. The 200 stores in **Lloyd Center** encircle an ice-skating rink.

SPECIALTY SHOPS

Specializing in items "made, caught, or grown" in the state, such as local jams and preserves, and smoked salmon, **Made in Oregon** also stocks a selection of products from the Pendleton Woolen Mills (see p111), as does the **Portland Pendleton Shop**.

An excellent selection of wines produced from the bounty of the state's many acclaimed vineyards is to be found at **Oregon Wines on Broadway**. There is a wine bar adjacent to the shop. **Columbia Sportswear** specializes in athletic wear made in the Pacific Northwest. Portland's very own **Norm Thompson** carries classic casual and outdoor clothing with a Pacific Northwest look. It also has a highly successful worldwide mail order business.

Powell's City of Books, with its inventory of over one million new and used books, is said to be the world's largest independent bookstore.

Gallery art on a First Thursday

Wares of all kinds on display at the popular Saturday Market

DIRECTORY

DEPARTMENT STORES AND SHOPPING CENTERS

Bridgeport Village
7455 SW Bridgeport Rd.
Tel (503) 968-1704.

Lloyd Center
NE Multnomah St & NE 9th Ave.
Tel (503) 282-2511.

Macy's
621 SW 5th Ave. **Map** 1 C5.
Tel (503) 223-0512.

Nordstrom
701 SW Broadway. **Map** 1 C5.
Tel (503) 224-6666.

Pioneer Place
700 SW 5th Ave. **Map** 1 C5.
Tel (503) 228-5800.

SPECIALTY SHOPS

Columbia Sportswear
911 SW Broadway. **Map** 1 C5.
Tel (503) 226-6800.

Made in Oregon
Suite 1300, 340 SW Morrison St.
Map 1 C5.
Tel (503) 241-3630.
(One of several locations).

Norm Thompson
www.normthompson.com

Oregon Wines on Broadway
515 SW Broadway. **Map** 1 C5.
Tel (503) 228-4655.

Portland Pendleton Shop
900 SW 5th Ave. **Map** 3 C1.
Tel (503) 242-0037.

Powell's City of Books
1005 W Burnside St. **Map** 1 B4.
Tel (503) 228-4651.

WHAT TO BUY

Wine connoisseurs will not want to miss the offerings of Oregon's vineyards, especially the pinot noirs. Smoked salmon and oysters from Oregon waters also rank high among local delicacies. A wool blanket or plaid shirt or scarf from Oregon's famed Pendleton Woolen Mills (see p111) is high on the list of popular gifts, as is the art – including masks, carvings, and jewelry – of Native Americans of the Pacific Northwest.

Entertainment in Portland

Portland has a vibrant and growing cultural scene. The performing arts thrive in the many venues located throughout the city, with theater and music offerings being especially plentiful. And, of course, Portland has its fair share of big-ticket rock concerts and professional sports matches.

INFORMATION

Portland has become the first US city to launch a "Twisitor Center," a virtual visitor center, Travel Portland (www.travel portland.com). Twitter technology is used to connect travelers with those who can answer their questions and help plan their trips.

The free weekly *Willamette Week* newspaper runs comprehensive entertainment listings. The *Oregonian*, the city's major daily, prints listings in its Friday edition. The Travel Portland website also provides information on events around town.

BUYING TICKETS

Tickets for many events can be purchased by phone or in person from **Ticketmaster** and **Tickets West**.

FREE EVENTS

Every Wednesday at noon, **The Old Church** *(see p62)* hosts a free organ concert. Free noontime concerts are also held at **Pioneer Courthouse Square** *(see p60)*.

During summer, the **Oregon Zoo Amphitheater** *(see p73)* is the setting for concerts several nights a week (tickets can be booked through Ticketmaster).

THEATER

Topping the list of Portland's theater troupes are the **Artists Repertory Theatre**, the oldest theater group in

The façade of the Portland Center for the Performing Arts

the city; **Portland Center Stage**, with a repertoire of classic and contemporary plays; and the **Miracle Theatre Group** is dedicated to the Hispanic arts and community.

DANCE

Based at the **Portland Center for the Performing Arts**, the **Oregon Ballet Theatre** performs classical and contemporary pieces, including the *Nutcracker* during the holiday season and new works showcased in late spring.

MUSIC

The oldest symphony orchestra on the West Coast, the **Oregon Symphony** has garnered considerable praise under conductor and music director Carlos Kalmar. The **Portland Baroque Orchestra** presents a program of early music, fall through spring, while the **Portland Opera** stages five works a year.

The **Crystal Ballroom**, opened in 1920, hosts popular musical acts; it is famous for its "floating" dance floor, which rests on ball bearings.

A favored jazz haunt of locals is **Jimmy Mak's Bar & Grill** in the Pearl District,

The modern Rose Garden Arena, in the Rose Quarter complex

DIRECTORY

TICKET OUTLETS

Ticketmaster
Tel (503) 224-4400.

Tickets West
Tel (503) 224-8499.

THEATER

Artists Repertory Theatre
Tel (503) 241-1278.

Miracle Theatre Group
Tel (503) 236-7253.

Portland Center Stage
Tel (503) 445-3700.

DANCE

Oregon Ballet Theatre
Tel (503) 222-5538.

Portland Center for the Performing Arts
Tel (503) 248-4335.

MUSIC

Crystal Ballroom
Tel (503) 225-0047.

Jimmy Mak's Bar & Grill
Tel (503) 295-6542.

Oregon Symphony
Tel (503) 228-1353.

Portland Baroque Orchestra
Tel (503) 222-6000.

Portland Opera
Tel (503) 241-1802.

SPORTS VENUES

Jeld-Wen Field
Tel (503) 553-5400.

Rose Garden Arena
Tel (503) 797-9619.

where world-class jazz can be enjoyed. Music can be accompanied by Greek and Middle Eastern cuisine.

SPECTATOR SPORTS

The **Rose Garden Arena**, part of the Rose Garden complex *(see p69)*, is home to the Portland Trailblazers basketball team and Portland Winter Hawks hockey team.

Fans can watch the Portland Timbers play soccer at the handsomely renovated **Jeld-Wen Field**.

Getting Around Portland

The results of Portland's efforts to prevent urban sprawl and congestion are noticeable in the compact metropolis. Central Portland is easy to navigate. One can walk just about anywhere, and extensive bus, light rail, and streetcar systems put most places within easy reach. Not only is public transportation readily available, in much of the city center the MAX and streetcars are also free.

Old-fashioned streetcar near Jamison Square

Bicycle parked on a Portland downtown street, a common sight

STREET LAYOUT

The Willamette River, which is spanned by eight downtown bridges, divides Portland into east and west. Burnside Street bisects the city into north and south. As a result, Portland is divided into quadrants, reflected in street addresses, most of which begin with a "Northwest," "Northeast," "Southwest," or "Southeast."

Avenues in Portland are numbered and run north–south; streets are named and run east–west. The streets north of Burnside run alphabetically, making them easy to find – for example, Couch is next to Burnside and Davis is next to Couch. South of Burnside, however, street names run in a random order. Street numbers that are odd are usually on the west and north sides, even numbers usually on the east and south.

Several highways crisscross Portland. The I-5, the main West Coast north–south route, runs through the city, while the I-84 runs from the east bank of the Willamette River east toward Idaho and beyond. The I-205 forms a perimeter around the city's outskirts and runs by the airport; the I-405 loops around the southern and western edges of downtown.

WALKING

Portland's downtown is so compact that it is easy to get almost anywhere on foot, and walkways on some bridges make most eastside neighborhoods accessible to pedestrians. Powell's City of Books (see p55) offers a free walking map. Maps are also available at **Travel Portland**, at Pioneer Courthouse Square (see p60).

BICYCLING

Portland is a bicycle-friendly city. Bikes are permitted on public transit, most public buses are equipped with bike racks, and many streets have designated bicycle lanes.

Helmets are mandatory for cyclists under 16 years of age, and all cyclists who ride after dark must equip their bicycles with a red reflector that can be seen from the rear and a flashing white light that is visible from ahead. The **Bicycle Transportation Alliance**, a cycling advocacy group, provides route maps and other useful cycling information.

TAXIS

Taxis do not cruise the streets in Portland looking for fares as they do in many other cities. You can find a cab outside major downtown hotels or call one of the city's taxi companies. Fares can be paid with major credit cards.

PUBLIC TRANSIT

Portland's public transit (except buses) is free within the 300 blocks of the Fareless Square, in the city center. The Fareless Square is bordered by the I-405 to the south and west; Northwest Irving Street to the north; and the Willamette River to the east, with the exception of the Rose Quarter and Lloyd Center, which also fall within the zone.

The Portland transportation authority, **Tri-Met**, provides three types of public transit: light rail, buses, and streetcars.

The Metro Area Express (MAX) light rail system serves the Portland metropolitan area. Its blue-line trains run through downtown between Hillsboro in the west and Gresham in the east, while the red line connects downtown with the airport. The yellow line runs across north Portland, from the Rose Quarter to the Expo Center. The green line connects Union Station to Portland State University.

Trains run roughly every 10 to 15 minutes, with a reduced late-night schedule.

Most Tri-Met bus routes include stops along the downtown transit malls on

A MAX train servicing Portland's historic Old Town

5th and 6th Avenues, from which many downtown attractions are an easy walk.

The Portland Streetcar travels through central Portland and makes many stops along 10th and 11th Avenues. At the south waterfront it connects with the Aerial tram, which takes passengers to Oregon Health and Science University.

Outside the Fareless Square, the fare on MAX trains, buses, and streetcars varies depending on the distance traveled. There are three zones; the adult fare for one zone is $2.05, increasing to $2.35 for three zones. The fare is reduced for seniors and for children aged 7 to 17. As many as three children under age 7 can ride for free when accompanied by an adult. Transfers are free and allow for interchangeable travel on the three forms of transit. Books of ten tickets are available at a discount. All-day tickets offering unlimited rides anywhere in the system and seven- or 14-day passes are also available. MAX tickets must be validated at one of the machines located throughout the trains.

Tri-Met buses, MAX trains, and Portland Streetcars all accommodate passengers with disabilities.

DRIVING

Compared with many other cities, Portland is relatively easy to drive in. Some of the major arteries out of downtown – such as US 26 West, I-84, I-85, and Macadam Boulevard – can become congested between 5 and 6pm, but at most other times, barring accidents and road work, traffic flows easily.

The many one-way streets downtown ease traffic congestion. Cars are prohibited on parts of 5th and 6th Avenues designated as transit malls, which accommodate public trains and buses. It is legal to make a right turn on a red light, but only after coming to a full stop.

Speed limits are generally 25 mph (40 km/h) in residential areas, and 20 mph (32 km/h) in business and

Portland Streetcar at the Portland State University Station

school districts. Drivers and passengers are required to wear seatbelts and motorcyclists must wear helmets.

If you need assistance, maps, or guidebooks, contact the local office of the **American Automobile Association (AAA)**.

PARKING

Metered street parking is available downtown, but the ease of finding a space greatly depends on the time of day. The parking time permitted varies from 15 minutes to three hours, one hour being the norm. An economical alternative is one of the city's many SmartPark garages.

On most downtown streets, the city has introduced a park-and-display system. Machines accept payment in cash or by credit card and issue a ticket – valid for up to three hours, depending on the amount paid – to be displayed on the inside of the windshield. Metered parking is generally

Union Station, with its prominent tower, welcoming train passengers

in effect Monday through Saturday, from 8am to 7pm, and Sunday from 1pm to 7pm, excluding state holidays.

TOWING

Parking wardens are a vigilant presence on downtown streets. Check posted street parking rules, as they may limit parking during rush hours or specify other regulations, such as stopping being permitted only to load or unload. If your car has been towed, call the **Portland Police Auto Records Department**. A processing fee and towing charge will be levied.

DIRECTORY

USEFUL NUMBERS

American Automobile Association (AAA)
Tel (800) 222-4357.
www.aaa.com

Bicycle Transportation Alliance
Tel (503) 226-0676.

Portland Police Auto Records Department
Tel (503) 823-0044.

Travel Portland
Tel (503) 275-9750 or *(877) 678-5263.*

Tri-Met Customer Service
Tel (503) 238-7433.
www.trimet.org

TAXIS

Broadway Cab
Tel (503) 227-1234.

Radio Cab
Tel (503) 227-1212.

PORTLAND STREET FINDER

The key map below shows the area of Portland covered by the *Street Finder* maps, which can be found on the following pages. Map references for sights, hotels, restaurants, shops, and entertainment venues given throughout the Portland chapter of this guide refer to the grid on the maps. The first figure in the reference indicates which map to turn to (1 to 4), and the letter and number that follow refer to the grid reference on that map.

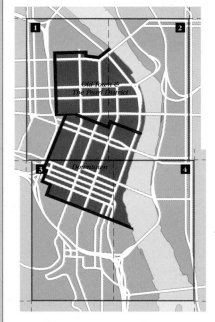

KEY

■	Major sight
■	Minor sight
■	Station building
🚆	Train station
🚌	Bus station – long distance
🚋	Streetcar
Ⓜ	MAX
🅿	Parking
ℹ	Information
➕	Hospital
🚓	Police station
✝	Church
⊠	Post office
═══	Railroad line
→	One-way street

SCALE OF MAPS 1–4

0 meters   150
0 yards   150

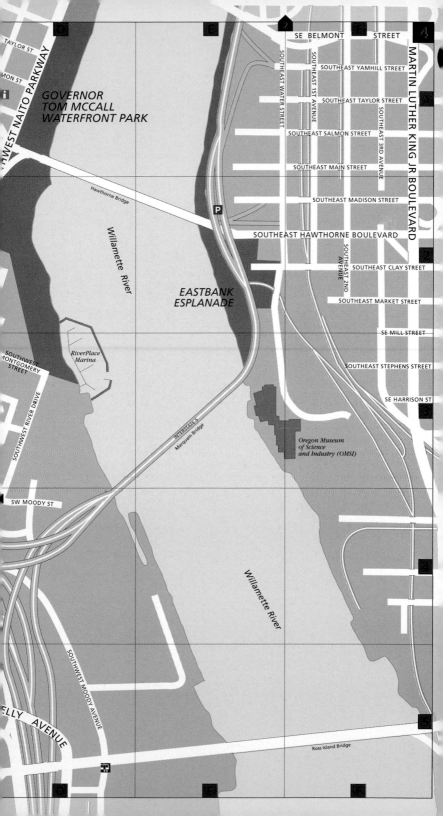

OREGON

*O*regonians and their visitors alike run out of adjectives to describe the scenic wonders contained within the 97,000 sq miles (251,200 sq km) of the tenth largest US state. Here, snow-capped mountains pierce the clouds, waves break on rocky shores, rivers sprint through gorges, dense forests cling to ravines, and desert vistas stretch beneath skies that, indeed, are not cloudy all day.

A forest-cloaked headland, tidal estuary, or stretch of isolated beach appears around every bend of the 350-mile (560-km) Oregon coastline. In the north, the mighty Columbia River flows through a magnificent gorge where waterfalls plummet from cliffs. Those traveling alongside the river follow in the footsteps of explorers Lewis and Clark, who canoed the rushing waters in 1805. The Snake River, a tributary of the Columbia River, tumbles through inhospitable desert at the bottom of 8,000-ft (2,440-m) Hells Canyon, the deepest gorge in North America.

Looking at such rugged landscapes, it is easy to imagine the hardships hundreds of thousands of pioneers encountered as they migrated west along the Oregon Trail. Then, of course, there are the mountains – the Coast range taking shape above coastal headlands, the Cascades peaks soaring above the central valleys, the Wallowas and Blues rising from high desert country in the east. These landscapes provide more than memorable views. Hiking trails lace the forests, and rushing white-water rivers, such as the Rogue and Deschutes, brim with trout, salmon, and sturgeon, attracting white-water rafters and anglers. Lakes sparkle with crystal-clear water; the most awesome of them, Crater Lake, is the deepest in North America. And the slopes of Mount Hood are covered with snow – and skiers – all year.

Oregon serves up cosmopolitan pleasures, too. Portlanders are quick to claim their city as one of the most sophisticated and cultured anywhere. But even out-of-the-way places, such as Ashland, of Shakespeare Festival fame, stage notable events.

Wherever a traveler goes or whatever a traveler does in Oregon, the glimmer of a distant mountain peak and the scent of pine in the air will add an extra zest to the experience.

Cowboys in the sagebrush-dotted ranching settlement of Jordan Valley

◁ The Heceta Head Lighthouse (c.1894), Florence, casting the strongest light on the Oregon coast

Exploring Oregon

Travelers in Oregon will find that almost any drive inevitably takes them through beautiful landscapes. From Portland, day trips can easily be made to the Columbia River Gorge and Mount Hood, to the north and central coasts, and to the wine country and historic towns of the Willamette Valley. From the Pacific beaches, breathtakingly scenic drives lead across the Coast Range to Bend and Central Oregon, and from there through pine forests and high desert country to such natural wonders as Crater Lake, Steens Mountain, and Hells Canyon.

Bybee-Howell House, a Sauvie Islar landmark, northwest of Portland

SIGHTS AT A GLANCE

Ashland **27**
Astoria **2**
Bandon **12**
Bend **21**
Cannon Beach **3**
Cape Perpetua
 Scenic Area **9**
Eugene **17**
Florence **10**
Jacksonville **26**
John Day Fossil Beds
 National Monument **31**
Jordan Valley **29**
Joseph **34**
Lincoln City **6**
Madras and Warm Springs **18**
Malheur National
 Wildlife Refuge **30**
McMinnville **14**
Newberry National
 Volcanic Monument **22**
Newport **7**
Oregon Caves
 National Monument **25**
Oregon Dunes National
 Recreation Area **11**
Pendleton **32**
Salem **16**
Silverton **15**
Sisters **19**
Smith Rock State
 Park **20**
Three Capes
 Scenic Route **5**
Tillamook **4**
Wallowa Lake **35**
Yachats **8**

Tours

Cascade Lakes Highway
 pp104–105 **23**
Columbia River Gorge and
 Mount Hood pp90–91 **1**
Crater Lake National
 Park pp106–107 **24**
Elkhorn Drive National
 Scenic Byway pp112–13 **33**

Hells Canyon National
 Recreation Area pp114–15 **36**
Steens Mountain p109 **28**
Wine Country of the North
 Willamette Valley pp98–9 **13**

For additional map symbols *see back flap*

GETTING AROUND

I-5, running north–south, and I-84, running east to Idaho and the Midwest, are Oregon's two major routes. Hwy 26 runs through lovely landscape from the coast across Mount Hood into eastern Oregon. Hwy 101 follows the coast; Hwy 97, another scenic north–south route, skirts the Cascade Mountains and Crater Lake. Car is the most convenient way to travel in Oregon. Amtrak offers three train routes: one east to Chicago, two along the coast. Bus service is limited.

Hood River, a small town on the Columbia River Gorge

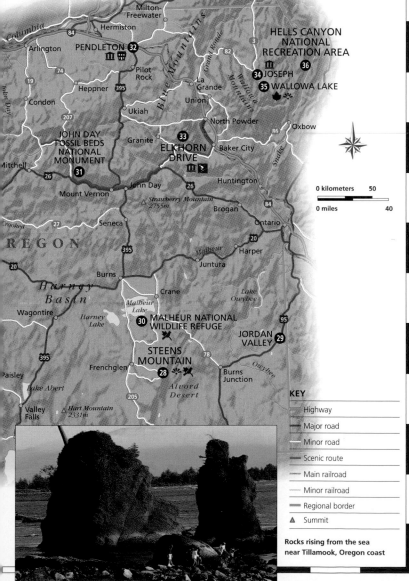

KEY

	Highway
	Major road
	Minor road
	Scenic route
	Main railroad
	Minor railroad
	Regional border
▲	Summit

Rocks rising from the sea near Tillamook, Oregon coast

Columbia River Gorge and Mount Hood Driving Tour ❶

Mount Hood Railroad sign

This easy outing from Portland encompasses a diverse sampling of Oregon scenery, including the banks of the Columbia River as it flows through a magnificent gorge and the spectacular summit of Mount Hood. Along the way, the route takes in five waterfalls, the bountiful orchards that surround the Hood River, and picturesque Timberline Lodge. Other features of this tour include scenic overlooks, rushing streams, mountain lakes, enormous glaciers, and dense forests.

Oneonta Gorge ③
Hardier hikers will enjoy walking through this dramatic gorge. It can also be viewed at the south end of a trail starting in Horsetail Falls.

Bonneville Dam ④
A tour of this 1930s dam reveals massive hydroelectric powerhouses, as well as underwater views of migrating salmon, and a fish hatchery.

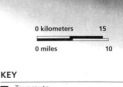

Multnomah Falls ②
The fourth highest waterfall in the US tumbles 620 ft (188 m) in two picturesque cascades.

Vista House ①
This historic, octagonal structure perched high above the river offers breathtaking views of the gorge and mountains.

Timberline Lodge ⑪
Artisans hired by the federal Works Project Administration crafted every detail of this beautiful 1930s ski lodge, from the wrought-iron door handles to its massive wood beams.

0 kilometers   15

0 miles   10

KEY

■■ Tour route

═ Other road

❄ Viewpoint

ℹ Information

Ruthton Point ⑤
This cape situated in a small state park makes a perfect stopping-off point from which to view the mighty Columbia River Gorge and the surrounding Cascade mountain range.

TIPS FOR DRIVERS

Tour length: *146 miles (235 km).*
Starting point: *I-84 in Portland.*
Stopping-off points: *The most scenic places to enjoy a meal are the two historic lodges on the loop, one at Multnomah Falls in the gorge and the other at Timberline atop Mount Hood. At both, salmon, trout, and other fresh Pacific Northwest cuisine can be enjoyed in front of a blazing hearth.*

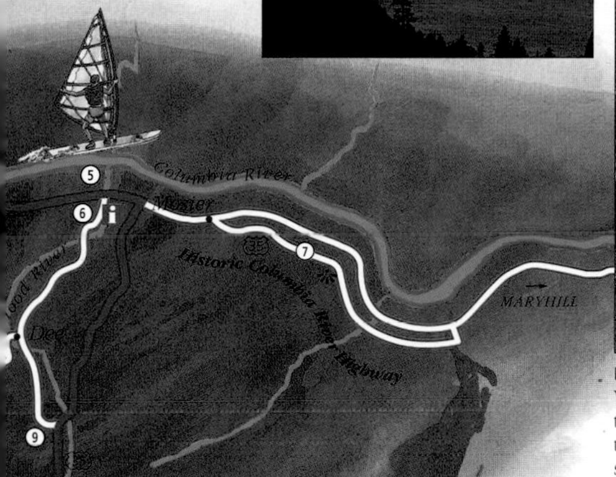

Hood River ⑥
Winds and river currents create the ideal conditions that render this riverside town the windsurfing capital of the world. Landlubbers enjoy the bounty of local fruit orchards.

Historic Columbia River Highway ⑦
Blasted out of the steep cliffs and opened in 1915, this narrow road was designed to maximize the view yet limit environmental damage as much as possible.

Parkdale ⑨
This pretty little town on the eastern slopes of Mount Hood is the terminus of the Mount Hood Railroad, which passes through apple and pear orchards to Hood River.

Hood River Valley ⑧
This beautiful and fertile valley offers blossoming fruit trees in season and magnificent views of majestic Mount Hood throughout the year.

Barlow Pass ⑩
Wheel tracks still rut this section of the Oregon Trail, which is so steep that wagons were often lowered down the hills with ropes.

Astoria ❷

Road map 1 A3. 🏠 *9,500.* ⓘ *111
W Marine Dr, (800) 875-6807.*
www.oldoregon.com

Throughout the damp winter
of 1805–1806, explorers Lewis
and Clark *(see p37)* passed
the time making moccasins,
preserving fish, and recording
in their journals accounts of
bear attacks and the almost
continual rain at a crude stockade near Astoria. This stockade
at **Lewis and Clark National
Historical Park – Fort Clatsop
Unit** was rebuilt again after
the first replica was destroyed
by fire in 2005. In 1811, John
Jacob Astor sent fur traders
around Cape Horn to establish
a trading post in this location
at the mouth of the Columbia
River, making Astoria the
oldest American settlement
west of the Rocky Mountains.

These days, the town is a
major port for fishing fleets
and commercial vessels; its
Victorian homes climb a
hillside above the river.
One such home, the stately
**Captain George Flavel House
Museum**, retains the cupola
from which he and his
wife once observed river
traffic. An even better view
can be enjoyed from atop the
164-step spiral staircase of the
Astoria Column, encircled
with bas-relief friezes paying
homage to the region's past –
from the Native Americans
to the arrival of the Great
Northern Railway in 1892.

The town honors its sea-
going past at the **Columbia**

Cannon Beach's famous Haystack Rock at sunset

River Maritime Museum,
where riverside galleries house
fishing dories and Native
American dugout canoes. The
lightship *Columbia*, berthed
in front, once guided ships
across the treacherous mouth
of the river – where more
than 200 shipwrecks in the
past century have earned for
local waters the moniker
"graveyard of the Pacific."

🏛 Lewis and Clark
**National Historical Park –
Fort Clatsop Unit**
6 miles (10 km) southwest of Astoria,
off Hwy 101. **Tel** *(503) 861-2471.*
⏰ *9am–6pm daily (Labor Day–mid-
Jun: to 5pm).* ● *Dec 25.* 🖾 🔖 🛈

🏛 Captain George Flavel
House Museum
441 8th St. **Tel** *(503) 325-2203.*
⏰ *May–Sep: 10am–5pm daily;
Oct–Apr: 11am–4pm daily.* ● *Jan 1,
Thanksgiving, Dec 24 & 25.* 🖾

🏛 Astoria Column
Atop Coxcomb Hill, off 16th St.
Tel *(503) 325-2963.* ⏰ *dawn–dusk
daily.* **www**.astoriacolumn.org

🏛 Columbia River
Maritime Museum
1792 Marine Dr. **Tel** *(503) 325-2323.*
⏰ *9:30am–5pm daily.* ● *Thanksgiving, Dec 25.* 🖾 🛈 **www**.crmm.org

Environs
Fort Stevens State Park,
10 miles (16 km) west of
Astoria, dates back to the
Civil War, when it guarded
the Columbia River from
Confederate incursions. The
only time the fort saw action
was on June 21, 1942, when
a Japanese submarine fired
17 rounds toward the
concrete bunkers that were
still buried in the dunes.

🍃 Fort Stevens State Park
Off Hwy 101. **Tel** *(503) 861-1671.*
⏰ *dawn–dusk daily.* ● *Dec 25.*
🖾 🛈 **www**.visitftstevens.com

**The Astoria Column, with a scenic
lookout of the port at its top**

Cannon Beach ❸

Road map 1 A3. 🏠 *1,600.* ⓘ *2nd
& Spruce Sts, (503) 436-2623.*
www.cannonbeach.org

Despite its status as Oregon's
favorite beach town, Cannon
Beach retains a great deal of
quiet charm. The surrounding
forests grow almost up to
Hemlock Street, where buildings clad with weathered cedar
shingles house art galleries.

Haystack Rock, one of the
tallest coastal monoliths in the
world, towers 235 ft (72 m)
above a long beach and tidal
pools teeming with life.

Ecola State Park, at the
beach's north end, carpets
Tillamook Head, an 1,100-ft
(335-m) basalt headland, with
verdant forests accessible via
Tillamook Head Trail. Viewpoints look across raging surf
to **Tillamook Rock Lighthouse**,
built in 1880 and soon known
as "Terrible Tillie," as waves,
logs, and rocks continually
washed through the structure.
Decommissioned in 1957, the
lighthouse is now a private
mortuary. Tillamook Rock, a
wildlife refuge closed to the
public, is home to nesting
murres and cormorants.

🍃 Ecola State Park
2 miles (3 km) north of Cannon
Beach, off Hwy 101. **Tel** *(503) 436-
2844.* ⏰ *dawn–dusk daily.* 🖾

**Picturesque house on Cannon
Beach's Hemlock Street**

Packaging cheese at the Tillamook County Creamery Association

Tillamook ●

Road map 1 A3. 4,600. 3705 Hwy 101 N, (503) 842-7525. **www**.tillamookchamber.org

Tillamook sits about 10 miles (16 km) inland from the sea in rich bottomland fed by five rivers that empty into Tillamook Bay. Green pastures, nurtured by more than 70 inches (178 cm) of rain a year, sustain 40,000 cows that supply milk for the historic **Tillamook County Creamery Association**. Here, visitors can view the facilities and sample its output of 78 million lb (35 million kg) of cheese per year, including smoked cheddar and pepper jack.

During World War II, Tillamook was the base for giant blimps that patrolled the coast for Japanese submarines. One of the hangars – at 1,100 ft (335 m) long and 15 stories tall the largest wood structure in the world – houses the **Tillamook Air Museum**, which boasts a fine collection of flying boats, early helicopters, and some 30 other restored vintage aircraft.

Tillamook County Creamery Association
4175 Hwy 101 N.
Tel (503) 815-1300. mid-Jun–Labor Day: 8am–8pm daily; Labor Day–mid-Jun: 8am–6pm daily. Thanksgiving, Dec 25. **www**.tillamook.com

Tillamook Air Museum
6030 Hangar Rd.
Tel (503) 842-1130. 9am–5pm daily. Thanksgiving, Dec 25. **www**.tillamookair.com

Three Capes Scenic Route ●

Road map 1 A3. **Oregon State Parks Association Tel** (800) 551-6949. **www**.oregonstateparks.org

Along this 35-mile (56-km) loop that follows the marshy shores of Tillamook Bay, roadside markers recount the fate of Bayocean, a resort that thrived in the early 20th century but was washed away in winter storms. For most of the drive, though, nature is the main attraction.

One of the several beaches on the Pacific coast, north of Tillamook

The rocks below **Cape Meares State Scenic Viewpoint** and Cape Meares Lighthouse are home to one of the largest colonies of nesting seabirds in North America. In **Cape Look-out State Park**, trails pass through old-growth forests to clifftop viewpoints – good places to spot migrating gray whales – and to a sand spit between the ocean and Netarts Bay. In the **Cape Kiwanda Natural Area**, waves crash into massive sandstone cliffs and offshore rock formations. Pacific City, at the route's south end, is home to a fleet of fishing dories that daringly ply the surf on their way out to sea.

The **Oregon State Parks Association** provides detailed information about the sights along this stunning route.

Massive sandstone cliffs at Cape Kiwanda, along the Three Capes Scenic Route

Colorful kites at one of Lincoln City's many kite shops

Lincoln City ❻

Road map 1 A3. 🏛 8,000.
ℹ 4039 NW Logan Rd, (541) 994-3070. **www**.lcchamber.com

Lincoln City is a long stretch of clutter and congestion along Highway 101. The town does, however, boast several natural attractions. Formerly called Devil's River and abbreviated by Christians who disliked the name, the D River flows only 120 ft (36 m) – from Devil's Lake to the Pacific Ocean – making it the world's shortest river. The 7.5-mile- (12-km-) long beach, littered with driftwood and agates, is popular with kite enthusiasts who enjoy the strong winds off the sea.

To the north, the steep cliffs of **Cascade Head Preserve** rise out of the surf, then give way to mossy rainforests of Sitka spruce and hemlock and a maritime grassland prairie. Many rare plants and animals, including the Oregon silverspot butterfly, thrive in the preserve, which can be explored on steep but well-maintained trails.

🎋 Cascade Head Preserve
2 miles (3 km) north of Lincoln City, off Hwy 101. **Tel** (503) 230-1221.
Lower trail ◯ dawn–dusk daily.
Upper trail ◯ mid-Jul–Dec.

Environs
At Depoe Bay, a little fishing port 12 miles (19 km) south of Lincoln City, rough seas blast through narrow channels in the basalt rock, creating geyser-like plumes that shoot as high as 60 ft (18 m). A local amusement is watching the fishing fleet "shoot the hole," or navigate the narrow channel that cuts through sheer rock walls between the sea and the tiny inland harbor, which lays claim to being the smallest navigable harbor in the world.

More excitement may be in store at the Otter Crest State Scenic Viewpoint atop Cape Foulweather, so named by Captain James Cook in 1778 because of the 100-mph (160-km/h) winds that regularly buffet it. This promontory provides an excellent view of the adjacent **Devil's Punchbowl State Natural Area**, where the foaming sea thunders into rocky hollows formed by the collapse of sea caves. Tidal pools on the rocky shore below are

Fish market sign in Newport

known as marine gardens because of the colorful sea urchins and starfish that inhabit them.

♣ Devil's Punchbowl State Natural Area
15 miles (24 km) south of Lincoln City, off Hwy 101. **Tel** (800) 551-6949. ◯ dawn–dusk daily.

Newport ❼

Road map 1 A3. 🏛 10,000.
ℹ 555 SW Coast Hwy, (541) 265-8801. **www**.discovernewport.com

This salty old port on Yaquina Bay is home to the largest commercial fishing fleet on the Oregon coast and supports many oystering operations. The town is well accustomed to tourists, too. Shingled resort cottages in the Nye Beach neighborhood date from the 1880s, and in the late 1990s travelers came from around the world to visit Keiko, an orca whale that resided in the internationally renowned **Oregon Coast Aquarium** and gained stardom in the *Free Willie* films. Keiko died in 2003, but the aquarium still teems with visitors and sealife. Rockfish and anchovies swim around pier pilings in the Sandy Shores exhibit, jellyfish float through the Coastal Waters exhibit, and sea horses and sea dragons cling to sea grass in Enchanted Seas. In Passages of the Deep, sharks swim alongside glass viewing

Picturesque fishing boats moored in Newport's harbor

tunnels that are suspended in a 1.32-million-gallon (5-million-liter) tank. Outdoors, tufted puffins and murres fly through North America's largest seabird aviary, and sea otters, sea lions, and seals frolic in saltwater pools.

At the **Hatfield Marine Science Center**, headquarters of Oregon State University's marine research programs, thoughtful exhibits encourage visitors to explore oceanic science in many fascinating ways, from viewing plankton through a microscope to spotting patterns of sand build-up in time-lapse photography. An octopus that occupies a tank near the entrance is referred to as the "tenacled receptionist."

Yaquina Head Outstanding Natural Area, a narrow finger of lava that juts into the Pacific Ocean on the north end of town, makes it easy to watch marine animals in their natural habitats. Platforms at the base of the restored Yaquina Head Lighthouse are within close sight of rocks where seabirds nest and sea otters play in the sea spray. Wheelchair-accessible paths lead to the edge of tidal pools occupied by kelp crabs, sea urchins, sea anemones, sea stars, and octopi. The interpretive center looks at human and nonhuman inhabitants of the headland; shell debris attests to the presence of the former more than 4,000 years ago.

Newport's working waterfront stretches along the north side of Yaquina Bay. Here,

The quiet and unspoiled shoreline near Yachats

the masts of the fishing schooners tower over shops and restaurants, and crab pots and pesky sea lions trying to steal bait are as much of an attraction as underwater shows and waxwork replicas of sea animals.

➤ Oregon Coast Aquarium
2820 SE Ferry Slip Rd. **Tel** *(541) 867-3474.* ◯ *Memorial Day–Labor Day: 9am–6pm daily; Labor Day–Memorial Day: 10am–5pm daily.* ◯ *Dec 25.* ⟐ ⟐ ⟐ ⟐ ⟐ **www**.aquarium.org

➤ Hatfield Marine Science Center
2030 SE Marine Science Dr. **Tel** *(541) 867-0100.* ◯ *Memorial Day–Labor Day: 10am–5pm daily; Labor Day–Memorial Day: 10am–4pm Thu–Mon.* ◯ *Jan 1, Thanksgiving, Dec 25.* ⟐ *by donation.* **http://**hmsc.oregonstate.edu

⟐ Yaquina Head Outstanding Natural Area
3 miles (5 km) north of Newport, off Hwy 101. **Tel** *(541) 574-3100.* ◯ *dawn–dusk daily.* **Interpretive center:** *10am–4:30pm daily.* **Lighthouse:** *10am–4pm daily (noon–4pm winter).* ⟐ ⟐

Yachats ❽

Road map 1 A3. ⟐ 635.
🛈 *241 Hwy 101, (541) 547-3530.* **www**.yachats.org

The town of Yachats (pronounced "ya-hots"), once home to the Alsea people who gave Yachats its name, is the sort of place a shore-lover dreams about: small, unspoiled, and surrounded by forested mountainsides and surf-pounded, rocky headlands. In the center of town, the Yachats River meets the sea in a little estuary shadowed by fir trees and laced with tidal pools. The rocky shoreline and a stunning sunset can be admired from the **Yachats Ocean Road State Natural Site**, a seaside loop on the south side of town.

♣ Yachats Ocean Road State Natural Site
South of Yachats River, west of Hwy 100. **Tel** *(800) 551-6949.* ◯ *dawn–dusk daily.*

ORCAS

The largest members of the dolphin family, orcas are found throughout the world's oceans, especially in cold waters. They are also known as killer whales. Along the coast of

Orcas swimming in the cold waters off the coast of Oregon

the Pacific Northwest, transient orcas roam the ocean from California to Alaska in groups of up to 60 whales. Resident orcas, on the other hand, remain faithful to a given location; up to 300, organized into matrilinear pods, live off Vancouver Island *(see pp254–5)* in summer.

Shark-watching from the Oregon Coast Aquarium's suspended tunnel

Heceta Head Lighthouse, near Cape Perpetua, in operation since 1894

Cape Perpetua Scenic Area **9**

Road map 1 A4. *Interpretive center* 2400 Hwy 101. *Tel (541) 547-3289.* ☐ *10am–5:30pm daily.* ● *major hols.* ⚘ ▮

Cape Perpetua is the highest – albeit often cloud-shrouded – viewpoint on the coast. A road ascends to the top at 800 ft (245 m), but those with time and stamina may prefer to make the climb on trails that wind through the old-growth rainforests from the interpretive center. An easy hike of about a mile (1.5 km) along the Giant Spruce Trail leads to a majestic, 500-year-old Sitka spruce.

From Cape Perpetua, Hwy 101 descends into **Heceta Head State Park**, where trails offer spectacular ocean views. Birds nest on the rocks and sea lions and gray whales swim just offshore. High above the surf rises Heceta Head Lighthouse, first lit in 1894 with a beacon that can be seen 21 miles (34 km) out to sea. Guided tours are likely to include imaginative accounts of hauntings by the wife of a lightkeeper; despite this ghostly presence, the lightkeeper's house is a popular bed-and-breakfast.

A herd of Steller sea lions inhabits the **Sea Lion Caves**, the only rookery for wild sea lions found on the North American mainland. An

elevator descends 208 ft (63.5 m) from the clifftop to platforms near the floor of the 12-story cavern. Some 200 animals live in the cave during fall and winter; in spring and summer they breed on rock ledges just outside the entrance, where they also bear and nurse their young. Burly bulls weighing up to 2,000 lb (900 kg) boisterously guard groups of 15 to 30 cows and the newborn pups.

⚘ **Heceta Head State Park**
Hwy 101, 19 miles (30.5 km) south of Yachats. *Tel (541) 547-3696.* ☐ *dawn–dusk daily.* **Lighthouse** ⚘ ▮ *Memorial Day–Labor Day: 11am–5pm daily; Labor Day–Memorial Day: call for times.*

➤ **Sea Lion Caves**
91560 Hwy 101 N, 11 miles (17.5 km) north of Florence. *Tel (541) 547-3111.* ☐ *8:30am–7pm daily.* ● *Dec 25.* ⚘ ▮ www.sealioncaves.com

Florence **10**

Road map 1 A4. ▓ *8,200.* ▮ *290 Hwy 101, (541) 997-3128.* www.florencechamber.com

It is easy to speed through Florence en route to the nearby sand dunes. The old town, though, tucked away along the banks of the Siuslaw River, warrants a stop. Many of its early 20th-century brick and wood buildings now house art galleries, and a sizeable commercial fishing fleet docks alongside them. The fishing boats not only add a great deal of color to the surroundings but also provide the bounty that appears in the riverside fish markets and restaurants.

Fishing boats in the harbor at Florence, on the Siuslaw River

Environs
At nearby **Darlingtonia State Natural Site**, a short trail loops through a bog where Darlingtonia, also known as cobra lily, thrive. These rare, tall, carnivorous plants are reminiscent of the human-eaters of horror films. Their sweet smell traps insects, which fall to the bottom of the plant stem where they are slowly digested.

⚘ **Darlingtonia State Natural Site**
5 miles (8 km) north of Florence, off Hwy 101. *Tel (800) 551-6949.* ☐ *dawn–dusk daily.* ♿

Dune buggy, Oregon Dunes National Recreation Area

Oregon Dunes National Recreation Area **11**

Road map 1 A4. ▮ *855 Highway Ave, Reedsport, (541) 750-7000.* ☐ *dawn–dusk daily.* ⚘ www.fs.fed.us

Massive sand dunes stretch south from Florence for 40 miles (64 km). The desert-like landscape has been created over thousands of years, as winds, tides, and ocean currents force sand as far as 2.5 miles (4 km) inland and sculpt it into towering formations that reach heights of as much as 300 ft (90 m). Not just sand but streams, lakes, shore pine forests, grasslands, and isolated beaches attract a wide variety of recreation enthusiasts to this area.

Boardwalks make it easy to enjoy stunning vistas from Oregon Dunes Overlook, about 20 miles (32 km) south of Florence, whereas the mile-long Umpqua Scenic Dunes Trail, 30 miles (48 km) south of Florence, skirts the tallest dunes in the area.

Sea stacks rising majestically from the ocean off Bandon, the lights of houses seen in the background

Bandon ⓬

Road map 1 A4. 🏘 *2,900.*
ℹ *300 2nd St, (541) 347-9616.*
www.bandon.com

The small town of Bandon, near the mouth of the Coquille River, is so weather-beaten, it is difficult to imagine that in the early 20th century it was a major port of call for cargo ships and passenger liners plying the route between Seattle and Los Angeles. These days, Bandon is famous for its cranberries, which are harvested in bogs north of the town.

Craggy rock formations rise from the sea just off Bandon's beach. These wind-sculpted shapes include Face Rock, allegedly an Indian maiden frozen into stone by an evil spirit. A wilder landscape of dunes and sea grass prevails at **Bullards Beach State Park**, which lies across the marshy, bird-filled Coquille Estuary from Bandon.

🐾 Bullards Beach State Park
2 miles (3 km) north of Bandon, off Hwy 101. Tel (541) 347-3501.
⏰ *dawn–dusk daily.*

Environs
In the early 1900s, lumber baron Louis J. Simpson built Shore Acres, an estate atop oceanside bluffs outside the town of Coos Bay, 25 miles (40 km) north of Bandon. It is now the site of **Shore Acres State Park**. Simpson enhanced this magnificent spot with formal gardens of azaleas, rhododendrons, and roses. An enclosed observatory offers visitors a stunning view of the ocean, while interpretive panels educate them about the history of the site. Although the mansion is long gone, the gardens continue to thrive next to **Cape Arago State Park**, where seals and sea lions bask in the sun on offshore rocks.

Cape Blanco State Park, 27 miles (43 km) south of Bandon, is the westernmost point in the 48 contiguous states and one of the windiest spots on earth, with winter gusts exceeding 180 mph (290 km/h). The park's lighthouse is the oldest on the Oregon coast, having been first lit in 1870.

Hwy 101 nears the California border in a stretch of dense forests, towering cliffs, and offshore rock formations. Some of the most spectacular scenery is within the boundaries of the **Boardman State Scenic Corridor**, 4 miles (6.5 km) north of Brookings – a little town where warm winter temperatures contribute to the town's fame as supplier of over 90 percent of the lily bulbs grown in North America.

🐾 Shore Acres State Park
Cape Arago Hwy, 13 miles (21 km) SW of Coos Bay. Tel (541) 888-4902. ⏰ *8am–dusk daily.* 📷 ♿

🐾 Cape Arago State Park
End of Cape Arago Hwy, 15 miles (24 km) southwest of Coos Bay. Tel (800) 551-6949. ⏰ *dawn–dusk daily.*

🐾 Cape Blanco State Park
9 miles (14.5 km) north of Port Orford, off Hwy 101. Tel (800) 551-6949. ⏰ *dawn–dusk daily.* **Lighthouse** ⏰ *Apr–Oct: 10am–3:30pm daily.* 📷

🐾 Boardman State Scenic Corridor
Hwy 101, 4 miles (6.5 km) north of Brookings. Tel (800) 551-6949. ⏰ *dawn–dusk daily.*

Driftwood on the beach near Bandon, looking toward the town

Wine Country of the North Willamette Valley ⑬

The rich, wet, temperate valley that surrounds the Willamette River as it flows north from Eugene to join the Columbia River has yielded a bounty of fruits and vegetables ever since Oregon Trail pioneers began farming the land in the mid-19th century. In the 1960s, the valley's soil was also found to be ideal for growing grapes, especially the pinot noir, pinot gris, and chardonnay varietals.

Wine grapes on the vine

Now, vineyards carpet the rolling hillsides, especially in Yamhill County. Though the wine country of North Willamette Valley is not as developed as that of Napa Valley, its output is arguably just as good. It is easy to conduct a taste test since dozens of wineries are conveniently located just off Hwy 99W between McMinnville and Newberg.

Farms dotting the valley slopes of Yamhill County

Typical of the valley, the lush vineyards at Domaine Serene

The Tasting Room ⑨
The wines of many small producers whose wineries are not open to the public are available here for tasting and purchase.

Eyrie Vineyards ⑧
This pioneering winery, established in 1966, produced the Willamette Valley's first pinot noir and chardonnay and the US's first pinot gris.

Yamhill

Carlton

McMinnville

SALEM

0 kilometers   4

0 miles   2

Anne Amie Vineyards ⑦
The views of the Willamette Valley are one attraction of this hilltop winery; several fine white wines are another.

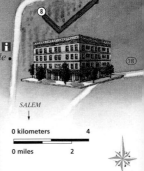

Argyle Winery ③
With 235 acres (95 ha) of vineyards, this winery specializes in sparkling wines. The tasting room is in a picturesque Victorian farmhouse.

TIPS FOR DRIVERS

Tour length: *About 35 miles (56 km).*
Starting point: *On 99W a few miles east of Newberg, which is 38 miles (58 km) west of Portland.*
Stopping-off points: *Dundee boasts many well-known restaurants, of which Tina's is arguably the star. Newberg, McMinnville, and Dayton also have good places to eat.*

Hoover-Minthorn House ①
An orphaned Herbert Hoover, who would become the 31st US president, came west from Iowa to live with his aunt and uncle in this handsome house in 1885, at the age of 11.

Rex Hill Vineyards ②
Shady hillside gardens and an antiques-filled tasting room warmed by a fire are lovely spots to taste this winery's award-winning pinot noirs.

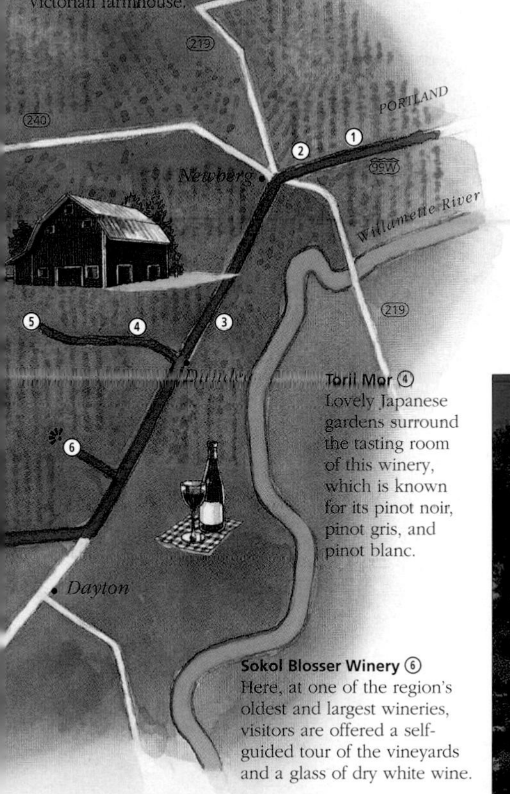

Toril Mor ④
Lovely Japanese gardens surround the tasting room of this winery, which is known for its pinot noir, pinot gris, and pinot blanc.

Sokol Blosser Winery ⑥
Here, at one of the region's oldest and largest wineries, visitors are offered a self-guided tour of the vineyards and a glass of dry white wine.

The Willamette River, meandering through the fertile North Willamette Valley

Maresh Red Barn ⑤
Wines from Maresh vineyard grapes, custom-made by three Oregon wineries, are on offer here. The vineyard, Oregon's fifth, grows pinot noir and pinot gris, among other varietals.

KEY

- Tour route
- Other road
- Viewpoint
- Information

Howard Hughes' "Spruce Goose" at the Evergreen Aviation & Space Museum

McMinnville 🔢

Road map 1 A3. 🏛 *32,000.*
ℹ *417 NW Adams St, (503) 472-6196.* **www**.mcminnville.org

In this prosperous town surrounded by the Willamette Valley vineyards, the Downtown Historic District is graced by the old Oregon Hotel, McMinnville Bank, and many other late 19th- and early 20th-century buildings. The excellent reputation of ivy-clad Linfield College, chartered in 1858, has long put McMinnville on the map, but these days the university shares the honor with the "Spruce Goose." This wooden flying boat, built in the 1940s, is housed in the **Evergreen Aviation & Space Museum**, where its 320-ft (97.5-m) wingspan spreads above early passenger planes, World War II fighters, and other vintage aircraft.

🏛 **Evergreen Aviation & Space Museum**
460 NE Capt. Michael King Smith Way. **Tel** (503) 434-4185. ◻ 9am–5pm daily. ◉ major hols. 📷 ♿ ◻
www.evergreenmuseum.org

Silverton 🔢

Road map 1 A3. 🏛 *7,500.*
ℹ *426 S Water St, (503) 873-5615.* **www**.silvertonchamber.org

This pleasant old farming town in the foothills of the Cascade Mountains is the entryway to 8,700-acre (3,520-ha) **Silver Falls State Park**, the largest state park in Oregon. The Trail of Ten Falls follows Silver Creek through a temperate rainforest of Douglas firs, hemlocks, and cedars to the trail's cataracts; the largest of them, South Falls, plunges 177 ft (54 m) down a mossy cliff into a deep pool.

At the southern edge of Silverton is the **Oregon Garden**. Rising high above the groomed landscape is a magnificent stand of oaks that are over 100 years old. The **Gordon House**, set in a shady grove near the garden's entrance, is the only structure in Oregon designed by renowned architect Frank Lloyd Wright.

The 1894 Deepwood Estate in Salem

🌿 **Silver Falls State Park**
Hwy 214, 10 miles (16 km) east of Salem. **Tel** (800) 551-6949.
◻ dawn–dusk daily. 📷
www.oregon.gov

🌿 **Oregon Garden**
879 W Main St. **Tel** (503) 874-8100.
◻ May–Sep: 10am–6pm daily; Oct–Apr: 10am–4pm daily. ◉ Jan 1, Thanksgiving, Dec 24 & 25. 📷 ♿
📷 ◻ **www**.oregongarden.org

Salem 🔢

Road map 1 A3. 🏛 *154,500.*
ℹ *181 High St NE, (800) 874-7012.* **www**.travelsalem.com

Salem was a thriving trading post and lumber port on the Willamette River when it became the capital of the Oregon Territory in 1851.

At the edge of Bush's Pasture Park stands **Bush House Museum**, an 1878 home with ten marble fireplaces and a conservatory said to be the first greenhouse west of the Mississippi River, and the historic **Deepwood Estate**. The **Mission Mill Museum** preserves some of the state's earliest structures: the 1841 home of Jason Lee, who helped found Salem; the 1847 home of state treasurer John Boon; and the Kay Woolen Mill, where waterwheels from the 1890s remain intact. The state's early history is also in evidence around the **Oregon State Capitol**. A gilded pioneer stands atop the rotunda of the building. Marble sculptures of a covered wagon and of Lewis and Clark *(see p37)* flank the entrance, and the murals inside depict Captain Robert Gray's discovery of the Columbia River in 1792.

On the Willamette University campus is **Waller Hall**, the oldest college building in Oregon, constructed in 1867; and the striking **Hallie Ford Museum of Art**, which houses an outstanding collection of 20th-century Native American basketry and paintings.

The Oregon State Capitol Building in Salem

🏛 Bush House Museum
600 Mission Street SE. ***Tel*** *(503) 363-4714.* 🕐 *noon–4pm Wed–Sun.* ● *major hols.* 🎟 👥 *compulsory.*

🏛 Deepwood Estate
1116 Mission St SE. ***Tel*** *(503) 363-1825.* 🕐 ***Grounds:*** *dawn–dusk daily.* ***House:*** *May–Sep: 9am–noon Wed–Mon; Oct–Apr: 11am–3pm Wed, Thu & Sat.* ● *major hols.* 🎟 👥
www.historicdeepwoodestate.org

🏛 Mission Mill Museum
1313 Mill St SE. ***Tel*** *(503) 585-7012.* 🕐 *10am–5pm Mon–Sat.* 🎟 👥
www.missionmill.org

🏛 Oregon State Capitol
900 Court St NE. ***Tel*** *(503) 986-1388.* 🕐 *8am–5:30pm Mon–Fri.*

🏛 Waller Hall
900 State St. 🕐 *8am–5pm Mon–Fri.*

🏛 Hallie Ford Museum of Art
700 State St. ***Tel*** *(503) 370-6855.* 🕐 *10am–5pm Tue–Sat, 1–5pm Sun.* ● *major hols.* 🎟 ♿ 🛍

Bush House Museum, built in 1878, a historic landmark in Salem

Eugene ⓱

Road map 1 A4. 👥 *156,000.* ℹ *754 Olive St, (541) 484-5307.* **www**.travellanecounty.org

The University of Oregon brings no small amount of culture and animation to the second largest city in Oregon, which straddles the banks of the Willamette River at the south end of the river valley. The peak-roofed, glass-and-timber **Hult Center for the Performing Arts**, designed by the New York firm Hardy Holzman Pfeiffer Associates and completed in 1982, is considered to be one of the best-designed performing arts complexes in the world. The **University of Oregon Museum of Natural and Cultural History** counts among its holdings the world's oldest shoes – a pair of sandals dating from 9500 BC.

Local artisans sell their wares weekly at the **Saturday Market**, a large collection of stalls on the downtown Park Blocks; and the **5th Street Public Market**, a collection of shops and restaurants in a converted feed mill, bustles with locals and the more than 17,000 university students who make good use of the city's many bicycle and rollerblading paths, pedestrian malls, and parks.

Local arts and crafts at the Saturday Market in Eugene

🏛 Hult Center for the Performing Arts
1 Eugene Center. ***Tel*** *(541) 682-5087.* **www**.hultcenter.org

🏛 University of Oregon Museum of Natural and Cultural History
1680 E 15th Ave. ***Tel*** *(541) 346-3024.* 🕐 *11am–5pm Wed–Sun.* ● *major hols.* 🛍

🛒 Saturday Market
8th Ave & Oak St. ***Tel*** *(541) 686-8885.* 🕐 *Apr–Nov: 10am–5pm Sat.* **www**.eugenesaturdaymarket.org

🛒 5th Street Public Market
High & 5th Sts. 🕐 *10am–7pm Mon–Sat, 11am–5pm Sun.*

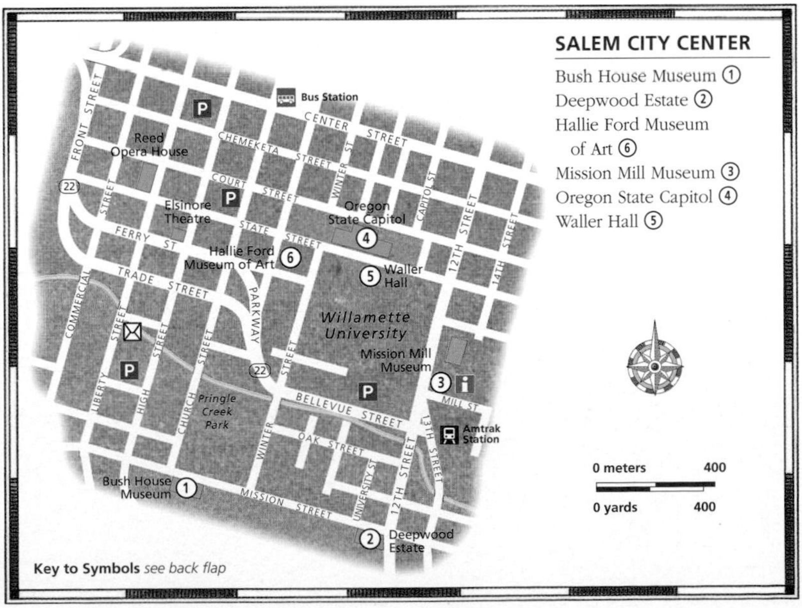

Bus Station
CENTER STREET
CHEMEKETA STREET
COURT STREET
STATE STREET
FERRY ST
TRADE STREET
BELLEVUE STREET
OAK STREET
MISSION STREET
MILL ST
FRONT STREET
COMMERCIAL STREET
LIBERTY STREET
HIGH STREET
CHURCH STREET
WINTER ST
CAPITOL ST
12TH STREET
13TH STREET
14TH STREET
UNIVERSITY ST
PARKWAY
Reed Opera House
Elsinore Theatre
Hallie Ford Museum of Art
Oregon State Capitol
Waller Hall
Willamette University
Mission Mill Museum
Pringle Creek Park
Amtrak Station
Bush House Museum
Deepwood Estate
22
SALEM CITY CENTER
Bush House Museum ①
Deepwood Estate ②
Hallie Ford Museum of Art ⑥
Mission Mill Museum ③
Oregon State Capitol ④
Waller Hall ⑤
0 meters 400
0 yards 400
Key to Symbols see back flap

Swimming pool fed by hot springs at the Warm Springs Reservation resort

Madras and Warm Springs ⑱

Road map 1 B3. *Madras* 🛈 *274 SW 4th St, (541) 475-2350.* www.madraschamber.com *Warm Springs* 🛈 *1233 Veterans St, (541) 553-1161.* www.warmsprings.com

Madras is a desert ranching town surrounded by rimrock and vast tracts of wilderness recreation lands. **Crooked River National Grassland** provides endless vistas as well as fishing and rafting opportunities on two US National Wild and Scenic Rivers – the Deschutes and the Crooked – that weave through the 112,000 acres (45,300 ha) of juniper and sage brush. **Cove Palisades State Park** surrounds Lake Billy Chinook, where deep waters reflecting the surrounding basalt cliffs are popular with boaters.

The Treaty of 1855 between the US government and the Wasco, Walla Walla, and Paiute tribes established lands for the tribes on the 640,000-acre (259,000-ha) Warm Springs

Reservation, located on the High Desert plateaus and forested Cascade slopes of central Oregon. These Confederated Tribes preserve their heritage at the **Museum at Warm Springs** with a stunning collection of basketry and beadwork, haunting historic photographs that chronicle the hardships of assimilation, and videotapes of tribal ceremonies. The Tribes also manage a casino and a resort, where a large pool is heated by hot springs.

🎣 **Crooked River National Grassland**
10 miles (16 km) south of Madras, off Hwy 26. ◯ *dawn–dusk daily.* 🛈 *813 SW Hwy 97, Madras.* **Tel** *(541) 475-9272.*

🌊 **Cove Palisades State Park**
15 miles (24 km) southwest of Madras, off Hwy 97. **Tel** *(541) 546-3412.* ◯ *dawn–dusk daily.* 🏞

🏛 **Museum at Warm Springs**
2189 Hwy 26, Warm Springs. **Tel** *(503) 553-3331.* ◯ *9am–5pm daily.* 🔴 *Sun & Mon (Nov–Apr), Jan 1, Thanksgiving, Dec 25.* 🏞 🛈 www.museumatwarmsprings.org

Sisters ⑲

Road map 1 B4. 🏔 *1,500.* 🛈 *291 E Main Ave, (541) 549-0251.* www.sisterscountry.com

Sisters is a ranching town that cashes in on its cowboy history with Old West-style storefronts and wood sidewalks. The setting, though, is authentic – the peaks of the Three Sisters, each exceeding 10,000 ft (3,000 m), tower majestically above the town and the surrounding pine forests, alpine meadows, and rushing streams.

Environs
The McKenzie Pass climbs from Sisters to a 1-mile (1.6-km) summit amid a massive lava flow. The **Dee Wright Observatory** provides panoramic views of more than a dozen Cascades peaks and buttes and of the sweeping lava fields, which can be examined at close range on the half-mile (0.8-km) Lava River Interpretive Trail.

The cold and clear waters of the Metolius River flow through fragrant pine forests on the flanks of Mount Jefferson. Near Camp Sherman, a tiny settlement of cabins 14 miles (22.5 km) west of Sisters, the river bubbles up from springs beneath Black Butte. The view from the scenic overlook above the headwaters usually includes fly-fishing enthusiasts casting their lines into one of the state's best trout streams.

🎣 **Dee Wright Observatory**
Hwy 242, 15 miles (24 km) west of Sisters. ◯ *mid-Jun–Oct: dawn–dusk daily.* 🔴 *Oct–mid-Jun.*

Galloping horses near Sisters, the towering peaks of the Three Sisters mountains visible in the distance

Bend's High Desert Museum, showcasing life in central and eastern Oregon

Smith Rock State Park 𝟐𝟎

Road map 1 B4. **Tel** (541) 548-7501. ⬜ dawn–dusk daily. 🏞️
www.oregon.gov

At Smith Rock, the Crooked River flows beneath towering rock faces of welded tuff – volcanic rock that was compressed under intense heat and pressure. These unusually shaped peaks and pinnacles – with compelling names like Morning Glory Wall and Pleasure Palace – are a lure for risk-taking rock climbers, who ascend the sometimes more than 550-ft (168-m) sheer faces on over 1,300 climbing routes. The less intrepid can enjoy the spectacle from roadside viewpoints or from one of the many hiking trails that follow the base of the cliffs.

Bend 𝟐𝟏

Road map 1 B4. 👥 75,000.
ℹ️ 777 NW Wall St, (541) 382-3221.
www.bendchamber.org

Busy Bend, once a sleepy lumber town, is alluringly close to the ski slopes, lakes, streams, and the many other natural attractions of Central Oregon. While unsightly development is quickly replacing juniper- and sage-covered grazing lands on the outskirts, the old brick business district retains a good deal of small-town charm. Drake Park is a grassy downtown retreat on both banks of the Deschutes River, and **Pilot Butte State Scenic Viewpoint**, atop a

volcanic cinder cone that rises 500 ft (150 m) from the center of town, overlooks the High Desert and nine snowcapped Cascade peaks.

The **High Desert Museum** celebrates life in the rugged, arid High Desert terrain that covers much of central and eastern Oregon. Walk-through dioramas use dramatic lighting and sound effects in authentic re-creations of Native American dwellings, a wagon camp, a silver mine, and other scenes of desert settlement. Outdoors, a trail crossing the floor of a forest of ponderosa pine leads to replicas of a settler's cabin and a sawmill, and to natural habitats, including a trout stream and an aviary filled with hawks and other raptors.

🌸 **Pilot Butte State Scenic Viewpoint**
East end of Greenwood Ave. **Tel** (800) 551-6949. ⬜ dawn–dusk daily.

🏛️ **High Desert Museum**
59800 S Hwy 97. **Tel** (541) 382-4754. ⬜ May–Oct: 9am–5pm daily, Nov–Apr: 10am–4pm daily. ⬤ Jan 1, Thanksgiving, Dec 25. 🏞️☐🔲
www.highdesertmuseum.org

Newberry National Volcanic Monument 𝟐𝟐

Road map 1 B4. ⬜ Apr–Oct: dawn–dusk daily. 🏞️ **www**.fs.usda.gov

The 50,000 acres (20,000 ha) of the Newberry National Volcanic Monument encompass eerie and bleak landscapes of black lava, as well as sparkling mountain lakes,

waterfalls, hemlock forests, and snow-capped peaks. Exhibits at the **Lava Lands Visitor Center** explain how Newberry Volcano has been built by thousands of eruptions that began about 600,000 years ago – the last eruption occurred in about AD 700 – and which, seismic activity suggests, may begin again. Other exhibits highlight central Oregon's cultural history. Well-marked roads and interpretive trails lead to major sites within the monument.

At Lava River Cave, a passage extends almost a mile (1.5 km) into a lava tube, a channel through which molten lava once flowed. At Lava Cast Forest, a paved loop trail transverses a forest of hollow molds formed by molten lava, which created casts around tree trunks. A road ascends into the 18-mile- (29-km-) wide crater, where Paulina and East Lakes sparkle amid pine forests. It then skirts a massive field of shiny black lava known as the Big Obsidian Flow as it climbs to the 7,987-ft (2,434-m) summit of Paulina Peak, the highest point within Newberry Monument.

In addition to magnificent scenery, the monument provides opportunities for hiking, fishing, boating, and other recreational activities.

Lava Lands Visitor Center
58201 Hwy 97. **Tel** (541) 593-2421. ⬜ May–Jun: 9am–5pm Thu–Mon; Jul–Aug: 9am–5pm daily; Sep–mid-Oct: 9am–5pm Thu–Mon.

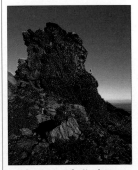

A rock outcrop at the Newberry National Volcanic Monument

Cascade Lakes Highway [23]

Entering
Cascade
Lakes
Oregon Scenic
Byway
Highway sign

This loop is often called Century Drive because the circuit is just under 100 miles (160 km) long. A stunning display of forest and mountain scenery unfolds in this relatively short distance. Most memorable are the many vistas of sparkling lakes backed by craggy Cascade peaks. Trails into the deep wilderness, idyllic picnic and camping spots, lakes and streams brimming with trout and salmon, and ski slopes and rustic resorts are likely to tempt even the most time-pressed traveler to linger on this scenic byway for as long as possible.

Mount Bachelor [7]
Some of the best skiing and snowboarding in the Pacific Northwest is here, on Mount Bachelor's 71 runs. There are also numerous trails for cross-country skiing and snowshoeing.

Devil's Garden [5]
Astronauts trained on foot and in moon buggies for their historic 1969 moonwalk on this enormous 45-sq-mile (117-sq-km) lava flow.

Sparks Lake [6]
This large shallow trout lake, surrounded by mountains, lava formations, and meadow, was considered by photographer Ray Atkeson to be the most scenic place in Oregon.

Elk Lake [4]
Conveniently located along the Cascade Lakes Highway, Elk Lake is a popular destination for sailing, windsurfing, and fishing. The store at the Elk Lake Resort rents canoes, motorboats, rowboats, and paddleboats.

Osprey Observation Point [3]
Crane Prairie Reservoir hosts a large colony of osprey that plunge from the sky like meteorites to pluck fish out of the water.

5
6
4
Hosmer Lake
Blow Lake
Lava Lake
Little Lava Lake
46
Cultus Lake
Crane Prairie Reservoir
3
42

Dutchman Flat ⑧
Quiet and seclusion are the rich rewards for hiking a short distance to this picturesque desert area.

NEWBERRY NATIONAL VOLCANIC MONUMENT ①

High Desert Museum ①
This museum shows the desert in its full glory and explains its evolution, flora, and fauna. Visitors can see live animals in their natural habits.

Lava Butte ②
A paved road ascends to the top of this extinct volcanic cone, affording spectacular views of the Cascade Mountains.

0 kilometers   5
0 miles   4

KEY

■ Tour route
═ Other road
ℹ Information
☆ Viewpoint

Striking view from Newberry National Volcanic Monument

Crater Lake National Park Tour ㉔

Oregon's only National Park surrounds a lake that, at 1,949 ft (594 m), is the deepest in the US and the ninth deepest in the world. Creation of Crater Lake began about 7,700 years ago when Mount Mazama erupted and then collapsed, forming the caldera in which the lake now sits. The crater rim

Golden-mantled ground squirrel

rises an average of 1,000 ft (300 m) above the lake. On the drive that circles the lake, the many overlooks, 90 miles (144 km) of trails, and a beautiful lodge afford stunning views.

Merriam Point ④
This promontory is an excellent spot from which to admire the west side of the lake, with the cone-shaped Wizard Island and its surrounding black volcanic blocks.

The Watchman ③
This viewpoint, reached after a moderate climb, is named for its historic fire tower, and is the closest lookout to Wizard Island.

Rim Villa

Wizard Island ②
Wizard Island is a small volcanic island in the shape of a cone jutting 764 ft (233 m) above the surface of the lake. At the summit is a crater 300 ft (90 m) across.

Mazama Village

Crater Lake Lodge ①
This rustic hotel perched on the caldera rim has welcomed guests since 1915. Extensive renovations have restored the structural integrity of the building, once at risk of collapsing under its own weight and that of the 15 ft (4.5 m) of snow that can accumulate in winter. Magnificent views can be enjoyed from here.

Tourists departing on a boat tour from Cleetwood Cove, on the north shore of the lake

TIPS FOR DRIVERS

Tour length: *33 miles (53 km).*
Starting point: *Steel Information Center, on Rim Drive 4 miles (6.5 km) north of Rte 62.*
When to go: *Rim Drive is open from the end of June to mid-October, weather permitting.*
Stopping-off points: *Meals are offered at Crater Lake Lodge and Annie Creek Restaurant near Mazama (Jun–mid-Oct); snacks are sold in Rim Village. Two-hour narrated boat trips (late Jun–mid-Sep: 10am–4pm daily) depart from Cleetwood Cove.*

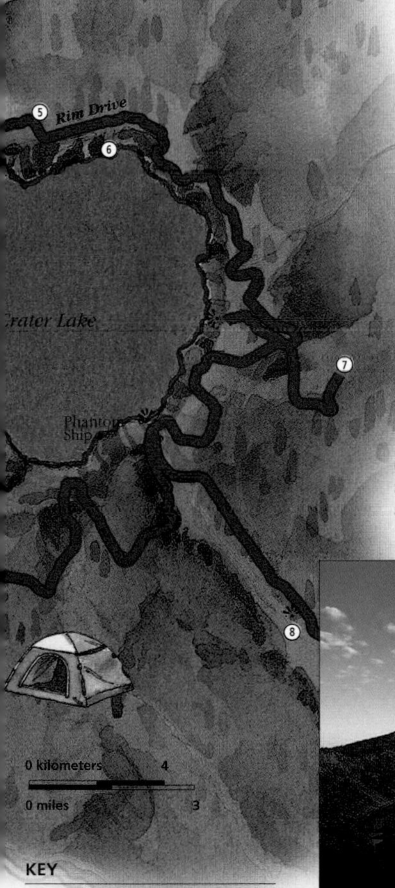

Rim Drive [5]
On this 33-mile (53-km) circuit, spectacular vistas of the lake, the islands, and the surrounding mountains unfold at every turn.

Cleetwood Trail [6]
This 1-mile (1.6-km) strenuous trail, which drops a steep 700 ft (210 m), provides the only access to the lake. In summer, a boat tour departs from the dock at the base of the trail.

Mount Scott [7]
When weather allows, views from this peak – at 8,929 ft (2,722 m) the highest point in the park – extend as far as California's Mount Shasta, located 100 miles (160 km) to the south.

The Pinnacles [8]
An eerie landscape of pumice spires, known as fossil fumaroles, rises from the caldera's eastern base. Many of the spires are hollow.

Castle Crest – Wildflower Trail [9]
Spectacular wildflowers bloom in July and August alongside this easy-to-walk 0.4-mile (0.6-km) trail.

KEY

- Tour route
- Other road
- Viewpoint
- Information

Sinnott Memorial Overlook [10]
Breathtaking views reward the short descent to this point just below the caldera rim, where park rangers give geology talks.

A park ranger giving a tour in the Oregon Caves National Monument

Oregon Caves National Monument ㉕

Road map 1 A5. ℹ️ *Oregon Route 46, Cave Junction, (541) 592-2100.* ⏰ *9:30am–5pm daily.* 🅿️ *hourly Apr–Oct.* **www**.nps.gov

Visitors on the 70-minute guided tours of these vast underground caverns follow lighted trails past strange formations, cross underground rivers, squeeze through giant ribs of marble, and clamber up and down staircases into enormous chambers hung with stalactites. Discovered in 1874 by a hunter chasing his dog into a dark hole in the side of Elijah Mountain, the caves have been formed by the steady trickling of water over the past hundreds of thousands of years. Above ground, three trails cross a remnant old-growth coniferous forest and lead to an ancient and noble Douglas fir, famous for having the widest girth of any known tree in Oregon.

Jacksonville ㉖

Road map 1 A4. 🏘️ *2,600.* ℹ️ *185 Oregon St, (541) 899-8118.* **www**.jacksonvilleoregon.org

In this Gold Rush boomtown, time has more or less stood still since the 1880s, when Rich Gulch Creek ceased to yield gold and it was decided that main railroad lines would bypass the town.

With more than 80 brick and wood-frame 19th-century buildings, Jacksonville has

been designated a National Historic Landmark. A walking tour (a map is available from the information center in the old railroad depot) shows off the town's wealth of architecture and history. The **Beekman House** (c.1876) is a museum that offers a glimpse of how the town's prosperous burghers once lived, with original funishings and actors dressed in costumes of the period. The beautiful hillside estate of 19th-century photographer Peter Britt is the setting of the annual **Britt Festivals**, the Pacific Northwest's premier outdoor performing arts summer festival. Internationally famous dancers and artists representing various music genres – including jazz, folk, bluegrass, pop, musical theater, and classical – perform beneath a canopy of Ponderosa pines *(see p31).*

🏛️ **Beekman House**
352 E California St.
***Tel** (541) 773-6536.* ⏰ *by appointment.* 🅿️ 🅿️
🎭 **Britt Festivals**
216 W Main St, Medford.
***Tel** (541) 773-6077.*
www.brittfest.org

Jacksonville's Beekman House, built during the Gold Rush

Ashland ㉗

Road map 1 A5. 🏘️ *20,000.* ℹ️ *110 E Main St, (541) 482-3486.* **www**.ashlandchamber.com.

At first glance, it may be difficult to believe that every year some 350,000 theater goers descend on Ashland, an amiable town surrounded by farms and orchards. What draws them is the **Oregon Shakespeare Festival**, established in 1935, and now presenting, between February and October, an annual schedule of 11 plays by Shakespeare, in addition to other works by classic and contemporary playwrights. Theater buffs can also view props and costumes from past performances at the Festival Exhibit Center, and take backstage tours of the festival's three venues: the 1,200-seat, open-air Elizabethan Theatre; the Angus Bowmer Theatre, which seats 600 people; and the modern New Theatre.

🎭 **Oregon Shakespeare Festival**
15 S Pioneer St. ***Tel** (541) 482-4331.*
www.osfashland.org

A Renaissance stage set at the Oregon Shakespeare Festival

Environs
Many commercial outfitters launch raft and jet boat trips from Grants Pass, 40 miles (64 km) north of Ashland on I-5. The Rogue River rushes 215 twisting miles (346 km) through Siskiyou National Forest and other wilderness before reaching the Pacific Ocean. Elk, mountain lions, and bears are often seen roaming the riverbanks, and bald eagles fly overhead.

Steens Mountain Tour ㉘

Alpine lupines in a mountain meadow

Scenery does not get much more rugged and grand than it does here on this 9,700-ft (2,960-m) mountain. Steens Mountain is a fault-block, formed when land on two sides of a geological fault rose and fell to different levels. As a result, the west slope of this mountain rises gradually from sagebrush country through stands of aspen, juniper, and mountain mahogany, while the east face drops precipitously for more than a mile (1.6 km). Pronghorn, bighorn sheep, and wild horses roam craggy gorges and alpine tundra carpeted with wildflowers, and eagles and falcons soar overhead. The Steens Mountain National Back Country Byway traverses this remarkable landscape.

TIPS FOR DRIVERS

Tour length: *58 miles (93.5km).*
Starting point: *North Loop Road in Frenchglen.*
When to go: *The entire Steens Loop Road is closed from November to June due to snow cover, though snow squalls and lightning storms can occur in any season.*
Getting around: *This dirt and gravel road is steep in parts. It is not suitable for vehicles with low clearance.*
Stopping-off points: *Many scenic overlooks, picnic spots, and some campgrounds are located on the route. Frenchglen has lodging and restaurants.*

Donner und Blitzen River ①
An army officer named this rushing torrent "Thunder and Lightning" while attempting to cross it during a thunderstorm in 1864.

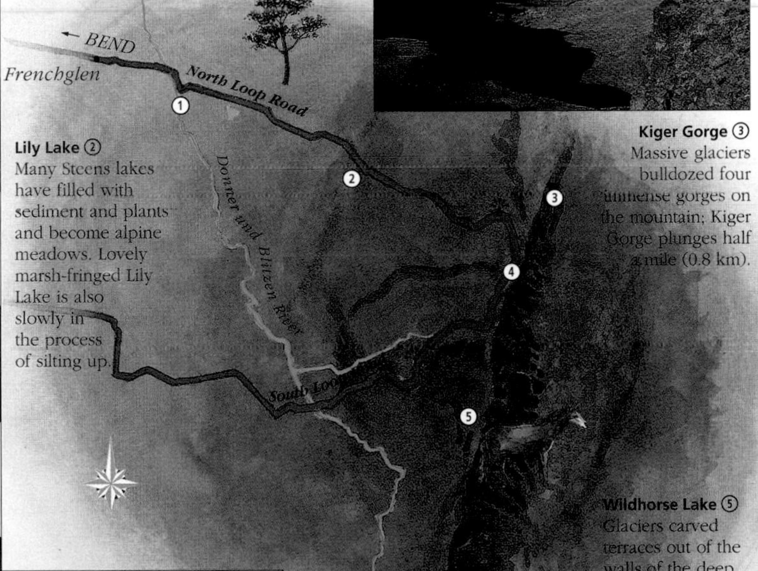
← BEND
Frenchglen
North Loop Road
Donner und Blitzen River
South Loop Road
0 kilometers 8
0 miles 6
KEY
Tour route
Viewpoint

Lily Lake ②
Many Steens lakes have filled with sediment and plants and become alpine meadows. Lovely marsh-fringed Lily Lake is also slowly in the process of silting up.

Kiger Gorge ③
Massive glaciers bulldozed four immense gorges on the mountain; Kiger Gorge plunges half a mile (0.8 km).

Wildhorse Lake ⑤
Glaciers carved terraces out of the walls of the deep gorge that encircles this sparkling lake.

East Rim Viewpoint ④
This perch is a full mile (1.6 km) above the alkali flats of the Alvord Desert; sitting in the rain shadow of the mountain, this desolate desert receives a mere 6 inches (15 cm) of rain a year.

The seemingly endless desert landscape of the Jordan Valley

Jordan Valley ㉙

Road map 1 C4. 🏃 239. ℹ️ 306 Blackaby St, (541) 586-2460.

This scruffy desert ranching settlement is one of only a few towns in sparsely populated Malheur County, where just 28,000 people inhabit 10,000 sq miles (25,900 sq km). Jordan Valley makes two claims to fame. A legacy of the Basque sheepherders who settled the town in 1890 is the ball court, built in 1915, for playing pelota, a game that resembles American handball. A windswept, sagebrush-filled cemetery 17 miles (27 km) south of town on Hwy 95 is the final resting place of Jean Baptiste Charbonneau, son of the Indian guide Sacagawea *(see p37)*. Born in 1805, Jean was taken across the country with the Lewis and Clark party, which his mother helped guide. Years later, he died of a chill at a stagecoach stop near Jordan Valley in 1866.

Malheur National Wildlife Refuge ㉚

Road map 1 C4. **Tel** (541) 493-2612. *Refuge and museum* 🔘 dawn–dusk daily. 🔘 major hols. *Visitors' center* 🔘 mid-Mar–mid-Oct: 8am–4pm daily; mid-Oct–mid-Mar: 8am–4pm Mon–Thu. 🔘 major hols. 🔥 www.fws.gov

One of the nation's largest wildlife refuges, Malheur spreads across 186,500 acres (75,500 ha) of the Blitzen

Valley floor. More than 320 species of birds and 58 species of mammals inhabit the wetlands, meadows, and uplands, ensuring prime wildlife viewing for visitors. Sandhill cranes, tundra swans, snowy white egrets, white-faced ibis, pronghorn antelope, mule deer, and redband trout are among the most numerous of the refuge's denizens.

Spring and fall are the best times to view birds, which alight in the refuge on their annual migrations up and down the Pacific Flyway, a major north–south route for migrating North American waterfowl. A small museum houses specimens of birds commonly seen in the refuge. Starting at the center, the Central Patrol Road traverses the 40-mile (64-km) length of the refuge and provides access to the prime viewing spots. The P Ranch, at the south end, is the historic spread of Peter French, who settled the Blitzen Valley in the 1880s.

Environs
From the refuge, the 69-mile (111-km) **Diamond Loop National Back Country Byway** heads into sage-covered hills and red rimrock canyons. Along the route are Diamond Craters, a volcanic landscape formed between 17,000 and 25,000 years ago; the Round Barn, a distinctive 19th-century structure with a round stone corral surrounded by a circular paddock; and Diamond, a small, poplar-shaded ranch town where the number of guests staying at the hotel

determines whether the town's population exceeds the single digits.

🐾 **Diamond Loop National Back Country Byway**
ℹ️ 28910 Hwy 20 W, Hines. *Tel* (541) 573-4400.

Resting mule deer in the Malheur National Wildlife Refuge

John Day Fossil Beds National Monument ㉛

Road map 1 B3. ℹ️ Hwy 19, 40 miles (64 km) west of John Day, (541) 987-2333. 🔘 dawn–dusk daily; *Thomas Condon Paleontology Center (Sheep Rock unit)* 🔘 9am–5pm daily. 🔘 major hols between Thanksgiving & Presidents' Day. www.nps.gov

Prehistoric fossil beds litter the John Day Fossil Beds National Monument, where sedimentary rocks preserve the plants and animals that flourished in jungles and savannas for 40 million years, between the extinction of the dinosaurs and the beginning of the most

Formations at John Day Fossil Beds National Monument's Sheep Rock unit

The magnificent Painted Hills at John Day Fossil Beds National Monument

recent ice age. The monument's 14,000 acres (5,700 ha) comprise three units: Sheep Rock, Painted Hills, and Clarno. At all three, trails provide opportunities for close-up observation of the fossil beds. Painted Hills presents the most dramatic landscapes: volcanic rock formations are vivid hues of red, pink, bronze, tan, and black. Clarno contains some of the oldest formations, dating back 54 million years and including some of the finest fossil plant remains on earth. At Sheep Rock, where formations date from 16 million to 6 million years ago, the visitors' center displays many important finds from the beds.

Enteledont skull and forelimb fossils

The fossil beds are named in honor of John Day, a fur trader from Virginia who arrived in Oregon in 1812 and for whom the John Day River is named, though Day himself apparently never actually set foot near the beds.

Pendleton ❷

Road map 1 C3. 🏠 *17,300.*
ℹ️ *501 S Main St, (541) 276-7411.*
www.pendletonchamber.com

Pendleton is the largest town in eastern Oregon, and it has an outsized reputation for raucous cowboys and lawless cattle rustlers to match. Visitors may be disappointed to learn, however, that these more colorful days belong to the past. **Pendleton Woolen Mills** *(see p76),* known for its warm clothing and blankets, particularly its "legendary" blankets whose designs are a tribute to Native American tribes, is now the big business in town. The mill wove its first Indian trade blanket in 1895. Native Americans used these blankets not only as standard clothing items but also in ceremonies and trade among each other, where the blankets were used as a measure of value and credit. Cowboy lore continues to come alive during the Pendleton Round-Up each September, when rodeo stunt performers and some 50,000 spectators crowd into town. Previous rodeos are honored in the photographs and other memorabilia at the **Round-Up Hall of Fame**.

The **Pendleton Underground Tours** reveal much about the town's notoriety. The tours begin in an underground labyrinth of opium dens, gaming rooms, and prohibition-era drinking establishments and include stops at the Cozy Room bordello and the cramped 19th-century living quarters of Chinese laborers.

Another chapter of local history is commemorated at the **Tamástslikt Cultural Institute**. Re-creations of historic structures and handsome exhibits of war bonnets and other artifacts depict the horse culture, seasonal migrations, forced resettlements, and current success of the Cayuse, Umatilla, and Walla Walla tribes, who have lived on the Columbia River plateau for more than 10,000 years.

🎪 **Pendleton Woolen Mills**
1307 SE Court Pl. **Tel** *(541) 276-6911.* **Salesroom** ⬜ *8am–6pm Mon–Sat, 9am–5pm Sun.* ⬤ *Jan 1, Thanksgiving, Dec 25.* 📷 *9am, 11am, 1:30pm, 3pm Mon–Fri.* 🅿️
www.pendleton-usa.com

🏛 **Round-Up Hall of Fame**
1205 SW Court Ave.
Tel *(541) 276-2553.* ⬜ *10am–4pm Mon–Sat.* ⬤ *major hols.*
www.pendletonroundup.com

🎫 **Pendleton Underground Tours**
37 SW Emigrant Ave. **Tel** *(541) 276-0730.* ⬜ *Mar–Oct: 9:30am–3pm Mon–Sat; Nov–Feb: call for hrs.*
⬤ *major hols.* 📷 🅿️ **www**.
pendletonundergroundtours.org

🏛 **Tamástslikt Cultural Institute**
47106 Wildhorse Blvd. **Tel** *(541) 966-9748.* ⬜ *Apr–Oct: 9am–5pm daily; Nov–Mar: 9am–5pm Mon–Sat.*
⬤ *Jan 1, Thanksgiving, Dec 25.* 📷
📷 🅿️ **www**.tcimuseum.com

Environs
The town of La Grande, 52 miles (84 km) southeast of Pendleton, is best known as the jumping-off point for trips into the scenic wilds of the Blue and Wallowa Mountains and Hells Canyon *(see pp112–15).*

In downtown La Grande, charming turn-of-the-19th-century buildings now house shops and cafés.

A rodeo rider at the popular
Pendleton Round-Up

Elkhorn Drive National Scenic Byway Tour [33]

Covered wagon of the type used by pioneers

This drive through a mountain range takes in some of the finest scenery in Eastern Oregon. To the west, the route climbs across the Elkhorn Range of the Blue Mountains, where dense pine forests interspersed with crystal-clear lakes give way to historic gold-mining towns. To the east, seen across Baker Valley, rise the snow-capped summits of the spectacular Wallowa mountain range.

Anthony Lakes (6)
A string of mountain lakes sparkle amid forests of ponderosa pines. In winter, skiers and snowmobile enthusiasts glide across this hilly terrain on deep powder.

Granite (5)
When pioneer gold mining days came to a close, the town of Granite changed from a boomtown into a ghost town.

Elkhorn Drive National Scenic Byway
6
BLUE MOUNTAINS
North Fork John Day
ELKHORN RANGE
Mount Ireland
5
4
Sumpter
3
McEwen
JOHN DAY
26
Powder River
Phillips Reservoir
KEY
Tour route
Other road
Information
0 km 8
0 miles 5

Sumpter Dredge (4)
This massive dredge once dug its way across the valley floor in search of gold. The hulking wood and steel beast is now the centerpiece of a unique heritage site.

**National Historic Oregon Trail
Interpretive Center** ①
Here, replicas of pioneer
scenes, accompanied by the
sounds of jangling oxen, re-
create life on the Oregon Trail.

**WALLOWA
MOUNTAINS**

*HELLS
CANYON*

Baker City
ⓘ ②

Baker City ②
Some rather grand
downtown blocks
and fine Victorian
residences are
reminders of
the fame and
prosperity that
gold mining once
brought to this
now quiet
ranching town.

Sumter Valley Railway ③
A narrow-gauge steam train
once again chugs along a
historic route originally built
to haul lumber and gold.
Hawks and other wildlife
usually provide an escort.

Joseph ㉞

Road map 1 C3. 🏚 *1,100.* ⓘ *Wallowa Mountains Visitor Center, 88401
Hwy 82, Enterprise, (541) 426-5546.*

Joseph is named for Chief
Joseph, leader of the Nez-
Perce people *(see p25)*. In
1877, he led his tribe on a
1,800-mile (2,880-km) flight
to resist resettlement from
their lands in the Wallowas;
they were apprehended
near the Canadian border
and relocated to a reservation
in Washington State.

The brick storefronts, snow-
capped Wallowa Mountains,
and outlying grasslands lend
Joseph a frontier-town air still.
These days, though, recreation enthusiasts outnumber
ranchers, and artisans,
particularly sculptors,
have established
galleries. Housed
in the historic
former location
of a newspaper
office, hospital,
and bank, the
**Wallowa
County
Museum**,
devoted to Chief
Joseph's famous
retreat, is here. Chief Joseph
Days, held in July, feature a
rodeo and carnival. The town
hosts several other festivals,
including the Annual Arts Festival and the Wallowa Mountain Quilt Show, both in June.

**Bronze horse
sculpture in Joseph**

🏛 **Wallowa County Museum**
110 S Main St. **Tel** (541) 432-6095.
◯ *Memorial Day–3rd weekend
Sep: 10am–5pm daily.* 📷

**Restored historic corner
building in Joseph, Oregon**

**Motorboat moored on the blue
waters of Wallowa Lake**

Wallowa Lake ㉟

Road map 1 C3.

The crystal-clear waters
of this long glacial lake
sparkle at the foot of the
Wallowa Mountains, which
form a 10,000-ft- (3,050-m-)
high, 40-mile- (64-km-) long
wall of granite. Though the
lake was a popular tourist
retreat over 100 years ago,
the forested shoreline
is remarkably
unspoiled. Much
of it falls within
the boundaries
of national forest
lands and Wallowa
State Park.
One of the few
commercial structures
on the lake is **Wallowa Lake
Lodge**, a beautifully restored
log building dating from
the 1920s. It still provides
accommodation and meals.
The popular **Wallowa Lake
Tramway** whisks riders up
3,700 ft (1,100 m) to the
summit of Mount Howard,
where spectacular views
of the lake below and the
Wallowa mountains can be
enjoyed. Deep wilderness is
only a short hike or pack trip
away from the lake in the
Eagle Cap Wilderness, which
climbs and dips over some
360,000 acres (146,000 ha)
of mountainous terrain to
the west of the lake.

🌿 **Wallowa Lake State Park**
6 miles (10 km) south of Joseph
off Hwy 82. **Tel** (541) 432-4185.
◯ *dawn–dusk daily.*
www.oregon.gov
🚠 **Wallowa Lake Tramway**
59919 Wallowa Lake Hwy,
Joseph. **Tel** (541) 432-5331.
◯ *mid-May–Sep.* 📷
www.wallowalaketramway.com

Hells Canyon National Recreation Area Tour [36]

Local prickly pear cactus

Some of the wildest terrain in North America clings to the sides of craggy, 9,400-ft (2,865-m) peaks at Hells Canyon and plunges to the famed basin far below, where the Snake River rushes through North America's deepest river-carved gorge. Visitors are awed by the massive canyon walls rising 7,993 ft (2,436 m) and delight in the dense upland pine forests and delicate flower-covered alpine meadows – 652,000 acres (264,000 ha) in all. Much of the terrain is too rugged to cross, even on foot, making sections of the Snake River accessible only by boat. Many visitors settle for the stunning views from several lookouts, and not one is disappointed.

Hells Canyon National Recreation Area viewpoint

Buckhorn Lookout ①
One of several spectacular overlooks in the Hells Canyon area, this remote spot offers superb views of the Wallowa-Whitman National Forest and the Imnaha River canyon.

Nee-Me-Poo Trail ②
Hikers on this national trail follow in the footsteps of Chief Joseph and 700 Nez Percé Indians who, in 1877, embarked on an 1,800-mile (2,880-km) trek toward freedom in Canada *(see p25)*.

Hells Canyon Reservoir ⑥
Formed by Oxbow Dam to the south and Hells Canyon Dam to the north, this 25-mile- (40-km-) long reservoir is part of a huge power-generating complex on the Snake River. A private road along the east shore provides boaters with access to the river.

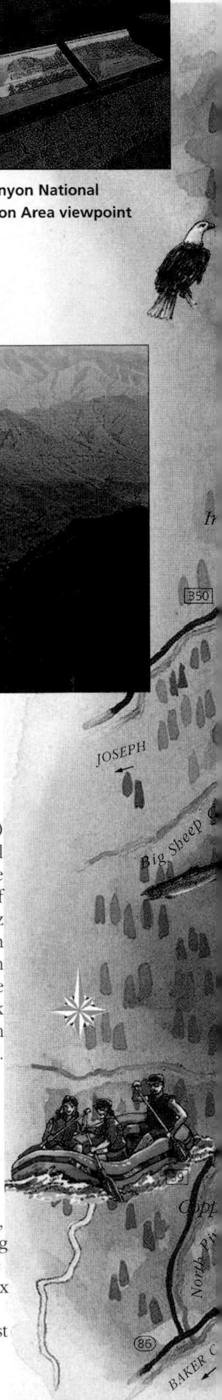

TIPS FOR DRIVERS

Tour length: *214 miles (345 km), including all turnoffs.*
Starting point: *Oregon SR 350, 8 miles (13 km) east of Joseph.*
When to go: *Summer months only. Some roads are not suitable for every type of vehicle. For information, call the area's Visitor Center at (541) 426-5546.*
Stopping-off points: *Picnic areas are abundant. Imnaha offers restaurants and lodging.*

Pittsburg Landing
493
Snake River
4240
Seven Devils Mountains
Hells Canyon Dam
454

Imnaha River ③
A road from the town of Imnaha follows this frothy river through a pine-scented valley, passing isolated ranches and a fish weir where Chinook salmon can be seen swimming upstream on their annual migration from the distant Pacific Ocean.

KEY

- Tour route
- Other road
- Information
- Viewpoint

Hat Point Road ④
A dizzying drive up a steep 23-mile (37-km) gravel road leads to Hat Point, which is located at an altitude of 7,000 ft (2,100 m).

0 kilometers 18
0 miles 14

Wild and Scenic River ⑤
A 31.5-mile (50.5-km) stretch of the Snake River, from Hells Canyon Dam to Upper Pittsburg Landing, is designated a Wild River. Experienced guides pilot rafters over the many stretches of rapids. Searing mid-summer temperatures and inhospitable terrain, as well as rattlesnakes and an occasional patch of poison ivy, make an overland trek along-side the river more challenging.

HELLS CANYON ADVENTURES
A boat negotiating rapids on a trip on the Snake River

SEATTLE

Seattle at a Glance

Seattle's history, commerce, and quality of life are closely tied to its waterfront location on Puget Sound. The Klondike Gold Rush National Historical Park recalls the city's pivotal role as an embarkation point for the gold rush of 1897–8. The Seattle Aquarium explores Puget Sound's diverse natural habitat. Embracing both the past and the future, Seattle's architectural icons include a number of historic buildings, the once-futuristic Space Needle, and the provocative EMP Museum.

Map of Seattle on a manhole cover

EMP Museum
This museum is dedicated to the history and exploration of music and science fiction (see pp146–7).

Space Needle
Built for the 1962 World's Fair, the 605-ft (184-m) Space Needle is Seattle's official landmark. A 43-second elevator ride whisks visitors to the observation deck and a 360-degree view (see pp144–5).

Maritime Event Center, Pier 66
Opened in 1998, this cleverly designed museum on Seattle's working waterfront engages visitors with interactive exhibits showcasing the region's maritime and fisheries industries (see p136).

Seattle Aquarium
Offering a window into Pacific Northwest marine life, this popular aquarium has an underwater glass dome which surrounds visitors with sharks, salmon, octopus, and other Puget Sound creatures (see pp138–9).

◁ Sailboats on Lake Union, Seattle

Benaroya Hall
*Home of the Seattle Symphony, this
$118 million complex occupies an entire
city block. Its 2,500-seat Taper Auditorium is internationally acclaimed for
its superior acoustics* (see p129).

**Fairmont
Olympic Hotel**
*This stately hotel
is listed on the
National Register
of Historic Places*
(see p128).

0 meters 200
0 yards 200

Seattle Art Museum
*An acclaimed expansion has vastly
increased exhibition space for this
museum's 23,000 works of art,
ranging from ancient Egyptian
reliefs to contemporary American
installations* (see pp128–9).

Smith Tower
*Once the world's tallest
office building outside
of New York City, this
42-story tower boasts the
last manually operated
elevators of their kind on
the West Coast* (see p124).

CITY
FISH MARKET

Pike Place Market
*Dating from 1907, the oldest
farmer's market in the
country is a beloved Seattle
landmark and a National
Historic District* (see p134).

**Klondike Gold Rush
National Historical Park**
*This indoor park located
in the Pioneer Square
Historic District celebrates
Seattle's role in North
America's last great
gold rush* (see p125).

PIONEER SQUARE AND DOWNTOWN

The birthplace of Seattle, Pioneer Square was the city's original downtown, established in 1852 when Arthur and David Denny arrived with a handful of fellow pioneers. Emerging from the ashes of the Great Fire of 1889, the rebuilt commercial area prospered as the 19th century drew to a close. By the time the much-touted Smith Tower opened in 1914, however, the city core had begun spreading north and Pioneer Square was less and less a prestigious business address. Today, the revitalized Pioneer Square – a National Historic District – is a thriving arts center, with First Thursday gallery walks and venues for author readings. A short walk leads to downtown – home to the city's modern skyscrapers, upscale shops, and luxury hotels, as well as green spaces such as Freeway Park. Lending cultural panache is the boldly designed Seattle Art Museum and the state-of-the-art Benaroya Hall.

Dragon, International District

SIGHTS AT A GLANCE

Buildings and Shops
Benaroya Hall 10
Central Library 12
Columbia Center 7
Fairmont Olympic Hotel 8
Pioneer Building 2
Smith Tower 1

Museums
Seattle Art Museum 9

Parks and Districts
Freeway Park 11
International District 6
Klondike Gold Rush National Historical Park 5
Occidental Square 4
Waterfall Garden Park 3

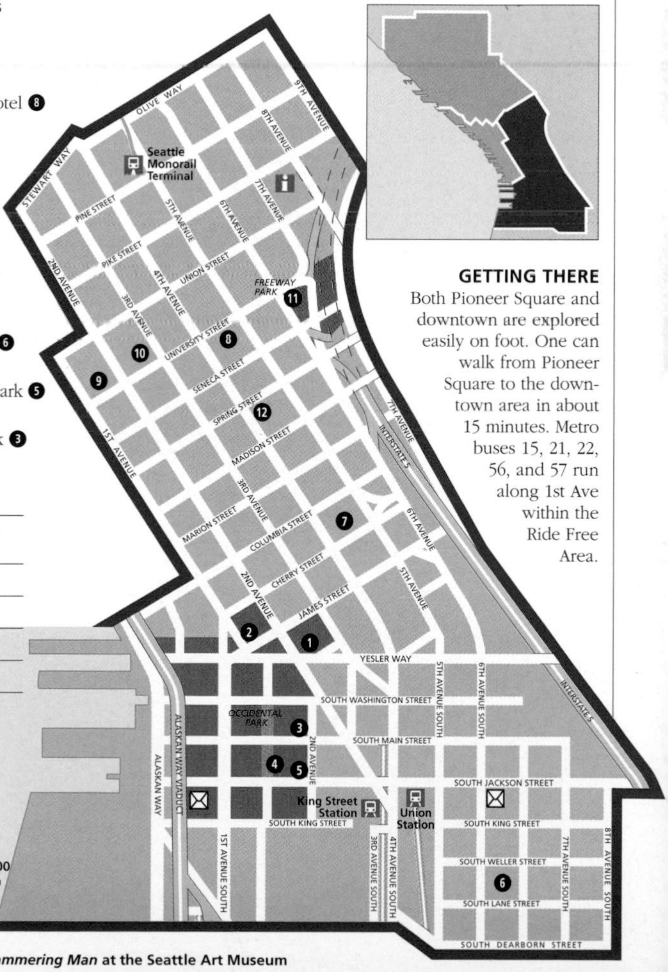

GETTING THERE

Both Pioneer Square and downtown are explored easily on foot. One can walk from Pioneer Square to the downtown area in about 15 minutes. Metro buses 15, 21, 22, 56, and 57 run along 1st Ave within the Ride Free Area.

KEY

- ■ Street-by-Street map *See pp122–3*
- 🚝 Monorail terminal
- 🚆 Train station
- ℹ Information
- ✉ Post office

◁ Jonathan Borofsky's *Hammering Man* at the Seattle Art Museum

Street-by-Street: Pioneer Square

Pioneer Square, Seattle's first downtown and later a decrepit skid row, is today a revitalized business neighborhood and National Historic District. The tall totem poles gracing the square are reminders of the Coast Salish Indian village that originally occupied this spot. The grand Victorian architecture, social service missions, and upscale shops that line the bustling streets and cobblestone plazas are further reminders of the area's checkered past and redevelopment since the 1960s. Many of the buildings standing today were constructed in the years between the Great Fire of 1889 and the Klondike Gold Rush of 1897–8, both pivotal events in Seattle's history. While the buildings look much as they did a century ago, their tenants have changed dramatically. Where saloons, brothels, and mining company headquarters once flourished, art galleries, boutiques, and antique shops now reside.

Pioneer Place
This small triangular park is graced with a Tlingit totem pole. A bust of Chief Seattle looms above the fountain.

Occidental Square
The Fallen Firefighters' Memorial in this square consists of four life-sized bronze statues designed and sculpted by Hai Ying Wu in 1998, as a tribute to Seattle's firefighters who have died in the line of duty ❹

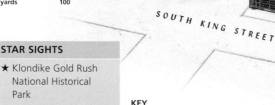

YESLER W

VIADUCT

ALASKAN WAY

1ST AVENUE

SOUTH JA

SOUTH KING STREET

International District

0 meters   100
0 yards   100

STAR SIGHTS

★ Klondike Gold Rush National Historical Park

★ Pioneer Building

KEY

– – – Suggested route

LOCATOR MAP
See Street Finder map 4

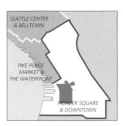

★ **Pioneer Building**
Completed in 1892 in the Romanesque Revival style, this building faces onto Pioneer Place. Bill Speidel's Underground Tour (see p124) starts from here ❷

Downtown

2ND AVENUE

SOUTH WASHINGTON STREET

UTH MAIN STREET

EET

The Smith Tower, an imposing terra-cotta building and Seattle landmark, is named after typewriter tycoon Lyman C. Smith, who commissioned the building in 1914.

Occidental Square

dental Walk

★ **Klondike Gold Rush National Historical Park**
This park, devoted to the story of North America's last great gold rush, has historical photographs such as this one, depicting prospectors arriving in Seattle ❺

Smith Tower ❶

506 2nd Ave. **Map** 4 D3. *Tel (206) 622-4004.* 🚌 *39, 42, 136, 137.* **Observation deck** ◯ *Apr & Oct: 10am–5pm daily; May–Sep: 10am–dusk daily; Nov–Mar: 10am–4pm Sat & Sun.* ● *Easter, Thanksgiving, Dec 25.* 🎫 *to observation deck.* ♿ *except observation deck.* 🎟 *for groups.* **www**.smithtower.com

When it opened in 1914, the 42-story Smith Tower was heralded as the tallest office building in the world outside New York City, and for nearly a half century it reigned as the tallest building west of Chicago.

Commissioned by rifle and typewriter tycoon Lyman Cornelius Smith, Seattle's first skyscraper is clad in white terracotta. While its height – 489 ft (149 m) from the curbside to the top of the tower finial – is no longer its claim to fame, the city's landmark does boast the last manually operated elevator of its kind on the West Coast. For a fee, you can ride one of the gleaming brass-cage originals to the 35th-floor Chinese Room. The carved wood and porcelain-inlay ceiling and the ornate Blackwood furniture adorning this banquet room were gifts to Smith from the last empress of China. The deck here offers panoramic views of Mount Rainier, the Olympic and Cascade mountain ranges, and Elliott Bay.

The onyx and marble lobby, which has been restored to its former glamour, is presided over by 22 carved chieftains.

Decorative brass elevator doors of the 1914 Smith Tower

Pioneer Building ❷

600 1st Ave. **Map** 4 D3. 🚌 *15, 18, 21, 22.* **Underground Tour Tel** *(206) 682-4646.* 🎫 📷 *call for hours & reservations.* **www**.pioneer-building.com

Completed in 1892, three years after the Great Fire flattened the core business district, the Pioneer Building was voted the "finest building west of Chicago" by the American Institute of Architects. It is one of more than 50 buildings designed by Elmer Fisher *(see p148)* following the devastating fire of 1889. Still imposing without its tower, destroyed in a 1949 earthquake, the brick building houses offices and Doc Maynard's Saloon,

starting point of Bill Speidel's **Underground Tour**. This 90-minute walk offers a lively look at Seattle's colorful past and the original streets beneath the modern city, including the 1890s stores abandoned in the 1900s when engineers raised streets. Beware: the subterranean portion is musty and dusty.

Waterfall Garden Park ❸

219 2nd Ave S. **Map** 4 D3. *Tel (206) 624-6096.* 🚌 *15, 18, 21, 22, 56.* ◯ *9am–3pm daily.*

A peaceful, secluded oasis in the middle of busy Pioneer Square, this little park is the perfect place to relax and enjoy a picnic. The sounds of the man-made waterfall cascading over huge rocks soften any street noise. There are several tables and chairs set out around the waterfall, some in the shade and some catching the few rays of sun that peer through the Japanese maples.

The park was designed by Masao Kinoshita and built in 1977 by the Annie E. Casey Foundation to honor the workers of the United Parcel Service (UPS). Jim Casey of Seattle was one of the founders of UPS, which was originally formed as the American Messenger Service in a saloon at this site in 1907.

The stately Smith Tower, once the tallest building outside New York

---

THE GREAT SEATTLE FIRE

On June 6, 1889, in a cabinet shop near Pioneer Square, a pot of flaming glue overturned, igniting wood shavings. The tide, which the city's water system depended on, was low at the time, and little water came out of the hydrants initially. The fire spread rapidly, engulfing 60 city blocks before burning itself out. Miraculously, no one died in the blaze, and it came to be seen as a blessing in disguise. Sturdy brick and stone buildings were erected where flimsy wood structures once stood; streets were widened and raised; and the sewer system was overhauled. From the ashes of disaster rose a city primed for prominence as the 20th century approached.

The aftermath of the Great Seattle Fire of 1889, devastating to a city built of wood

For hotels and restaurants in Seattle see pp286–8 and pp303–6

Occidental Square ❹

Occidental Ave between S Main & S Jackson Sts. **Map** 4 D3. 🚌 *15, 18, 21, 22, 56.*

The brick-paved plaza known as Occidental Square offers relief from the busy traffic of Pioneer Square. The tree-lined pedestrian walk is flanked by upscale shops, galleries, and coffeehouses, many housed in attractive Victorian buildings.

Across South Main Street is Occidental Park, where the ambiance changes considerably because of the local contingent of homeless people and panhandlers. Of special note here are four cedar totem poles carved by Northwest artist Duane Pasco and the Fallen Firefighters' Memorial, a moving tribute to the 34 Seattle firefighters who have died in the line of duty since the Seattle Fire Department was founded in 1889.

The striking cedar totem poles in Pioneer Square's Occidental Park

Klondike Gold Rush National Historical Park ❺

319 2nd Ave S. **Map** 4 D3. *Tel* (206) 220-4240. 🚌 *15, 18, 21, 22, 56.* ⬤ *9am–5pm daily.* ⬤ *Jan 1, Thanksgiving, Dec 25.* ♿ **www**.nps.gov

In 1895, gold was discovered in a tributary of the Klondike River, in the middle of the Canadian Yukon wilderness.

Exhibit at the Klondike Gold Rush National Historical Park

This discovery triggered a frenzied stampede, as 100,000 gold seekers from around the world rushed to the Klondike to find their fortunes.

The largest and closest US city to the gold fields, Seattle became the primary outfitting and embarkation point for the stampede north. Tens of thousands of miners passed through the city, purchasing $25 million worth of food, clothing, equipment, pack animals, and steamship tickets. While few Klondikers struck it rich during the Gold Rush of 1897–8, Seattle merchants made a fortune and established the city's reputation as the premier commercial center of the Pacific Northwest.

Established by Congress in 1976, Klondike Gold Rush National Historical Park comprises five units – three in Canada, one in Skagway, Alaska, and one in Seattle's Pioneer Square Historic District. Housed in the restored Hotel Cadillac building, the Seattle visitors' center celebrates the city's role in North America's last great gold rush. On display here are evocative black-and-white photographs and simulations of the "ton of provisions" that Canadian law required each prospector to bring with him, including 350 pounds (160 kg) of flour and 150 pounds (68 kg) of bacon. Personable park rangers staff the center, offering insights into this fascinating period in American history.

Open year-round, the park offers an expanded program in the summer. Activities include ranger-led walking tours of Pioneer Square, gold-panning demonstrations, and scheduled screenings of

Gold Rush-themed films. (These films are shown at other times of the year by request.)

International District ❻

East of 6th Ave S, south of Yesler Way. **Map** 4 E4. 🚌 *7, 14, 36.*

Located southeast of Pioneer Square, the International District was settled by Asian-Americans in the late 19th century. This bustling area continues to serve as the cultural hub for the city's Chinese, Korean, Japanese, Filipino, Vietnamese, and Laotian residents.

In addition to its fine ethnic restaurants, the area is home to **Uwajimaya** (600 5th Avenue South), the largest Asian market in the Pacific Northwest. The **Wing Luke Asian Museum** (719 South King Street), a Smithsonian affiliate, is named after the first Asian Pacific American elected to office in the Pacific Northwest. The museum highlights the history, culture, and art of Asian Pacific Americans.

Items for sale at Uwajimaya, in Seattle's International District

The tall Columbia Center, dwarfing the Smith Tower

Columbia Center **❼**

701 5th Ave. **Map** 4 D2.
Tel *(206) 386-5564.* 🚌 *16, 358.*
Observation deck ◯ *8:30am–4:30pm Mon–Fri.* ⬤ *public hols.*
🎦 *to observation deck.* ♿

The tallest building in Seattle, Columbia Center (formerly known as the Bank of America Tower) is the tallest building – according to the number of stories – west of the Mississippi River. Rising 1,049 ft (320 m) above sea level, the 1.5-million-sq-ft (139,500-sq-m), 76-story skyscraper was designed by Chester Lindsey Architects and completed in 1985 at a cost of $285 million. In 1998, it was sold for $404 million.

A prestigious business address for more than 5,000 Seattle-area workers, the shimmering black tower also attracts visitors to its 73rd-floor observation deck, which offers spectacular vistas of the Cascade and Olympic mountain ranges, Mount Rainier, Lake Washington, and Puget Sound, as well as views of the city and its many suburbs.

The four-level retail atrium houses shops, food vendors, and, on the third floor, the *City Space* art gallery, which features the works of artists who have been commissioned for projects by the city.

Fairmont Olympic Hotel **❽**

411 University St. **Map** 4 D1.
Tel *(206) 621-1700.* 🚌 *17, 19, 24, 26, 28.* ♿ 🏨 🍸 🅿️ *See **Where to Stay** p287.* www.fairmont.com

When it debuted in 1924, the Olympic Hotel was *the* place to see and be seen – not surprising since the bondholders who funded the $4 million construction were among the city's most socially prominent citizens. Designed by the New York firm of George B. Post and Sons, the Italian Renaissance-style building features high, arched Palladian windows, gleaming oak-paneled walls, and terrazzo floors laid by Italian workmen who were sent to Seattle for the task.

More than $800,000 was spent on furnishings, including hundreds of antique mirrors, Italian and Spanish oil jars, and bronze statuary. A glamorous venue for parties, weddings, and debutante balls, the Olympic reigned as the *grande dame* of Seattle hotels for half a century before losing her luster.

In 1979, the hotel was listed on the US National Register of Historic Places. A year later, the Four Seasons hotel chain assumed management of the building and gave the hotel a $62.5 million facelift – the most costly hotel restoration in the US at that time – returning the landmark hotel to her original grandeur. Fairmont Hotels and Resorts assumed management in 2003.

The striking modern façade of the Seattle Art Museum

Seattle Art Museum **❾**

1300 First Ave. **Map** 3 C2. **Tel** *(206) 654-3100.* 🚌 *174.* ◯ *10am–5pm Wed–Sun (to 9pm Thu & Fri).* ⬤ *major hols.* 🚫📷 ♿ 🎦 🛍 🅿️ 🖥
📷 www.seattleartmuseum.org

At the museum's south entrance is a giant *Hammering Man*. A tribute to workers, Jonathan Borofsky's 48-ft (15-m) animated steel sculpture "hammers" silently and continuously from 7am to 10pm daily, resting only on Labor Day.

The museum building is no less impressive. Designed by the Philadelphia firm Venturi Scott Brown and Associates, the original bold limestone and sandstone building was completed in 1991 at a cost of $62 million. An acclaimed expansion in a light-filled building designed by Brad Cloepfil is shared with Washington Mutual Bank.

The opulent interior of the Fairmont Olympic Hotel

◁ **The Seattle skyline, framed by the Space Needle and Mount Rainier**

The museum's permanent collection includes 25,000 objects ranging from ancient Egyptian relief sculpture and wooden African statuary to Old Master paintings and contemporary American art.

Traveling exhibits are featured on the second floor. Permanent collections of Asian, African, and Northwest Coast Native American art figure prominently on the third floor. Highlights here include the 14-ft- (4-m-) tall red-cedar Native houseposts carved with bears and thunderbirds boasting 11-ft (3.5-m) wingspans, from the village of Gwa'yas-dams in British Columbia. The fourth floor houses European and American art, including works by contemporary Pacific Northwest artists such as Morris Graves, Jacob Lawrence, and Dale Chihuly.

Also in this museum family is the Seattle Asian Art Museum, in Volunteer Park *(see p153)*, housing extensive Asian art collections. The Seattle Art Museum's third venue is the Olympic Sculpture Park *(see p144)*, an outdoor "museum" on the north end of Seattle's waterfront.

Dale Chihuly's *Benaroya Hall Silver Chandelier,* one of a pair

Benaroya Hall ⓿

200 University St. **Map** 3 C1.
Tel *(206) 215-4800.* 🚌 *many.*
🎦 *noon & 1pm Tue & Fri.* 🚫 🔥 🖥
🏳 www.seattlesymphony.com

Home of the Seattle Symphony and occupying an entire city block, the $118.1 million Benaroya Hall contains two performing halls, including the 2,500-seat Taper Auditorium,

Benaroya Hall, grand home of the Seattle Symphony

acclaimed for its superior acoustics. The multi-level Grand Lobby, dramatic at night when lit, offers stunning views of Puget Sound and the city skyline.

Even if time doesn't permit attending a symphony performance, visitors can gain an appreciation of this magnificent facility by taking one of the excellent tours offered, learning how this acoustical masterpiece was created atop a railroad tunnel. Visitors can also admire Benaroya Hall's impressive private art collection, which includes *Echo,* Robert Rauschenberg's evocative 12-ft (3.5-m) mural painted on metal; *Schubert Sonata,* sculptor Mark di Suvero's towering steel wind vane; and Dale Chihuly's pair of chandelier sculptures – 1 silver, 1 gold – each with some 1,200 pieces of blown glass wired to a steel armature.

Within the hall's open space along 2nd Avenue is the Garden of Remembrance, a park commemorating Washington citizens killed in battle.

Freeway Park ⓫

Seneca St & 6th Ave. **Map** 4 D1.
🚌 *2, 13.* 🕐 *6am–11:30pm daily.* 🔥

Tucked into the heart of Seattle's bustling commercial district, and adjoining the Washington State Convention and Trade Center, 5-acre (2-ha) Freeway Park straddles the I-5, which runs through downtown. Inside the park, thundering waterfalls drown out the traffic

roar, and shady footpaths invite leisurely strolling. Outdoor music concerts are held here in summer.

Central Library ⓬

1000 Fourth Ave. **Map** 4 D2. ***Tel*** *(206) 386-4636.* 🚌 *many.* 🕐 *10am–8pm Mon–Thu, 10am–6pm Fri & Sat, noon–6pm Sun.* 🌑 *New Year's Day.*
🚫 🔥 🖥 🏳 www.spl.org

This striking glass and steel structure, completed in 2004, was designed by the award-winning Dutch architect Rem Koolhaas as a replacement for the city's 1960 Central Library. The unusual shape of the building was once a source of controversy, but the Central Library is now regarded as one of Seattle's architectural highlights. The 11-floor library includes works of art worth a staggering $1 million and an innovative "Books Spiral," allowing visitors maximum access to the collection. In its first year, some 8,000 people visited the library every day to benefit from its 1.45 million books. Other facilities include Internet access, 400 computers for public use, and separate centers for children, teenagers, and adult readers.

Seattle's strikingly modern Central Library, designed by Rem Koolhaas

PIKE PLACE MARKET AND THE WATERFRONT

Neon sign advertising fresh fish at Pike Place Market

Situated above the shores of Elliott Bay, Seattle's Pike Place Market is both a venerable landmark and a veritable feast for the senses. Exuberant and engaging, this 9-acre (3.5-ha) National Historic District is known as much for its colorful personalities as it is for its abundance of local produce. Pike Street Hillclimb, a system of stairs and elevators, connects the market to Seattle's bustling waterfront, with its briny scents, squawking sea gulls, fish and chip joints, and fine seafood restaurants. Marine activity abounds, as this working waterfront is the departure point for freighters, ferries, cruise ships, and harbor tour boats. The Bell Street Pier (Pier 66) is home to restaurants, a pleasure craft marina, and a cruise ship terminal, while at Pier 57, the Seattle Aquarium showcases Pacific Northwest marine life. The adjacent Seattle IMAX Dome offers the ultimate 3D experience.

SIGHTS AT A GLANCE

Aquariums
Seattle Aquarium pp138–9 ❻

Shops, Markets, and Restaurants
Athenian Inn ❹
Pike Place Market ❶
Pike Place Starbucks ❸
Upper Post Alley ❷
Ye Olde Curiosity Shop ❾

Ferry Terminal
Washington State Ferries Terminal ❺

Parks
Waterfront Park ❽

Piers
Pier 66 ❼

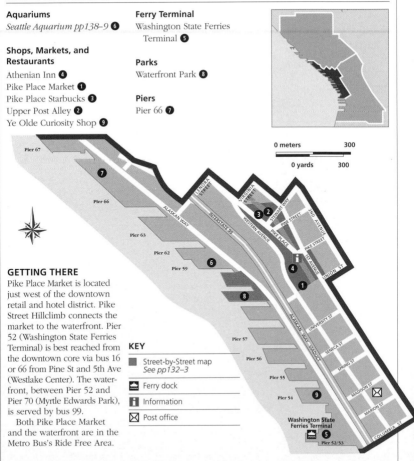

0 meters 300
0 yards 300

GETTING THERE
Pike Place Market is located just west of the downtown retail and hotel district. Pike Street Hillclimb connects the market to the waterfront. Pier 52 (Washington State Ferries Terminal) is best reached from the downtown core via bus 16 or 66 from Pine St and 5th Ave (Westlake Center). The waterfront, between Pier 52 and Pier 70 (Myrtle Edwards Park), is served by bus 99.

Both Pike Place Market and the waterfront are in the Metro Bus's Ride Free Area.

KEY

▪ Street-by-Street map
  See pp132–3

⛴ Ferry dock

ℹ Information

⊠ Post office

Washington State Ferries Terminal ❺
Pier 52/53

◁ **Luscious locally grown cherries on display at a Pike Place Market fruit stall**

Street-by-Street: Pike Place Market

Newsstand sign in Pike Place Market

Pike Place Market is said to be the soul of Seattle. Established in 1907, it is the oldest continuously operating farmer's market in the US. Over the years, the market has mirrored national waves of immigration, with new arrivals from countries including Mexico, Ethiopia, and Cambodia flocking here to set up small businesses. Bustling with some 100 farmers, 200 artists and craftspeople, engaging street performers, and 500 residents, the district contains art galleries, ethnic and specialty groceries, bistros, and an eclectic mix of shops.

★ Upper Post Alley
This pedestrian walkway is lined with specialty shops, restaurants, and pubs. Its sister Lower Post Alley is home to similar businesses **2**

UPPER POST ALLEY

PIKE PLACE

PIKE PLA

WESTERN A

Waterfront

Pike Place Starbucks
This building, a former feed store, is the site of the first Starbucks coffee shop, which moved here from its original Western Avenue location in 1976. The Starbucks sign in the window sports the chain's original logo depicting a bare-breasted siren, based on a 16th-century Norse woodcut **3**

Athenian Inn
This historic restaurant in Pike Place Market is as well known for its appearance in the Tom Hanks movie Sleepless in Seattle *as it is for its seafood and diner-style sandwiches, which can be enjoyed while sitting at a booth overlooking Elliott Bay* **4**

STAR SIGHTS

★ Pike Place Fish

★ Rachel

★ Upper Post Alley

| 0 meters | 40 |
| 0 yards | 50 |

KEY

- - - Suggested route

For hotels and restaurants in Seattle see pp286–8 and pp303–6

Market sign and clock, c.1927, one of Seattle's oldest neon works

LOCATOR MAP
See Street Finder map 3

Newsstand
*There are several news-
stands in and around
Pike Place Market,
offering a wide range of
US and international
publications.*

★ **Rachel**
*Rachel, an enormous piggy bank, stands
at the main entrance to Pike Place Market.
Sculpted by Pacific Northwest artist Georgia
Gerber, it raises funds for low-income families.*

★ **Pike Place Fish**
*Fish-flinging fishmongers are
a long-standing tradition at
this Pike Place Market store.*

Pike Place Market ❶

Bounded by Pike & Virginia Sts, from 1st to Western Aves. **Map** 3 C1. **Tel** *(206) 682-7453.* 🚌 *15, 18.* 🕐 *9am–6pm Mon–Sat, 11am–5pm Sun; may vary.* ⏺ *Jan 1, Thanksgiving, Dec 25.* ♿ 📷 **Market Heritage Tour**: Call for details: (206) 322-2219. **www**.pikeplacemarket.org

The heart of Pike Place Market is the **Main Arcade** (1914) and the adjacent **North Arcade** (1922). Here, low metal-topped counters display freshly picked seasonal fruit, vegetables, herbs, and flowers grown by local farmers. Shoppers at these lowstalls get to "meet the producer," as promised by the market's signature green sign. Each morning, the Market Master, whose role at the market dates back to 1911, does roll call, assigning stalls to farmers and craftspeople based on seniority. This often results in vendors selling their wares from a different stall each day.

A wide selection of fish on display at Pike Place Fish, in the Main Arcade

Freshly cut flowers from a market flower stall

Originally, the North Arcade consisted of two "rows." The Dry Row, along the west wall, had no access to running water. The Wet Row, with access to running water, was also closest to the exposed arcade entrance and thus the damp weather. Today, craftspeople sell from the dry tables and farmers from the wet tables, the run-off still being channeled along a trough. Highstalls leased by commercial greengrocers on a permanent basis are also to be found in the Main Arcade. Both imported and locally grown produce are on offer here.

Pike Place Fish, located in the Main Arcade, is not Pike Place Market's only seafood vendor. It is, however, certainly the best known. Situated beneath the market's landmark clock, this busy stall always draws a crowd, thanks to the loud, lively banter and high-spirited antics of its fishmongers, who are amazingly adept at tossing fish over the heads of cheering spectators to co-workers behind the shop's counter. The repartee is as fresh as the seafood, which ranges from wild king salmon and Dungeness crab to rainbow trout and live clams. Should tourists care to buy, Pike Place Fish will ship their seafood home.

To the south of the arcades is the **Economy Market**, a 1907 structure which was incorporated into the market

THE HISTORY OF PIKE PLACE MARKET

Hungry for fresh produce and fair prices, Seattleites mobbed Pike Place Market when it opened August 17, 1907, at Pike Street and 1st Avenue, as an effort by the city council to eliminate "greedy middlemen" and allow farmers to sell directly to the public. Sensing opportunity, local Frank Goodwin used his Klondike gold to build permanent arcades. At its height in the 1930s, hundreds of farmers sold their produce at the market. But by World War II, it had fallen on hard times: Japanese Americans made up to 80 percent of the sellers at the wet tables; their internment *(see p40)* had a disastrous effect. In the years that followed, the decline continued as

suburbs and supermarkets became entrenched in the American way of life. By the late 1960s, developers were lobbying to tear it down. Rallied by architect Victor Steinbrueck, Seattleites rebelled, voting in 1971 to make the market a historic district.

Local farmers selling their produce at Pike Place Market, May 1912

One of many stands displaying artwork at the market

in 1916, and where, among other things, damaged goods were sold at a discount.

Across Pike Street are the **Corner Market** (1912) and **Sanitary Market** (1910) – two of the several buildings constructed during the market's first two decades as it prospered, and so named because horse-drawn carts were not allowed inside. Today all three market buildings house retail shops, restaurants, and cafés.

> **🐟 Pike Place Fish**
> Pike Place Market (Main Arcade). **Tel** (206) 682-7181. ⏱ 6:30am–6pm Mon–Sat, 7am–5pm Sun. ♿ www.pikeplacefish.com

A local clown entertaining visitors to Pike Place Market

Upper Post Alley ➋

Stewart to Virginia Sts between Pike Pl & 1st Ave. **Map** 3 B1. 🚌 15, 18. ♿

Upper Post Alley has a decidedly European ambience. Along this brickpaved passageway are two of the city's favorite haunts. **The Pink Door** (1919 Post Alley) is an Italian trattoria identified only by an unmarked pink door. Come summer, the restaurant's terrace, with its impressive harbor view, is popular with locals – and tourists who happily stumble upon the elusive restaurant. Across the alley, **Kell's Irish Restaurant and Pub** (1916 Post Alley) pours Guinness and offers live Celtic music in cozy surroundings.

Above the shops of Upper Post Alley are condominiums and apartments, many housing the market's some 500 residents, many of whom are low-income seniors.

Pike Place Starbucks ➌

1912 Pike Pl. **Map** 3 B1. **Tel** (206) 448-8762. 🚌 15, 18. ⏱ 6am–7:30pm Mon–Fri, 6:30am–7:30pm Sat & Sun. ♿ www.starbucks.com

Seattle is said to be the most caffeinated city in the US, a distinction Seattleites don't refute. To see where the coffee craze started, visit Pike Place Starbucks, the first shop in the omnipresent chain.

Opened in 1971, at 2000 Western Avenue, Starbucks Coffee, Tea and Spices moved to its Pike Place location in 1976. Named after the first mate in Herman Melville's *Moby Dick*, the company's first logo – a voluptuous two-tailed mermaid encircled by the original name – still greets visitors at this small store.

In the early days, Starbucks did not sell coffee by the cup; the focus was on whole-bean coffee. Occasionally, they offered tasting samples in porcelain cups, creating loyal customers by educating them on the finer points of quality coffee. A decade later, in 1982, inspired by the coffee culture of Milan, Italy, Starbucks opened its second location, also in Seattle. Today, visitors to the flagship store can choose from a long list of coffee drinks, as can the millions of customers around the world. Indeed, according to the company, 40 million customers visit Starbucks each week.

Starbucks' original sign, at its first location

The entrance to the Athenian Inn in Pike Place Market

Athenian Inn ➍

1517 Pike Pl (Main Arcade). **Map** 3 C1. **Tel** (206) 624-7166. 🚌 15, 18. ⏱ 6:30am–8:30pm daily. ♿ 1st floor only.

The Athenian Inn has been in operation nearly as long as the market itself. Opened by three brothers in 1909, it evolved from a bakery and luncheonette to a tavern and, later, a restaurant. It was, in 1933, one of the first restaurants in Seattle to get a liquor license. Neither flashy nor fancy, this diner serves old-time favorites like corned beef hash, accompanied by generous helpings of local color. However, the best reason to visit the Athenian Inn is not for the food but for the view of Elliott Bay. Nab one of the wooden booths at the back of the restaurant and you will see the Duwamish waterway, with its impressive container-ship loading facility; West Seattle; Bainbridge Island; and ferries skimming across the bay.

If the inn seems oddly familiar as you pass by its U-shaped counter, that may be because of its supporting role in the 1993 movie *Sleepless in Seattle*.

The sign for Pike Place Market, high above the market's rooftop

Washington State Ferries Terminal at Pier 52, on Seattle's waterfront

Washington State Ferries Terminal ❺

Pier 52, 801 Alaskan Way. **Map** 3 C2. 🚌 *15, 18, 21, 22, 56.* ***Ferry schedules Tel** (206) 464-6400 (recording).* 🚻 www.wsdot.wa.gov

Both a highly efficient transit system and a top tourist attraction, Washington State ferries transport 26 million residents and travelers a year. Seattle's main terminal is Colman Dock, located on the waterfront at the foot of Columbia Street.

The original wharf was built in 1882 by Scottish engineer James Colman to accommodate steamships. Destroyed seven years later in the Great Fire, it was immediately rebuilt to service Puget Sound's "mosquito fleet" of private ferries. It was also a bustling hub for ships bound for the northern gold fields during the gold rushes of the 1890s.

In 1908, Colman extended the dock, adding a domed waiting room and a clock tower. The elegant tower toppled four years later when the ocean liner *Alameda* rammed the pier. The tower's replacement met with similar misfortune when it was scorched in a 1914 pier fire.

Although not as architecturally interesting as its predecessors, the present terminal, which was built in 1964, does an admirable job accommodating the many passengers traveling to Bremerton and Bainbridge Island. The terminal also serves foot passengers traveling to Vashon Island.

A popular tourist activity is the 35-minute ferry ride to

Winslow on Bainbridge Island, where galleries, shops, restaurants, and a waterfront park are all within walking distance of the ferry dock, making for a pleasant day trip.

Seattle Aquarium ❻

See pp138–9.

Pier 66 ❼

Bell St Pier, Pier 66, Alaskan Way. **Map** 3 A1. 🚌 *15, 18, 21, 22, 56, 99.* www.portseattle.org **Maritime Education Initiative (at the Maritime Event Center) Tel** (206) 269-4108. ☐ *Mon by appt only.* www.maritimeeducationinitiative.org

One of the liveliest parts of the waterfront is the Port of Seattle's Pier 66, also known as Bell Street Pier. It is home to a thriving cruise ship terminal, a pleasure craft marina, a conference center, and a handful of eateries.

There is a constant hub of activity, with Bell Street Pier

Terminal and Smith Cove Terminal (at Pier 91, north of downtown) together greeting more than 200 cruise ships every year, most of which are bound for Alaska.

Pier 66 is also home to the Bell Harbor Marina, a small in-city marina for pleasure boats. For spectacular views of the moored boats here, visitors can gaze out from Bell Street Pier's rooftop plaza.

Visitors may also wish to stop off at The Maritime Event Center on the pier. This interactive nautical museum also serves as an events venue. It is open to families and school groups on Mondays, as part of the local community's Maritime Education Initiative. It displays a range of hands-on exhibits designed to give visitors of all ages an insight into the many different facets of the local maritime industry. Kids and adults can give orders from the captain's chair, track down ships using binoculars, paddle a virtual kayak, learn how to move cargo with a crane, drive a remote control tug boat, and identify real-life vessels using a touchscreen. There is also the chance to learn about the fishing industry, to try your hand at operating a fish conveyer, or to experience what it's like to be rescued at sea.

On and around the pier is a variety of restaurants, from take-out fish and chips to more comfortable and relaxed dining *(see pp303–4).*

The Maritime Event Center, Pier 66

A sunny day at Seattle's Waterfront Park

Waterfront Park ❽

Pier 57–59, 1301 Alaskan Way.
Map 3 B1. **Tel** *(206) 684-4075*.
🚌 *15, 18, 21*. **Park** ⏰ *6am–10pm daily*. ♿

The Waterfront Park comprises the area between Pier 57 and Pier 59. The park offers excellent views of the Seattle skyline and the waterfront, and visitors have even been known to spot a seal! At the north end of the park is *The Waterfront Fountain*, by James FitzGerald and Terry Copple. Made of casted and welded bronze, the sculpture is composed of a number of cubical structures. At its south end is a large abstract statue of Christopher Columbus gazing out across the water. Other interesting sculptures as well as picnic tables and benches are dotted around the park.

The Waterfront Streetcar, officially known as the George Benson Waterfront Streetcar Line, began in 1982 and was the first streetcar to run in Seattle since 1941. It used to be a great way to see Seattle's best attractions but was suspended in 2005, when the maintenance barn and one of the stations were demolished to make room for the Seattle Art Museum's Olympic Sculpture Park. The track and other eight stations remain, but it is unclear whether it will ever be operational again. The route has been replaced by Metro bus Route 99. The buses have been made to look like streetcars.

Ye Olde Curiosity Shop ❾

Pier 54, 1001 Alaskan Way. **Map** 3 C2. **Tel** *(206) 682-5844*. 🚌 *15, 18, 21, 22, 56, 57*. ⏰ *mid-Apr–Sep: 9am–9:30pm daily; Oct–mid-Apr: 10am–6pm Sun–Thu, 9am–9pm Fri & Sat*. ⏰ *Jan 1, Thanksgiving, Dec 25*. ♿ www.yeoldecuriosityshop.com

The quintessential curio shop, this Seattle institution has been a fixture of the city's waterfront since 1899. Among the legendary curiosities are shrunken heads, a pig with three tails, and a well-preserved mummy that

Sign for Ye Olde Curiosity Shop, a Seattle institution since 1899

was discovered in the Arizona desert a century ago. Oddities include a prayer engraved on a grain of rice and oil paintings on the heads of pins.

But there is much more to this tightly packed store than quirky curios. From its first days of business, this waterfront shop has been an Indian trading post. Today, the crafts of the region's Native Americans are sold through the store which has also provided a number of private collections and prestigious museums, including the Smithsonian Institute in Washington, DC, with Native American art and artifacts.

Joseph Edward Standley of Ohio started this family-run shop in 1899 – reportedly earning only 25 cents in the first three days. But Standley persevered. In 1909, he sold his ethnological collection, which had garnered a gold medal at Seattle's World Fair that year, to New York's Museum of the American Indian, for $5,000, establishing the shop with collectors.

IVAR'S ACRES OF CLAMS

A waterfront landmark since 1938, the seafood restaurant Ivar's Acres of Clams on Pier 54 was founded by Seattle-born Ivar Haglund (1905–85), a radio and television personality and self-promoter. Eighteen years before opening his popular restaurant, Haglund established Seattle's first aquarium, also on Pier 54, scooping the "exhibits" out of Puget Sound himself. Wearing his trademark captain's hat, Haglund entertained visitors by singing songs he had written about his favorite sea critters. The aquarium's other attraction was a fish-and-chips counter across from the seal cage. It was the seed for Haglund's foray into the

Hungry visitors and sea gulls – all are welcome at Ivar's

food-service business, an enterprise that grew to include three restaurants, nearly 30 fish bars throughout the Pacific Northwest, and Ivar's own brand of clam chowder. Known for his silly puns ("Keep Clam" remains the company motto) and frequent publicity stunts (he once hoisted a 16-ft/5-m salmon windsock to the flagpole atop stately Smith Tower), Haglund was – and remains – a colorful Seattle icon. Two months after his death in 1985, the city celebrated his 80th birthday with a boat parade in Elliott Bay. And each Independence Day, as Seattleites watch the lavish "Fourth of Jul-Ivar's" fireworks display over the bay, they remember with fondness the "firecracker" who started the tradition back in 1964.

Seattle Aquarium ❻

One of the top aquariums in the country, the Seattle Aquarium offers a fascinating window into Pacific Northwest marine life, showcasing more than 400 different species of fish, plants, and mammals indigenous to the area. Sea otters and seals cavort in pools, and feeding time is especially entertaining. Visitors can also learn about the aquarium's ecological and conservation work with the local environment, and even meet the wildlife in one of the interactive exhibits.

Encountering local sea creatures in the Life on the Edge exhibit

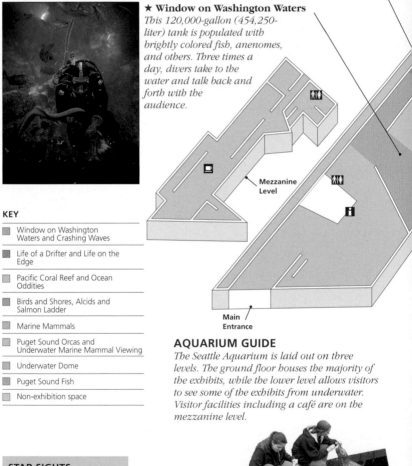

★ Window on Washington Waters
This 120,000-gallon (454,250-liter) tank is populated with brightly colored fish, anenomes, and others. Three times a day, divers take to the water and talk back and forth with the audience.

Mezzanine Level

Main Entrance

KEY

- ▢ Window on Washington Waters and Crashing Waves
- ▢ Life of a Drifter and Life on the Edge
- ▢ Pacific Coral Reef and Ocean Oddities
- ▢ Birds and Shores, Alcids and Salmon Ladder
- ▢ Marine Mammals
- ▢ Puget Sound Orcas and Underwater Marine Mammal Viewing
- ▢ Underwater Dome
- ▢ Puget Sound Fish
- ▢ Non-exhibition space

AQUARIUM GUIDE

The Seattle Aquarium is laid out on three levels. The ground floor houses the majority of the exhibits, while the lower level allows visitors to see some of the exhibits from underwater. Visitor facilities including a café are on the mezzanine level.

STAR SIGHTS

- ★ Marine Mammals
- ★ Underwater Dome
- ★ Window on Washington Waters

Caring for two of Seattle Aquarium's plentiful seal population

Birds and Shores
Learn how local sea birds make their homes in inhospitable conditions. Birds including this tufted puffin and common murres can be seen nesting, foraging, and more.

VISITORS' CHECKLIST

Pier 59, 1483 Alaskan Way.
Map *3 B1.* **Tel** *(206) 386-4300.*
15, 18, 21, 22, 56. 99
Pike. 9:30am–5pm daily;
9:30am–3pm some public hols. www.
seattleaquarium.org

★ **Marine Mammals**
This popular attraction features the antics of the aquarium's sea otters, harbor seals, and fur seals. Visitors can also see these mammals in an underwater viewing area on the lower level.

ower evel

★ **Underwater Dome**
Travel through a short tunnel to this stunning undersea dome, which offers a panoramic view from inside a 400-gallon (1,514,160-liter) tank housing sharks, salmon, octopus, and many others.

Puget Sound Fish
Packed with bright, exotic fish such as this canary rockfish, Pacific spiny lumpsuckers, and midshipmen fish, Puget Sound Fish is a great chance for kids to snap some colorful photos.

SEATTLE CENTER AND BELLTOWN

Located north of downtown, Seattle Center is the proud legacy of the city's 1962 World's Fair. Best known to tourists as the home of the Space Needle, the center boasts numerous cultural venues and excellent museums, including the innovative EMP Museum, designed by architect Frank Gehry and funded by Microsoft billionaire

Hendrix gold record, EMP Museum

Paul Allen *(see p159)*. Just to the south of Seattle Center lies trendy Belltown, its hub stretching from Virginia to Vine Streets along 1st Avenue. Here, among the pricey condominiums, visitors will find high-end hair salons, upscale clothing boutiques, antique shops, home accessories stores, trendy restaurants, and a fashionable crowd.

SIGHTS AT A GLANCE

Museums and Theaters
The Children's Museum **7**
EMP Museum pp146–7 **5**
Olympic Sculpture Park **1**
Pacific Science Center and
  Boeing Imax Theater **2**

Buildings
Austin A. Bell Building **8**
KeyArena **6**
Space Needle **3**
Virginia Inn **9**

Other Attractions
Seattle Monorail **4**

GETTING THERE

The Monorail runs from the downtown Westlake Center station (5th Avenue at Pine Street) to Seattle Center. Seattle Center is explored easily on foot. Belltown, just north of Pike Place Market, is a 15-minute walk from downtown. Most of Belltown falls within the Ride Free Area. Buses 3, 4, and 16 run north–south on 3rd Avenue.

KEY

   Street-by-Street map
   See pp142–3

   Streetcar

   Seattle Center Monorail

   Bus station

   Post office

0 meters 500
0 yards 500

◁ **The Space Needle, soaring above Frank Gehry's EMP Museum**

Street-by-Street: Seattle Center

The Seattle Center grounds have long been a lively gathering spot for city residents and visitors. In the 1800s, this prized parcel of land was the setting for Indian potlatches. In 1962, it was transformed into a fairground for the World's Fair – Century 21 Exposition *(see p145)*. Today, the 74-acre (30-ha) site is one of the most visited urban parks in the US. Strolling the pedestrian boulevards, you'll see several legacies of the World's Fair.

Whale tail, *Neototems* **Children's Garden**

Among the most notable and noticeable is the Space Needle, which now shares the spotlight with such innovative structures as the EMP Museum. Performing arts companies, sports teams, and a children's museum all call Seattle Center home.

Marion Oliver McCaw Hall is home to the Seattle Opera and Pacific NW Ballet.

MERCER STREET

International Fountain
A mainstay of the 1962 World's Fair, redesigned in 1995, this fountain features 283 water shooters and propels 9,000 gallons of water up to 120 ft (37 m).

Seattle Repertory Theatre
"The Rep" presents both contemporary and classic plays on its two stages: the Bagley Wright Theatre and the Leo K. Theatre.

1ST AVENUE NOR

KeyArena
Now a sports and concert venue, the arena was built in 1962 for Seattle's second World's Fair **6**

KEY

- - - Suggested route

| 0 meters | 40 |
| 0 yards | 50 |

Downtown

D STREET

★ Space Needle
The once futuristic Space Needle is a prominent feature of Seattle's skyline ❸

LOCATOR MAP
See Street Finder map 1

SEATTLE CENTER
& BELLTOWN

PIKE PLACE MARKET
& THE WATERFRONT   PIONEER SQUARE
& DOWNTOWN

Pacific Science Center
Interactive exhibits devoted to science, mathematics, and technology; two IMAX theaters; and a planetarium are housed in the center's five buildings ❷

DENNY WAY

WEST THOMAS

STREET

★ EMP Museum
This exceptional museum situated at the base of the Space Needle was designed by the architect Frank Gehry ❺

Fisher Pavilion, facing the South Fountain Lawn, is a popular venue for trade shows and festivals.

★ Seattle Center Monorail
The monorail enters a tunnel within the EMP Museum at the Seattle Center station using a GPS. The train is cantilevered as it hits the outbound curve ❹

STAR SIGHTS

★ EMP Museum

★ Seattle Center Monorail

★ Space Needle

Perrre's Ventaglio III, one of the pieces in the Olympic Sculpture Park

Olympic Sculpture Park ❶

2901 Western Ave. **Map** 1 B5.
Tel (206) 654-3100. 🚇 Seattle Center. 🚌 1, 2, 13, 15, 18, 99. ☐ dawn–dusk daily. PACCAR Pavilion: May–Labor Day: 10am–5pm Tue–Sun; Labor Day–Apr: 10am–4pm Tue–Sun. 🍴 🎁 ♿ **www**.seattleartmuseum.org

Opened to the public in January 2007 as part of the Seattle Art Museum, the Olympic Sculpture Park sits on what used to be a 9-acre (3.5-ha) industrial site, now transformed into a unique green space for public recreation and outdoor art. The innovative design for the park included environmental restoration schemes such as the creation of a salmon habitat and tree planting.

The park is made up of three areas linked by a 2,200-ft (670-m) Z-shaped path. Visitors can see over 20 modern sculptures scattered throughout a variety of typical Pacific Northwest landscapes such as *The Valley*, an evergreen forest similar to those found in the lowland coastal regions and *The Shore*, which features a beach and a naturally developing tidal garden.

The PACCAR Pavilion is the park headquarters. It houses a car park and a Seattle Art Museum shop as well as a café where visitors can buy food for picnics. Guided tours of the park are also available starting from the Pavilion.

Pacific Science Center and Boeing IMAX Theater ❷

200 2nd Ave N. **Map** 1 B4. **Tel** (206) 443-2001. 🚇 Seattle Center. 🚌 19, 24, 33. ☐ 10am–6pm daily; IMAX open daily, call (206) 443-4629 for films and showtimes. ⬤ Thanksgiving, Dec 25. 🎟 (additional charge for laser & IMAX shows). ♿ **www**.pacificsciencecenter.org

The Pacific Science Center features six interconnected buildings surrounding five 110-ft (33.5-m) arches that rise over reflecting pools and fountains. While enjoyed by all ages, the science and math exhibits are especially appealing to kids.

Dinosaurs: A Journey Through Time takes visitors back to the Mesozoic Era to meet lifelike robotic dinosaurs. In Body Works, visitors can pedal on the Calorie Bicycle to see how much energy they produce and in Tech Zone, they can challenge an industrial robot to games of tic-tac-toe. Also popular with youngsters is Kids Works, which allows budding meteorologists to see themselves on television. Insect Village features huge robotic insects and a mini-zoo where brave visitors can touch a cockroach. The Tropical Butterfly House is filled with exotic free-flying butterflies. Outside, visitors can spin a 2-ton granite ball or ride the High Rail Bicycle perched 15 ft (4.5 m) above the ground on a one-inch (2.5-cm) rail.

The Center also houses a planetarium, laser theater, and the futuristic 400-seat Boeing IMAX Theater, which has six screens showing documentaries on the natural world, space exploration, and a variety of children's films and animations.

Pacific Science Center and Boeing IMAX Theater

The magnificent Space Needle, the pride of Seattle

Space Needle ❸

400 Broad St. **Map** 1 C4. **Tel** (206) 905-2100. 🚇 Seattle Center. 🚌 3, 4, 16. ☐ 9am–midnight daily. ♿ 🍴 **www**.spaceneedle.com

What started as a rough sketch on the back of a paper placemat has become Seattle's internationally recognized landmark and number one tourist attraction. Built for the 1962 World's Fair, the 605-ft (185-m) Space Needle was the brainchild of Edward Carlson, the fair's chairman, who was inspired by Germany's Stuttgart Tower. The final design by John Graham and Company, architects of the first shopping mall in the US, was approved just 18 months before the fair's opening date; the Space Needle was built in 12 months, for a relatively inexpensive $4.5 million. At the time, it was the tallest building west of the Mississippi River.

Supported by three curved steel legs, the needle's glass-enclosed tophouse features an observation deck and, below it, a revolving restaurant – the second in the world – turned by a one-and-a-half-horsepower motor.

The underground foundation, buried 30 ft (8 m) deep and stretching 120 ft (37 m) wide, took 467 cement trucks to fill – a mission that was accomplished in less than 12 hours. The tower is attached to the foundation with 72 30-ft- (9-m-) long bolts.

Solidly constructed, the Space Needle has weathered several earthquakes and has closed fewer than ten times in its history because of high winds. (While the structure itself can withstand winds up to 200 mph [322 km/h], its elevators can't.)

During the Seattle World's Fair, nearly 20,000 people a day rode the high-speed elevators to the top, enduring waits of up to three hours for the 43-second ride. Thankfully, the wait is much shorter today, and the view just as spectacular. Weather permitting, visitors can enjoy panoramic views of the Olympic and Cascade mountain ranges, Mount Rainier, Lake Union, Elliott Bay, and downtown Seattle.

In 1982, a "skyline level" was added 100 ft (30 m) above the ground. In 1999, on its 37th birthday, the Space Needle was proclaimed the city's official landmark by Seattle's Landmarks Preservation Board. And in 2000, a $20 million revitalization included construction of a glass pavilion, which encircles the base of the tower.

Seattle Monorail pulling into the Space Needle terminal

Seattle Monorail ❹

Stations at Westlake Center (5th Ave & Pine St) & at Seattle Center (across from Space Needle). **Map** 1 C4–3 C1. **Tel** (206) 905-2620. ◯ 9am–11pm daily; departs every 10 mins. 🅿 ♿ **www**.seattlemonorail.com

Built for Seattle's second World's Fair in only ten months, its foundations buried 25 ft (7.5 m) below street level, Seattle's Alweg monorail provided a link between the fairgrounds (now the Seattle Center) and downtown Seattle. At the time, it was described as a preview of the mass transit system of the future. Traveling between downtown and the foot of the Space Needle, the Monorail's high-speed trains carried as many as 8 million passengers during the fair's six-month duration.

Today, this "futuristic" transit system is used by 2.5 million passengers per year, many of them locals who ride the Monorail to festivals, concerts, and sporting events at the Seattle Center. The fastest full-sized monorail system in the US, the Seattle Monorail covers the 1-mile (1.6-km) distance in 2 minutes, at a speed of up to 60 miles (97 km) per hour, zipping through the EMP Museum, which was built around and over the Monorail's tracks.

The Space Needle's observation deck, offering stunning views

SEATTLE WORLD'S FAIR

Officially known as the Century 21 Exposition, Seattle's second World's Fair was conceived as a way to commemorate the 50th anniversary of the Alaska-Yukon-Pacific Exposition held here in 1909. Billed as "America's Space Age World's Fair," the new exposition was dedicated to science and life in the 21st century. Ambitious plans and a desire to design a civic center that would be enjoyed by the community for generations to come pushed the original opening date back a few years, from 1959 to 1962.

Among the fair's most ambitious buildings and lasting legacies are the Space Needle, the Monorail, the US Science Pavilion (now the Pacific Science Center), and the Washington State Coliseum (now KeyArena). Designed to appear futuristic, in keeping with the Century 21 theme, the buildings now have a rather retro appeal, especially the Space Needle.

The fair drew 9,634,600 people. Today, more than five decades later, Seattleites and tourists continue to flock to the Seattle Center to enjoy a festival, cultural performance, or sporting event; visit a museum; or simply stroll the tree-lined, fountain-filled grounds.

Seattle's towering Space Needle under construction in 1961

EMP Museum [5]

Opened in 2000, Seattle's EMP Museum celebrates American popular music, with rare memorabilia, interactive exhibits, and a live performance space – all housed in an exuberant structure that swoops and swirls at the base of the Space Needle. Designed by Frank Gehry, an architect with a penchant for atypical shapes and angles, innovative building materials, and bold colors, the building is said to resemble a smashed electric guitar. The museum was conceived by Microsoft co-founder Paul Allen *(see p159)*. EMP incorporates the world's first science-fiction museum, which features multimedia exhibits documenting the history of science fiction in literature and film.

The Building
From the air, the seemingly random jumble of shapes and tortured metal designed by architect Frank Gehry takes form as the carcass of a smashed guitar.

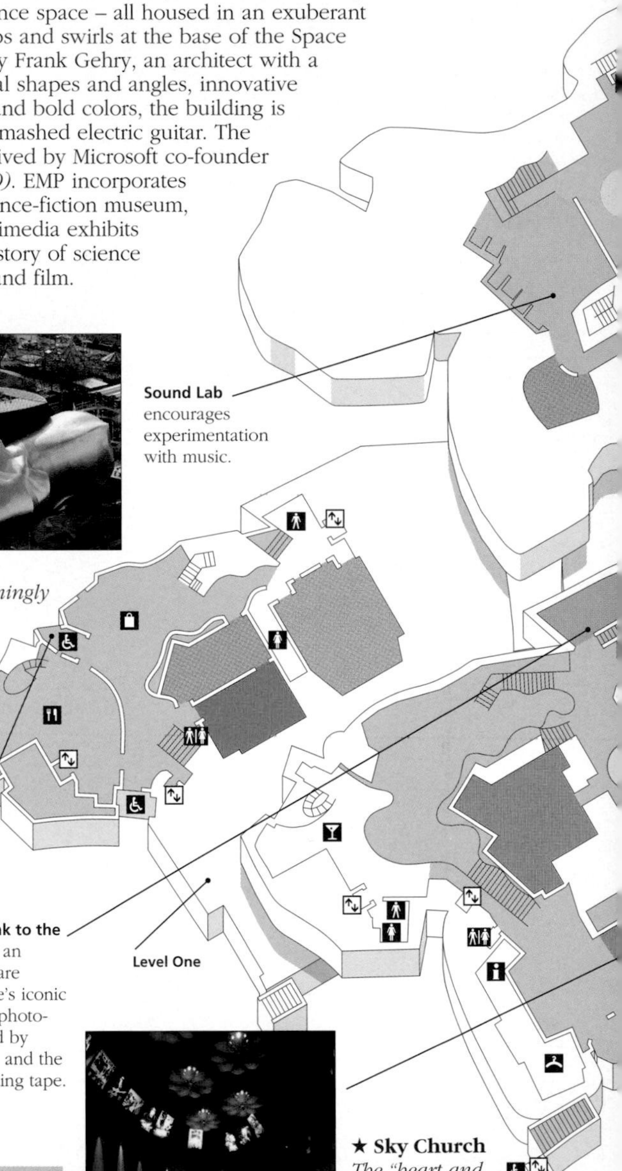

Sound Lab encourages experimentation with music.

Main Entrance

The "Nirvana: Taking Punk to the Masses" exhibit features an extensive collection of rare memorabilia from Seattle's iconic grunge band, including photographs, a guitar smashed by lead singer Kurt Cobain, and the band's first demo recording tape.

Level One

★ Sky Church
The "heart and soul" of EMP, this great hall is used as a performance space, which includes the world's largest video screen.

STAR SIGHTS
★ Guitar Gallery
★ On Stage
★ Roots and Branches
★ Sky Church

VISITORS' CHECKLIST

325 5th Ave N. **Map** 1 C4.
***Tel** (206) 770-2700.*
Seattle Center. 3, 4, 16.
Memorial Day–Labor Day:
10am–7pm daily; Labor Day–
Memorial Day: 10am–5pm daily.
Thanksgiving, Dec 25.
www.empsfm.org

★ On Stage
*Be a rock star, even if
you've never played an
instrument! On Stage
transports you to the center
stage of a large arena, complete with
smoke, lights, and a virtual audience
of screaming fans. To add to the
experience, visitors can watch your
performance live on closed-circuit TV.*

Level Three

★ Guitar Gallery
*In this gallery, famous guitars are
on display, including one that
belonged to Eddie van Halen.*

The Exhibition features a range of
displays that take visitors through the
sci-fi universe, from Mary Shelley's
Frankenstein to *Avatar*. The implications
of new technology are explored and
fantastic worlds created.

**Level Two,
Main Level**

MUSEUM GUIDE
*EMP has three levels.
The main galleries and
exhibits are on Levels
Two and Three. The
lower level offers a
theater for lectures, films,
and classes; a digital
lab offering access to
the EMP digital collection;
and a restaurant
that serves regional
American cuisine.*

★ Roots and Branches
*This sculpture offers a dynamic,
interactive, and historical journey into the origins and evolution
of American popular music. An
audio/visual tour explores American musical roots and influences.*

KEY

	On Stage
	Sound Lab
	Demo Lab
	The Rec Room
	JBL Theater
	Learning Labs
	Nirvana: Taking Punk to the Masses
	EMP Sci-Fi Store
	The Exhibition
	Sky Church
	Special exhibits gallery
	Guitar Gallery
	Roots and Branches
	Non-exhibition space

KeyArena ⑥

305 Harrison St. **Map** 1 B4.
Tel** (206) 684-7200.* ***Event tickets
***Tel** (800) 745-3000.* 🚇 *Seattle
Center.* 🚌 *1, 2, 13, 14, 15, 18.* ♿
*See **Shopping in Seattle** p160.*
www.keyarena.com

In its first life, KeyArena
was the Washington State
Coliseum, offering Seattle
World's Fair visitors a glimpse
into the 21st century. Hailed
as an architectural masterpiece
in 1962 for its shape (a hyper-
bolic paraboloid) and lack
of interior roof supports, this
4-acre (1.5-ha) structure at
the western end of the Seattle
Center was designed by
Paul Thiry (1904–93), main
architect of Seattle's second
World's Fair *(see p145)*, to
last well into the 21st century
as a sports and convention
facility. Fairgoers fondly recall
the coliseum's giant glass
Bubbleator, which transported
150 passengers at one time
high up into the World of
Tomorrow exhibit.

After the fair, the futuristic
building was converted into
a sports arena. In 1964, it
hosted the Beatles' first
Seattle concert and, since
then, has become one of the
top big-ticket concert venues
on the country's west coast.

In 1995, architectural firm
NBBJ led a $74 million
renovation in which the
interior was completely
remodeled – the plastic,
wood, steel, copper, and
concrete from the gutted
interior either recycled in the
renovation or sold. Renamed,
the 17,000-seat KeyArena
is now home to Seattle's
women's professional basketball team the Storm, and
it is also a favored venue
for entertainment acts.

Seattle's Children's Museum,
popular for interactive exhibits

The Children's Museum ⑦

305 Harrison St. **Map** 1 B4.
***Tel** (206) 441-1768.* ⬜ *10am–5pm
Mon–Fri, 10am–6pm Sat & Sun.*
⬛ *Jan 1, Labor Day weekend,
Thanksgiving, Dec 25.* 🚇 *Seattle
Center.* 🚌 *1, 2, 3, 4, 13, 14,
15, 16, 18.* ♿ 🅿 **www**.
thechildrensmuseum.org

While most of Seattle Center
is a delight for kids, the
Children's Museum, founded
in 1979 by parents and edu-
cators, is especially popular
with youngsters. Located on
the first level of the Seattle
Center's Center House, the
nonprofit interactive museum
features eight permanent galleries, one temporary gallery,
and three studio spaces.

Permanent exhibits include
Global Village, where young
visitors are introduced to the
cultures and lifestyles of their
contemporaries around the
world. Children can visit a
tailor shop in Ghana and taste
sushi in Japan. In the Mountain Forest exhibit, kids learn
about Washington's natural
environment as they hike

through a re-creation of a
Pacific Northwest forest,
complete with a bat-inhabited
cave, a waterfall, and flowing
lava. Interactive elements
include sliding down a glacier.

Pulleys, pipes, mazes,
and levers challenge hand–
eye coordination in Cog City.
Kids can experience the laws
of physics first-hand by
directing balls through a
busy cityscape. The museum
also has an interactive exhibit
designed especially with
toddlers in mind. Discovery
Bay's aquarium contains kelp
and a touch pool.

Three to four changing
exhibitions throughout the
year guarantee that there is
always something new to
see. The museum also
features an artist-in-residence
and a drop-in arts studio
for kids – the first of its
kind in the region.

Brick façade of the Austin A. Bell
Building, with its Gothic features

Austin A. Bell Building ⑧

2326 1st Ave. **Map** 1 C5. 🚌 *15, 18,
21, 22, 56.* ⬛ *to the public.*

The Austin A. Bell Building
was designed by Elmer
Fisher, Seattle's foremost commercial architect at the end of
the 19th century and designer
of more than 50 buildings in
the years surrounding the
Great Fire of 1889. While
most were in Pioneer Square,
including the still-standing
Pioneer Building *(see p124)*, a
few Fisher-designed structures
graced the Belltown (then
Denny Hill) area, chief among
them this building.

The unique geometric roof of KeyArena at the Seattle Center

For hotels and restaurants in Seattle see pp286–8 and pp303–6

Combining Richardsonian, Gothic, and Italianate design elements, the handsome four-story brick structure was commissioned in 1888 by Austin Americus Bell, the wealthy son of Seattle pioneer William M. Bell, for whom Belltown is named. It was to be an apartment building and the young Bell's first major building project in the city. However the 35-year-old entrepreneur did not live to see his building completed. Suffering from ill health and depression, Bell took his own life in 1889. His wife saw the project through to completion, and had Bell's name etched into the top of the building's façade. Its interior was destroyed by fire in 1981, but the exterior survived relatively unscathed.

Listed on the National Register of Historic Places, the Austin A. Bell Building now houses pricey condominiums on its upper three floors and a coffee shop at street level.

The European-style Virginia Inn, a favorite pub among Belltown locals

Virginia Inn ❾

1937 1st Ave. **Map** 3 B1.
Tel (206) 728-1937. 📷 15, 18, 21, 22, 56. ⬜ 11:30am–midnight Sun–Thu, 11:30am–2am Fri & Sat. ♿ 🚻
Ⓨ www.virginiainnseattle.com

Located on the southern boundary of Belltown, the Virginia Inn has been a popular watering hole since before the area came to be called Belltown. Established in 1903, it has operated continuously, first as a beer parlor for

waterfront workers, right through the Prohibition period (1920–33), when it served as a cardroom and lunch spot.

In the 1970s, the pub began to attract an arty clientele, who joined the old-timers at the long elegant bar. Over time the local community has changed as low-income housing was replaced by upmarket condominiums, and the clientele altered accordingly. The Virginia Inn has now become known

as Seattle's hottest art bar, with rotating exhibits by local artists adorning the walls. Each exhibition is displayed for two months at a time.

The pub is a good place to sample a local microbrew from of the 16 beers on tap (or even try one from its good selection of Belgian beers). It also has an excellent wine list and specialty cocktails. The brick-and-tile Virginia Inn has something of a European feel to it – without the cigarette fumes.

A café-cum-laundromat, one of Belltown's many eclectic businesses

BELLTOWN HISTORY

With its broad avenues lined with hip clubs, chic restaurants, and eclectic shops, Belltown has been compared to Manhattan's Upper West Side. What Belltown conspicuously lacks is the one thing for which the rest of the city is famous: hills. This was not always the case. Originally home to a very steep slope, the area took on a new identity between 1905 and 1930 when Denny Hill was regraded and washed into Elliott Bay. In all, more than 50 city blocks were lowered by as much as 100 ft (30 m), turning Denny Hill into the Denny Regrade, a lackluster name for an unremarkable area of town inhabited by labor union halls, car lots, inexpensive apartments, and sailors' taverns. (Ironically, the intent of the regrade project was to encourage business development by making the area easier to navigate.)

For decades, the area's identity was its very lack thereof. This began to change in the 1970s when artists, attracted by cheap rents and abundant studio space, started moving to the Regrade. It was also during the 1970s that a neighborhood association renamed the area Belltown, after William M. Bell, one of the area's pioneers. By the 1980s, as Seattleites and suburbanites began taking an interest in cosmopolitan urban living, condominiums began appearing on Belltown's periphery. Fueled by the software boom of the 1990s, the area experienced a huge building boom, attracting well-paid high-tech types to its amenity-rich towers. Although today Belltown bears little resemblance to its early days, a few original structures remain; among them the Virginia Inn and the Austin A. Bell Building.

Belltown coffee shop sign

FARTHER AFIELD

Seattle's outlying areas offer plenty of opportunities for exploration and recreation. Immediately to the south sit two spectacular professional sports stadiums – the pride and joy of the US Northwest's baseball and football fans. To the east, two of Seattle's prominent hills, First and Capitol, offer notable museums, grand cathedrals, and an eclectic assortment of shops and restaurants. For active outdoor pursuits, Green Lake, Discovery Park, and Alki Beach all feature paths for strolling, jogging, biking, rollerblading, or hiking. Those wanting to go the distance can opt for the Burke-Gilman Trail, stretching from Fremont to Kenmore. The city is also home to Woodland Park Zoo, one of the top zoos in the US, and the University of Washington, the heart of the University District. Other Seattle neighborhoods, such as Ballard, Fremont, and Madison Park, each with its own distinct character, are ideal destinations for a day trip.

Signpost in Fremont

SIGHTS AT A GLANCE

Neighborhoods
Ballard **13**
Capitol Hill **4**
First Hill **3**
Fremont **12**
Madison Park **7**
University District **6**

Parks, Gardens, Museums and Zoos
Alki Beach **15**
Burke-Gilman Trail **8**

Discovery Park **14**
Gas Works Park **9**
Green Lake **10**
Museum of Flight **16**
Volunteer Park **5**
Woodland Park Zoo pp156–7 **11**

Sports Stadiums
CenturyLink Field **2**
Safeco Field **1**

KEY

■ Central Seattle
■ Urban area
▬ Major highway
▬ Highway
═ Major road

5 miles = 8 km

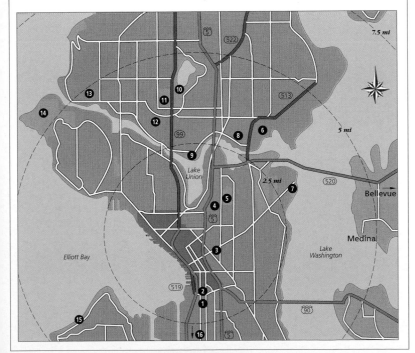

Safeco Field ❶

1250 1st Ave S. **Map** 4 D5.
Tel (206) 346-4000. 🚏 15, 18.
🎫 Apr–Oct: 10:30am, 12:30pm,
2:30pm daily (except days of afternoon
games; no 2:30pm tour on days of
evening games); Nov–Mar: 12:30pm
& 2:30pm Tue–Sun. 📷 ♿

Although Seattle is a rainy
city, Seattle baseball fans
have not endured the disap-
pointment of a rainout since
the American League's Seattle
Mariners christened Safeco
Field on July 15, 1999. Its size
is impressive, encompassing
nearly 20 acres (8 ha) and
seating over 47,000 fans, who
enter the stadium through the
curved entranceway, behind
the field's home plate.

The stadium's state-of-the-
art retractable roof can cover
the playing field with a simple
push of a button. This massive
9-acre (3.5-ha) roof contains
enough steel to build a skyscraper 55 stories tall. Utility
came with a hefty price tag,
however – an unprecedented
$516 million. Designed by the
Seattle firm NBBJ and completed in 1999, Safeco Field
became the nation's most
expensive stadium ever built.

With its sweeping views of
the Seattle skyline, $1.3 mil-
lion in public art, and such
amenities as a children's play-
field and picnic patio, Safeco
Field provides an excellent
atmosphere in which to
watch a Major League
ballgame. While many games
are sold out, tourists may visit
the stadium by taking one of
the regularly scheduled tours.

CenturyLink Field ❷

800 Occidental Ave S. **Map** 4 D4.
Tel (206) 381-7555. 🚏 15, 18.
🎫 Jun–Aug: 12:30pm & 2:30pm
daily; Sep–May: 12:30pm & 2:30pm
Fri & Sat (except days of major
events). **Events Tel** (206) 381-7582.
📷 ♿ www.centurylinkfield.com

The designers of CenturyLink
Field, which opened in 2002,
were intent on factoring
the city's often inclement
winter weather into its design.
So despite the harsh winds
and rains associated with
winter in Seattle, the stadium
was left roofless. The end
result is a spacious, open-air
stadium with unobstructed
views of the Seattle skyline.
With two massive 760-ft
(232-m) eaves, nearly 70 percent of the 67,000 spectator
seats are shielded from falling
rain. Some visiting teams that
are unfamiliar with Pacific
Northwest weather, however,
have found it to be an
inhospitable environment.
The stadium is home to the
NFL's Seattle Seahawks.

Just as the stadium design
by Minneapolis-based Ellerbe
Becket is unconventional, so,
too, is the mix of art scattered
within it, which draws visitors
from around the world. The
four Native American-inspired
steel discs by New Mexican
artist Bob Haozous are
especially striking. The discs,
each 24 ft (7 m) in diameter,
represent people's interaction
with and connection to the
earth and nature.

**Entrance and rotunda of the
Frye Art Museum on First Hill**

First Hill ❸

Bounded by E Pike St, E Yesler Way,
12th Ave E & I-5. **Map** 4 E1.
🚌 3, 4, 12.

Nicknamed Pill Hill for its
several hospitals and numerous doctors' offices, First Hill
lies just east of downtown.
A pedestrian-friendly district
(more than 40 percent of
its residents walk to work),
First Hill was Seattle's first
neighborhood, home to the
city's pioneer families. It
still boasts a number of
the original mansions
from Seattle's earliest days.

First Hill's most recognizable
landmark, **St. James Cathedral**,
(804 9th Avenue) is a parish
church and the cathedral of
the Catholic Archdiocese of
Seattle. Designed by the New
York firm Heins and LaFarge,
the Italian Renaissance
structure dating to 1907
features two tall spires, which
are illuminated at night.

One block southeast of
St. James Cathedral, the **Frye
Art Museum** showcases the
extensive art collection of
Seattle pioneers Charles
and Emma Frye, which
features 19th- and 20th-
century French, German,
and American paintings.
Temporary exhibitions are
held throughout the year.

🏛 **Frye Art Museum**
704 Terry Ave. **Tel** (206) 622-9250.
⏰ 11am–5pm Tue–Sun (to 7pm
Thu). ⚫ Jan 1, Jul 4, Thanksgiving,
Dec 25. 🎫 ♿ 📷 📷
www.fryemuseum.org

The brick and steel façade of Safeco Field, home of the Seattle Mariners

For hotels and restaurants in Seattle see pp286–8 and pp303–6

Capitol Hill ❹

Bounded by Montlake Blvds E & NE, E Pike & E Madison Sts, 23rd Ave E & I-5. **Map** 2 F5. 🚌 7, 9, 10.

Northeast of downtown, lively Capitol Hill is a colorful and diverse urban neighborhood where no one blinks at spiked purple hair and multiple body piercings.

The district's commercial hub and major avenue is Broadway (East Roy to East Pike Streets). Referred to as the "living room of Capitol Hill," it offers shopping (from books to home accessories to vintage clothing), a number of ethnic restaurants, and bronze footsteps embedded in the sidewalk to teach passersby the tango and fox trot.

While people-watching is a major source of entertainment, Capitol Hill also features two vintage movie houses: the **Egyptian** (805 East Pine Street) and the **Harvard Exit** (807 East Roy Street). Both theaters specialize in independent and foreign films.

The hill is also home to **St. Mark's Episcopal Cathedral** (1245 10th Avenue East) (1931), belonging to the Diocese of Olympia. It is known for its magnificent Flentrop organ, installed in 1965 and consisting of 3,944 pipes that range in size from 1 inch (2.5 cm) to 32 ft (9.7 m).

The internationally acclaimed **Cornish College of the Arts** (710 East Roy Street) features a full roster of student exhibits and performances.

Volunteer Park's Seattle Asian Art Museum, in an historic Art Deco building

Volunteer Park ❺

1247 15th Ave E. **Tel** *(206) 684-4075.* 🚌 *7, 9, 10.* ⭕ *6am–11pm daily.*

Located at the north end of Capitol Hill, elegant Volunteer Park was designed in 1904–1909 by the Olmsted Brothers, the US's most famous landscape-architecture firm. The 48-acre (19.5-ha) park is named for the Seattle men who enlisted to fight in the Spanish-American War of 1898.

The Olmsteds' design called for an observation tower. The city obliged by building a 75-ft (23-m) brick water tower with an observation deck open to the public. A steep climb up the 106-step spiral staircase rewards visitors with spectacular views of the Space Needle, Puget Sound, and the Olympic mountain range.

A children's playground, wading pool, tennis courts, and bandstand make the park a favorite outing for families.

Volunteer Park is the site of the **Seattle Asian Art Museum**, located in a 1933 Art Deco building which formerly housed the Seattle Art Museum *(see pp128–9).* The Seattle Asian Art Museum's renowned collection includes works from Japan, Korea, China, and Southeast Asia.

Highlights of the rotating collection include wood and lacquer furniture from imperial China and 14th-century Chinese sculpture. Other gems of the collection are the Korean ceramics and metalware, and bronze figures of Buddha and Bodhisattva that date back to the country's Unified Shilla dynasty (57–935).

Across from the museum is the **Volunteer Park Conservatory**, a botanical garden also home to plants confiscated by US customs. The conservatory consists of five houses. Four showcase bromeliads, palms, ferns, and cacti, respectively. The seasonal display house includes lilies, poinsettias, azaleas, and a 75-year-old Jade plant that blooms November to January.

🏛 **Seattle Asian Art Museum**
1400 E Prospect St. **Tel** *(206) 654-3100.* ⭕ *10am–5pm Tue, Wed & Fri–Sun, 10am–9pm Thu.* ● *Jan 1, Labor Day, Thanksgiving, Dec 25.* 🎟 *by donation; free 1st Thu & Sat of month.* ♿ 📷
www.seattleartmuseum.org

🏛 **Volunteer Park Conservatory**
1400 E Galer St. **Tel** *(206) 684-4743.* ⭕ *10am–4pm Tue–Sun.* 🎟 *by donation.* ♿ 📷
www.seattle.gov

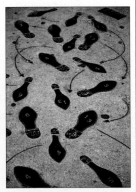

Dance Steps on Broadway, by Jack Mackie, in Capitol Hill

Summer flowers outside the Conservatory at Volunteer Park

The University of Washington campus, with its mix of architectural styles

University District ⑥

Bounded by NE 55th St, Portage Bay, Montlake Blvd NE & I-5.
🚌 7, 25, 43, 70, 71, 72, 73.
ℹ️ Ground floor, Odegaard Undergraduate Library, near 15th Ave NE and NE 41st, (206) 543-9198.

Eclectic and energetic thanks to the vibrant youth culture surrounding a major university campus, the University District makes for an interesting half- or full-day excursion. The hub of the district is the University of Washington. The premier institution of higher learning in the Northwest US, this university is internationally known for its excellent research and graduate programs.

Located on the site of the 1909 World's Fair, the beautiful 643-acre (260-ha) parklike campus is home to more than 43,000 students and 500 buildings in a mix of architectural styles. Just inside the main campus entrance is the **Burke Museum of Natural History and Culture**, featuring dinosaur fossils and a notable collection of Northwest Native art. On the western edge of the campus sits the **Henry Art Gallery**, the first public art museum in the state of Washington. The museum has a special focus on photography and digital and projected media.

The university's main avenue is **University Way Northeast**, known to locals as "The Ave." Located just west of campus, it is lined with bookstores, pubs, inexpensive restaurants, and shops. At the opposite end of the spectrum, University Village, located east of the campus, offers an upscale shopping and dining experience.

A must-see, especially spring through autumn, is the **Washington Park Arboretum**, a 230-acre (93-ha) garden and living plant museum, with 4,600 species, including 139 on the endangered list. The arboretum also features a Japanese garden with sculptures and wildlife, carp-filled ponds, and an authentic open teahouse for ceremonies once a month.

Neo-Gothic building, university campus

🏛 **Burke Museum of Natural History and Culture**
NE 45th St & 17th Ave NE. **Tel** (206) 543-5590. ⭘ 10am–5pm daily, 10am–8pm 1st Thu of month. ⭘ Jan 1, Jul 4, Thanksgiving, Dec 25. 🎫 (free 1st Thu of month; separate adm to some exhibits). ♿ 🔲 🅰
🅿 www.burkemuseum.org

🏛 **Henry Art Gallery**
NE 41st St & 15th Ave NE. **Tel** (206) 543-2280. ⭘ 11am–4pm Wed, Sat & Sun, 11am–9pm Thu & Fri. ⭘ Jan 1, Jul 4, Thanksgiving, Dec 25. 🎫 (by donation on Thu). ♿ 🎫 for groups in advance. 🔲 🅰 🅿 www.henryart.org

🌿 **Washington Park Arboretum**
2300 Arboretum Dr E.
Tel (206) 543-8800. 🚌 11, 43, 48.
Visitors' center ⭘ 9am–5pm.
Grounds ⭘ dawn–dusk.
🎫 to Japanese Garden. ♿ 🅰
www.washington.edu

Madison Park ⑦

Bounded by E Madison St, Lake Washington Blvd & Lake Washington.
🚌 11.

Seattle's lakeside community of Madison Park is one of the city's most affluent. Its tree-shaded streets, lined with charming older homes, most built between 1910 and 1930, are ideal for leisurely strolling.

The area was established in the early 1860s when Judge John J. McGilvra purchased 420 acres (170 ha) of land, cutting a road through the forest from downtown Seattle to his property, which was later named Madison Street after former US President James Madison (1751–1836). In the 1880s, McGilvra divided his land into lots, decreeing that only "cottages" could be built on them. He also set aside 24 acres (10 ha) for public use. This parcel of land is now known as Madison Park. By the end of the 19th century, this park had become the most popular beach in the city, complete with an ornate boathouse, piers, a wooden promenade, a greenhouse, and floating bandstands. Reminiscent of a friendly village, the neighborhood's commercial area today offers a number of popular restaurants, upscale boutiques, and home accessories shops.

Children playing on Madison Park's sandy lakeside beach

Burke-Gilman Trail **8**

Numerous access points; main access point at Gas Works Park. 25, 43.

When the sun comes out in Seattle, cyclists, speed-walkers, joggers, rollerbladers, and lovers of the outdoors flock to the scenic Burke-Gilman Trail. Built on an old railway bed, this 27-mile (43-km) paved trail is used by more than one million people each year. It is both a popular recreation corridor and a pleasant, automobile-free commuter route for residents.

Although the Burke-Gilman Trail was extended west through Fremont (see p158) to 8th Avenue Northwest, it officially begins at Gas Works Park, at the north end of Lake Union. From there, it follows the shores of Lake Washington, beginning at the University of Washington and extending all the way to the city of Kenmore, where it connects with the Sammamish River Trail.

A warning to pedestrians: bicyclists comprise roughly 80 percent of all trail users, making attentiveness and keeping to the right-hand side a must.

Gas Works Park **9**

2101 N Northlake Way. **Tel** (206) 684-4075. 26. 6am–10pm daily. **www**.seattle.gov

Huge rusty pipes and pieces of decrepit machinery are not typically found in a park. But Gas Works Park on Lake Union is anything but typical. Established in 1906 as a gasification plant by the Seattle Gas Company for extracting gas from coal, Gas Works was once a primary source of power for Seattle. Shut down in 1956, the plant's machinery and towers stood dormant until 1975, when the site was reno-vated into an award-winning park under the direction of landscape architect Richard Haag. With its renovation, Gas Works became the first industrial site in the world to be converted into a public

Stunning view of the Seattle skyline from Gas Works Park

park. Today, Gas Works Park is a scenic, 21-acre (8.5-ha) knoll offering vast recreation-al opportunities and magnifi-cent views of Lake Union and downtown Seattle. Besides serving as a model for urban renewal, the park is a haven for kite flying, kayaking, picnicking, and viewing the July 4 fireworks.

Boaters enjoying an outing on Seattle's Green Lake

Green Lake **10**

7201 E Green Lake Dr N. **Tel** (206) 684-4075. 16, 26. 24 hrs daily.

On any given day – and especially a sunny one – Green Lake hosts a spirited parade of people, from joggers, walkers, cyclists, and skaters to bird-watchers, dog walkers, and pram-pushing parents.

For wheeled sports, the 2.8-mile (4.5-km) asphalt path circling the lake is ideal. Joggers and walkers can use the adjacent 3.2-mile (5-km) trail, which runs closest to the lake and has a crushed granite surface.

Attracting more than a million outdoor enthusiasts a year, this 324-acre (131-ha) park is populated by as many as 7,200 people a day on summer weekends. While kayaking, windsurfing, and paddleboating are popular pursuits during the warmer months, and boats can be rented at the lake, swimming may be restricted due to algae blooms and other problems caused by water stagnation.

Likened to New York's Central Park – albeit on a smaller scale – the lake and its surrounding park is a lively gathering spot for Seattle residents and a welcome recreational oasis in a high-density urban area. In addition to the lake, the park grounds include an indoor public pool, outdoor wading pool, tennis courts, soccer field, outdoor basket-ball court, baseball diamond, and pitch-and-putt golf course. The park is also home to many different species of wildlife, including ducks, turtles, squirrels, and eagles.

Jogger on the path that runs along Green Lake

Woodland Park Zoo ⓫

Designed in 1899 by city landscape consultant John Olmsted, Woodland Park Zoo is one of the oldest zoos on the West Coast and one of Seattle's major attractions. Of the nearly 300 animal species that reside at the 92-acre (37-ha) zoo, most live in environments that closely resemble their native habitats. Unlike typical zoo models where animals are grouped by species, Woodland Park creatures are grouped in ecosystems. Six of the zoo's naturalistic exhibits have won top honors from the Association of Zoos and Aquariums. Among these are the Elephant Forest – with its enormous elephant pool, Thai logging camp replica, and temple-like nighttime shelter – and the Trail of Vines, which includes the first open-forested canopy for orangutans to be created at a zoo.

African Savanna giraffes

★ Jaguar Cove
Visit the tropical world of the jaguar, the largest cat in the Western Hemisphere. This is one of the most naturalistic exhibits dedicated to jaguars in any zoo.

★ Tropical Rain Forest
The gorilla exhibit in the Tropical Rain Forest includes the endangered western lowland gorilla, a gentle giant that can eat as much as 70 lbs (32 kg) of food each day.

Family Farm
A popular seasonal Contact Area is one of the features of the Family Farm, as is the year-round "Bug" World, exhibiting earth's smallest animals.

STAR SIGHTS

★ African Savanna

★ Jaguar Cove

★ Northern Trail

★ Tropical Rain Forest

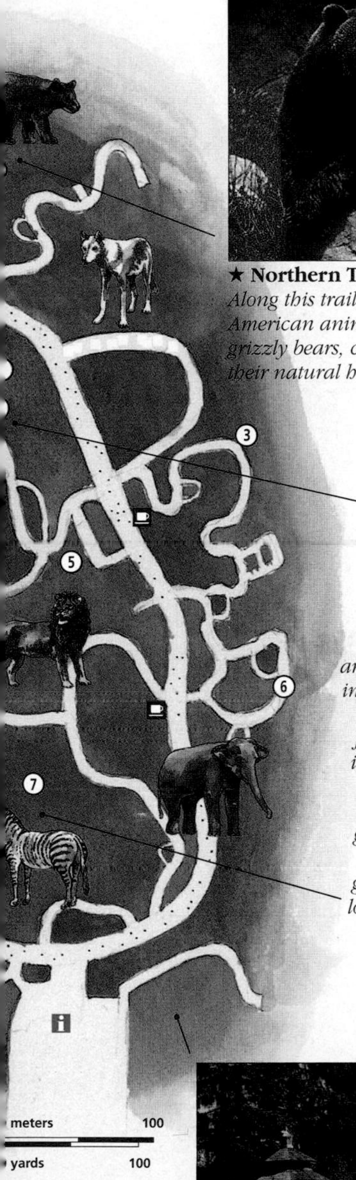
3
5
6
7
meters 100
yards 100

★ Northern Trail
Along this trail, indigenous North American animals, including grizzly bears, can be viewed in their natural habitats.

VISITORS' CHECKLIST

N 50th St & Fremont Ave N.
Tel *(206) 548-2500.* 🚌 *5.*
🕐 *May–Sep: 9:30am–6pm daily; Oct–Apr: 9:30am–4pm daily.* ⛔ *Dec 25.* ♿
☕ 🍴 🛍 **www**.zoo.org

Willawong Station
The bird-feeding experience offers an opportunity to feed free-flying birds, primarily small colorful Australian parrots, while learning about responsible care for birds in the wild and at home.

★ African Savanna
Many species are found here, including zebras, hippos, and gazelles, which roam freely with the herd of imposing giraffes near a replica African village. There is a giraffe-feeding station where visitors may get up close to feed the long-necked creatures.

Woodland Park Rose Garden
Located near the zoo's main entrance, the award-winning, fully organic garden features more than 5,000 rose bushes.

KEY

African Savanna 7
Australasia 1
Carousel 14
Family Farm 8
Humboldt Penguin Exhibit 13
Jaguar Cove 10
Northern Trail 2
Temperate Forest 9
Trail of Adaptations 5
Tropical Asia: Elephant Forest 6
Tropical Asia: Trail of Vines 3
Tropical Rain Forest 11
Willawong Station 4
Zoomazium 12

People Waiting for the Interurban, an aluminum sculpture in Fremont

Fremont ⑫

Bounded by N 50th St, Lake Washington Ship Canal, Stone Way Ave N & 8th Ave NW. 🚌 26, 28.

In the 1960s, when it was a community of students, artists, and bohemians attracted by low rents, Fremont declared itself an "artists' republic." By the late 1990s, the neighborhood's character began to shift, after a high-tech firm settled its Seattle office here. However, Fremont has managed to hold on to cherished traditions, such as the Summer Solstice Parade and an outdoor cinema series, and today, it is still one of Seattle's funkiest districts.

Public art is a fixture of Fremont. A 13.5-ft- (4-m-) tall statue of Lenin towers above pedestrians at Fremont Place, and a 15-ft- (4.5-m-) tall Volkswagen-eating troll lurks under the north end of the Aurora Bridge. On 34th Street, near the drawbridge, sculptor Richard Beyer's *People Waiting for the Interurban* is

The historic landmark belltower in Ballard

regularly clothed by locals. The dog's human face is modeled after an honorary mayor, with whom the artist had a dispute.

Ballard ⑬

Bounded by Salmon Bay, Shilshole Bay & Phinney Ridge. 🚌 15, 17, 18.

Settled by Scandinavian fishermen and loggers in 1853, Ballard was incorporated into Washington State in 1889 and annexed to Seattle in 1907. At the turn of the 19th century, Ballard was a mill town, producing an impressive three million wooden shingles a day. Many of the mill jobs were held by Scandinavian immigrants. Located north of the shingle mills, Ballard Avenue was the commercial center of this then-booming area. Its buildings recall the area's industrial growth and strong Scandinavian heritage; many are open to the public. In 1976, King Carl XVI Gustav of Sweden read the proclamation establishing Ballard Avenue a Historic District.

The area's proud Scandinavian heritage is celebrated at the annual Norwegian Constitution Day Parade every May 17, at the excellent **Nordic Heritage Museum** (3014 Northwest 67th Street), and at the Bergen Place mural, located in Bergen Place Park. Ballard

greets the thousands of container ships, tugboats, fishing boats, and pleasure craft that make their way through the **Hiram M. Chittenden Locks** each year. Located at the west end of Ballard, the locks allow boats to travel between saltwater Puget Sound and freshwater Lake Union and Lake Washington. The best times to observe migrating salmon on the fish ladder are June through October. One of the city's major – and free – tourist attractions, the locks' grounds include 7 acres (3 ha) of botanical gardens.

🏛 **Hiram M. Chittenden Locks**
3015 NW 54th St. **Tel** (206) 783-7059. **Grounds** ⬜ 7am–9pm daily. **Visitors' center** ⬜ May–Sep: 10am–6pm daily; Oct–Apr: 10am–4pm Thu–Mon. ♿ 🎦 Mar–Apr & Oct–Nov: 2pm Thu–Mon; May–Sep: 1pm, 2pm Mon–Fri, 11am, 1pm, 3pm Sat–Sun.

Discovery Park ⑭

3801 W Government Way. **Tel** (206) 386-4236. 🚌 24, 33. **Park** ⬜ 6am–11pm daily. **Visitors' center** ⬜ 8:30am–5pm Tue–Sun. ⬤ major hols. **www**.seattle.gov

Located on Magnolia Bluff, overlooking Puget Sound, 534-acre (216-ha) Discovery Park is Seattle's largest park. It occupies most of the former Fort Lawton site, a defensive base for soldiers during World Wars I and II and the Korean War. Built at the turn of the 20th century, the still-occupied Officers' Quarters are listed

The West Point Lighthouse, off the South Beach Trail, Discovery Park

The gigantic Fremont troll, waiting for unsuspecting cars

For hotels and restaurants in Seattle see pp286–8 and pp303–6

A cyclist on Alki Beach, a stunning view of Seattle in the background

on the National Register of Historic Places. A visitors' center at the east entrance offers trail maps and interactive exhibits for kids.

Home to over 250 species of birds and other wildlife, the park offers more than 7 miles (11 km) of hiking trails, including the 2.8-mile (4.5-km) Loop Trail, which circles the park and passes through forests, meadows, and dunes. For beach exploration, the park has two very different habitats: the rocky North Beach and the sandy South Beach.

Discovery Park is also home to the **Daybreak Star Cultural Center**. Operated by the United Indians of All Tribes Foundation, this cultural and educational center houses a collection of Native American art. The annual summer Pow Wow features some 500 dancers, 30 drum groups, arts and crafts, and a salmon bake.

🏛 Daybreak Star Cultural Center
Near north parking lot of Discovery Park. *Tel (206) 285-4425.*
🚻 🅿 *10am–5pm Mon–Sat, noon–5pm Sun.* 🚻

Alki Beach ⑮

1702 Alki Ave SW. *Tel (206) 684-4075.* 🚌 *37, 56.*

When the first European settlers landed on Alki Beach on a stormy November day in 1851, they were welcomed by Chief Seattle and his Duwamish tribe *(see p25)*. Today, this lively beach is the coolest place in town to be on a warm day.

The beach offers spectacular views of Puget Sound, the Olympic Mountains, and the Seattle skyline.

Museum of Flight ⑯

9404 E Marginal Way S.
Road map 1 A2. *Tel (206) 764-5720.* 🕐 *10am–5pm daily.*
⬤ *Thanksgiving, Dec 25.* 🎟 🚻 📷
🏠 🖥 www.museumofflight.org

The west coast's largest air and space museum, the Museum of Flight takes visitors on a fascinating journey from the earliest days of aviation to the Space Age. The museum features 39 historic airplanes, of which more than half are suspended from the ceiling of the six-story Great Gallery.

Visitors can sit in the cockpit of an SR-71 Blackbird or F/A-18 Hornet, and board the first Air Force One, the US presidential jet.

The restored Red Barn, Boeing's original 1910 airplane factory and a National Historic Site, is part of the museum. Its exhibits include the world's first fighter plane.

The Personal Courage Wing, which opened in 2004, houses the Champlin Fighter collection containing 28 historical aircraft, mainly from World Wars I and II.

Especially popular are the museum's simulators, including the challenging space-docking simulators in which participants try to link up with the Hubble space telescope.

Aviatik D-1 in the Personal Courage Wing of the Museum of Flight

THE MEN BEHIND MICROSOFT

Seattle is home to two of the world's wealthiest men and most accomplished entrepreneurs. Bill Gates and Paul Allen met at a prestigious Seattle prep school. Sharing a fascination for computers, the boys soon landed jobs with a company that paid them in computer time instead of cash. There they pored over manuals and explored the computer system inside and out. In 1973, Gates left for Harvard University but kept in touch with Allen, with whom he vowed to go into business one day. By 1975, Bill Gates was the US's most successful college dropout, having left Harvard to devote his energies to the company he founded with his friend. Microsoft went on to become the goliath of the computer software industry. In 1985, its headquarters settled in Redmond, a suburb of Seattle. In 1986, the company began public trading. Today, Microsoft employs over 90,000 people in 135 countries.

Bill Gates, co-founder of Seattle-based Microsoft

Shopping in Seattle

Shopping aficionados will not be disappointed in Seattle. From 5th Avenue's ritzy boutiques to funky shops on Fremont's streets, you'll find plenty of irresistible buys. Without a car, you can shop until you drop downtown, at Pioneer Square, Pike Place Market, and Belltown, or hop on a bus and explore the shopping options farther afield.

Westlake Center shopping mall, in downtown Seattle

SHOPPING DISTRICTS

Seattle has several interesting shopping districts. Upscale clothing boutiques, antique shops, and home accessory stores make their home in trendy Belltown *(see p141)*. Downtown *(see p121)*, chic boutiques mingle with top retailers and multilevel malls. At Pike Place Market *(see p134)* you'll find produce as well as antiques, art, crafts, jewelry, vintage apparel, and cookware. Pioneer Square *(see p121)* features bookstores, art galleries, antique shops, and a plethora of Oriental rug stores.

DEPARTMENT STORES AND SHOPPING CENTERS

Seattle-based **Nordstrom** opened its opulent flagship department store in 1998. Known for its wide selection of shoes, the fashion specialty store pampers shoppers with excellent customer service and, at this location, a luxurious full-service day spa. **Macy's** department store downtown sells everything from linens and lingerie to loveseats and luggage. Downtown Seattle also has several notable malls. The poshest is **Pacific Place**, a five-level complex featuring

dozens of upscale apparel, jewelry, and home accessory stores. Two blocks west, **Westlake Center** is home to top national and regional retailers and a sprawling food court. Barneys New York and Furla are among the prestigious retailers at **City Centre**. Located two blocks south of Pacific Place and Westlake Center, this classy mall boasts an impressive collection of contemporary glass art.

Located just outside downtown Seattle, **University Village** is the area's most high-end open-air shopping center. Locally owned specialty shops share the pedestrian-friendly Village with national retailers such as Barnes & Noble, Restoration Hardware, and Pottery Barn.

SPECIALTY SHOPS

You will find 150,000 titles at the **Elliott Bay Book Company**. **Made in Washington**, which sells everything from smoked salmon to handmade pottery, offers one-stop shopping for top-quality, locally made merchandise and food items. The **REI** (Recreational Equipment Inc.) flagship store sells all kinds of outdoor gear, and features an indoor climbing wall. **Sur La Table** offers the latest culinary utensils and kitchenware. **Ye Olde Curiosity Shop** *(see p137)* is a jam-packed curiosity shop, known for

One of Seattle's many specialty shops, this one selling pottery

both its kitschy souvenirs and fine Native American crafts.

WHAT TO BUY

Smoked salmon, and coffee beans from small local roasting companies, such as Tully's, Espresso Vivace, and Caffè Appassionato, are Seattle specialties. Hand-blown glass and pottery are popular souvenirs. More conventional items include Space Needle-inspired items, and bags with Pike Place Market motifs.

Entertainment in Seattle

With Seattle's varied offerings, from baseball to ballet, and book readings to Broadway musicals, visitors won't be lacking for entertainment. The city is home to one of the top opera companies in the US, a critically acclaimed symphony orchestra, and a Tony Award-winning repertory theater company.

Window of the Crocodile Café, a Belltown favorite for live music

INFORMATION

The city's daily newspaper, the *Seattle Times*, offers complete entertainment listings for the week in its Friday "Ticket" supplement. For daily listings, visit the newspaper's website at www.seattletimes.com.

BUYING TICKETS

Tickets for sporting events and many performing arts events can be purchased through **Ticketmaster**.

FREE EVENTS

Free art and literary events abound in Pioneer Square: First Thursday Gallery Walks through museums, galleries, bars, and shops occur on the first Thursday evening of each month; and the Elliott Bay Book Company hosts author readings several times each week.

FILM

Seattle has a thriving film scene, with the **Landmark Theatres** group and **Northwest Film Forum** screening art house and independent films. One of the most respected and comprehensive film festivals in the US is the **Seattle International** Film Festival (SIFF) which screens more than 300 new works during May and June.

THEATER

Many of Seattle's performing arts venues are located at the Seattle Center, including the respected **Seattle Repertory Theatre**, which presents nine plays from September to May, and the **Intiman Theatre**, which stages classic and contemporary plays March through December. The popular **Seattle Children's Theatre**, the second largest children's theater in the country, stages performances from September to June.

DANCE

Internationally acclaimed, the **Pacific Northwest Ballet** performs at Marion Oliver McCaw Hall. Its *Nutcracker* is a must-see during the holiday season.

MUSIC

The distinguished **Seattle Symphony** performs September through June at the stunning Benaroya Hall (*see p129*). Marion Oliver McCaw Hall at Seattle Center is home to the acclaimed **Seattle Opera**, which attracts audiences from around the world with its productions of Wagner's *Ring* cycle every four years. For live blues, jazz, rock, and folk music, there are many venues to choose from in Pioneer Square, as well as in Belltown and Ballard.

Young musicians performing in downtown Seattle

DIRECTORY

TICKET OUTLETS

Ticketmaster
Tel General: (800) 745-3000.
Arts: (800) 982-2787.
www.ticketmaster.com

FILM

Landmark Theatres
Tel (206) 633-0059.
www.landmarktheatres.com

Northwest Film Forum
Tel (206) 829-7863.
www.nwfilmforum.org

SIFF
Tel (206) 633-7151.
www.siff.net

THEATER

Intiman Theatre
Tel (206) 269-1900.
www.intiman.org

Seattle Children's Theatre
Tel (206) 441-3322.
www.sct.org

Seattle Repertory Theatre
Tel (206) 443-2222.
www.seattlerep.org

DANCE

Pacific Northwest Ballet
Tel (206) 441-2424.
www.pnb.org

MUSIC

Seattle Opera
Tel (206) 389-7676.
www.seattleopera.com

Seattle Symphony
Tel (206) 215-4747.
www.seattlesymphony.org

SPECTATOR SPORTS

Spectator sports are big in Seattle. Seattleites are justifiably proud of their two stadiums – Safeco Field (*see p152*), home of the Seattle Mariners baseball team, and CenturyLink Field (*see p152*), where the National Football League's Seattle Seahawks play. The city's professional women's basketball team, the Storm, plays at the Seattle Center's KeyArena (*see p148*). For sporting events tickets, call **Ticketmaster**.

Getting Around Seattle

Seattle may be a hilly city but its main tourist areas – Pioneer Square, downtown, Pike Place Market, the waterfront, Seattle Center, and Belltown – are relatively flat, close to each other, and easy to navigate on foot. The city's buses serve these areas and all Farther Afield sights and neighborhoods. A two-minute ride on the Monorail connects downtown to the Seattle Center.

Area is delineated by Jackson Street to the south, 6th Avenue to the east, Battery Street to the north, and the waterfront to the west. Bus schedules are available from the **Seattle Convention and Visitors Bureau** at the Washington State Convention and Trade Center (800 Convention Place) and from the Metro

STREET LAYOUT

Interstate-5 runs north–south through the middle of Seattle. In the downtown area, avenues run north–south, and streets run east–west. With only a few exceptions, avenues are numbered and streets are named (for example, 3rd Avenue and Spring Street). Many of Seattle's streets and avenues run one-way. For a good selection of local street maps, as well as state and recreational maps, visit **Metsker Maps of Seattle**, in Pioneer Square.

The Metro Bus running along Seattle's waterfront

BICYCLING

Cyclists may wish to avoid Seattle's busy streets and head to one of the area's popular bike trails. The 27-mile (43-km) paved Burke-Gilman Trail *(see p155)* stretches from Fremont to Kenmore. Bike rental shops such as **All About Bike and Ski** and the **Bicycle Center of Seattle** are located near the trail. A 2.8-mile (4.5-km) path that encircles Green Lake *(see p155)* is ideal for shorter spins. **Gregg's Greenlake Cycle**, located beside the lake, rents touring, mountain, and hybrid bicycles.

Transit customer service office at Westlake Station, on the mezzanine level. The **Metro Transit Rider Information** phone line provides route and other information.

The 2.6-mile (4-km) **South Lake Union Streetcar** connects downtown Seattle with the fast-growing South Lake Union neighborhood. It runs every 15 minutes from 6am until 9pm weekdays (to 11pm on Saturdays) and from 10am to 7pm on Sundays and holidays. Tickets can be purchased at the 11 streetcar stops, and Metro transfers are also valid.

A Seattle taxi cab, a common sight on downtown streets

WALKING

Seattle is a great city for walking. Though it is quite hilly, the downtown area is compact enough to walk in its entirety, and locals are generally happy to offer directions. Keep in mind that jay-walking (crossing the street other than at designated crossings) is illegal in Seattle. Tourist offices provide free maps that will help visitors navigate the downtown area.

Traffic sign to help pedestrians

TAXIS

Taxis can usually be flagged outside every major downtown hotel and attraction, as well as on main streets and at taxi stands, found at bus stations and the airport. Taxis can also be ordered by telephone. Fares start at $2.50, and increase at a rate of approximately $2.50 per mile.

PUBLIC TRANSIT

Traveling by metro offers inexpensive transportation throughout the city. Buses are equipped with wheelchair lifts. Between 6am and 7pm, bus transportation is free in downtown Seattle. The Ride Free

The 14-mile (23-km) **Sound Transit** light rail system connects downtown Seattle with Sea-Tac airport, a journey taking approximately 36 minutes. Trains operate from 5am to midnight Monday to Saturday, and 6am to 11pm on Sunday. Tickets can be bought at the stations. There are stops at the International District/ Pioneer Square, the stadiums and SODO, Beacon Hill, Mount Baker, Southeast Seattle, and Tukwila. Further extensions are under way.

A fare payment system, ORCA (One Regional Card for All) has been launched for light rail, streetcar and buses.

The Seattle Monorail, linking downtown to the Seattle Center

Another convenient and inexpensive way to travel within the city is the **Seattle Monorail** *(see p145)*. Linking downtown Seattle to the Seattle Center *(see pp142–3)*, it operates Monday through Friday from 7:30am to 11pm, and Saturday through Sunday from 8:30am to 11pm. It departs every 10 minutes from the station at Seattle Center (across from the Space Needle) and from Westlake Center, at 5th Avenue and Pine Street. The 1-mile (1.6-km) trip takes two minutes.

FERRIES

Several of Seattle's outlying areas can be reached via the **Washington State Ferries** *(see p136)*, which offer scenic rides through the San Juan Islands and to other destinations around Puget Sound.

A Seattle bus stop sign

Sail from downtown Seattle's Pier 52 to nearby Bremerton and Bainbridge Island, or from Pier 50 to Bremerton and Vashon Island. Ferries leaving from Pier 52 carry automobiles and passengers, whereas those from Pier 50 are passenger-only. Several private companies offer ferry rides along similar routes as well as narrated tours of the Seattle waterfront.

DRIVING

The traffic in downtown Seattle can be daunting. Avoid driving during weekday rush hours, 7 to 9:30am and 3 to 7pm. Unless posted otherwise, the speed limit on arterial (city) streets is 30 mph (48 km/h). The speed limit for non-arterial (residential) streets is 25 mph (40 km/h). A right-hand turn on a red light is permitted after coming to a full stop. Traffic circles (raised islands in intersections) are common in many neighborhoods. Drivers should yield to the motorist on the left, then proceed to the right.

Seat belts, safety seats for young children, and motorcycle helmets are mandatory. **American Automobile Association (AAA)** members can obtain free maps and tour books from the Seattle office.

PARKING

Parking downtown is generally expensive. However, one of the best-kept secrets is the underground parking garage beneath Pacific Place *(see p160)*, where budget-savvy Seattleites usually park. On-street parking is available for cars in some areas of the city, but be aware that strict time limits apply and that these differ from street to street.

TOWING

If your car is towed from a street within the city limits, call the **Seattle Police, Auto Records Department**. Staff here will tell you which impound yard your car has been taken to. Be prepared to provide the car's license plate number and the location from which the vehicle was towed. If you are renting a car, be sure to carry the vehicle license number with you. If the car was towed from a private lot, call the number posted on the sign.

A local seaplane, offering visitors a bird's-eye view of Seattle

DIRECTORY

USEFUL NUMBERS

All About Bike and Ski
Tel (206) 524-2642.

American Automobile Association (AAA)
Tel (206) 448-5353.
www.aaa.com

Bicycle Center of Seattle
Tel (206) 523-8300.

Gregg's Greenlake Cycle
Tel (206) 523-1822.

Metro Transit Rider Information
Tel (206) 553-3000.

Metsker Maps of Seattle
Tel (206) 623-8747 or (800) 727-4430.
www.metskers.com

Seattle Convention and Visitors Bureau
Tel (206) 461-5800.
www.visitseattle.org

Seattle Monorail
Tel (206) 905-2620.

Seattle Police, Auto Records Department
Tel (206) 684-5444.

Sound Transit
Tel (206) 398-5000.
www.soundtransit.org

South Lake Union Streetcar
Tel (206) 553-3000.
www.seattlestreetcar.org

Washington State Ferries
Tel (206) 464-6400 for Seattle schedule. **www**.wsdot.wa.gov

TAXIS

Far West Taxi
Tel (206) 622-1717.

Yellow Cab
Tel (206) 622-6500.

The Washington State Ferries service, linking Puget Sound communities

SEATTLE STREET FINDER

The key map below shows the area of Seattle covered by the *Street Finder* maps, which can be found on the following pages. Map references for sights, hotels, restaurants, shops, and entertainment venues given throughout the Seattle chapter of this guide refer to the grid on the maps. The first figure in the reference indicates which map to turn to (1 to 4), and the letter and number that follow refer to the grid reference on that map.

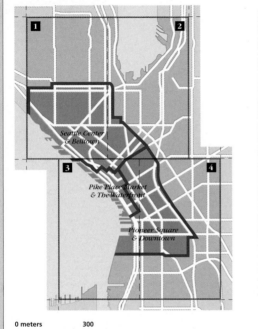

SCALE OF MAPS 1–4

0 meters   300
0 yards   300

KEY TO STREET FINDER

■	Major sight
■	Minor sight
■	Station building
🚉	Train station
🚍	Bus station – long distance
🚊	Streetcar
🚝	Monorail
P	Parking
ℹ	Information
✚	Hospital
🚔	Police station
✝	Church
⊠	Post office
⛴	Ferry boarding point
– –	Ferry route
=	Railroad line
→	One-way street

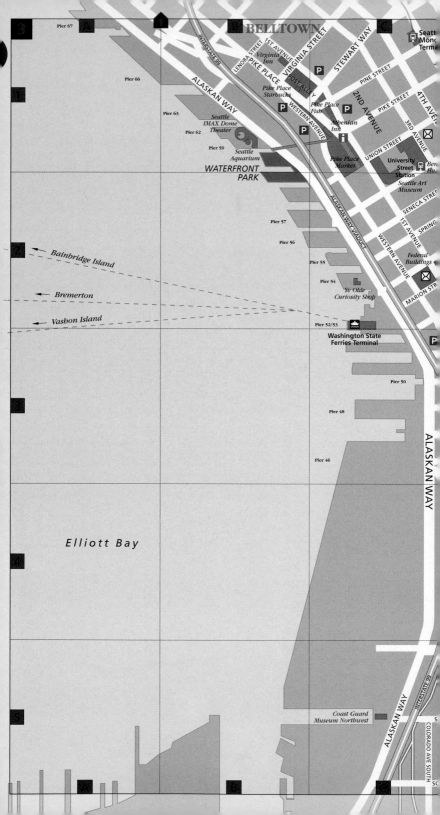

3 Pier 67 **A** **1** **B** **BELLTOWN** **C** Seat
Mono
Term

Pier 66

INTERSTATE 99

LENORA STREET

1ST AVENUE

PIKE PLACE

VIRGINIA STREET

STEWART WAY

PINE STREET

1 Pier 63

Virginia
Inn

POST ALLEY

P

PIKE STREET

2ND AVENUE

4TH AVE

Pier 62 Pike Place
Starbucks

WESTERN AVENUE

Pike Place
Fish P

3RD AVENUE

Seattle
IMAX Dome
Theater

ALASKAN WAY

P

Athenian
Inn

UNION STREET

X

Pier 59 Seattle
Aquarium

i

University
Street
Station Ben
Ha

**WATERFRONT
PARK**

Pike Place
Market

Seattle Art
Museum

SENECA STREE

2 ← Bainbridge Island

Pier 57

ALASKAN WAY VIADUCT

1ST AVENUE

SPRING

Pier 56

WESTERN AVENUE

Federal
Buildings

X

← Bremerton

Pier 55

MARION STR

Pier 54

Ye Olde
Curiosity Shop

← Vashon Island

Pier 52/53

**Washington State
Ferries Terminal**

P

3 Pier 50

Pier 48

Pier 46

ALASKAN WAY

Elliott Bay

4

5 *Coast Guard
Museum Northwest*

ALASKAN WAY

INTERSTATE 99

S

COLORADO AVE SOUTH

SO

A **B** **C**

WASHINGTON

Named for the first president of the US, Washington was the 42nd state to enter the Union, in 1889. Washington is located in the far northwestern corner of the country, sharing a border with Canada. Within its 68,139 sq miles (176,466 sq km) of land lies an extraordinary geographical diversity; each of the state's three distinct regions has its own geology, personality, and climate.

The coastal region – bordered by the Pacific Ocean to the west, the Strait of Juan de Fuca to the north, Oregon to the south, and Puget Sound to the east – is dominated by the beautiful Olympic National Park and other great tracts of forest. Highlights include the charming Victorian seaport of Port Townsend, the spectacular views from the top of Hurricane Ridge, the expansive Crescent Lake, the towering moss-draped trees of the Hoh Rainforest, and miles of scenic coastline, which receive the highest amounts of rainfall in the state.

Western Washington contains the state's most populous areas, which lie in the corridor along Interstate-5, especially between Tacoma and Seattle. In the far northwest, scattered off the coast, are the San Juan Islands, with 247 days of sunshine a year.

The Cascade mountain range, which runs between western and eastern Washington, provides wonderful opportunities for skiing, hiking, and numerous other outdoor activities. Mount Rainier, the highest peak in the range, is Washington's most-visited attraction.

The dry, sunny eastern region, stretching from the Cascades to the Idaho border, contrasts with the dense, damp greenness of western Washington. Both the fertile Yakima Valley, the fifth largest producer of fruits and vegetables in the US, and the Walla Walla Valley are known for their many excellent wineries. Farther north, the magnificent Grand Coulee Dam harnesses the power of the mighty Columbia River to provide irrigation water for more than half a million acres (202,000 ha) of farmland.

Sea kayaks at Snug Harbor in Mitchell Bay, on the west side of San Juan Island

◁ Snow trekkers on the trail from Paradise to Camp Muir, Mount Rainier

Exploring Washington

Washington's many attractions are sprinkled
liberally throughout the state, which consists of
three distinct regions: coastal, western, and eastern.
The Olympic Peninsula, in the coastal region, provides
visitors with a choice of ocean, lake, forest, or mountain
playgrounds. Western Washington's favorite islands,
among them Bainbridge, Whidbey, and the San Juans,
all offer charming towns, miles of terrain for cycling,
and the opportunity to slip into "island time" for a day
or two. A drive to the eastern region – at its best in
late spring to mid-fall – leads to the western-themed
Winthrop and the breathtaking peaks of North
Cascades National Park.

**Sailboats moored at Point Hudson
marina, Port Townsend**

SIGHTS AT A GLANCE

SEE ALSO

**The dramatic metal cone of
Tacoma's Museum of Glass**

KEY

━━ Highway
━━ Major road
═══ Minor road
━━ Scenic route
━━ Main railroad
▬▬ International border
━━ Regional border
▲ Summit
╳ White Pass

Mount Rainier, as seen from Mount Rainier National Park

Oroville
Northport
Orient
Metaline Falls
ORTH CASCADES ATIONAL PARK
31
Tiffany Mountain △ 2512m
Tonasket
395
Republic
Colville
20
Mt Loganん 2770m
Mazama
97
20
19 WINTHROP
Franklin D. Roosevelt Lake
Chewelah
17 STEHEKIN
20
153
Hunters
Newport
acier Peak 13m
Lake Chelan
Columbia
155
395
Deer Park
Pateros
21
25
Manson
20 GRAND COULEE DAM
Wilbur
Spokane
21 SPOKANE
2 16 LAKE CHELAN
2
Davenport
Entiat
Coulee City
90
Cheney
15 LEAVENWORTH
21
Odessa
28
195
Tekoa
Roslyn
28
Ephrata
Sprague
90 97
Quincy
Ritzville
23
Ellensburg
90
Moses Lake
Columbia Basin
Colfax
Vantage
17
395
Pullman
12
82
Othello
26
Yakima
24
Connell
YAKIMA VALLEY 22
Eltopia
12
Sunnyside
Dayton
Clarkston
Toppenish
Richland
Pasco
124
97
Prosser
Kennewick
24 23 WALLA WALLA
GOLDENDALE OBSERVATORY STATE PARK
82
WALLA WALLA VALLEY WINE TOUR
25
Paterson
26 MARYHILL
14
Columbia

GETTING AROUND

Bellingham, Seattle, Tacoma, and Olympia are all accessed by I-5, the state's main north–south interstate. I-90, the major east–west artery, leads from Seattle to Spokane. Five mountain passes and the Columbia Gorge link western and eastern Washington. US Hwy 2 crosses Stevens Pass to Leavenworth. State Hwy 20 (North Cascades Hwy), usually closed in winter, passes through Winthrop. Amtrak offers a rail service, and Greyhound, a bus service, to most of Washington's major cities. Washington State Ferries sail to destinations including around Puget Sound and the San Juan Islands.

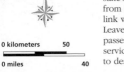

0 kilometers   50
0 miles   40

Olympic Peninsula Tour ❶

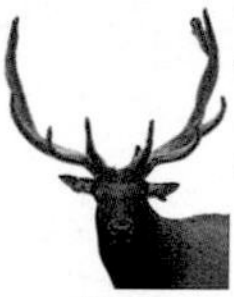

The shy Roosevelt elk

The Olympic Peninsula, in the far northwestern corner of Washington, offers many opportunities for spectacular sightseeing. The centerpiece of the peninsula is Olympic National Park, a UNESCO biosphere reserve and World Heritage Site. Encompassing 923,000 acres (373,540 ha), the park contains mountains with snowcapped peaks, as well as lakes, waterfalls, rivers, and rainforests. Opportunities for outdoor activities abound in the peninsula; among the most popular pursuits are deep-sea- and fly-fishing, kayaking, white-water rafting, mountain biking, and bird-watching.

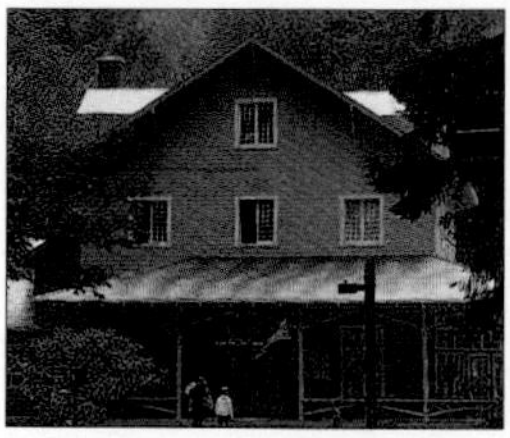

Lake Crescent ⑤
Lake Crescent Lodge is an historic resort on the shores of Lake Crescent. The lake's crystal-clear fresh water, which reaches a depth of 625 ft (190 m), makes it a favorite location for divers.

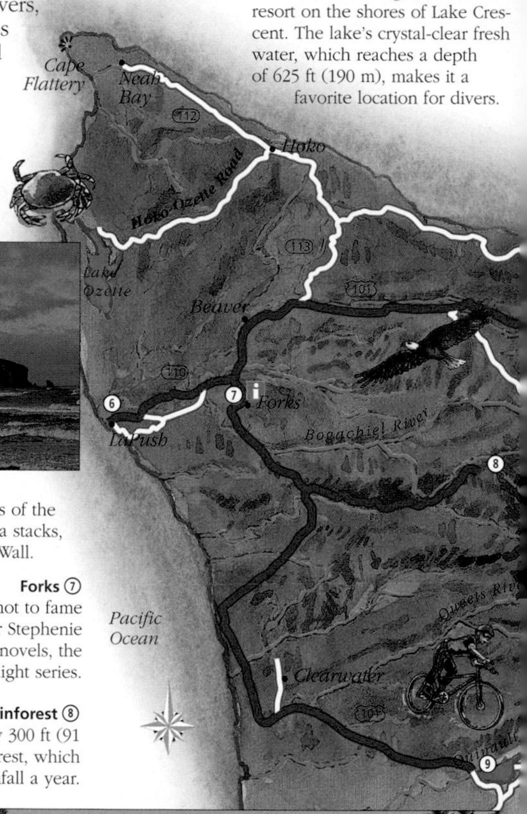

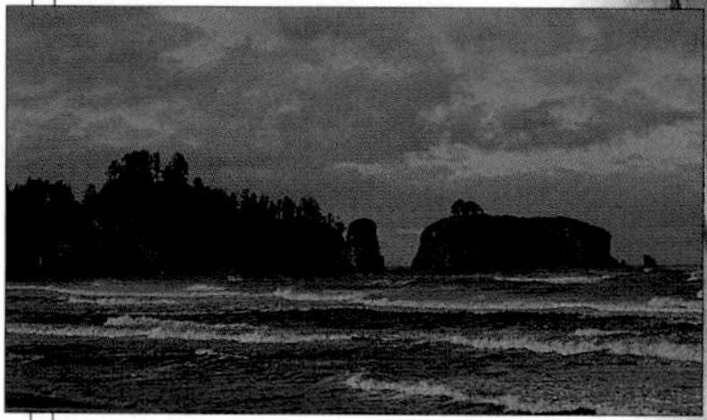

Rialto Beach ⑥
This long beach offers terrific views of the Pacific coast, with its tide pools, sea stacks, rocky islands, and the Hole in the Wall.

Forks ⑦
This former logging town shot to fame in 2005 as the setting for Stephenie Meyer's bestselling vampire novels, the Twilight series.

Hoh Rainforest ⑧
Ancient trees tower to nearly 300 ft (91 m) in this old-growth forest, which receives 14 ft (4 m) of rainfall a year.

0 kilometers 20

0 miles 15

KEY

- Tour route
- Other road
- Information
- Airport
- Ferry
- Viewpoint

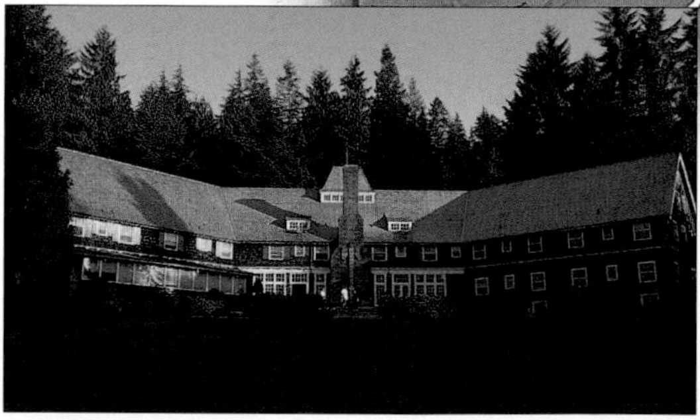

Lake Quinault ⑨
Snow-capped mountains encircle this lake and Lake Quinault Lodge.

Hurricane Ridge ④
The ridge's summit, at 5,230 ft (1,594 m), is covered with flowers in spring and offers panoramic views. Skiing and snowshoeing are popular winter activities here.

Sequim ③
Sitting in the rain shadow of the Olympic Mountains, Sequim features an elk viewing site and the Olympic Game Farm, home to endangered wild animals.

TIPS FOR DRIVERS

Tour length: *272 miles (438 km) including all detours off Hwy 101.*
Starting point: *Port Gamble on Hwy 104. Here, cross the Hood Canal Bridge to begin the tour.*
Stopping-off points: *As well as the numerous public campsites and lodges situated in or near Olympic National Park (see p289), a wide variety of restaurants and accommodations is to be found throughout this popular area.*

Port Gamble ①
Located on the Kitsap Peninsula, this former logging town has retained its original New England Victorian–style homes, country store, and church. The 1982 movie *An Officer and a Gentleman* was filmed here.

Port Townsend ②
This seaport, a National Historic Landmark, is known for its Victorian architecture and vibrant arts community *(see pp176–7)*. The town is also an excellent base from which to make kayaking, whale-watching, and cycling day trips.

Mount Olympus ⑩
With its West Peak rising 7,965 ft (2,428 m), this three-peaked, glacier-clad mountain is the highest in Washington's Olympic range.

Port Townsend ❷

**Shop sign,
Port Townsend**

Port Townsend was founded in 1851, almost 60 years after Captain Vancouver first saw its harbor and named it for his friend, the Marquis of Townshend. By the late 19th century, it was a bustling maritime community, with more ships in its port than in any other city in the US with the exception of New York. Convinced that Port Townsend would be the end point for a transcontinental railroad, residents went on a building spree, erecting lavish mansions and grand buildings in anticipation of its becoming the "New York of the West." That dream never materialized, but most of the original structures from that era have survived. The city today enjoys a booming tourism business, thanks to its Victorian buildings. Port Townsend is one of only three seaports on the National Registry as a historic landmark.

**Ann Starrett Mansion, with its
unusual eight-sided domed tower**

Exploring Port Townsend

Port Townsend is easily explored on foot. Water Street, the Downtown Historic District's main boulevard, is lined with brick-and-stone buildings housing art galleries, upscale shops, and restaurants. Many of the city's Victorian homes, churches, and inns are in the Uptown Historic District, between Clay and Lincoln Streets. The center of the uptown business district is Lawrence and Tyler Streets. Maps and information about tours are available at the visitors' center.

🏛 Jefferson County Courthouse

1820 Jefferson St. **Tel** (360) 385-9100. ◯ 9am–5pm Mon–Fri. ◐ public hols. ♿
The jewel of Port Townsend's Victorian architecture, this neo-Romanesque building was designed in 1892 by Seattle architect Willis A. Ritchie, who ordered its bricks be hauled west from St. Louis, rather than using the soft, local ones. The building's 124-ft- (38-m-) tall clock tower, its clockwork also dating to 1892, has long been a landmark for sailors.

**Jefferson County
Courthouse tower**

🏛 Jefferson County Historical Society

540 Water St. **Tel** (360) 385-1003. ◯ 11am–4pm daily. ◐ Jan 1, Thanksgiving, Dec 25. 🎟 ♿ 📷
www.jchsmuseum.org
Occupying the old City Hall (1891), this building once housed the town's fire station, jail, court room, and city offices. Today it is home to the city council, as well as an excellent museum that showcases the county's heritage through artifacts, archives, and photographs. Highlights of the exhibits include a display on the area's Native peoples. The Then and Now exhibit features interactive scenes from local history.

🏠 Ann Starrett Mansion

744 Clay St. **Tel** (800) 321-0644. ◯ to hotel guests only. www.starrettmansion.com
Built in 1889 by wealthy contractor George Starrett as a wedding gift for his bride, Ann, this grand Queen Anne-style mansion has received national recognition for its architecture, frescoed ceilings, and three-tiered spiral staircase topped by a domed ceiling. A National Historic Landmark, it now serves as a hotel.

🏠 Rothschild House

Franklin & Taylor Sts. **Tel** (360) 379-8076. ◯ May–Sep: 11am–4pm daily. ◑ Oct–Apr. 🎟
A departure from Port Townsend's more elaborate homes, this estate reflects the simplicity of the New England-style design that predated Victorian architecture. Built in 1868 for David C.H. Rothschild, it was donated by the sole remaining family member to the Washington State Parks and Recreation Commission in 1959.
Restored and listed on the National Register of Historic Places, the house contains original furnishings.

⛪ St. Paul's Episcopal Church

1020 Jefferson St. **Tel** (360) 385-0770. ◯ 9am–noon Mon–Thu. ✝ 8am & 10am Sun. ♿ www.stpaulspt.org
The oldest surviving church in Port Townsend – and the oldest Episcopal church in continuous use in

Union Wharf, jutting out from Port Townsend's waterfront

Washington – the Gothic Revival-style St. Paul's was built in 1865. Originally located below the bluff, the church was placed on logs and rolled to its present location in 1883 with the help of horses and a windlass.

🏛 Fire Bell Tower

Tyler & Jefferson Sts.

Located on the bluff overlooking downtown, the 1890 fire bell tower was once used to summon the town's volunteer fire fighters. The number of rings indicated which part of town the fire was in. The tower is placed first on Washington, DC's list of Ten Most Endangered Historic Treasures.

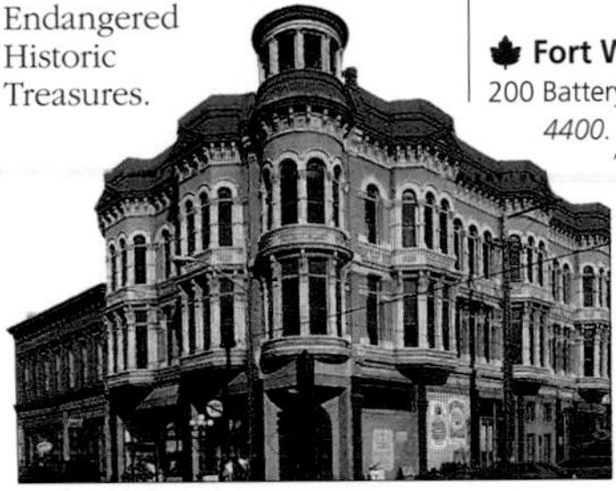

The prominent 1889 Hastings Building, today housing offices and upmarket shops

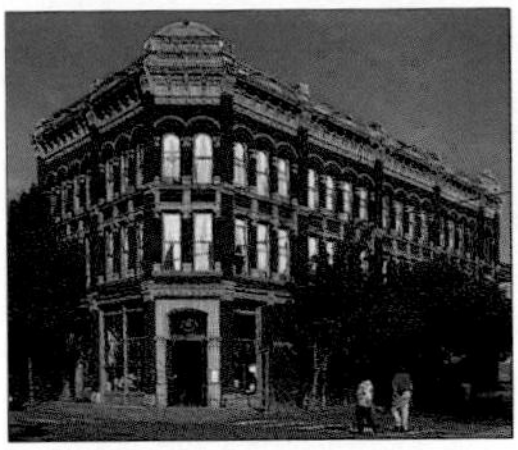

Water Street's N.D. Hill Building, used as a hotel since 1889

🏛 Haller Fountain

Taylor & Washington Sts.

Donated to the city in 1906 by city resident Theodore Haller, the fountain's centerpiece, a bronze maiden, made her debut in the Mexican exhibit at the 1893 World's Columbian Exposition in Chicago.

🍁 Fort Worden State Park

200 Battery Way. ***Tel*** *(360) 344-4400.* **www**.parks.usa.gov

This former military base is now a 440-acre (178-ha) state park. Visitors can explore the fort's bunkers and tour the **Commanding Officer's Quarters** (1904). A museum refurbished in late Victorian style, it offers a glimpse into the lives of the officers in the early 20th century. The **Puget Sound Coast Artillery Museum** is devoted to harbor-defense operations from the late 19th century through World War II.

VISITORS' CHECKLIST

Road map 1 A2. 👥 *8,900.* ⛴ *from Keystone on Whidbey Island.* ℹ *440 12th St, (360) 385-2722.* **www**.ptguide.com

🏛 Commanding Officer's Quarters

Tel *(360) 344-4452.* ○ *Mar, Apr & Oct: noon–4pm daily; May–Sep: 11am–5pm daily.* 📷 ♿

🏛 Puget Sound Coast Artillery Museum

Tel *(360) 385-0373.* ○ *11am–4pm daily.* ● *major hols.* 📷 ♿

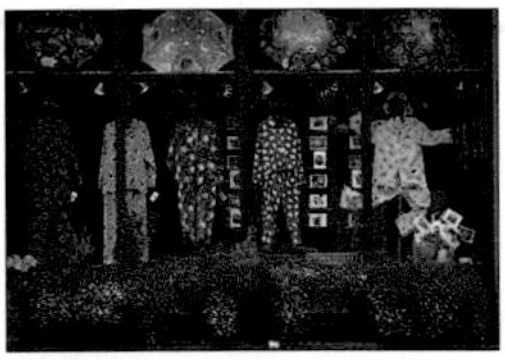

Store window display on Port Townsend's historic Water Street

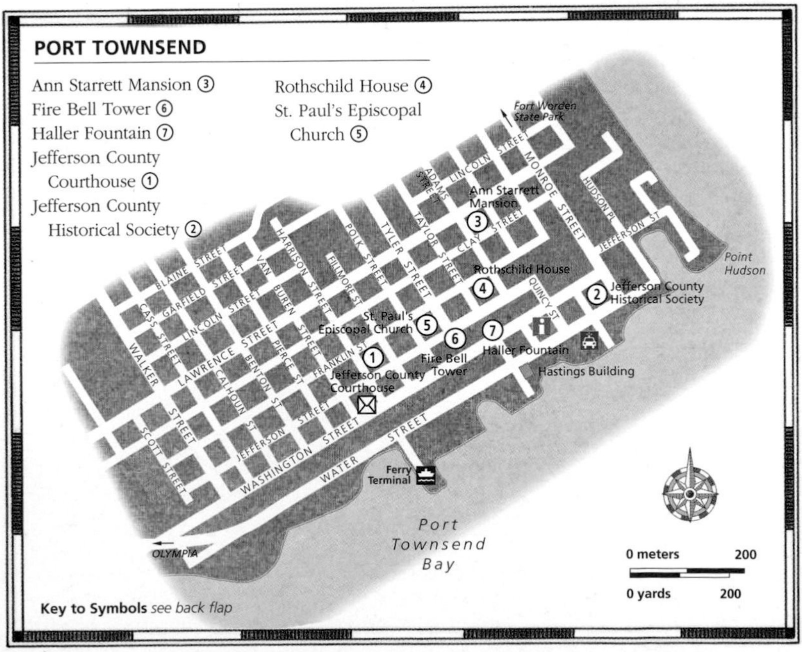
PORT TOWNSEND
Ann Starrett Mansion ③
Fire Bell Tower ⑥
Haller Fountain ⑦
Jefferson County Courthouse ①
Jefferson County Historical Society ②
Rothschild House ④
St. Paul's Episcopal Church ⑤
Fort Worden State Park
Point Hudson
Port Townsend Bay
Ferry Terminal
Hastings Building
OLYMPIA
LINCOLN STREET
MONROE STREET
HUDSON PL
JEFFERSON ST
ADAMS STREET
CLAY STREET
TAYLOR STREET
TYLER STREET
POLK STREET
FILLMORE ST
HARRISON STREET
VAN BUREN
BLAINE STREET
GARFIELD STREET
CASS STREET
WALKER STREET
LAWRENCE STREET
CALHOUN ST
BENTON ST
PIERCE ST
FRANKLIN ST
QUINCY ST
SCOTT STREET
JEFFERSON STREET
WASHINGTON STREET
WATER STREET
0 meters 200
0 yards 200
Key to Symbols see back flap

San Juan Islands

A Washington state ferry sailing from the mainland to the islands

Scattered between the Washington mainland and Vancouver Island, the San Juan archipelago consists of over 450 islands, 172 of them named. Ferries sail from Anacortes to the four largest islands: Lopez, Shaw, Orcas, and San Juan. Lopez is affectionately called "Slopez" because of its laid-back nature. Gently rolling roads, numerous stopping points, and friendly drivers make it a popular destination for cycling. Horseshoe-shaped Orcas, the hilliest island in the chain, offers breathtaking views from atop 2,409-ft (734-m) Mount Constitution. The best destination for walk-on passengers, San Juan Island is home to Friday Harbor, the largest town in the archipelago. The nationally renowned Whale Museum is located here. Primarily residential, Shaw Island does not offer visitor facilities.

Sailboats in the Channel
Sailors love the many harbors and good winds in the San Juan Channel.

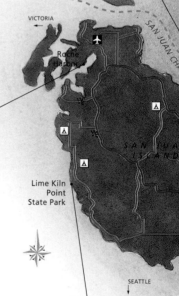
VICTORIA
Roche Harbor
SAN JUAN CHA
SAN JUAN ISLAND
Lime Kiln Point State Park
SEATTLE

★ Roche Harbor
A charming seaside village, Roche Harbor features a marina, Victorian gardens, a chapel, and the historic Hotel de Haro, built in 1886.

0 kilometers   2
0 miles   1

STAR SIGHTS

★ Deer Harbor

★ Friday Harbor

★ Lopez

★ Roche Harbor

Lime Kiln Point State Park
This state park, with its picturesque lighthouse, completed in 1919, is the only park in the US dedicated to whale-watching.

For hotels and restaurants in this region see pp288–90 and pp306–8

★ Deer Harbor
Sea kayakers flock to Deer Harbor and the other waters surrounding the islands of Orcas, Lopez, and San Juan.

VISITORS' CHECKLIST

Road map 1 A1. 🚢 Washington State Ferries from Anacortes or Sidney, BC, to the San Juan Islands. **Tel** (206) 464-6400.
www.wsdot.wa.gov
ℹ️ (888) 468-3701.
www.visitsanjuans.com

★ Lopez
Despite its gently rolling hills, Lopez is the flattest of the San Juan Islands, making it a popular destination for recreational cyclists.

★ Friday Harbor
The largest town in the San Juans, Friday Harbor offers a number of restaurants, inns, galleries, and shops – all within easy walking distance of the ferry dock.

KEY

▬	Major road
▬	Minor road
--	Ferry route
Ⓐ	Camping
☆	Viewpoint
✈	Airport
ℹ	Information

Bellingham ❹

Road map 1 A1. ✈ *Bellingham Airport.* 👥 *81,000.* ℹ *(800) 487-2032.* **www**.bellingham.org

Overlooking Bellingham Bay and many of the San Juan Islands, Bellingham has been inhabited by the Lummi Indians for thousands of years. The area – consisting of the four original towns of Whatcom, Sehome, Bellingham, and Fairhaven – was settled in 1853 and consolidated in 1904. The town's historic architecture includes Old Whatcom County Courthouse (1308 East Street), the first brick building north of San Francisco, built in 1858, and the majestic City Hall, built in 1892 in the Victorian Second Empire style. The latter is now the heart of the **Whatcom Museum of History and Art**, a four-building campus that includes a children's museum. Highlights of the museum include exhibits on the Northwest Coast First Nations and on the birds of the Pacific Northwest.

South of downtown, the historic Fairhaven district is an artsy enclave of Victorian buildings housing galleries, restaurants, bookstores, and coffeehouses.

Just up the hill from downtown Bellingham sits the campus of **Western Washington University**, with a famous collection of outdoor sculptures, including artworks by internationally recognized

Boats journeying along the Skagit River in La Conner

American artists Richard Serra, Mark di Suvero, and Richard Beyer.

🏛 **Whatcom Museum of History and Art**
121 Prospect St. **Tel** *(360) 778-8930.*
⏷ *noon–5pm Tue–Sun.* ⬤ *major hols.* **Family Interactive Gallery**:
10am–5pm Tue–Sun. ✎ ⬤ ▢ ▢
www.whatcommuseum.org

🏛 **Western Washington University**
ℹ *S College Dr & College Way.*
Tel *(360) 650-3424.* **Visitors' center** ⏷ *mid-Jun–mid-Sep: 7am–5pm Mon–Fri; mid-Sep–mid-Jun: 7am–8pm Mon–Fri.* ⬤ *major hols.* ⬤ **www**.wwu.edu

Tower of Bellingham's former City Hall

Environs

South of Bellingham, Chuckanut Drive (Hwy 11) is a scenic 21-mile (34-km) loop with outlooks to Puget Sound and the San Juan Islands. Along the way are hiking and biking trails, restaurants, and oyster farms selling fresh oysters in season. Fifty-five miles (88.5 km) east of Bellingham is 10,778-ft- (3,285-m-) high Mount Baker, where the ski and snowboarding season runs from November through April.

La Conner ❺

Road map 1 A2. 👥 *890.* ⬤ ℹ *(888) 466-4778.* **www**.laconnerchamber.com

Long associated in the minds of Washingtonians with tulips, the town of La Conner draws thousands to the Skagit Valley Tulip Festival. And although the town's famous fields are abloom with spectacular color come springtime, there is more to La Conner than flowers. A magnet for artists since the 1940s, this tiny town is a thriving arts community. The highly respected **Museum of Northwest Art** showcases works by Mark Tobey, Guy Anderson, Morris Graves, and Kenneth Callahan (all of whom were inspired by the Skagit Valley's unique light), as well as Dale Chihuly and other prominent Pacific Northwest artists.

Listed on the National Register of Historic Places, La Conner was founded in the early 1860s. It was originally called Swinomish, after the area's first residents, the Swinomish Indians. In 1869, wealthy merchant John Conner renamed the town after his wife, Louisa Ann Siegfried, by combining her first two initials and her married name. Louisa Ann was the town's first non-Indian woman resident. For a glimpse into her life – and those of other early settlers – visit the **Skagit County Historical Museum**.

🏛 **Museum of Northwest Art**
121 S 1st St. **Tel** *(360) 466-4446.*
⏷ *noon–5pm Sun & Mon, 10am–5pm Tue–Sat.* ⬤ *major hols.* ✎ ⬤ ▢ **www**.museumofnwart.org

🏛 **Skagit County Historical Museum**
501 S 4th St. **Tel** *(360) 466-3365.*
⏷ *11am–5pm Tue–Sun.* ✎ ⬤ ▢

Crab traps on a boat ready to set out from Bellingham Harbor

For hotels and restaurants in this region see pp288–90 and pp306–8

Whidbey Island ⑥

Road map 1 A2. 🏔 *60,000*. 🚢
ℹ *107 S Main St, Coupeville,
(360) 678-5434.*

Whidbey Island boasts five
state parks and two charming
seaside villages. **Coupeville**'s
Victorian homes, old barns,
and quaint waterfront recall
the town's beginnings.
Nearby, the extensive Ebey's
Landing National Historical
Reserve includes the historic
army post, **Fort Casey State
Park**. At the island's south
end, the arts community of
Langley has historic buildings,
upscale shops, art galleries,
and bed-and-breakfasts.

🌺 **Fort Casey State Park**
1280 Engle Rd. *Tel (360) 678-4519*.
🕐 *8am–dusk*. **www**.parks.usa.gov

Bainbridge Island ⑦

Road map 1 A2. 🏔 *22,000*. 🚢
ℹ *395 Winslow Way E, (206) 842-
3700*. **www**.bainbridgechamber.com

A 35-minute ferry ride from
Seattle, this island makes for a
pleasant outing. Near the ferry
terminal, a path leads through
Waterfront Park to downtown
Winslow's galleries, shops, and
cafés. The island's charming
inns make it a popular stop
for travelers to the Kitsap and
Olympic Peninsulas. **Bloedel
Reserve**, with its Japanese
garden, English landscape, and
bird refuge, is worth a visit.

🌺 **Bloedel Reserve**
7571 NE Dolphin Dr. *Tel (206) 842-
7631*. 🕐 *10am–4pm Tue–Sun
(Jun–Aug: to 7pm); reservations
only*. 🌑 *Dec 25*. 📷 ♿

Isolated coastline in one of
Whidbey Island's state parks

Tillicum Village ⑧

Blake Island State Park. **Road map**
1 A2. *Tel (206) 622-8687*. 🕐 *two
trips per day: 11:30am–3:30pm,
4:30–8:30pm (schedule varies)*.
🌑 *Jan–Feb*. 🚢 *tours depart from
Pier 55, Seattle Central Waterfront*.
♿ 📷 🍴 **www**.tillicumvillage.com

Tillicum Village, located in
Blake Island State Park, offers
visitors a fascinating cultural
and culinary experience.
Guests are taken on a four-
hour tour of the village which
starts with a cruise from Pier
55 on Seattle's Waterfront.
Once at the village, visitors
can observe whole Chinook
salmon being prepared and
cooked around alder wood
fires, in the traditional style of
the Northwest Coast Indians.
A buffet-style meal is served,
followed by a performance
of the "Dance on the Wind"
stage show, a combination of
traditional songs, dances, and
stories about the Northwest
Coast Native culture. Also
held here are demonstrations

of the traditional carving
techniques and the creation
of local artwork.

Blake Island State Park is
named after Captain George
Blake, commander of the US
Coast Survey vessel in 1837.
The park is the ancestral campground of the Suquamish and
Duwamish Indian tribes and
boasts unspoilt scenery. The
475-acre (192-ha) island is an
excellent example of Pacific
Northwest lowland forest
and is home to numerous
native trees and shrubs as
well as deer, otter, squirrels,
mink, and many varieties
of bird. The island's large
number of walking trails and
a 5-mile (8-km) saltwater
beach make it an excellent
destination for hikers.

Tour group arriving in Tillicum
Village, Blake Island State Park

Chateau
Ste. Michelle ⑨

14111 NE 145th St, Woodinville.
Road map 1 A2. *Tel (425) 488-
1133*. 🕐 *10am–5pm daily*. 🌑 *Jan 1,
Easter, Thanksgiving, Dec 25*. ♿
🚢 *10:30am–4:30pm daily*. 📷
***Summer concerts, cooking
classes***. **www**.ste-michelle.com

Washington's oldest winery,
Chateau Ste. Michelle is
located on an 87-acre (35-ha)
wooded estate in Woodinville,
15 miles (24 km) northeast
of Seattle. This location
produces all Chateau Ste.
Michelle's white wines. (The
red wines are made in eastern
Washington, where grapes for
both the white and red wines
are grown.) Complimentary
cellar tours and wine tastings
are offered daily. The
winery's summer concert
series draws top blues, jazz,
classical, and contemporary
talents to its outdoor grass
amphitheater, where concert-
goers savor wine and picnics
while enjoying the music.

Chateau Ste. Michelle, founded in 1934, Washington's oldest winery

The magnificent cascades of
Snoqualmie Falls

Snoqualmie Falls ⑩

Road map 1 B2.

The most famous waterfall in
the state, Snoqualmie Falls is
Washington's second most
visited tourist attraction after
Mount Rainier. This 268-ft
(82-m) waterfall on the
Snoqualmie River draws one
and a half million visitors
each year. Long regarded as a
sacred site by the Snoqualmie
Indians and other local Native
American tribes, the cascade
also fascinated the naturalist
John Muir who, in 1889,
described it as the most
interesting he had ever seen.

An observation deck 300 ft
(91 m) above the river
provides an excellent view
of the thundering water. For
a closer look, visitors can
follow a steep half-mile (0.8
km) trail down to the river.

Tacoma ⑪

Road map 1 A2. 🏛 200,000.
✈ Seattle-Tacoma International
Airport. ℹ 1516 Pacific Ave, (253)
627-2836. **www**.traveltacoma.com

Washington's third largest city,
Tacoma was founded as a sawmill town in the 1860s. With
the arrival of the railroad in
the late 1880s it prospered,
becoming a major shipping
port for commodities important
to a growing nation: lumber,
coal, and grain. Many Pacific
Northwest's railroad, timber,
and shipping barons settled
in Tacoma's Stadium District.
This historic area, with its
stately turn-of-the-19th-century

mansions, is named for
Stadium High School, which
is also known as the "Castle."
Designed in the 1890s to be
a luxury hotel, the French
chateau-style building was
converted in the early 1900s
into a high school.

The undisputed star of the
city's revitalized waterfront is
the striking **Museum of Glass**.
Opened in July 2002, this landmark building was designed by
top Canadian architect Arthur
Erickson to showcase contemporary art, with a focus on
glass. The 75,000-sq-ft (6,968-
sq-m) museum includes a
spacious glass-blowing studio
housed within a dramatic 90-
ft (37-m) metal-encased cone.

The stunning Chihuly Bridge
of Glass, a collaboration between Austin, Texas architect
Arthur Andersson and world-
renowned Tacoma glass artist
Dale Chihuly, serves as a
pedestrian walkway linking
the museum to down-
town Tacoma and
the innovative
**Washington
State History
Museum**. Tales of
Washington's past
are related using
interactive exhibits,
high-tech displays,
and theatrical storytelling by
characters in period costume.

The spectacular home of
the **Tacoma Art Museum** was
designed by architect Antoine
Predock to be a dynamic cultural center and a showpiece
for the city. The 50,000-sq-ft
(4,645-sq-m), stainless-steel-
wrapped museum boldly
showcases the growing
collection of works from the
18th century to the present

Sign denoting the old
town of Tacoma

The imposing Stadium High School,
in Tacoma's Stadium District

day. These include a large
assembly of Pacific Northwest
art, European Impressionist
pieces, Japanese woodblock
prints, American graphic art,
and Chihuly glass. In keeping
with its vision of creating a
place that "builds commu-
nity through art," the
museum's facilities
include the Bill
and Melinda Gates
Resource Center,
providing visitors
with access to
a wide array
of reference
materials and state-of-the-art
research equipment. As well,
kids of all ages can make use
of the in-house, interactive
art-making studio, ArtWORKS.

Tacoma's most popular
attraction is Point Defiance
Park, ranked among the 20
largest urban parks in the
US. Encompassing 700 acres
(285 ha), its grounds include
Fort Nisqually, the first European settlement on Puget

The modern stainless steel exterior of the Tacoma Museum of Glass

For hotels and restaurants in this region see pp288–90 and pp306–8

E.T. the walrus, at Point Defiance Zoo and Aquarium, Tacoma

Sound and a major fur-trading establishment; seven specialty gardens; a scenic drive; hiking and biking trails; beaches; a boat marina; and a picnic area. Fishing is permitted, and gear is available for rental.

Highlighting a Pacific Rim theme, the world-class **Point Defiance Zoo and Aquarium** is home to over 9,000 animals. A vantage point at the west end of the park offers terrific views of Mount Rainier, Puget Sound, and the Tacoma Narrows Bridge, one of the longest suspension bridges in the United States.

🏛 **Museum of Glass**
1801 E Dock St. *Tel (253) 284-4750 or (866) 468-7386.* ⬜ *Memorial Day–Labor Day: 10am–5pm Mon–Sat, noon–5pm Sun; Labor Day–Memorial Day: 10am–5pm Wed–Sat, noon–5pm Sun.* ⬤ *Jan 1, Thanksgiving, Dec 25.* 🖼 ♿ 🎫
🖥 📷 www.museumofglass.org

🏛 **Washington State History Museum**
1911 Pacific Ave. *Tel (888) 238-4373.* ⬜ *Jun–Aug: 10am–5pm Mon–Sat, noon–5pm Sun; Sep–May: 10am–5pm Tue–Sat, noon–5pm Sun.* ⬤ *major hols.* 🖼 ♿ 🎫 *for groups.* www.wshs.org

🏛 **Tacoma Art Museum**
1701 Pacific Ave. *Tel (253) 272-4258.* ⬜ *Memorial Day–Labor Day: 10am–5pm Tue–Sat, noon–5pm Sun; Labor Day–Memorial Day: 10am–5pm Wed–Sat, noon–5pm Sun.* ⬤ *major hols.* 🖼 *(free 5–8pm 3rd Thu of month).* ♿ 🎫 🖥 📷
www.tacomaartmuseum.org

🦭 **Point Defiance Zoo and Aquarium**
5400 N Pearl St. *Tel (253) 591-5337.* ⬜ *9:30am–4pm daily (Apr–May & Sep: to 5pm; Jun–Aug: to 6pm). Hours can vary; check in advance.* ⬤ *3rd Fri in Jul, Nov–Feb: Tue & Wed, Thanksgiving, Dec 25.* 🖼 ♿ 🖥 📷 www.pdza.org

Environs

Just 11 miles (17 km) from Tacoma, across the Narrows on the Kitsap Peninsula, is the charming fishing village of **Gig Harbor**, named by Captain Charles Wilkes, who, from 1838 to 1842, charted the area from his gig. The community's boutiques, galleries, and waterfront restaurants reflect the proud Scandinavian and Croatian heritage of many of its 6,500 inhabitants.

The bastion at Fort Nisqually historic site in Point Defiance Park

Olympia ⓬

Road map 1 A2. 🏠 *43,000.*
🛈 *809 Legion Way SE, (360) 357-3362.* www.thurstonchamber.com

Washington's state capital since 1853, Olympia was named for its magnificent view of the Olympic Mountains. Located 60 miles (97 km) south of Seattle at the southern tip of Puget Sound, the city is known first and foremost for its lovely **State Capitol Campus**, dominated by the 28-story domed Legislative Building. With its stunning buildings, landscaped grounds (designed in 1928 by the Olmsted Brothers and known for their spectacular bulb and annual plantings),

fountains, and monuments, this capital campus is one of the most beautiful in the nation. The centerpiece is the **Legislative Building** (the Capitol). Its 287-ft (87-m) brick-and-sandstone dome is one of the tallest masonry domes in the world.

The **State Archives** stores Washington's historical records and artifacts. Visitors can view such treasures as documents from the Canwell Committee, which blacklisted suspected Communists in the 1950s.

Tree-lined streets, old homes, a picturesque waterfront, and a thriving cultural community all contribute to Olympia's charm. Tucked among downtown Olympia's historic buildings are restaurants, galleries, and shops. Within walking distance are attractions such as the lively **Olympia Farmers Market**, offering local produce, seafood, baked goods, and crafts, along with dining and entertainment.

Percival Landing (4th Avenue between Sylvester and Water Streets), a 1.5-mile (2.5-km) boardwalk along Budd Inlet, offers views of the Olympic Mountains, Capitol Dome, and Puget Sound.

State Capitol Campus
🛈 *416 Sid Snyder Ave SW, (360) 902-8881.* ⬤ *Jan 1, Thanksgiving, Dec 25.* **Legislative Bldg** ⬜ *7am–5pm Mon–Fri, 11am–4pm Sat & Sun.* ⬤ *Jan 1, Thanksgiving, Dec 25.* 🎫 *hourly 10am–2pm.* **Temple of Justice:** *8am–5pm Mon–Fri.* ♿

🏛 **State Capital Museum**
211 21st Ave SW. *Tel (360) 753-2580.* ⬜ *10am–4pm Sat (by appt).* ⬤ *major hols.* 🖼 ♿

🏛 **State Archives**
1129 Washington St SE. *Tel (360) 586-1492.* ⬜ *8:30am–4:30pm Mon–Fri.* ♿ www.sos.wa.gov

🛒 **Olympia Farmers Market**
700 N Capitol Way. *Tel (360) 352-9096.* ⬜ *Apr–Oct: 10am–3pm Thu–Sun; Nov–Dec: 10am–3pm Sat & Sun.* ♿

The imposing Legislative Building on the State Capitol Campus, Olympia

Mount Rainier National Park ⓫

Jeep with outdoor equipment

Established in 1899, Mount Rainier National Park encompasses 337 sq miles (872 sq km), of which 97 percent is designated Wilderness. Its centerpiece is Mount Rainier, an active volcano towering 14,410 ft (4,392 m) above sea level. Surrounded by old-growth forest and wildflower meadows, Mount Rainier was named in 1792 by Captain George Vancouver for fellow British naval officer Peter Rainier. Designated a National Historic Landmark District in 1997, the park, which features 1920s and 1930s National Park Service rustic architecture, attracts two million visitors a year. The summer draws hikers, mountain climbers, and campers; the winter lures snowshoers and cross-country skiers.

Mount Rainier Nisqually Glacier
Close to the Paradise entrance, the Nisqually Glacier is one of the most visible on Mount Rainier. It is currently retreating.

Mount Rainier Narada Falls
One of the more spectacular and easily accessible cascades along the Paradise River, Narada Falls is just a short, steep hike from the Nisqually road. The falls plummet 168 ft (51 m).

National Park Inn
This small and cozy inn, located in Longmire and open year-round, is a perfect spot from which to enjoy the stunning view of Mount Rainier.

STAR SIGHTS

★ Emmons Glacier

★ Paradise

★ Sunrise

★ **Emmons Glacier**
*Emmons Glacier, on Mount Rainier's
eastern slope, is, at 4.3 sq miles (11.1 sq km),
the largest glacier in the lower 48 states.*

★ **Sunrise**
*Open only during the
summer, Sunrise is, at
6,400 ft (1,950 m), the
highest point to which
you can drive in the park.*

★ **Paradise**
*Paradise, the park's
most popular destination,
is open year-round and
has an excellent visitors'
information center.*

KEY

▬	Minor road
▬	Dirt or four-wheel-drive road
▪ ▪	Hiking trail
Ⓐ	Camping
🏞	Picnic area
ⓘ	Information
🔆	Viewpoint
🍴	Restaurant

GETTING AROUND

From the southwest (Hwy 706), enter the park via Nisqually
gate. Open year-round, this is the only entrance in winter.
Drive 6 miles (10 km) to Longmire, where facilities include an
inn and museum, and the Wilderness Information Center, open
from late May to October. The 12-mile (19-km) road between
Paradise and Longmire is steep and winding; drive carefully.
Carry chains when traveling by car during winter. The National
Park Service (tel: (360) 569-2211) offers a free weekend shuttle
to Paradise from Ashford or Longmire (Jun–Sep).

Downhill skiing on the sparkling snow-covered slopes of Washington's Crystal Mountain

Crystal Mountain ⓮

Road map 1 B2. **Tel** (360) 663-2265. ⬭ hrs vary depending on facility & season; call for details. 🔟 ▢ 🔳 See **Where to Stay** p288. www.crystalmountainresort.com

Located near the northeast corner of Mount Rainier National Park and rising above the town of the same name, Crystal Mountain is Washington's largest and only destination ski area.

Attracted by reports of local gold finds in the late 1800s, the first visitors to the area were miners intent on making their fortunes. However, by the end of World War I, these claims had not yielded the riches envisioned, and investment in this area then known as the Summit Mining District severely declined.

Its recreational attributes were discovered in 1949 when attempts to put a chair lift on Mount Rainier failed, and a group of avid Puget Sound skiers began looking for another spot to develop as a ski area. Crystal Mountain opened for business in 1962, receiving national attention three years later when it hosted the National Alpine Championships, an event that attracted skiing legends such as Jimmie Heuga, Billy Kidd, and Jean-Claude Killy.

The ski area, with over 50 named runs, encompasses 2,300 lift-serviced acres (930 ha) and another 300 acres

(121 ha) of backcountry terrain. Eleven lifts, including two high-speed, six-passenger chairs, transport more than 19,000 skiers per hour. There is also an extensive network of trails for cross-country skiers.

During summer, mountain biking, hiking, and chair-lift sightseeing are Crystal Mountain's main attractions. On weekends, high-speed lifts whisk passengers to the 6,872-ft (2,095-m) summit and its panoramic views of the Olympic and Cascade Mountains, with Mount Rainier dominating the western horizon. Herds of elk and black-tailed deer grazing the grassy slopes are often spotted from the lifts.

Snowboarding in the stunning backcountry at Crystal Mountain

Leavenworth ⓯

Road map 1 B2. 🚶 2,000. 🚌 940 Highway 2, (509) 548-5807. 🌐 www.leavenworth.org

Crossing over the Cascade Mountains from the western part of the state, first-time visitors to Leavenworth never fail to be surprised to encounter an enchanting Bavarian-style village seemingly straight out of a fairy tale. But this small town was not always so charming. In the early 1960s it was a dying logging town, with plenty of drive-through traffic but no real business to sustain it. Inspired by Leavenworth's spectacular mountain backdrop, a tourism committee decided to develop a Bavarian village theme to revitalize the town. Buildings were remodeled to echo Bavarian architecture and, today, every commercial building in town, Starbucks and McDonald's included, looks as though it belongs in the Alps.

Leavenworth now bustles with festivals, art shows, and summer theater productions, attracting more than a million visitors each year. Among its most popular festivals are Maifest, with its 16th-century costumes, maypole dances, Tyrolean Haflinger horses, and

Shop sign in the Bavarian-themed village of Leavenworth

jousting; the Leavenworth International Accordion Celebration, in June, with competitions and concerts; Oktoberfest, the traditional celebration of German beer, food, and music; and Christ-kindlmarkt, an open-air Christmas market. In addition to its many shops and restaurants featuring Bavarian specialties, the **Leavenworth Nutcracker Museum** showcases 6,000 nutcrackers from 38 countries, some dating back 1,800 years.

🏛 **Leavenworth Nutcracker Museum**
735 Front St. *Tel (509) 548-4573.*
🕐 *May–Oct: 2–5pm daily;*
Nov–Apr: 2–5pm Sat & Sun.
📷 🎫 *for groups by appt.* ♿
www.nutcrackermuseum.com

Leavenworth's traditional horse-drawn 13-barrel beer wagon

Lake Chelan 🔟

Road map 1 B2. 🎿 *3,500.*
🛈 *102 E Johnson Ave, (509) 682-3503.* www.lakechelan.com

Chelan, a resort town on the southeast end of Lake Chelan, has been a popular summer vacation destination for generations of western Washingtonians seeking the sunny, dry weather on the eastern side of the state. Basking in the rain shadow of the Cascade Mountains, the town

Cyclists stopping for a refreshment at the Alley Cafe in Leavenworth

enjoys 300 days of sunshine each year.

Its namesake claims the distinction of being the third deepest lake in the country, reaching 1,500 ft (457 m) at its deepest point. Fed by 27 glaciers and 59 streams, the lake, which is less than 2 miles (3 km) wide, stretches for 55 miles (89 km). In the summer, it buzzes with activity: water-skiing, boating, snorkeling, fishing, and wind surfing.

Strolling through the town, visitors can admire the vintage **Ruby Theatre** (135 East Woodin Avenue). Listed on the National Register of Historic Places, it is one of the oldest continuously running movie theaters in the Northwest US. The 15 murals painted on area buildings are another highlight of the town. Depicting the agricultural, recreational, cultural, and ecological history of the Lake Chelan Valley, all contain an image – obvious in some murals,

Sign welcoming visitors to Lake Chelan

obscure in others – of an apple, a crop that thrives in the area's soil, fertile thanks to the glaciers that melted here thousands of years ago.

Environs
Manson, 9 miles (14 km) along the north shore from downtown Chelan, is a charming town. Along with shops, restaurants, and recreational activities, the town boasts the Scenic Loop Trail, offering easy exploration of the nearby orchards and hilly countryside. Many businesses offer free route maps.

Stehekin 🔟

Road map 1 B2. 🎿 *70.* 🛈 *Golden West Visitor Center, by the Ferry Building, (360) 854-7365.* www.stehekinvalley.com

At the northernmost tip of Lake Chelan, nestled at the base of the North Cascade Mountains, rustic Stehekin invites travelers to slow down and savor life without the distractions of televisions or telephones. You won't find one single automated bank machine in this tiny community, but you will discover some of the most beautiful scenery in the state – accessible only by foot, horseback, plane, or boat.

Since the early 20th century, the Lady of the Lake boat service has ferried passengers from Chelan to Stehekin. This ride takes 4 hours; faster options include the *Lady Express* (just over 2 hours) and the high-speed *Lady Cat*, which zips to Stehekin in an hour.

Bird-watching, biking, hiking, horseback riding, fishing, and rafting the Stehekin River are all popular summer activities in the Stehekin Valley; cross-country skiing and snowshoeing are popular in winter.

Rainbow Falls, a 312-ft (95-m) waterfall near Stehekin Landing, is worth a visit (call 509/682-4494 for tour details).

View of glacier-fed Lake Chelan, in its arid setting

North Cascades National Park Tour ⑱

The North Cascades National Park is a breathtakingly beautiful ecosystem of jagged snowcapped peaks, forested valleys, and cascading waterfalls. Its many wonders can be accessed from the scenic North Cascades Highway, which bisects the park. With more than 300 glaciers, the 684,300-acre (276,935-ha) park is the most heavily glaciated region in the lower 48 states. It is home to a variety of animals, including bald eagles, beavers, gray wolves, and black and grizzly bears. The park and the adjacent Ross Lake and Lake Chelan National Recreation Areas attract over 400,000 visitors each year. The North Cascades Highway and the Lake Chelan National Recreation Area are linked by hiking trails to the quiet town of Stehekin on Lake Chelan, which is serviced by a ferry from Chelan *(see p187)*.

Mount Shuksan ④
One of the state's highest mountains at 9,131 ft (2,783 m) and a dominant feature of the park, Mount Shuksan consists of a form of basalt known as Shuksan greenschist.

Gorge Creek Falls ③
Plunging 242 ft (74 m) into Gorge Lake, the Gorge Creek Falls are visible from an overlook just off the North Cascades Highway. A fully accessible, paved trail leads to the overlook.

North Cascades Visitor Center ②
Commanding an impressive view of the Picket Range, the visitor center, near Newhalem, offers interpretive displays, multimedia presentations, and daily ranger-guided programs in summer.

Skagit River ①
The second longest river in Washington, the Skagit is popular for steelhead and salmon fishing. The river has been dammed in three locations in the park, creating lakes and providing hydroelectric power for the state.

KEY

■	Tour route
=	Other road
••	Trail
❖	Viewpoint
ℹ	Information

TIPS FOR DRIVERS

Tour length: *56 miles (90 km).*
Starting point: *State Route 20 (North Cascades Highway) at the entrance to Ross Lake National Recreation Area, approximately 5 miles (8 km) north of Marblemount.*
When to go: *Mid-Apr–mid-Oct, when all of Route 20 is open.*
Stopping-off points: *There are restaurants in Marblemount and Winthrop but in the park itself there are only picnic facilities. It is a good idea to bring along your own provisions. You can stock up on groceries and buy hot soup and coffee at the Skagit General Store in Newhalem.*

Diablo Lake ⑤
Diablo Lake owes its rich turquoise color to sediment from glacier-fed streams. Boat tours of Diablo Lake are offered Thursday to Monday in July and August; Saturday and Sunday in June and September.

ROSS LAKE NATIONAL RECREATION AREA
6
North Cascades Highway
Ruby Creek
Rainy Pass
7
McAlester Trail
Rainbow Creek Trail
LAKE CHELAN NATIONAL RECREATION AREA
Glory
8
Stehekin
Lake Chelan
0 kilometers 15
0 miles 10

Ross Lake Overlook ⑥
At this lookout, dramatic vistas of 24-mile- (40-km-) long Ross Lake, created by the damming of Skagit River, come into view.

Washington Pass Overlook ⑦
This overlook, 5,477 ft (1,669 m) above ground level, offers heart-pounding views of the steep pass up Liberty Bell Mountain.

Rainbow Falls ⑧
Accessible on foot after a 20-mile (32-km) hike from Rainy Pass or a short hike from Stehekin, these spectacular falls are located on a creek leading into Lake Chelan.

The jagged peak of Glory Mountain's 7,228-ft- (2,203-m-) high summit

Horseback riders enjoying the scenery along a Winthrop trail

Winthrop ⑲

Road map 1 B1. 🚶 *350.*
ℹ️ *202 Hwy 20, (509) 996-2125.*
www.winthropwashington.com

The wild west lives on in Winthrop. In the spring or fall, more than one astonished traveler has witnessed a genuine cattle drive – right down the main street.

The town was founded in 1891 by Guy Waring, a Boston-bred businessman whose Winthrop enterprises included the Duck Brand Saloon. The saloon, now home to the Winthrop Town Hall, is still standing, as is Waring's pioneer log house, which sits on the grounds of the **Shafer Museum**, along with other relics from the past.

By the 1960s, Winthrop resembled any other small, non-descript town in the American West before its merchants, eager to revive the local economy, "renovated" the town to give it an Old West ambience. A popular overnight

and vacation destination for tourists exploring the North Cascades, the Winthrop area offers a wealth of outdoor recreation possibilities.

🏛 **Shafer Museum**
285 Castle Ave. *Tel* (509) 996-2712. ☐ May & Sep: 10am–5pm Sat & Sun; Memorial Day–Labor Day: 10am–5pm daily. 🅿️ by donation.

Spokane ㉑

Road map 1 C2. 🚶 *208,000.*
✈ *Spokane International Airport.*
ℹ️ *201 W Main Ave, (509) 747-3230.* **www**.visitspokane.com

Washington's largest inland city, Spokane is the commerce and culture center for the Inland Northwest. Founded in 1873 by real estate developer James Nettle Glover, the city suffered a disastrous fire in 1889. It responded by rebuilding in brick and terra-cotta. Many handsome reminders of the building boom remain.

Grand Coulee Dam ⑳

Considered one of the modern engineering wonders of the world, Grand Coulee Dam is the largest concrete dam in North America and the third largest producer of electricity in the world. Spanning the mighty Columbia River – the second largest river in the US – it generates more power than a million locomotives, supplying electricity to 11 western states. Construction of the dam began in 1933 and took over nine years. The dam was built primarily to supply irrigation water to eastern Washington, where inadequate rainfall threatened the livelihood of the region's farmers.

VISITORS' CHECKLIST

Road map 1 C2. *Tel* (509) 633-9265. ☐ daily. Jun–Aug: 8:30am–10:30pm; Sep: 8:30am–9:30pm; Oct–May: 9am–5pm. 🅿️

Irrigation Canal

Twelve irrigation pipes at the canal headworks pump water to Lake Roosevelt.

INSIDE THE DAM

The power plants house the generators and turbines.

The dam, nearly a mile (1.6 km) long, towers almost 550 ft (152 m) above bedrock.

Trash-racks prevent debris from entering the generators.

Four gantry cranes are located on the dam to move heavy equipment.

The spillway doubles as a screen in summer for spectacular nightly laser shows.

Columbia River

Lake Roosevelt

A third power plant featuring reversible pumps was added in the 1970s.

The concrete poured to build the dam amounts to almost 12 million cubic yards (9 million cubic m) – enough to build a 6-ft- (2-m-) wide sidewalk around the equator.

For hotels and restaurants in this region see pp288–90 and pp306–8

View of the Spokane River, the town in the background

Regional history is showcased at the **Northwest Museum of Arts and Culture**. Nearby **Campbell House** (1898) is an interactive museum.

The smallest city ever to host a world's fair (Expo '74), Spokane's fair site is now **Riverfront Park**, a 100-acre (40-ha) expanse in the heart of the city that offers views of dramatic Spokane Falls. Other attractions are an IMAX theater and a 1909 carousel carved by Charles Looff, of Coney Island fame. A 37-mile (60-km) trail connects Riverside State Park.

🏛 **Northwest Museum of Arts and Culture**
2316 W 1st Ave. **Tel** *(509) 456-3931.*
⭘ *Jun–Sep: 10am–5pm Tue–Sun (call ahead).* 🌑 *major hols.* 🏷 ♿
🖥 📷 www.*northwestmuseum.org*

Environs
Just 6 miles (10 km) northwest of Spokane, **Riverside State Park** offers plenty of freshwater shoreline. The Bowl and Pitcher, with its suspension bridge and volcanic formations, is stunning.

🌿 **Riverside State Park**
9711 W Charles St, Nine Mile Falls.
Tel *(509) 465-5064.* ⭘ *dawn–dusk.*

Yakima Valley ㉒

Road map 1 B2. 📍 *10 N 8th St, Yakima, (800) 221-0751.*
www.*visityakima.com*

Boasting rich volcanic soil, an abundance of irrigation water, and 300 days of sunshine per year, the Yakima Valley is the fifth largest producer of fruits and vegetables in the US, and home to more than 40 regional wineries.

For a taste of the valley's award-winning wines, drive 10 minutes south of Yakima on I-82. Begin the wine tour at Exit 40 (Sagelands Vineyard), then continue on the Yakima Valley Highway. Columbia Crest and Preston Winery have some of the best tours.

The outstanding weather and beautiful landscape lend themselves to outdoor recreations. The two mountain passes, White Pass and Chinook Pass, offer great hiking, mountain biking, and skiing in the winter months, streams encourage fishing, and boating is available on lakes. The area is also rich in wildlife including bald eagles.

Luscious grapes on the vine in the wine-growing area of Yakima Valley

Walla Walla ㉓

Road map 1 C3. 📍 *30,000.*
📍 *26 E Main, (877) 998-4748.*
www.*wallawalla.org*

Located in the southeast corner of the state, Walla Walla is a charming and pretty town – and a green oasis in the midst of an arid landscape. The town features a large number of National Register buildings, lovely parks, and a wealth of public art. **Whitman College**, one of the nation's top-rated liberal arts colleges, is just three blocks from downtown. The attractive campus is a delight to stroll, as is the surrounding neighborhood, with its tree-shaded streets lined with historic homes.

A popular destination for wine connoisseurs, the Walla Walla area offers more than 100 wineries *(see pp192–3)* – several right in the heart of downtown Walla Walla. Among the town's other claims to fame are its delicious sweet onions and its annual Hot Air Balloon Stampede, a rally of some 45 pilots, held in May. The stampede also features live music, antiques and arts-and-crafts booths, and various events.

For a historical perspective on the area, visit **Fort Walla Walla Museum**, a pioneer village consisting of 17 original and replica buildings, including a schoolhouse, jail, and train station, as well as the **Whitman Mission National Historic Site**. Here, the story of pioneer missionaries Marcus and Narcissa Whitman and their subsequent massacre by the Cayuse Indians is told. On weekends, the Living History Company honors the area's history through music and dance.

🏛 **Fort Walla Walla Museum**
755 Myra Rd. **Tel** *(509) 525-7703.*
⭘ *Apr–Oct: 10am–5pm daily, Nov & Dec: 10am–4pm daily.* 🏷
♿ *(call ahead).* 📷 *by appt.*
www.*fortwallawallamuseum.org*

🏛 **Whitman Mission National Historic Site**
Hwy 12. **Tel** *(509) 522-6360.*
⭘ *8am–6pm daily (Oct–May: to 4:30pm).* 🌑 *Jan 1, Thanksgiving, Dec 25.* 🏷 ♿ *(except Monument Hill).* www.*nps.gov*

Balloons over Walla Walla during the annual Hot Air Balloon Stampede

Walla Walla Valley Wine Tour ㉔

Walla Walla Valley grapes

Although grape-growing in the Walla Walla Valley dates back to the mid-1800s, it wasn't until 1977 that the valley's first winery was established. Seven years later, the region was recognized as an American Viticultural Area. Today, the Walla Walla area boasts more than 100 wineries and 1,200 acres (485 ha) of vineyards.

Lying at the same latitude as the great wine-producing regions of France, the valley enjoys long, sunny days and cool evenings, which together with ideal soil conditions create the perfect environment for growing grapes. The region has won national and international recognition for its wines and is especially known for its reds – in particular, cabernet sauvignon, merlot, and syrah.

L'Ecole No. 41 ③
The cellars at this winery are located in a 1915 schoolhouse, colorfully depicted on the wine-bottle labels.

Lower Dry Creek Road

YAKIMA

Walla Walla River

Woodward Canyon ①
This winery is known for its award-winning merlots, cabernets, and chardonnays.

Goldendale Observatory State Park ㉕

1602 Observatory Dr, Goldendale. **Road map** 1 B3. **Tel** *(509) 773-3141*. **Observatory** ◻ *Apr–Sep: 2–5pm, 8pm–midnight Wed–Sun; Oct–Mar: 2–5pm, 7–10pm Fri–Sun.* 🎟 *by donation.* ♿ *partial.* 📷 *Library.*

Perched atop a 2,100-ft (640-m) hill, the Goldendale Observatory, with its 20-ft-(6-m-) diameter dome, has more than a dozen telescopes with which to observe the countryside and night sky. The highlight is a 24.5-inch (62-cm) reflecting Cassegrain, one of the largest telescopes in the US available for public viewing. During the day, visitors can enjoy great views of Mount Hood and the Klickitat Valley. By night, they can

observe the sky from a site well away from city lights. Daily programs on telescopes and sky-watching are offered.

Maryhill ㉖

Road map 1 B3.

A remote sagebrush bluff overlooking the Columbia River is where entrepreneur Sam Hill chose to build his palatial residence. In 1907, he purchased 7,000 acres (2,833 ha), with the vision of creating a utopian colony for Quaker farmers. He called the community Maryhill, in honor of his daughter, Mary. Utopia never materialized, however. No one wanted to live in such a desolate place, and Hill was persuaded to turn his

unfinished mansion into a museum. The **Maryhill Museum of Art** houses the throne and gold coronation gown of his friend Queen Marie of Romania, 87 sculptures and drawings by Auguste Rodin, an impressive collection of Native art, and many other treasures. The beautifully landscaped grounds include a lovely picnic area.

At the original Maryhill town site, 2.5 miles (4 km) east of the museum, is a replica Stonehenge built by Hill to honor locals killed in World War I.

🏛 **Maryhill Museum of Art**
35 Maryhill Museum Dr, Goldendale. **Tel** *(509) 773-3733.* ◻ *mid-Mar–mid-Nov: 10am–5pm daily.* 🎟 ♿
📷 📷

Mount St. Helens National Volcanic Monument ㉗

Road map 1 A3. **Tel** *(360) 449-7800.* 🎟 🍴 📷 www.fs.fed.us

On the morning of May 18, 1980, Mount St. Helens literally exploded. Triggered by a powerful earthquake, the conical peak erupted,

Maryhill Museum of Art, overlooking the Columbia River Gorge

For hotels and restaurants in this region see pp288–90 and pp306–8

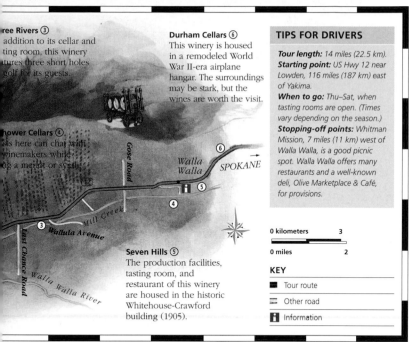

ree Rivers ③
addition to its cellar and
ting room, this winery
tures three short holes
golf for its guests.

Durham Cellars ⑥
This winery is housed
in a remodeled World
War II-era airplane
hangar. The surroundings
may be stark, but the
wines are worth the visit.

TIPS FOR DRIVERS

Tour length: 14 miles (22.5 km).
Starting point: US Hwy 12 near
Lowden, 116 miles (187 km) east
of Yakima.
When to go: Thu–Sat, when
tasting rooms are open. (Times
vary depending on the season.)
Stopping-off points: Whitman
Mission, 7 miles (11 km) west of
Walla Walla, is a good picnic
spot. Walla Walla offers many
restaurants and a well-known
deli, Olive Marketplace & Café,
for provisions.

hower Cellars ④
ts here can chat with
winemakers while
ng a merlot or syrah.

Gose Road

*Walla
Walla*

SPOKANE

ℹ ⑤

④

③ *Wallula Avenue*

Mill Creek

East Chance Road

Walla Walla River

Seven Hills ⑤
The production facilities,
tasting room, and
restaurant of this winery
are housed in the historic
Whitehouse-Crawford
building (1905).

0 kilometers   3

0 miles   2

KEY

■ Tour route

═ Other road

ℹ Information

**Mount St. Helens and surrounding
area after the 1980 explosion**

spewing a cubic mile
(4.17 cubic km) of rock into
the air and causing the largest
avalanche in recorded history.
In the blink of an eye, the
mountain lost 1,314 ft (400 m),
and 234 sq miles (606 sq km)
of forestland were destroyed.
The eruption also claimed
57 human lives and those of
millions of animals and fish.

Following the eruption, the
US Congress created the
110,000-acre (44,000-ha)
monument to allow the
environment to recover
naturally and to encourage
research, recreation, and
education. NASA scientists
have placed high-tech
monitoring devices inside
the volcanic crater to detect
an impending eruption.

Roads and trails allow visitors to explore this fascinating
region by car and on foot.

On the mountain's west side,
Highway 504 leads to five
visitor centers. The first is the
**Mount St. Helens National
Volcanic Monument Visitor
Center** (tel. 360/274-0962),
at exit 49 from Interstate 5,
featuring interpretive exhibits
of the mountain's history. **The
Hoffstadt Bluffs Visitor Center**
(tel. 360/274-5200), at milepost 27, gives visitors their first
full view of Mount St. Helens
and offers helicopter tours
into the blast zone from May
to September. The **Forest
Learning Center** (tel. 360/414-
3439), at milepost 33, open
in the summer only, teaches
about reforestation efforts.
Johnston Ridge Visitor Center
(tel. 360/274-2140), at milepost 52, offers a close-up view
of the crater and lava dome.

Fort Vancouver ㉘

Road map 1 A3. **Tel** (360) 816-
6230. ☐ mid-Mar–Oct: 9am–5pm
daily; Nov–mid-Mar: 9am–4pm daily.
◉ Jan 1, Thanksgiving, Dec 24, 25 &
31. ☐ partial. ☐ **www**.nps.gov

Between 1825 and 1849, this
was an important trading outpost for British-based Hudson's

**The three-story bastion, dating from
1845, at Fort Vancouver**

Bay Company, the giant fur-
trading organization *(see p38)*.
Located close to major tributaries and natural resources,
it was the center of political
and commercial activities in
the Pacific Northwest during
these years. During the 1830s
and 1840s, the fort also
provided essential supplies
to settlers. A National Historic
Site, Fort Vancouver features
accurate reconstructions of
nine of the original buildings,
including the jail, fur store,
and wash house, all on their
original sites. Guided tours
and re-enactments offer a
window into the fort's past.

VANCOUVER

Vancouver's Best

Lively and livable, Vancouver is a young city with an eclectic sense of identity. The city's passion for the outdoors began with Stanley Park when it opened in 1888 and the love affair continues. The art and culture of coastal First Nations people is a source of pride, with totem poles and other artwork evident in the park and throughout the city. The cityscape reflects both old and new, from the century-old buildings of Gastown to Science World's geodesic dome, built for the 1986 world exposition. As the gateway to the Pacific Rim, Vancouver boasts the largest Asian population in North America; its Chinatown is the second largest in North America, after that of San Francisco.

Inukshuk, English Bay

Vancouver Art Gallery
Emily Carr's works are featured in the gallery, which has a lovely flower garden on its north side (see p211).

Vanier Park
Across English Bay from downtown, Vanier Park features a planetarium and two museums. Restored boats are docked in nearby Heritage Harbour (see pp220–21).

0 meters   800
0 yards   800

Granville Island Public Market
Bustling and bright, this former industrial site is a must-visit for its fresh produce stalls, baked goods, and arts-and-crafts tables. Enjoy a snack or meal here, accompanied by live entertainment provided by the market's numerous buskers (see p219).

Yaletown
Funky restaurants, brewpubs, and shops make Yaletown a great destination day or night (see pp220–21).

Canada Place
The Canada Place promenade offers a terrific view of Vancouver's port, busy with seaplanes, cruise ships, and harbor craft (see p202).

Harbour Centre
Enjoy panoramic views of Vancouver and beyond from the Lookout observation deck, 553 ft (169 m) above the city (see p203).

Water Street
A world first, the cast bronze-and-gold steam clock was installed in 1977, instantly becoming one of the city's most beloved land-marks (see p203).

Science World
OMNIMAX shows inside the geodesic dome are just one of Science World's highlights (see p213).

Chinatown
Straddling Pender Street, the classically proportioned Chinatown Millennium Gate was erected in 2002 as the gateway to historic Chinatown, with its 19th-century buildings and lively street market (see p204).

Dr. Sun Yat-Sen Chinese Garden
Built in the classical style of Chinese gardens, this serene enclave in China-town was the first full-sized example of its kind built outside China (see p205).

WATERFRONT, GASTOWN, AND CHINATOWN

Vancouver's waterfront, the city's birthplace, thrives with activity, the five-sailed roof of Canada Place at its helm. The harbor view from here is memorable, as is that from the Vancouver Lookout atop the Harbour Centre tower. Clustered near the waterfront are shops, restaurants, and some of Vancouver's most interesting attractions. Nearby Gastown began as a haven for gold-seekers, loggers, and a host of

Pavilion at Dr. Sun Yat-sen Garden

ruffians. This changed when, in 1885, Canadian Pacific Railway (CPR) chose the town as its western terminus. After the Great Fire of 1886, the newly renamed Vancouver – a CPR marketing decision – settled into respectability. Boutiques and restaurants now occupy the area's historic buildings and Chinatown sprung up next door. Today, its bustling sidewalks and night markets highlight an enduring presence.

SIGHTS AT A GLANCE

Museums and Galleries
Chinese Cultural Centre Museum and Archives **10**
Vancouver Police Museum **7**

Historic Buildings
Marine Building **1**
Waterfront Station **3**

Gardens and Viewpoints
Canada Place **2**
Dr. Sun Yat-Sen Chinese Garden **9**
Harbour Centre **4**

Historic Squares, Streets, and Districts
Chinatown **8**
Maple Tree Square **6**
Water Street **5**

KEY

▢ Street-by-Street map
See pp200–201

🚇 SkyTrain station

⛴ SeaBus terminal

ℹ️ Information

🚓 Police station

0 meters 400
0 yards 400

North Vancouver

CANADA PLACE

Waterfront — SeaBus

WATERFRONT ROAD

Burrard

BURRARD STREET
WEST PENDER STREET
HORNBY STREET
HOWE STREET
WEST CORDOVA STREET
WEST HASTINGS STREET

Granville

GRANVILLE STREET
SEYMOUR STREET
RICHARDS STREET
HOMER STREET
HAMILTON STREET
DUNSMUIR STREET

VICTORY SQUARE

WATER STREET
MAPLE TREE SQUARE
CAMBIE STREET
ABBOTT STREET
CARRALL STREET
COLUMBIA STREET
MAIN STREET

PORTSIDE PARK

ALEXANDER STREET
POWELL STREET
GORE AVENUE
EAST CORDOVA STREET
EAST HASTINGS STREET

EAST PENDER STREET

DR. SUN YAT-SEN CHINESE GARDEN

KEEFER PLACE
Stadium
EXPO BOULEVARD
DUNSMUIR VIADUCT

GETTING THERE
Waterfront SkyTrain Station and the SeaBus terminal provide access to Waterfront and Gastown. The Main Street SkyTrain station is three blocks from Chinatown. Many bus routes serve Waterfront and Gastown, including numbers 1, 3, 4, 7, 8, 23, 35, and 50. Chinatown is served by routes 3, 4, 7, 19, and 22.

◁ **Reflections of the Art Deco Marine Building on the façades of downtown high-rises**

Street-by-Street: Waterfront and Gastown

The landmark steam clock

One of Vancouver's oldest areas, Gastown, which faces the waters of Burrard Inlet, is bounded by Columbia Street to the east and Burrard Street to the west. The district grew up around a saloon opened in 1867 by "Gassy Jack" Deighton, whose statue stands in Maple Tree Square. Gastown is a charming mix of cobblestone streets and restored 19th-century public buildings and storefronts. Chic boutiques and galleries line Water Street, and delightful restaurants and cafés fill the mews, courtyards, and passages. Visitors can watch the steam rise from the steam clock every 15 minutes, as well as be entertained by street performers.

Canada Place
Canada Place is a waterside architectural marvel of white sails and glass that houses a hotel, two convention centers, and a cruise ship terminal.

The SeaBus
This catamaran ferries passengers across Burrard Inlet between the central Waterfront Station and Lonsdale Quay in North Vancouver. The ride offers stunning views of the harbor.

Waterfront Station occupies the imposing 19th-century Canadian Pacific Railway building.

★ Harbour Centre
Harbour Centre is a modern high-rise building best known for Vancouver Lookout, a viewing deck 550 ft (167 m) above the city. On a clear day it is possible to see as far as Vancouver Island.

STAR SIGHTS
★ Harbour Centre
★ Water Street

LOCATOR MAP
See Street Finder map 3

★ Water Street
Much of the historic charm of Gastown can be seen here. Water Street boasts brick streets and cobblestones, as well as shops and cafés.

The steam clock is said to be one of the world's only steam-powered clocks. It chimes every hour on the hour.

The Inuit Gallery displays original Inuit art such as sculpture and prints.

"Gassy Jack" Statue
Gastown is named after "Gassy Jack" Deighton, an English sailor noted both for his endless chatter and for the saloon he opened here for the local sawmill workers in 1867.

KEY

– – – Suggested route

0 meters   100
0 yards   100

Shopping on West Cordova Street, with its wide range of small galleries and trendy boutiques, is a delightful experience.

Hotel Europe
Reminiscent of New York's Flatiron Building, this triangular structure at the corner of Powell and Alexander Streets was built in 1908–9 as a hotel. It now houses apartments.

Marine Building ❶

355 Burrard St. **Map** 3 A1.
🚇 *Waterfront.* 🚌 *17, 22.*
⛴ *SeaBus: Waterfront.*

Architects McCarter and
Nairne described the Marine
Building as "a great crag
rising from the sea." Their
design, built in 1929 in an
extravagant Art Deco style
near the waterfront, cost its
Toronto developers $2.35
million before they went
broke. The 25-story buff-
brick tower, meant to house
Vancouver's marine-related
businesses, was sold in
1933 for a mere $900,000 to
Ireland's Guinness family.

This now-beloved office
building has seen $20 million
worth of restoration and
repair since the mid-1980s.
Outside and in, it is the most
impressive of all Vancouver's
historic buildings. On the
façade, terra-cotta marine
fauna, including sea horses,
frolic amid frothy waves. The
main entrance, with its double revolving doors, features
bronze grilles and brass bas-
relief castings of starfish, crabs,
and seashells. A 40-ft- (12-m-)
high terra-cotta arch includes
depictions of a jutting ship's
prow and Canada geese.

The lobby is a dramatic step
back in time, with aqua-green
and blue tiles and carved
maritime-inspired friezes.
The elevator, inlaid with 12
varieties of BC hardwood,
whisks visitors up to the second floor, from where there is
a bird's-eye view of the lobby.

**Entrance to the Art Deco Marine
Building, with its bronze grilles**

Canada Place, resembling a sailing ship setting out to sea

Canada Place ❷

999 Canada Pl. **Map** 3 B1.
🚇 *Waterfront.* 🚌 *1, 3, 4, 7, 8, 50.*
⛴ *SeaBus: Waterfront.*
⭕ *daily.* ♿

Built for Expo '86, Canada
Place was the flagship
pavilion of the Government
of Canada. Today Canada
Place is home to a cruise
ship terminal, the Vancouver
Convention Centre, Vancouver's World Trade Centre,
and an upscale hotel.

The structure's five white
Teflon-coated fabric "sails,"
aside from being a pleasing
sight on the waterfront, make
possible a huge interior area
free of support structures. On
the west side of the complex,
a cooling fountain, shady
trees, and ample outdoor
seating provide an oasis in
the heart of the bustling city.

The three-block, open-air
Canada Place Promenade
juts into Vancouver Harbour
and offers a panorama of
busy sea and air traffic.
More than 2,800 cruise
ships a year dock alongside
the promenade en route to
Alaska or Seattle. Every year
on July 1 *(see p31)*, Canada
Place hosts a spectacular
celebratory fireworks display
over the harbor; the promenade offers the best view
in town.

During the 2010 Winter
Olympics, the Convention
Centre served as the hub for
all the press and international
broadcasting companies.

Waterfront Station ❸

601 W Cordova St.
Map 3 B2. 🚇 *Waterfront.*
🚌 *1, 3, 4, 7, 8, 50.* ⛴ *SeaBus:
Waterfront.* ♿ 🖥 📱

A busy transportation hub,
Waterfront Station is the
convergence point of the
SeaBus, SkyTrain, and
West Coast Express trains.
Built by Canadian Pacific
Railway, the current Waterfront Station is the third
passenger train station built
on the site *(see p211)*. The
first cross-Canada passenger
train pulled into the original
timber station on May 23,
1887. The second station
here was a chateau-style
structure built in 1898–9.

**The grand columned entrance
to Waterfront Station**

The present-day building was designed by the firm of Barott, Blackader and Webster and completed in 1914. It was restored in 1976–7 to make the most of its expansive waiting area, arches, and columns. Murals circling the upper walls portray romantic versions of Canadian landscapes. Shops and cafés now occupy the former waiting room.

Outside the station is *Wounded Soldier*, a sculpture by Charles Marega (1871–1939), Vancouver's premier artist of his day. Marega also carved the two stone lions that guard the Stanley Park entrance to Lions Gate Bridge.

Viewing platform at Harbour Centre's Vancouver Lookout

Harbour Centre ❹

555 W Hastings St. **Map** 3 B2. *Tel (604) 689-7304.* 🚇 *Waterfront.* 🚌 *23, 35.* ⛴ *SeaBus: Waterfront.* 🕐 *10am–6pm daily.* ♿📱📷

Glass elevators glide 553 ft (169 m) up the tower of Harbour Centre to **Vancouver Lookout**, an enclosed observation deck with a superb 360-degree view of Vancouver and informative plaques to help visitors identify the sights below. These interpretive panels locate, amongst other sights, the distinctive white roof of BC Place Stadium, Stanley Park, and Mount Baker, in neighboring Washington.

When it opened on August 13, 1977, Harbour Centre was the tallest building in British Columbia. Among the guests at the opening was the first man on the moon, Neil Armstrong, who left his footprint in cement as an official memento of the opening. A ticket to the observation deck is valid all day, so return to watch the sun set over Vancouver Island. Also at the top of tower is a revolving restaurant, providing fabulous views.

At street level, in Simon Fraser University's downtown campus, the small Teck Gallery showcases the work of Pacific Northwest artists. The two lower levels of Harbour Centre house a food fair, shops, and a well-stocked bookstore.

Vancouver Lookout
Harbour Centre. *Tel (604) 689-0421.* 🕐 *Apr–Sep: 8:30am–10:30pm daily; Oct–Mar: 9am–9pm daily.* 🧳♿📷 🖥 www.vancouverlookout.com

Water Street ❺

From Richards to Carrall Sts. **Map** 3 B2. 🚇 *Waterfront.* 🚌 *1, 50.* ⛴ *SeaBus: Waterfront.*

Water Street, with its distinctive red-brick paving, is Gastown's main thoroughfare and popular with tourists. Its turn-of-the-19th-century buildings house a mix of restaurants, nightclubs, boutiques, souvenir shops, rug merchants, offices, and First Nations art galleries.

Water Street's steam clock, drawing a crowd every hour

Water Street was not always so well-liked. Having slipped into decline after World War I, it wasn't until the 1960s that the area's potential was recognized and a wave of restoration begun. By 1971, Water Street was designated an historic area. Old-fashioned street lamps and mews enhance its historic flavor.

The world's first steam-operated clock stands 16 ft (5 m) tall at the corner of Water and Cambie Streets. Erected in 1977, it strikes its Westminster chimes on the hour and every 15 minutes emits a blast of steam. Other notable sights include The Landing, a seven-story heritage building; the 1899 Dominion Hotel; and the historically seedy Blood Alley.

THE GREAT FIRE OF 1886

On June 13, 1886, the lethal combination of a powerful westerly wind and sparks from a Canadian Pacific Railway brush fire near Drake and Homer Streets, in what is now Yaletown *(see pp220–21)*, burned through Vancouver's motley assortment of 1,000 wooden buildings. In 20 minutes, the city was devastated, barely two months after its incorporation. The raging fire – so hot it not only burned nearby St. James' Anglican Church but also melted its bell – killed at least 21 people; the exact number is unknown. Within 12 hours, rebuilding had begun. The Burns Block in Maple Tree Square *(see p204)* was built that same year and still exists.

City officials in front of a temporary city hall after the devastating fire of 1886

Statue of "Gassy Jack" Deighton
in Gastown's Maple Tree Square

Maple Tree Square ➏

Water St at Carrall St. **Map** 3 C2.
🚋 1, 50.

Search as you might, you
will not find a maple tree in
Gastown's Maple Tree Square.
The famous tree, destroyed in
the Great Fire of 1886 (see
p203), marked a popular meeting spot for local residents.

Standing in the square is
Okanagan artist Vern Simpson's 6-ft- (1.8-m-) tall ham-
mered copper statue of John
"Gassy Jack" Deighton, for
whom Gastown is named.
Commissioned in 1970, the
statue recognizes this voluble,
or "gassy," entrepreneur's
place in Vancouver history.

In 1867, Deighton built,
near Maple Tree Square, the
first watering hole on Burrard
Inlet. Deighton apparently
persuaded local millworkers
to build the Globe Saloon in
just 24 hours. Deighton died
on May 29, 1875, at age 45,
and was buried in an
unmarked grave in New
Westminster, some 13 miles
(20 km) from Gastown.

The restored Gaoler's
Mews in the square marks
the residence of Constable
Jonathan Miller, the town of
Granville's first policeman,
in 1871. The two adjacent
small log prisoner cells had
doors but no locks.

Vancouver Police Museum ➐

240 E Cordova St. **Map** 3 C2.
Tel (604) 665-3346. 🚋 3.
🕐 9am–5pm Mon–Sat.
⬤ major hols. 🎨 ♿ 🚻 📷
www.vancouverpolicemuseum.ca

Opened in 1986 to mark the
centennial of the Vancouver
police force and housed in
the former (1932–80)
Coroner's Court Building,
this museum includes the
city's original morgue. Step
into the autopsy laboratory to
view the forensic table where
actor Errol Flynn was declared
dead on October 14, 1959.
Scenes for TV series *The
X-Files* and *Da Vinci's Inquest*
have been filmed here.
A large mural depicts the
colorful history of the
police department;
historical action
settings re-create Van-
couver crime scenes.
Some 100 international
police uniforms and 200
police hats are displayed,
as well as street weaponry,
prohibited weapons,
antique firearms,
and a Thompson
submachine gun.

**Dragon atop
a lamppost, Chinatown**

Chinatown ➑

E Hastings to Union Sts, from Carrall to
Gore Sts. **Map** 3 C3. 🚈 Stadium. 🚋 3,
4, 7, 19, 22. 🎫 call (604) 632-3808.
www.vancouver-chinatown.com

Vancouver's Chinatown is
older than the city itself.
Pender Street, the main byway,
is straddled near Taylor Street
by Millennium Gate, a good

Chinatown's record-thin
Sam Kee Building (1913)

spot from which to view architectural details of the area's
restored buildings. The 1907
Chinese Freemasons Building
(1 W Pender St.) was
once home to Dr. Sun
Yat-Sen. The 1913
Sam Kee Building (8 W
Pender St.) is the result of
government expropriation
of property in order to
widen the street. In
defiance, the owner
built the world's thinnest
commercial building on
the 5-ft- (1.5-m-) wide
plot that was left. The 1889
Wing Sang Building (51–
67 E Pender St.),
the oldest in
Chinatown, had
an opium factory at its rear.

Known for traditional shops,
tearooms, and restaurants
offering *dim sum*, Chinatown
is largely a daytime place.
The exception is the open-air
Chinatown Night Market,
selling goods of all kinds.

🏮 **Chinatown Night Market**
E Pender & E Keefer Sts, Gore to Main
Sts. 🕐 May–Sep: 6:30–11pm Fri–Sun.

The ornate Millennium Gate welcoming visitors to Chinatown

A classical pavilion at the Dr. Sun Yat-Sen Chinese Garden

Dr. Sun Yat-Sen Chinese Garden ❾

578 Carrall St. **Map** 3 B3. **Tel** (604) 662-3207. 🚇 Stadium. 🚌 4, 7, 19, 22. ⏰ May–mid-Jun & Sep: 10am–6pm daily; mid-Jun–Aug: 9:30am–7pm daily; Oct–Apr: 10am–4:30pm Tue–Sun. 📷 ♿ 🛒 **www**. vancouverchinesegarden.com

Modeled after private gardens developed in the city of Suzhou during the Ming Dynasty, this is the first complete classical Chinese garden created outside China. A 52-member team of experts from Suzhou spent an entire year constructing the garden, building with materials shipped from China in more than 950 crates. No nails, screws, or power tools were used in constructing the buildings.

At first, the garden, named in honor of the founder of the Republic of China, seems a maze of walls within walls. Designed to appear larger than it really is, the garden is sprinkled with windows and moon gates – large circular openings in walls – that allow inviting glimpses of tiny courtyards wrapped around still smaller courtyards, miniature pavilions, intricate mosaic pathways, bridges, and galleries. Many of the plants and trees here symbolize human virtues: willow is a symbol of feminine grace; the plum and bamboo represent masculine strength.

Chinese Cultural Centre Museum and Archives ❿

555 Columbia St. **Map** 3 C3. **Tel** (604) 658-8880. 🚇 Stadium, Main. 🚌 3, 19, 22. ⏰ 9am–5:30pm Tue–Sun. ⬤ Jan 1, Dec 25 & 26. 📷 (except to gallery). ♿ 🛒 **www**.cccvan.com

The three-story Chinese Cultural Centre Museum and Archives building, styled after the architecture of the Ming Dynasty (1368–1644), is an impressive sight. At the edge of its curving tiled roof stand a pair of ornamental dragons, protecting the building from harm.

The museum and archives opened in 1998 as part of the Chinese Cultural Centre complex (50 East Pender Street). At the Pender Street entrance, the intricate red-and-green China Gate, which was originally displayed at the Expo '86 China Pavilion in Vancouver, is a distinguishing landmark for the complex.

The museum and archives are significant additions to Chinatown. On the first floor is the To-Yick Wong Gallery, with exhibits of both established and up-and-coming artists.

On the second floor, permanent exhibits of artifacts and photos, such as From Generation to Generation, portray the history of BC's Chinese population from the Gold Rush of 1858 to the present. The Chinese Canadian Military Museum is housed here also. Exhibits recount the lives of Chinese-Canadian veterans of World War II.

On the third floor, the S.K. Lee Academy hosts seminars and symposiums to promote cross-cultural understanding.

The Ming Dynasty-style Chinese Cultural Centre building

VANCOUVER'S CHINESE COMMUNITY

Vancouver's Chinatown, home to over 35,000 people of Chinese descent, is the largest in North America after San Francisco's. The success of the community, which sprang up as a shantytown in the 1880s after 18,000 Chinese immigrated to the city to build the cross-Canada railway (see p211), did not come easily. Chinatown's growth was seen as a threat to non-Asian seasonal workers. In 1885, a closed-door immigration policy became law. Many Chinese still came, but women were largely excluded; the men who stayed often supported families they would not see for decades. Racial tensions culminated in two major riots in Vancouver, in 1887 and 1907. The Chinese Immigration Act of 1923 caused the local Chinese population to decline further. But by the 1940s, Vancouver's Chinatown was drawing tourists, prompting the government, in 1947, to grant Chinese Canadians citizenship and reopen immigration. Encouraged by this policy shift, Chinese immigrants ventured beyond Chinatown to settle in other areas of the city. Today, a second Chinatown is located in Richmond.

A Chinatown storefront with a variety of foodstuffs on display

DOWNTOWN VANCOUVER

Downtown Vancouver is a compact hub of activity, where shopping, business, and arts and culture all play a major role. In 1895, when Christ Church Cathedral opened at the corner of Burrard and Georgia Streets, its comforting lights could be seen from the harbor below. Today, the little church is almost buried by a cluster of office towers as the modern city grows around it. Nevertheless, quiet enclaves, such as the courtyard at Cathedral Place, can still be found amid the hustle of pedestrians.

Stained glass, Christ Church Cathedral

One of the city's most famous landmarks is in the center of downtown: the historic Fairmont Hotel Vancouver, which still hosts royalty and other celebrities from around the world. The Vancouver Art Gallery, with its important collection of paintings by Emily Carr and the Group of Seven, is located in a former courthouse overlooking Robson Square – a wonderful place to sit and watch the world pass by. Robson Street, which cuts through the heart of downtown, is known for its excellent shopping and numerous restaurants.

SIGHTS AT A GLANCE

Museums and Galleries

BC Sports Hall of Fame and Museum 10
Science World 12
Vancouver Art Gallery 5

Churches and Buildings

BC Place Stadium 11
Cathedral Place 2
Christ Church Cathedral 1
Fairmont Hotel Vancouver 3
HSBC Building 4
Vancouver Central Library 9
Vogue Theatre 8

Squares

Robson Square and Law Courts 6

Shopping Streets

Robson Street 7

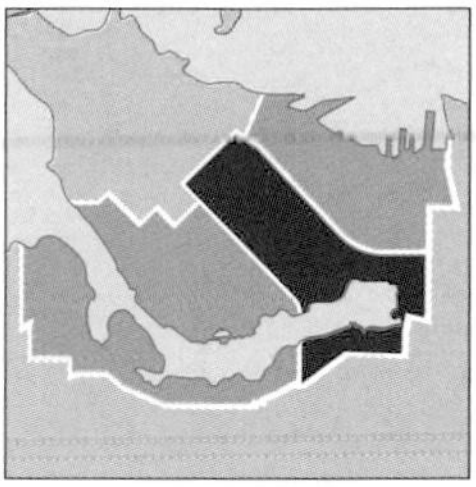

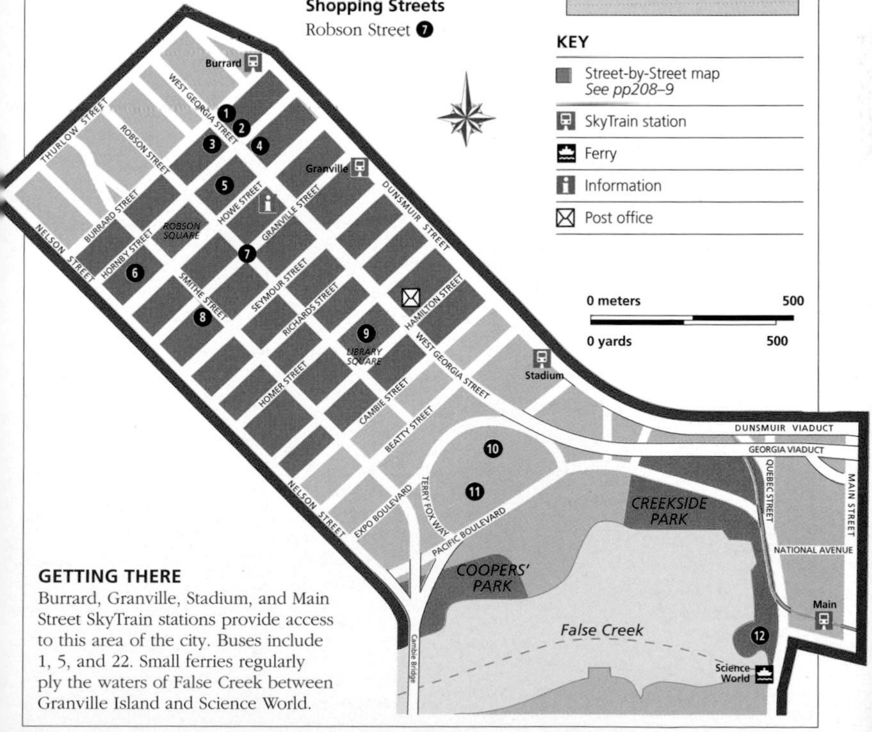

KEY

- ▪ Street-by-Street map *See pp208–9*
- 🚉 SkyTrain station
- ⛴ Ferry
- ℹ Information
- ✉ Post office

GETTING THERE

Burrard, Granville, Stadium, and Main Street SkyTrain stations provide access to this area of the city. Buses include 1, 5, and 22. Small ferries regularly ply the waters of False Creek between Granville Island and Science World.

◁ **Boats bobbing in a marina in False Creek against a backdrop of downtown apartment buildings**

Street-by-Street: Downtown

**Justice,
the Law Courts**

Vancouver's small downtown might have ended up an unlivable, daytime-only place crowded with office towers. That affliction has been avoided by preserving existing, often historic, apartment blocks, and by building new towers to accommodate inner-city dwellers. Although Vancouver is a relatively new city, it has taken care to preserve many of its historic buildings, which gives the downtown area a panache missing in many other North American city centers. A prime example is the Vancouver Art Gallery *(see p211)*, housed in the former provincial courthouse, designed in 1906 by the preeminent Victoria architect Francis Rattenbury.

Christ Church Cathedral
Stained-glass windows inside this cathedral, which was once a landmark for sailors, depict the lives of Vancouver heroes **1**

Cathedral Place
This elegant building is indicative of Vancouver's efforts to preserve the past while building with an eye to the future **2**

**Fairmont
Hotel Vancouver**
An historic building and Vancouver landmark, this building dates back to the 1920s. Much of the hotel's interior today has been restored to its former glory **3**

BURRARD ST

HORNBY STREET

HOWE

SMITHE S

NELSON STREET

**★ Robson Square
and Law Courts**
This complex, with expanses of glass over the Great Hall, is quintessentially West Coast in style **6**

0 meters	100
0 yards	100

KEY

– – – Suggested route

**★ Vancouver
Art Gallery**
Work from British Columbia's major artists is shown at this gallery, along-side exhibits by acclaimed inter-national artists **5**

HSBC Building
A stunning, seven-story brushed-aluminum pendulum, created by BC artist Alan Storey, swings gracefully through the HSBC building's wonderful tree-filled atrium ❹

LOCATOR MAP
See Street Finder map 2

★ **Vancouver Central Library**
A coliseum is set in the heart of the city thanks to Moshe Safdie's innovative design ❽

GRANVILLE STREET

WEST GEORGIA STREET

ROBSON STREET

RICHARDS STREET

MOUR STREET

HOMER STREET

HAMILTON STREET

Robson Street
Shops on this busy street are known worldwide as being the height of casual chic ❼

STAR SIGHTS

★ Robson Square and Law Courts

★ Vancouver Art Gallery

★ Vancouver Central Library

The stained-glass windows of Christ Church Cathedral

Christ Church Cathedral ❶

690 Burrard St. **Map** 2 F2. **Tel** (604) 682-3848. 🚇 Burrard. 🚌 22. ⬤ 10am–4pm Mon–Fri & Sun for services. ⬤ non-religious hols. ⬤ ✝ 8am & 10:30am Sun. **Concerts**. www.cathedral.vancouver.bc.ca

Originally known as "the light on the hill," Christ Church Cathedral was once a beacon for mariners entering Vancouver's harbor. After undergoing several expansions since its consecration in 1895, the oldest surviving church in Vancouver now sits in the midst of the downtown business center. Modeled after a Gothic parish church by its designer, Winnipeg architect C.O. Wickenden, the interior features arched ceiling beams of Douglas fir. The sandstone cathedral remains to this day a quiet sanctuary.

In 1929, the church became a cathedral and, in 1930, the spacious chancel was added. The overhead lanterns were installed in 1937. Plans to build a bell tower were halted when a city by-law restricting church bells was passed.

Thirty-two impressive British- and Canadian-made stained-glass windows feature scenes from Old and New Testament stories. Look for several unique windows that include images of Vancouver people and places. Three William Morris windows, on permanent loan from the Vancouver Museum, are set in the downstairs office vestibule. To see them, use the Burrard Street entrance.

As part of a major renovation in 2004, a new Kenneth Jones organ was installed in the cathedral.

Cathedral Place ❷

925 W Georgia St. **Map** 2 F2. **Tel** (604) 684-0925. 🚇 Burrard. 🚌 22. ⬤ 7am–6pm Mon–Fri, 9am–5pm Sat. ⬤ major hols. ⬤ ✪ www.925westgeorgia.com

Cathedral Place is a high-rise makeover of the 1929 Art Deco Georgia Medical Dental Building that once stood on this site. The 23-story postmodern tower was designed by Paul Merrick Architects and constructed in 1990–91.

Cathedral Place preserves the stylistic ambience of its predecessor. Sculpted figures on the 11th-story parapet are copies of the three famous terra-cotta nurses dressed in World War I uniforms that graced the Medical Dental building and were demolished along with that building. Lions that adorned the 3rd-story parapet are now at home at each of the entrances to Cathedral Place. Eight gargoyles on the 16th-story parapet echo those of the Hotel Vancouver across the street. The exterior of Cathedral Place is a collection of 20,000 pieces of Kansas limestone, polished, cut to shape, numbered, and then hoisted by crane.

The Art Deco-inspired lobby is dominated by the glass-and-steel illuminated sculpture *Navigation Device: Origin Unknown*, by Robert Studer. Some 17,000 pieces of Spanish granite are set geometrically into the floor. Behind the lobby is an outdoor grassy courtyard offering benches and serenity.

Cathedral Place, as seen from the Vancouver Art Gallery

The copper-roofed Fairmont Hotel Vancouver, a city landmark

Fairmont Hotel Vancouver ❸

900 W Georgia St. **Map** 2 F2. **Tel** (604) 684-3131. 🚇 Burrard. 🚌 22. ⬤ ✪ 🍴 ✫ ⬤ See **Where to Stay** p291. www.fairmont.com

The first Hotel Vancouver was built by the Canadian Pacific Railway (CPR) in 1887, two blocks east of where the current Vancouver icon stands. Construction of the current hotel, the fourth to bear the name, began in the late 1920s but came to a standstill after the stock market crash of 1929. When it was finally completed in 1939, the CPR closed the original hotel and entered into a joint-management contract for the new hotel with rival Canadian National Railway.

The building boasts a distinctive peaked green copper roof, a Vancouver landmark that has set the style for many downtown office towers. Ten craftsmen from ten countries worked for 12 months to carve the exterior stonework. Hermes, messenger of the gods in Greek mythology, is carved on the façade facing Georgia Street. Also visible are boats, trains, rams, winged goats, and griffins, noteworthy for their classic ugliness.

The hotel's lobby was restyled in 1996 by Fairmont Hotels, the current owners. The $12 million renovation restored the lobby according to the original architectural drawings. More than 8,000 sq ft (743 sq m) of marble were used.

HSBC Building ❹

885 W Georgia St. **Map** 2 F2.
🚇 Burrard. 🚌 22. **Tel** (604) 683-8144. ♿ ▣ ▯ **www**.885westgeorgia.com **Pendulum Gallery** ◯ 9am–6pm Mon–Wed, 9am–9pm Thu & Fri, 9am–5pm Sat. ⬤ major hols.

The skylit atrium is a striking entrance to the HSBC Building, a 24-story tower which houses, among others, offices of the Hong Kong Bank of Canada. A stunning seven-story kinetic pendulum hangs from the ceiling. Swinging in a graceful 20 ft (6 m) arc 11,232 times each day, the hollow 3,527-lb (1,600-kg) brushed-aluminum sculpture by BC artist Alan Storey is enhanced by the building's postmodern Classicism style.

The atrium's Pendulum Gallery shows include works of Canadian contemporary artists and international photographers. Local musicians sometimes play the baby grand piano next to the café.

The magnificent pendulum suspended in the HSBC Building

Vancouver Art Gallery ❺

750 Hornby St. **Map** 2 F2.
Tel (604) 662-4719. 🚇 Burrard. 🚌 5. ◯ 10am–5pm daily (to 9pm Tue). 🖼 ♿ ▮ ▣ ▯
www.vanartgallery.bc.ca

What was once British Columbia's imposing provincial courthouse now houses the Vancouver Art Gallery. The building was

Logger's Culls (c.1935) by Emily Carr, Vancouver Art Gallery

created in 1906 by Francis Rattenbury, an architect known for his Gothic design of Victoria's Parliament building and Empress Hotel (see pp248–9). The interior was modernized in 1983 by Arthur Erickson, another noted architect, who designed the UBC Museum of Anthropology (see pp230–31).

Among an impressive assortment of Canadian art, including works by the Group of Seven, the gallery houses the world's largest collection of paintings by one of Canada's best-loved artists, Emily Carr. Born in Victoria in 1871, Carr studied local Native cultures, capturing their way of life and the scenery of the western coastline in her sketchbook. She often depicted Haida artifacts such as totem poles in her pictures. Her palette is dominated by the blues, greens, and grays of the stormy West Coast.

Robson Square and Law Courts ❻

800 Hornby St. **Map** 2 F2–F3.
Tel (604) 660-8989. 🚇 Granville. 🚌 5. ◯ 9am–4pm Mon–Fri. ⬤ major hols. ♿ ▮

Designed by eminent BC architect Arthur Erickson, the four-level Robson Square stretches several blocks. On Robson Street's south side, on the square's first level, trees and a waterfall provide a shaded, soothing background to Alan Chung Hung's red steel sculpture, Spring. Steps to the right of the waterfall lead to a pool and parkette offering a good view north. From here, a walkway leads to the law courts, built from 1974 to 1979. Jack Harman's statue Themis Goddess of Justice overlooks the Great Hall. An impressive but controversial (it is prone to leaking) steel frame rises four stories above the hall.

THE IRON ROAD

In 1886, Prime Minister John A. Macdonald fulfilled his promise to build the Canadian Pacific Railway (CPR) to unite the new Dominion of Canada. The Iron Road linked eastern financial centers and the emerging lumber town of Vancouver. The first cross-Canada passenger train arrived in Vancouver on May 23, 1887 (see p202). The Iron Road was completed at last. Progress came at the price of many lives, including those of over 600 Chinese laborers, many of whom did the most dangerous of jobs, clearing and grading the roadbed and securing rail ties with gravel.

The first cross-Canada passenger train arriving in Vancouver in 1887

One of the many specialty stores on Robson Street

Robson Street ❼

Map 2 E1. 🚇 Burrard. 🚌 5.
www.robsonstreet.ca

Once known as Robson strasse due to a multitude of German businesses, Robson Street, named after former BC premier John Robson (1889–92), today boasts restaurants from just about every continent. Local urban chic, international celebrities, and tourists alike flock here, making people-watching from outdoor cafés a popular pastime.

Shopping is the street's main attraction. Soaps, accessories, chocolates, lingerie, men's wear, souvenirs, and even hologram products are sold in stylish shops stretching along Robson Street from Granville to Denman Streets. A music megastore at the corner of Robson and Burrard Streets is located in the old **Vancouver Public Library** building, constructed in 1957. A sentimental favorite among locals, it is famous for being the city's first modernist glass-curtain building. Some traces of the original structure remain.

All stores on Robson Street are open seven days a week, with extended evening hours.

Vogue Theatre ❽

918 Granville St. Map 2 F3.
Tel (604) 569-1144 (box office);
(604) 688-1975 (general inquiries).
🚇 Granville. 🚌 5. ⏰ Box office:
10am–6pm Mon–Sat, noon–4pm
Sun. **www**.voguetheatre.com

Designed in 1940 by Kaplan & Sprachman, the glamorous Art Deco Vogue Theatre was a defining architectural achievement for Vancouver at the time. With its symmetrical façades and 62-ft (19-m) neon sign topped by a silhouette of the Roman goddess Diana, the Vogue is a prominent landmark on busy Granville Street.

A National Historic Site of Canada, the Vogue has exceptional acoustics and hosts theater, live music, and movie events, including the Vancouver International Film Festival every fall.

The iconic Vogue Theatre, on Vancouver's Theatre Row

Vancouver Central Library ❾

350 W Georgia St. Map 3 A3.
Tel (604) 331-3603. 🚇 Granville,
Stadium. 🚌 15, 17. ⏰ 10am–
9pm Mon–Thu, 10am–6pm Fri & Sat,
noon–5pm Sun. 🔴 major hols.
♿ 🔲 📷 author readings, special
events. **www**.vpl.ca

Imaginative and daring, the design of the Vancouver Central Library was inspired by a Roman coliseum. The wraparound, sand-colored, precast concrete colonnade occupies a full city block. The nine-story library building features a dramatic concourse, the ceiling soaring six stories overhead. The top two floors are occupied by the offices of the provincial government. Adjacent to the library is a 21-story federal government office tower.

Designed by Moshe Safdie & Associates (designers of the National Gallery of Canada in Ottawa) with Downs/Archambault Partners (designers of Canada Place, *see p202*) and opened in 1995, the building was decried by some as not fitting into the Vancouver cityscape. The negative opinions have been toppled by the unanimous support the dramatic building has subsequently received.

Engineered to high seismic standards, the building is also notable because it is not cooled by air conditioning but by an ecologically sound air circulation system.

More than 1.3 million items, including books, periodicals, videos, CDs, and audiocassettes are housed in the 350,000-sq-ft (32,500-sq-m) library space, which draws over 7,000 people daily. Items are transported through the building via vertical and horizontal conveyor belts.

On the impressive concourse there are several cafés, where visitors can pause for a drink or a light snack. During the warmer months, the outdoor plaza is a popular meeting place.

The elliptical coliseum-style colonnade of the Vancouver Central Library

BC Sports Hall of Fame and Museum ⑩

Gate A, BC Place Stadium, 777 Pacific Blvd. **Map** 3 A3. **Tel** (604) 647-7414. 🚇 Stadium. 🚌 15, 17. ☐ 10am–5pm daily. 🌑 Jan 1, Dec 25. 🏷 🅰 🎟
www.bcsportshalloffame.com

Canada's largest sports museum, the BC Sports Hall of Fame and Museum is housed in 20,000 sq ft (1,858 sq m) of space inside the BC Place Stadium. Twenty galleries showcase BC's sports history, starting in the 1860s and include a Vancouver 2010 Games Gallery that celebrates hosting the Winter Olympics. Among the artifacts on display are medals, trophies, uniforms, equipment, murals, and photos. Clever games test visitors' knowledge. Interactive displays provide fascinating details of the lives of famous athletes, such as Olympic medalists sprinter Harry Jerome and skier Nancy Greene. A series of videos on the 1990s tells the exciting stories of the Vancouver Canucks' skate to the Stanley Cup finals, the BC Lions' Grey Cup victory, and Victoria's Commonwealth Games, all held in 1994.

Percy Williams statue at BC Sports Hall of Fame

Children will particularly enjoy the Participation Gallery, where they can run against the clock, rock climb, and see how fast they can pitch.

One of the most touching displays is that honoring runner Terry Fox (1958–81), who lost his leg to cancer. His run across Canada to raise money for cancer research was halted only by his death. The feat of local wheelchair athlete Rick Hansen is also highlighted. To raise public awareness of the potential of people with disabilities, Hansen set out in 1987 to wheel 24,855 miles (40,000 km) around the world. Two years later, he had earned the well-deserved title of Man in Motion.

The enormous air-supported dome of BC Place Stadium

BC Place Stadium ⑪

777 Pacific Blvd. **Map** 3 A4. **Tel** (604) 669-2300. 🚇 Stadium. 🚌 15, 17. ☐ hrs vary, depending on events. 🏷 🅰
www.bcplacestadium.com

With its white-domed roof standing out in the city's skyline, BC Place Stadium was, when it opened in 1983, Canada's first covered stadium and the largest air-supported dome in the world. The 10-acre (4-ha) stadium, consisting of enough cement to pour a sidewalk from Vancouver to Tacoma (see p182), can be converted in a matter of hours from a football field seating 60,000 to a cozier concert bowl seating 30,000. In 2011, the stadium reopened after 18 months of renovations that included the fitting of a fully retractable roof.

Science World ⑫

1455 Quebec St. **Map** 3 C4. **Tel** (604) 443-7443. 🚇 Main. 🚌 3. ☐ 10am–6pm daily. 🌑 Dec 25. 🏷 🅰 🍴 🅰
www.scienceworld.bc.ca

Overlooking the waters of False Creek, the 155-ft- (47-m-) tall steel geodesic dome built for Expo '86 now houses Science World, Vancouver's interactive science museum. The dome was designed by American inventor Richard Buckminster Fuller (1895–1983), who patented the geodesic dome in 1954. It is one of the city's most striking landmarks.

Science World hosts both traveling and permanent exhibitions. The latter include hands-on activities such as blowing square bubbles, wandering through the insides of a camera, and playing with magnetic liquids, making this a museum popular with children. In the Sara Stern Search Gallery, visitors can touch fur, bones, and animal skins, crawl into a beaver lodge or look into a beehive. KidSpace Gallery features a huge kaleidoscope kids can crawl into, and a flying saucer. The Our World and Eureka! exhibits are especially educational, exploring themes of sustainability, motion, and energy. There is also a wide spectrum of laser shows.

Science World is renowned for its OMNIMAX Theatre, located in the dome. A five-story screen 88 ft (27 m) in diameter shows films on subjects ranging from bears to Sir Ernest Shackleton's epic 1914 Antarctic journey.

The futuristic geodesic dome defines Vancouver's Science World

SOUTH GRANVILLE AND YALETOWN

The neighborhoods of South Granville and Yaletown are separated by a drive across Granville Bridge or a nautical ride across False Creek. On the south shore, South Granville offers a mix of grocers, cafés and restaurants, and upscale shops – clear signs that people live as well as work here. The numerous commercial art galleries justify the local moniker "gallery row." Nearby Vanier Park and Kitsilano Beach are favorite recreational areas.

Glass marine reliquary vase

Since the early 1990s, Yaletown, on the north shore of False Creek, has seen a dramatic transformation. Once an underused warehouse district, it is now a magnet for high-tech companies and downtown dwellers. High-rises and converted warehouses lend a flair both ultramodern and charmingly historic. Terrace cafés, designer outlets, and interior design stores draw visitors in the day; nightclubs and brew pubs attract revelers come evening.

SIGHTS AT A GLANCE

Museums, Galleries, and Art Schools
Emily Carr University of Art & Design ❷

Studios and Markets
Granville Island Public Market ❻
Kids Market ❸
New-Small and Sterling Studio Glass ❹

Waterways and Ferries
False Creek ❶
Granville Island Market Ferries ❼

Beaches, Parks, and Districts
Railspur Alley ❺
Sunset Beach ❾
Vanier Park ❽
Yaletown ❿

KEY

▦ Street-by-Street map
See pp216–17

⛴ False Creek ferry

ℹ Information

✝ Church

GETTING THERE
The area is reached by buses 1, 22, and 50. Granville Island is a 10-minute walk north of Granville Street and 4th Ave. Aquabus and False Creek Ferries link docks on False Creek to Granville Island.

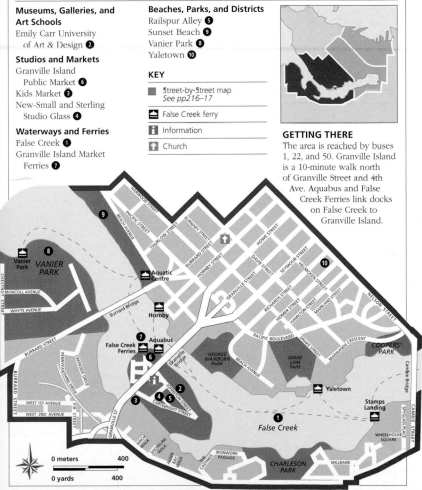

◁ **Bird's-eye view of Granville Island at dusk, the Burrard Street Bridge and North Shore mountains in the distance**

Street-by-Street: Granville Island

Granville Island Brewing Company sign

Granville Island had its beginnings in 1916, as an industrial area situated on land dredged from False Creek.

For decades, heavy industry belched out noxious fumes. By the 1950s, the area was nearly abandoned. In 1972, the Canadian government, backed by City Hall, took over the site, with a plan to make it a people place, and, in 1979, a public market opened. Today, stores, known for the originality of their wares, galleries, studios, and restaurants are housed in brightly painted converted warehouses and tin sheds. Granville Island, which is not an island at all but a peninsula, is also home to music, dance, and theater.

Marina on False Creek, downtown buildings in the background

★ Granville Island Public Market

Enjoy a wonderful diversity of locally grown fruits and vegetables in the colorful displays that make this market Vancouver's most popular attraction **6**

One of the many outdoor cafés and restaurants at Granville Island

Kids Market

The Kids Market is a child's fantasyland, with more than 20 shopkeepers selling everything from games and toys to pint-sized clothing **3**

★ **Emily Carr University of Art & Design**
Named in honor of one of BC's major artists (see p28), this respected school is located in a former warehouse ❷

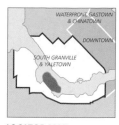

LOCATOR MAP
See Street Finder maps 1 & 2

New-Small and Sterling Studio Glass
Look through the windows of this glass-blowing studio and marvel as molten glass is transformed into beautiful works of art ❹

0 meters   80

0 yards   80

STON STREET

RTWRIGHT STREET

KEY

- - - - Suggested route

STAR SIGHTS

★ Emily Carr University of Art & Design

★ Granville Island Public Market

Railspur Alley
A sign from one of the boutiques on Railspur Alley, a lively street lined with quirky local stores and businesses ❺

View of False Creek, looking northeast toward Yaletown from Granville Island

False Creek ❶

Map 3 B4.

As the name suggests, False Creek is not a creek at all but a saltwater inlet in the heart of the city, extending east from Burrard Bridge to Science World *(see p213)*. In the 1850s, Captain G.H. Richards sailed up this body of water, which originally covered what is now Chinatown eastward to Clark Drive, hoping to find the Fraser River. Disappointed, he named it False Creek.

The mud flats Richards saw originally served as the winter fishing grounds of the Squamish people. By the late 1800s, sawmills had set up on the south shore, followed by the railyards of Yaletown *(see pp220–21)* on the north shore.

Today, paved seawalls flank both the north and south shores, allowing walkers, bicyclists, and rollerbladers to admire the views of downtown and the mountains.

Emily Carr University of Art & Design ❷

1399 Johnston St. **Map** 2 E5.
Tel (604) 844-3800. 🚌 50.
⛴ False Creek Ferries, Aquabus.
◯ 10am–6pm daily. ● mid-Dec–Jan 1. ♿ www.ecuad.ca

The unpainted corrugated metal exterior of the famed Emily Carr University of Art & Design (ECUAD) is perfectly in keeping with the industrial ambience of Granville Island.

Not surprisingly, industrial design is a major focus within the school's three degree-granting programs. Over 4,000 artists and designers have been trained at ECUAD and its several predecessors.

The school moved into three abandoned industrial buildings on Granville Island in 1980. The original building, on the north side of Johnston Street, houses the **Charles H. Scott Gallery**, which hosts regional, national, and international exhibits of contemporary art that complement the institute's curriculum. Student shows are held in the **Concourse Gallery**.

The school's newest addition on the south side of Johnston Street is a 58,000 sq ft (5,400 sq m) structure built for $14 million. A retractable roof can transform the concourse into an atrium within 45 seconds.

Well-known alumni include painter Jack Shadbolt, cartoonist Lynn Johnston, and author Douglas Coupland.

Eric Metcalfe's Attic Project at Emily Carr University of Art & Design

Kids Market ❸

1496 Cartwright St. **Map** 2 D5.
Tel (604) 689-8447. 🚌 50.
⛴ False Creek Ferries, Aquabus.
◯ 10am–6pm daily. ● Jan 1, Dec 25 & 26. ♿ www.kidsmarket.ca

Children will be dazzled by the Kids Market: two floors filled with toys, games, gadgets, clothing, and jewelry. The more than 20 retailers here provide an eclectic shopping experience. Clownin' Around Magic is filled with puzzles and magic tricks, Knotty Toys features handmade wooden toys, Little Treasures sells beachwear, while The Hairloft will fulfil every little girl's princess fantasy. There is also the Adventure Zone, with a supervised play area, picnic spot, and special events. Outside, Granville Island Waterpark is a joyful free-for-all of fountains, nozzles, and sprays.

Pousse-café vessels at New-Small and Sterling Studio Glass

New-Small and Sterling Studio Glass ❹

1440 Old Bridge St. **Map** 2 D5.
Tel (604) 681-6730. 🚌 50.
⛴ False Creek Ferries, Aquabus.
◯ 10am–6pm Mon–Sat, 11am–5pm Sun. ● Jan & Feb: Mon; Jan 1, Dec 25 & 26. ♿ 📷 📱
www.hotstudioglass.com

Many of the best-known glassblowers in BC have worked for New-Small and Sterling Studio Glass since it opened here in 1982. Visitors can watch owner David New-Small and other artists create vases, bowls, and artwork using traditional techniques dating back hundreds of years.

The studio specializes in freeblown glass, made without molds using steel blowpipes and pontils. One of four furnaces keeps 150 lbs (70 kg) of glass molten at 2,000°F (1,100°C) around the clock. The others are fired as needed to heat and shape works in progress. Complicated pieces require a team of glassblowers.

The adjacent shop is one of the best-known glass galleries in Western Canada.

Railspur Alley ❺

Railspur Alley. **Map** 2 D5.
🚌 50. 🚢 False Creek Ferries, Aquabus. 🍴 📷 📷
www.granvilleisland.com

In the heart of this former industrial district, tucked away off Old Bridge Street on Granville Island, you can find Railspur Alley, a quiet, charming street that has been remodeled and is filled with boutique shops and artisan businesses. A highlight is the cluster of 12 artists' studios, where visitors can watch artists at work and browse items for sale.

Other shops include Alarte Silks in the Alley Gallery, which has beautiful, hand-painted and wearable silk art, and Sadryna Design, which sells custom leather fashions with European flair. You can find belts and purses for sale as well as more theatrical stage costumes. Hartman Leather also sells handcrafted leather bags and belts, using top grain vegetable-tanned and latigo leathers.

Dalbergia Wood and Fine-Objects produces wooden furniture and sculptures with simple, clean lines. Fine art galleries Hilary Morris, Studio 13 Fine Art, and Peter Kiss Gallery round off the selection of art for sale.

The Artisan Sake Maker is Vancouver's only fresh, organic, premium sake producer, and the popular Railspur Alley Cafe and Bistro has an affordable and tasty menu. AGRO Café offers organic, fair-trade coffee direct from farmers in developing countries, as well as baked goods and a menu which changes seasonally.

Abundant fresh produce at Granville Island Public Market

Granville Island Public Market ❻

1689 Johnston St. **Map** 2 D4.
Tel (604) 666-5784. 🚌 50.
🚢 False Creek Ferries, Aquabus.
🕐 9am–7pm daily. 🌑 Jan 1, Dec 25 & 26. 🦽 **www**.granvilleisland.com

The Granville Island Public Market opened in 1979 in a former industrial building. Cleaned up and given new tin cladding, the public market building was the first renovated structure on the site to open for business. Food specialties at the market include high-quality fresh fruits and vegetables (many of them organic), meats, fresh pasta, cheese, breads and baked goods, chocolates, and herbs and spices. Flowers are also a big draw.

At the rear of the market, vendors sell the wares of local artisans and craftspeople – candles, custom jewelry, and hats. Exhibitors are selected for their high standards of design and production.

A food fair on the market's west side offers a variety of ethnic cuisines. From the benches outside on the wharf, visitors take in one of the best views of the False Creek marina and docks, as well as a spectacular view of downtown and the North Shore mountains. Street performers – from musicians to stilt-walkers to magicians – entertain outside, adding to the market's eclectic, vibrant ambience.

Granville Island Market Ferries ❼

Map 2 D4. *False Creek Ferries*
Tel (604) 684-7781. **www**.granville islandferries.bc.ca *Aquabus Tel* (604) 689-5858. **www**.theaquabus.com
🚌 50. 🕐 call for hrs. 🌑 Dec 25 & 26. 🦽 🦽 partial. See **Getting Around Vancouver** *p235*.

A ride aboard one of the ferries that service Granville Island and the surrounding area is one of the best ways to see the sights of False Creek, such as Granville Island, the Maritime and Vancouver Museums, and the Aquatic Centre. These small boats offer a striking perspective of the city's downtown and west side.

Two ferry companies operate from Granville Island. **False Creek Ferries**' vessels, depart daily from the wharf on the west side of the Granville Island Public Market. Routes cross False Creek to the south foot of Hornby Street and also go to Vanier Park *(see pp220–21)*. Another route goes to Science World *(see p213)*. The fleet includes four 20-passenger diesel ferries, plus six electric boats.

The **Aquabus** comprises 12 small vessels running three routes from the ferry dock west of Granville Island Public Market. The Hornby route takes passengers and bicyclists to the southern foot of Hornby Street. The Yaletown route drops passengers at the eastern foot of Davie Street. A third route encompasses Science World.

Both companies offer mini-cruises, including sunset cruises of False Creek, with frequent departures. The Aquabus evening cruise is aboard the *Rainbow Hunter*, a restored antique ferry.

An Aquabus vessel, belonging to one of two False Creek ferry services

Vanier Park 8

A ship in the harbor at the Maritime Museum

Vanier Park is a calming oasis on the city's west side. Although it is relatively small, it feels spacious. Boats sail by on English Bay, kites fly overhead, ferries dock and depart, and pedestrians and cyclists pass through on their way to Kitsilano Beach or Granville Island *(see pp216–19)*. Vanier Park was first inhabited by Coast Salish people. It is now the home of the Museum of Vancouver, the H.R. MacMillan Space Centre, Vancouver City Archives, and the Vancouver Maritime Museum. In late May, large white tents are set up for the week-long Vancouver International Children's Festival *(see p30)*. In summer, the Bard on the Beach Shakespearean Festival is held here.

ENGLISH BAY

HERITAGE HARBOUR

Gate to the Northwest Passage
This imposing giant red steel sculpture by Chung Hung overlooks English Bay.

| 0 meters | 150 |
| 0 yards | 200 |

Sunset Beach 9

Map 2 D3. 🚌 1.
🛳 *False Creek Ferries, Aquabus.*

The white sands of Sunset Beach, which marks the end of the English Bay seawall and the start of False Creek, make an ideal place to relax and do some serious sun-tanning or swimming. Summertime water temperatures rise to 65°F (18°C), and lifeguards are on duty from mid-May to Labor Day.

The western end of Sunset Beach provides a good view of the gray granite *Inukshuk*, which sits at the foot of neighboring English Bay Beach. This Inuit statue by Alvin Kanak, modeled on traditional markers used by

the Inuit for navigation, is a symbol of friendship.

The **Vancouver Aquatic Centre**, at the beach's east end, has a 164-ft- (50-m-) long Olympic-size swimming pool, and diving pools, a sauna, a whirlpool, and a steam room. False Creek Ferries dock behind the center, with routes to Vanier Park, Granville Island, and Science World.

Yaletown 10

Map 2 F3. 🚇 *Stadium*. 🚌 1.
🛳 *False Creek Ferries, Aquabus.*

Warehouses have been transformed into lofts, outdoor cafés have sprung up on old loading docks, and high-rise buildings have filled

Restaurant with outdoor seating on a street in Yaletown

in the horizon of Yaletown. The area was first settled by Canadian Pacific Railway (CPR) train crews and laborers after the CPR closed its construction camp in

Museum of Vancouver
The curved white roof of the Museum of Vancouver resembles a Haida woven hat. The Crab, a stunning stainless steel sculpture by George Norris, presides outside. Canada's largest civic museum boasts seven re-creations of Vancouver's history, including an immigrant ship and a fur-trading post.

VISITORS' CHECKLIST

Map 1 C3. 🚌 22. ⛴ *False Creek Ferries*. **H.R. MacMillan Space Centre Tel** (604) 738-7827. **www**.spacecentre.com **Maritime Museum Tel** (604) 257-8300. **www**.vancouver maritimemuseum.com **Museum of Vancouver Tel** (604) 736-4431. **www**.museumofvancouver.ca

H.R. MacMillan Space Centre
Space lore is presented in child-friendly hands-on displays and multimedia shows at the space center. The popular Cosmic Courtyard is an interactive gallery that focuses on space exploration.

Vancouver Maritime Museum
The West Coast's rich maritime history is featured in this museum, from seagoing canoes to a 1928 police schooner.

KEY

P Parking

⚘ Viewpoint

Yale, BC, on completion of the transcontinental railway to Vancouver in 1887. Yaletown remained the decaying heart of the city's industrial activity until the early 1990s, when a development plan began its transformation into a lively urban community.

A multitude of Yaletown condominiums now house a youthful, sophisticated crowd. Along with new residents came a new look. Dirty and neglected industrial warehouses on Homer, Hamilton, and Mainland Streets were given facelifts. The result is a landscape of bistros, cafés, restaurants, nightclubs, studios, galleries, hair salons, interior design stores, and international and local designer clothing outlets. On Beach

Avenue, the **Roundhouse Community Arts and Recreation Centre**, in a former CPR switching building, includes theater and gallery spaces and

a host of community arts and athletics programs. It also houses the locomotive that pulled the first passenger train to Vancouver in 1887.

JOE FORTES, THE HERO OF ENGLISH BAY

Vancouver's "Citizen of the Century" was a simple man named Seraphim "Joe" Fortes. Born in Barbados in 1865, he arrived in Vancouver in 1885 and was soon a regular at the English Bay Beach. He taught thousands of children to swim. As the city's first appointed lifeguard, he is credited with saving more than 100 lives. Joe's cottage was located right by the beach at the site of today's Alexandra Park. The Joe Fortes Memorial Drinking Fountain in the same park was designed by Charles Marega and installed in 1926, four years after Joe's death.

Joe Fortes in front of his cottage

FARTHER AFIELD

Detail of a totem pole in Stanley Park

Beyond downtown Vancouver lie such memorable attractions as Stanley Park and the Museum of Anthropology. Other intriguing sights are located in outlying cities, easily reached by car or public transit. The North Shore, once home to the Coast Salish people, consists of two cities. Lions Gate Bridge spans the First Narrows to West Vancouver, featuring 17 miles (28 km) of scenic shoreline. The bridge also leads to North Vancouver and the physical wonders of Capilano Canyon and Grouse Mountain. At the mouth of the Fraser River is fast-growing Richmond. With its Chinese malls and markets, this city superbly reflects Greater Vancouver's multicultural character. The riverside community of Steveston is noted for its historic cannery.

SIGHTS AT A GLANCE

Museums and Galleries
Museum of Anthropology pp230–31 **9**
West Vancouver Museum and Archives **2**

Areas of Natural Beauty
Capilano Suspension Bridge **3**
Grouse Mountain **4**
Marine Drive **1**
Stanley Park pp226–7 **7**

Markets
Lonsdale Quay Market **5**

Neighborhoods and Cities
Richmond **10**
Steveston **12**
West End **6**

Buildings
Chinese Buddhist Temple **11**
University of British Columbia **8**

KEY
■ Central Vancouver
■ Urban area
▬ Major highway
▬ Highway
═ Minor road
✈ Airport

5 miles = 8 km

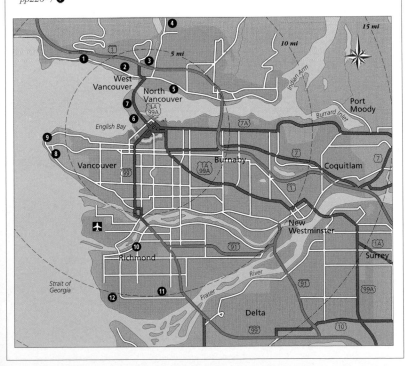

◁ Siwash Rock, alongside the seawall in Stanley Park, Vancouver

Capilano Suspension Bridge, not for the fearful

Marine Drive ❶

📷 250. **Tel** (604) 926-6614.
www.westvanchamber.com

Scenic Marine Drive winds
through West Vancouver and
makes for an ideal day trip.
Park Royal Shopping Centre,
with its 280 stores, is the area's
major mall. The nearby seaside
suburb of Ambleside boasts a
par-three golf course on the
Capilano Indian Reserve; a
popular seawall walkway; and
a park overlooking
Burrard Inlet, which
includes tennis
courts, a paddling
center, fitness
circuit, skate
board park, and
waterfowl pond.
At the end of the
Ambleside Sea
Walk, Dundarave
Pier offers a
wonderful view of
Vancouver and the
Strait of Georgia.
Both Ambleside
and Dundarave
are good places
to shop and dine.

From here westward,
Marine Drive clings to the
rocky shoreline, buffered by
some of Canada's priciest
real estate.

At Lighthouse Park, an easy
walk through old-growth
forest leads to the Atkinson
lighthouse, built in 1912.

Horseshoe Bay welcomes
visitors with a park, a marina,
and a Native art gallery. Ice
cream and fish and chips are
Horseshoe Bay specialties.

West Vancouver Museum and Archives ❷

680 17th St, West Vancouver.
Tel (604) 925-7295. 📷 251, 252.
⬜ 11am–5pm Tue–Sat. 🅿 public
hols & various other times; call for
details. 🎫 (free Tue). 🅿 🅿
www.westvancouvermuseum.ca

Small and inviting, the West
Vancouver Museum and
Archives is housed in the
stately former
home of Gertrude
Lawson, daughter
of John Lawson,
the first permanent
white settler in West
Vancouver. The
stones of the 1938
house were brought
from New Zealand
as ballast on a
sailing ship; others
came from the
Capilano River.
After Gertrude died
in 1989, the District
of West Vancouver
acquired the
property. The
house was restored and then
opened in 1995 as a museum.

**Atkinson Lighthouse,
just off Marine Drive**

The museum's exhibits relate
to West Vancouver heritage
and community interests, such
as local sporting history and
historic toys. West Vancouver
communities are sometimes
profiled and decorative arts
are particularly well represented. The gift shop sells
arts and crafts by local artists
and books on West Vancouver
history and architecture.

Capilano Suspension Bridge ❸

3735 Capilano Rd, North Vancouver.
Tel (604) 985-7474. 📷 232, 236.
🚢 SeaBus. ⬜ Jan–mid-May:
9am–5pm daily; mid-May–Aug:
8:30am–8pm daily; Sep: 9am–6pm
daily; Oct–Nov: 9am–5pm daily; Dec:
10am–9pm daily. 🌑 Dec 25. 🎫
🎫 May–Oct. ♿ partial. 🍴 🅿
www.capbridge.com

The first Capilano Suspension
Bridge, not much more than a
hemp rope and cedar planks,
was built in 1889 by Scotsman
George Mackay and Squamish
locals August and Willie Jack.
Mackay was drawn by Capilano
Canyon's wild beauty and built
a cabin overlooking it. Access
to the Capilano River below
was almost impossible. It is said
that Mackay built the bridge
so that his son, who loved
fishing, could reach the river.

The present bridge, dating
to 1956 and the fourth to be
constructed here, spans 450 ft
(137 m). Secured by 13 tons of
concrete, 230 ft (70 m) above
the canyon floor, it is the longest such bridge in the world.

Nature lovers are drawn here
by the views and the chance
to wander through old-growth
woods, past trout ponds and a
200-ft- (61-m-) high waterfall.
Other highlights include Totem
Park and the Big House, where
Native artists carve poles. The
Living Forest exhibit explains
the West Coast rainforest.
Treetops Adventures offers a
bird's eye view of the forest.

Costumed guides at the Capilano
Suspension Bridge

For hotels and restaurants in Vancouver see pp291–2 and pp308–11

View of Vancouver from Grouse Mountain

Grouse Mountain ❹

6400 Nancy Greene Way.
Tel (604) 980-9311. 🚌 232, 236.
🚠 SeaBus. 🕐 9am–10pm daily.
🅿️ ♿ 🍴 📷
www.grousemountain.com

From the summit of Grouse Mountain, visitors can experience British Columbia's dramatic landscape. On a clear day one can see as far as Vancouver Island in the west and the Columbia Mountains in the east.

The 2-mile (3-km) Grouse Grind trail, leading to the top of the 3,973-ft (1,211-m) mountain, lives up to its name. Most prefer to take the fully enclosed Skyride gondola.

Popular activities include skiing, snowboarding, skating, snowshoeing, and sleigh rides in the winter; mountain biking, hiking, forest walks, helicopter tours, and tandem paragliding in the summer. Ski and snowboarding schools, 12 ski runs, and equipment rentals are among the amenities here.

The Skyride gondola, Grouse Mountain

During the day, visitors are invited to watch the World's Greatest Lumberjack Show which sees two lumberjacks showcase their tree-climbing, axe-throwing, and log-rolling skills.

At the Refuge for Endangered Wildlife, an enclosed 2-acre (1-ha) natural habitat, home to orphaned grizzly bears and wolves, wildlife rangers give daily talks. The Theatre in the Sky presents a video that takes viewers on a stunning aerial tour of British Columbia.

Lonsdale Quay Market ❺

123 Carrie Cates Ct, North Vancouver. **Tel** (604) 985-6261.
🚠 SeaBus. 🕐 9am–7pm daily.
🔴 Jan 1, Dec 25. ♿ 📷 🍴 🎭 📷
📷 www.lonsdalequay.com

Opened in 1986, the striking concrete-and-glass building housing the Lonsdale Quay Market forms part of the North Shore SeaBus terminal. The market has a floor devoted to food, as well as an array of cafés and restaurants that serve a variety of ethnic cuisines. On the second floor, visitors will find specialty shops that sell hand-crafted products, such as jewelry, pottery, and textiles; and Kid's Alley, a row of child-oriented shops. The complex also includes a hotel, a pub, and a nightclub. In the summer, music festivals are held outside on the adjacent Plaza Deck, overlooking the city and port. Musical offerings include jazz, folk, African, and Celtic performances.

The fountain at Lonsdale Quay, Vancouver in the distance

Sailboat on English Bay, West End high-rises in the background

West End ❻

🚌 1, 5, 6. 🚇 Burrard.

Vancouver's West End is the most densely populated residential area in Canada, yet it maintains a relaxed and spacious ambience, in part because of its proximity to Stanley Park and English Bay. Offering everything from beaches to hip urban street-life, it is one of the best neighborhoods in Vancouver for strolling and taking in the delights of the city.

The West End, as one of Vancouver's earliest neighborhoods, has preserved several important historic buildings, such as the exquisite 1893 **Roedde House**, home to Vancouver's first bookbinder and now a museum, and the ivy-clad Sylvia Hotel, built in 1911.

West End streets are generally busy with pedestrians at all hours of the day or night. Robson, Denman, and Davie Streets are the main West End thoroughfares, with Burrard Street as its eastern boundary. Among the many shops and restaurants on Robson Street (see p212) is the Robson Public Market. Denman Street reflects the beach culture of English Bay with its casual clothing boutiques and cafés. It is also popular with Vancouver's gay community. Although Davie Street is more residential, it too has many cafés and restaurants.

The West End also offers plenty of green space in among the high-rise apartments and heritage homes.

🏛️ **Roedde House**
1415 Barclay St. **Tel** (604) 684-7040.
🕐 11am–5pm Tue–Sat, 2–4pm Sun. 📷 **www.**roeddehouse.org

Stanley Park 7

Girl in a Wetsuit sculpture

A magnificent 1,000-acre (404-ha) park of tamed wilderness a short ride from downtown Vancouver, Stanley Park was originally home to Musqueam and Squamish peoples. In 1888, Lord Stanley, Governor General of Canada, opened the park to all. More than eight million visitors a year make this Vancouver's top attraction. Many walk the 5.5-mile (8.8-km) perimeter seawall with its lovely views of the harbor, English Bay, and the Coast Mountains. Bicycles can be rented near the Denman Street entrance to the park. In addition to the Vancouver Aquarium, Stanley Park boasts rose gardens, a lake, a lagoon, and a totem pole display, as well as beaches, swimming pools, a miniature railway, tennis courts, and a pitch-and-putt golf course.

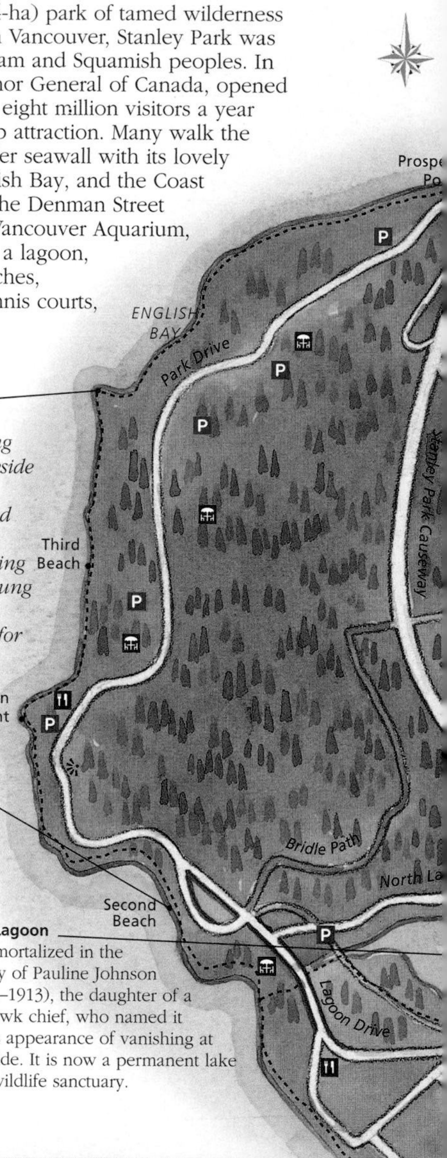
Prospe
Po
ENGLISH BAY
Park Drive
Stanley Park Causeway
Third Beach
Ferguson Point
Bridle Path
North La
Second Beach
Lagoon Drive

Siwash Rock
A volcanic formation jutting from the inlet beside the seawall, the rock has inspired many native legends. According to one, it is a young chief turned to enduring stone for his courage.

★ Second Beach
Second Beach is a hub of activity in the summer with a swimming pool, children's playground, picnic areas, and traffic school.

Lost Lagoon
is immortalized in the poetry of Pauline Johnson (1861–1913), the daughter of a Mohawk chief, who named it for its appearance of vanishing at low tide. It is now a permanent lake and wildlife sanctuary.

KEY

- Viewpoint
- Information
- Picnic area
- Path
- Seawall walk
- Restaurant
- Parking

Colorful flowerbeds in Stanley Park

For hotels and restaurants in this Vancouver see pp291–2 and pp308–11

★ The Seawall

The Seawall winds around the rim of the park past Girl in a Wetsuit (see p226), a sculpture by Elek Imredy. This curious sculpture, which sits on an offshore rock, was introduced to the park in 1972.

VISITORS' CHECKLIST

2099 Beach Ave.
Tel (604) 257-8400. 🚇 Burrard.
🚌 23, 35. ⬜ 24 hrs daily
(not all sights).🎫 to some
exhibits. ♿ 🚻 ⓫ 🚹 ♒ 🅿
Horse-drawn carriage tours
(Mar–Oct), call (604) 681-5115.
Stanley Park Shuttle (May–
Sep). **Special events**, call
(604) 473-6204.
www.vancouver.ca

0 meters   400
0 yards   500

BURRARD
INLET

BEAVER
LAKE

Pipeline Road

Seawall Walk

Brockton Point Trail

Avison Way

Brockton
Point

Hallelujah
Point

COAL HARBOUR

DEADMAN'S
ISLAND

W Georgia Street

OST
GOON

**Vancouver Aquarium
Marine Science Centre**
The surprisingly graceful white beluga whales are the stars of Canada's premier aquarium. The more than 165 displays also feature sea otters, wolf eels, and giant Pacific octopus.

Rose Garden
From May to September, the lovely formal Rose Garden, surrounded by a variety of perennial plantings, looks its very best.

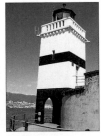

★ Brockton Point

Features of the point are a 1915 lighthouse and the Nine O'Clock Gun, a cannon that has stood sentinel in the park since 1894. Still fired nightly, its boom once helped sailors synchronize their chronometers.

Totem Park
Situated beside Brockton Oval, where the city's first cricket match was played in the late 1800s, this area displays eight totem poles. Created by the Haida, Kwakiutl, and other Aboriginal peoples, each totem tells its own story.

STAR SIGHTS

★ Brockton Point

★ The Seawall

★ Second Beach

Walter C. Koerner Library, University of British Columbia

University of British Columbia ❽

Tel (604) 822-2211. 🚌 4, 10, 99 B-Line. ♿ 🅿 www.ubc.ca

The University of British Columbia (UBC), founded in 1915, is one of Canada's leading medical doctoral universities. A 30-minute drive from the heart of downtown Vancouver, the 993-acre (402-ha) campus is an eclectic mix of architecture, the range of which can be seen by comparing the 1923 **Irving K. Barber Library** with the **Walter C. Koerner Library**, whose construction began in 1996. The former is a combination of imposing stone walls and medieval-style detail; the latter, designed with the help of Arthur Erickson, is a striking combination of concrete and glass.

Campus highlights include the **UBC Botanical Garden**, with 70 acres (28 ha) of rare or unusual plants, and the Rose Garden, boasting 300 varieties. The zinc-paneled **Chan Centre for the Performing Arts** (*see p233*) hosts classical and contemporary musicians, theater and opera productions, as well as film screenings. Works by leading Canadian and international contemporary artists are shown at the **Morris and Helen Belkin Art Gallery**. UBC's **Museum of Anthropology** (*see pp230–31*) is world-renowned. The **Pacific Museum of the Earth** is a treasure chest of minerals and fossils, including an impressive collection of BC jade. The award-winning cedar-and-glass **First Nations Longhouse** resembles a traditional longhouse. The **Asian Centre** houses a photographic exhibit of Asian Canadians and one of North America's largest collections of rare Chinese books. The Japanese-style Nitobe Memorial Garden, part of the Botanical Garden, is at the rear of the building. Campus maps are available from kiosks at the bus loop, Student Union Building, and Chan Centre.

🌸 **UBC Botanical Garden**
6804 SW Marine Dr. *Tel* (604) 822-9666. ⬜ 9am–5pm Mon–Fri, 9:30am–5:30pm Sat & Sun. 🎫 ♿ partial. 🎫 Mar–Oct. 🅿
www.ubcbotanicalgarden.org

🏛 **Morris and Helen Belkin Art Gallery**
1825 Main Mall. *Tel* (604) 822-2759. ⬜ 10am–5pm Tue–Fri, noon–5pm Sat & Sun. ⬛ major hols. ♿

🏯 **Asian Centre**
1871 West Mall. *Tel* (604) 822-2427. *Library* ⬜ 9am–5pm Mon–Fri.

Museum of Anthropology ❾

See pp230–31.

Richmond's Public Market

Richmond ❿

🏘 175,000. *Tel* (604) 271-8280 or (877) 247-0777. 🚌 98 B-Line. www.tourismrichmond.com

Built on a group of islands, Richmond was originally an isolated farming community settled by Europeans in the 1880s. Before that, the Coast Salish used the islands as temporary dwelling grounds, for fishing and collecting berries. Blueberry and cranberry are still important local crops, but Richmond today is predominantly a busy metropolis. Lulu Island, the largest island, is the site of the city proper.

Richmond is home to the second largest North American Asian community. **Yaohan Centre**, one of several Asian malls, sells everything from traditional Chinese herbs to the latest high-tech gadgetry to Taekwon-do classes. Tea ceremonies, foot massages, and face readings are some of the less conventional offerings. The **Richmond Centre** combines mainstream shopping with Asian influences.

Richmond also offers international dining, art galleries, and live performances at the **Gateway Theatre**. Outdoor activities include year-round golfing, and visiting the **Richmond Nature Park**, which features trails through forests, bogs, and pond habitats. Walking and cycling the West Dyke Trail are also popular. The area is also rich in wildlife including seals and whales.

🌸 **Richmond Nature Park**
11851 Westminster Hwy. *Tel* (604) 718-6188. ⬜ 7am–sunset daily.

The UBC's Irving K. Barber Library, its clock tower a campus landmark

Restaurants lining the boardwalk along Steveston's waterfront

Chinese Buddhist Temple ⓫

9160 Steveston Hwy, Richmond.
Tel (604) 274-2822. 🚌 98 B-Line, 403. ⏰ 9:30am–5:30pm daily.
🎫 (by donation).

The grace of Richmond's huge Chinese Buddhist Temple, completed in 1983 after much planning and fundraising by five Chinese immigrants, is immediately evident in the curved roof of golden porcelain tiles and the marble lions guarding the entrance. The temple's interior is richly adorned with sculptures of the Buddha, ornate murals, and sumptuous painting, woodwork, and embroidery. Visitors may encounter one of the daily ceremonies that take place and are welcome to observe the rituals.

Outside, a majestic stone path lined with Tang Dynasty lanterns and brilliant marigolds leads to the statue of the Maitreya Buddha. The

shade of twin gazebos and the restful sound of nearby fountains offer a soothing respite from the bustling city. The bonsai garden in the courtyard is a delight to stroll.

Steveston ⓬

Tel (877) 247-0777. 🚌 401, 402.
www.steveston.bc.ca

The village of Steveston, in Richmond, offers visitors a peek into British Columbia's fishing and agricultural heritage. Steveston is proud of its past, which dates back to the turn of the 19th century. The charming **Steveston Museum** is housed in the last of the original 350 Northern Banks that once operated in Western Canada. The **London Heritage Farm** features a restored 1880s farmhouse.

Steveston's waterfront is home to Canada's largest commercial fishing fleet. Freighters and fishing boats share the mouth of the Fraser River as they head for the Strait

of Georgia. On Fisherman's Wharf, shoppers can purchase fish and seafood directly off the fishing boats. Restaurants overlooking the water serve equally fresh fare. Harbor cruises go up the Fraser River. A block away, on Moncton Street, art shops and souvenir galleries mingle with local businesses. A short walk from the village center is 44-acre (18-ha) **Garry Point Park**, with beaches that offer vistas of Vancouver Island.

A highlight is the **Gulf of Georgia Cannery**. In the 1890s, 15 salmon canneries employed upwards of 10,000 men and women. Most of the Gulf of Georgia Cannery complex, a national historic site which includes an icehouse, a lead foundry, and an artifact collection featuring machinery from the early 1900s, sits on pilings built over the Fraser River. At its height, in 1897, the cannery produced over 2.5 million cans of salmon.

🏛 **Steveston Museum**
3811 Moncton St. *Tel* (604) 718-8439. ⏰ 9:30am–1pm, 1:30–5pm Mon–Sat. ● major hols.
🎫 donation. 🚻 1st floor only.
📷 by appt.

🚻 **London Heritage Farm**
6511 Dyke Rd. *Tel* (604) 271-5220.
Farm ⏰ Feb–Jun & Sep–mid-Nov: noon–5pm Sat & Sun; Jul–Aug: noon–5pm Wed–Sun; mid-Nov–Dec: noon–4pm Fri, noon–5pm Sat & Sun. 🎫 donation. 🚻 📷 by appt.
www.londonheritagefarm.ca

🚻 **Gulf of Georgia Cannery**
12138 4th Ave. *Tel* (604) 664-9009. ⏰ May–Sep: 10am–5pm daily. 🎫 🚻 📷 🚻 www.gulfofgeorgiacannery.com

The intricately carved Chinese Buddhist Temple and gate

THE MIGHTY FRASER RIVER

The majestic Fraser River travels from Mount Robson Provincial Park to the Strait of Georgia, near Vancouver. It broadens at Hope, transforming the Fraser Valley into lush farmlands. Once in the Vancouver area, it splits into two arms. One million migratory birds settle by the river near Steveston each winter, making this a great bird-watching area. The Fraser is also the largest salmon river in the world, though overfishing has severely reduced its runs.

The spectacular, winding Fraser Canyon

Museum of Anthropology ❾

Founded in 1947, this outstanding museum houses one of the world's finest collections of Northwest Coast First Nations peoples' art. Designed by Canadian architect Arthur Erickson in 1976, the museum is housed in a stunning building over-looking mountains and sea. The tall posts and huge windows of the Great Hall were inspired by the post-and-beam architecture of Haida houses and are a fitting home for a display of full-size totem poles, canoes, and feast dishes. Through the windows of the Great Hall, the visitor can see the magnificent outdoor sculpture complex, which includes two houses designed by contemporary Haida artist Bill Reid.

★ The Great Hall
The imposing glass and concrete structure of the Great Hall is the perfect setting for totem poles, canoes, and sculptures.

OUTDOOR HAIDA HOUSES AND TOTEM POLES

Set overlooking the water, these two Haida houses and collection of totem poles are faithful to the artistic tradition of the Haida and other tribes of the Pacific Northwest, such as the Nisga'a, Gitxsan, and Kwak-waka'wakw. Animals and mythic creatures representing various clans are carved in cedar on these poles and houses, made between 1959 and 1963 by Vancouver's favorite contemporary Haida artist Bill Reid and Namgis artist Doug Cranmer.

Carved red cedar totem poles

Carved Figures
These figures are on houseboards that once decorated the interior of a First Nations family house. Carved from cedar planks, the style is typical of Coast Salish sculpture.

Ceramic Jug
This beautifully decorated jug was made in Central Europe in 1674 by members of the Anabaptist religious sect. The foliage motifs are in contrast to the freely sketched animals that run around the base.

STAR EXHIBITS

★ The Great Hall

★ The Raven and the First Men by Bill Reid

★ **The Raven and the First Men** *(1980)*
Carved in laminated yellow cedar by Bill Reid, this modern interpretation of a Haida creation myth depicts the Raven, a wise and wily trickster, trying to coax mankind out into the world from a giant clamshell.

MUSEUM GUIDE

The museum's collections are on one level. The Ramp leads to the Great Hall, which features the cultures of Northwest coast First Nations peoples. The Multiversity Galleries contain artifacts from other cultures, and a range of 16th- to 19th-century European ceramics is housed in the Koerner European Ceramics Gallery.

Wooden Frontlet
Decorated with abalone shell, this wooden frontlet was a ceremonial headdress worn only on important occasions such as births and marriages.

Red Cedar Carved Doors

This detail comes from the set of stunning carved red cedar doors that guard the entrance to the shop. Created in 1976 by a group of First Nations artists from the 'Ksan cultural center near Hazelton, the doors show the history of the first people of the Skeena River region in British Columbia.

KEY

- ⬜ The Ramp
- ⬛ The Great Hall
- ⬜ The Rotunda
- ⬛ Multiversity Galleries
- ⬜ Koerner European Ceramics Gallery
- ⬜ Michael M. Ames Theatre
- ⬜ Temporary exhibition space
- ⬜ Non-exhibition space

Shopping in Vancouver

The shops in Vancouver and surrounding areas show-case goods and fashions from every continent. Funky boutiques and vintage clothing stores abound in Gastown, as do shops specializing in Native art. Other shopping districts also offer myriad goods, from upscale furniture to kitchenware and specialty items.

Window display at a clothing store on Vancouver's Granville Island

SHOPPING DISTRICTS

Robson Street *(see p212)* is Vancouver's major shopping promenade. Specialty shops and boutiques line the streets of Gastown, Kitsilano, Kerrisdale, Yaletown, and Ambleside *(see p224)*. South Granville is home to upscale clothing and furnishing stores. Granville Island *(see pp216–19)* offers an array of shops and galler-ies, as well as a huge food market. Visit Chinatown and the Punjabi market around Main Street and 49th Avenue for ethnic shopping. Richmond *(see p228)* is known for its Asian shopping malls.

Sign for Lonsdale Quay Market

DEPARTMENT STORES AND SHOPPING CENTERS

Most of the city's shopping centers are anchored by major department stores. **The Bay** sells quality Canadian and international brand-name clothing, and its own clothing lines. **Sears on Robson** features the Roots and Kenneth Cole labels, as well as big cosmetic houses.

At the 140-store **Pacific Centre** and the 500-store **Metropolis at Metrotown**, BC's largest shopping mall, goods range from brand-name fashions to smoked BC salmon. The smaller **Sinclair Centre** features international fashions in an Edwardian

Baroque-style building that was formerly a post office. On the North Shore, Lonsdale Quay Market *(see p225)* offers a harbor view as well as a food market and boutiques, while **Park Royal Shopping Centre** *(see p224)* houses a multitude of shops under two roofs.

SPECIALTY SHOPS

On the funkier side is **John Fluevog** with unique boot and shoe designs for both men and women. **Leone** houses sophisticated boutiques, with fashions from Yves St. Laurent, Prada, and Versace, among others. Internationally known **Roots** offers Canadian design in both casual and athletic wear, as well as leather goods.

The elegant selection at **Birks Jewellers** includes, along with fine jewelry, pens, watches, crystal, and classic gifts. The **Inuit Gallery**, one of several stores in Gastown specializing in Native art, carries high-quality Inuit prints and soapstone carvings, and Northwest Coast First Nations masks, bentwood boxes, prints, and jewelry.

Chocoholics will love **Rogers' Chocolates**, which first opened in 1885. There are two locations in Vancou-ver: one in Gastown and the other on Granville Island.

Store in Gastown selling western-style boots and other leather goods

DIRECTORY

DEPARTMENT STORES AND SHOPPING CENTERS

The Bay
674 Granville St. **Map** 3 A2.
Tel (604) 681-6211.

Metropolis at Metrotown
4800 Kingsway, Burnaby.
Tel (604) 438-4715.

Pacific Centre
700 W Georgia St. **Map** 3 A2.
Tel (604) 688-7235.

Park Royal
2002 Park Royal South,
West Vancouver.
Tel (604) 925-9576.

Sears on Robson
701 Granville St. **Map** 3 A2.
Tel (604) 685-7112.

Sinclair Centre
757 W Hastings St. **Map** 3 A2.
Tel (604) 488-0672.

SPECIALTY SHOPS

Birks Jewellers
698 W Hastings St. **Map** 3 A2.
Tel (604) 669-3333.

Inuit Gallery
206 Cambie St. **Map** 3 B2.
Tel (604) 688-7323.

John Fluevog
837 Granville St. **Map** 2 F3.
Tel (604) 688-2828.

Leone
757 W Hastings St. **Map** 3 A2.
Tel (604) 683-1133.

Rogers' Chocolates
The Landing, 389 Water St.
Map 3 B2. *Tel (604) 676-3452.*

Roots
1001 Robson St. **Map** 2 F2.
Tel (604) 683-4305.

WHAT TO BUY

Quality Canadian-made fashions, leatherwear, and handbags are good buys in Vancouver. First Nations and Inuit art – including carvings, prints, masks, and jewelry – is available at many stores and gallery shops. BC jade jewelry is also popular, as are Cow-ichan knit sweaters. Tradition-ally smoked wild sockeye salmon, often packaged in decorative cedar boxes, is another West Coast specialty.

Entertainment in Vancouver

Entertainment in Vancouver runs the gamut from world-class opera productions to amateur music concerts. Each year the city hosts folk music, jazz, theater, dance, comedy, literary, and film festivals, among others. Vancouver is one of Canada's top theater centers; homegrown talent mixes with performers from Europe and the US.

The Orpheum Theatre's spectacular gold-leaf interior, built in 1927

INFORMATION

The city's two dailies, the *Vancouver Sun* and *The Province*, publish events listings on Thursdays. The free weekly *Georgia Straight* also has extensive listings. *Where Vancouver*, available at downtown hotels and tourist kiosks, lists events and shows.

BUYING TICKETS

Tickets for most events can be purchased from **Ticketmaster** by phone or at one of its locations. Many venues also sell tickets directly. **Tickets Tonight**, in the main Tourist-info Centre *(see p234)*, sells full-price tickets for theater and sporting events, and half-price tickets for some performances on the day of. Discount tickets must be bought in person; others can be bought online.

FREE EVENTS

The Vancouver Central Library *(see p212)* hosts a variety of lectures and author readings; CBC *(see p209)* presents concerts and admits the public to many studio tapings. Annual and community festivals are listed in *Georgia Straight*.

THEATER

Classics by Shakespeare, Shaw, and others, along with modern US and Canadian plays, are features of the **Vancouver Playhouse**. The **Arts Club Theatre** owes its success to solid theatrical fare performed by BC's leading actors. A popular venue for musicals is the 1930 **Stanley Industrial Alliance Stage**, now restored to its sassy vaudeville style. The small **Firehall Arts Centre** showcases culturally diverse contemporary theater and dance.

Summer events include plays at the open-air Theatre under the Stars (tel. 604/734-1917) in Stanley Park and the Bard on the Beach Shakespeare Festival (tel. 604/739-0559) in Vanier Park.

DANCE AND MUSIC

With its inspiring modern repertoire, **Ballet British Columbia** performs at the **Queen Elizabeth Theatre**, as does the **Vancouver Opera**, founded in 1958 and presenting four operas each year. The ornate 2,700-seat **Orpheum Theatre** hosts a variety of concerts, including classical, jazz, and pop. It is also home to the **Vancouver Symphony Orchestra**, whose series include classical and family concerts, often with internationally recognized guest musicians. The 1,200-seat **Chan Centre for the Performing Arts** *(see p228)* showcases musical recitals and opera ensembles.

Performer in one of Vancouver Opera's many productions

DIRECTORY

TICKET OUTLETS

Ticketmaster
Tel (604) 280-4444.

Tickets Tonight
Tel (604) 684-2787.
www.ticketstonight.ca

THEATER

Arts Club Theatre
Tel (604) 687-1644.

Firehall Arts Centre
Tel (604) 689-0926.

Stanley Industrial Alliance Stage
Tel (604) 687-1644.

Vancouver Playhouse
Tel (604) 873-3311.

DANCE AND MUSIC

Ballet British Columbia
Tel (604) 732-5003.

Chan Centre for the Performing Arts
Tel (604) 822-9197.

Commodore Ballroom
Tel (604) 683-9413.

Orpheum Theatre
Tel (604) 665-3050.

Queen Elizabeth Theatre
Tel (604) 665-3050.

Vancouver Opera
Tel (604) 683-0222.

Vancouver Symphony Orchestra
Tel (604) 876-3434.

SPORTS VENUES

BC Place Stadium
Tel (604) 669-2300.

Nat Bailey Stadium
Tel (604) 872-5232.

Rogers Arena
Tel (604) 899-7400.

Commodore Ballroom, boasting a floating dance floor and table seating for 990, hosts an eclectic mix of local and international talent.

SPECTATOR SPORTS

Sporting events such as BC Lions CFL football and Vancouver Canucks NHL hockey games take place at **BC Place Stadium** and **Rogers Arena**. The Vancouver Canadians play baseball at **Nat Bailey Stadium** in Queen Elizabeth Park.

Getting Around Vancouver

Although somewhat sprawling, Vancouver is not so big as to be overwhelming. The Vancouver Touristinfo Centre, near Canada Place, provides information on sights, accommodation, and transit, as well as street maps. The various local tours on offer, such as the free tour of historic Gastown, are an excellent way of exploring the city.

CITY AND STREET LAYOUT

The many bridges spanning Vancouver's bodies of water can confuse visitors, as can the occurrence of "west" in the names of several areas in the city. The residential West End shares the downtown peninsula with the business and commercial district and with Stanley Park. The West Side stretches from Ontario Street, on the south side of False Creek, to the University of British Columbia and encompasses several neighborhoods, including Kitsilano and Kerrisdale. The community of West Vancouver is adjacent to North Vancouver, on the North Shore.

Before heading anywhere, it is wise to consult a good street map. The mountains, which are to the north, are a useful landmark for orientation.

Most streets run north–south and east–west, though some run on the diagonal. Some downtown streets are one-way. Outside the downtown core, avenues, divided east–west by Ontario Street, are numbered; north–south streets are named.

WALKING

Many of the city's attractions are within walking distance of the downtown core. Others are easily accessible by public transit. However, as the neighborhoods are somewhat scattered, it is often best to drive or use public transit to

The SeaBus heading from the North Shore to downtown Vancouver

get to a particular neighborhood and then walk around to soak up the atmosphere. Walking tours through various neighborhoods are available; for a tour of Gastown, contact **Walking Tours of Gastown**.

BICYCLING

Vancouver is a great city for cycling, with bikeways covering more than 249 miles (400 km). Bikeways can be found at False Creek, Stanley Park, the University of British Columbia, and elsewhere downtown.

The free brochure "Cycling in Vancouver" includes a map of bike routes. It is available at bicycle shops and bookstores, or by calling the **City of Vancouver Bicycle Hot Line**, which also provides details on where to rent bicycles.

Traffic-calming circles and other measures, such as cyclist-friendly sensors at traffic lights, slow vehicle traffic on city streets. Bicycle helmets are mandatory.

Vancouver taxi

TAXIS

Taxis are numerous in Vancouver and can be hailed on the street or ordered by telephone. Taxi fares start at $3.05 and increase at the rate of approximately $1.76 per half mile (1 km).

PUBLIC TRANSIT

The Greater Vancouver transportation authority, **TransLink**, operates an extensive public transit network. Transit maps are available for a minimal charge at major drugstores and supermarkets, some convenience stores, and the main location of the **Tourism Vancouver Visitor Centre**.

The SeaBus, a 400-seat catamaran, crosses Vancouver Harbour from the downtown Waterfront Station to Lonsdale Quay in North Vancouver every 15 to 30 minutes until around midnight.

SkyTrain, a driverless aboveground light rail system, travels between Waterfront Station and Surrey. Schedules vary, depending on the time of day and day of the week. Fares range from $2.50 to $5 and are based on a three-zone system. Tickets allow interchangeable travel on the SeaBus, SkyTrain, and buses, including TransLink trolleys. Children under the age of 4 ride free; those between the ages of 5 and 13, as well as people over age 65, pay a reduced fare. A transfer ticket is free and lasts for 90 minutes of travel in any direction. FareSaver books of ten tickets, usually available where transit maps are sold, provide a discount. A $9 day pass can be purchased at supermarkets and at SkyTrain ticket vending machines in the stations.

All trips after 6:30pm and on weekends and holidays are considered to be in one zone anywhere in the system.

The commuter rail service **West Coast Express** runs during peak periods on weekdays between Mission and Vancouver, stopping at several outlying municipalities.

The free Stanley Park shuttle bus at Brockton Point, one of its many stops

The West Coast Express, SkyTrain, SeaBus, and many of the bus routes are wheelchair accessible.

FERRIES

Two ferry companies operate ferries along False Creek: **False Creek Ferries** and **Aquabus** *(see p219)*. The ferries dock at Science World, Yaletown, the Vancouver Aquatic Centre, Granville Island, and Vanier Park. Adult single fares range from $3.25 to $6.50. False Creek Ferries' day pass ($15) allows unlimited one-day travel. The Aquabus all-day pass is also $15.

The SkyTrain, linking downtown with Vancouver suburbs

DRIVING

Despite some downtown congestion, traffic in Vancouver usually flows reasonably well. Streets are generally easy to navigate, although street signage is sometimes nonexistent. Some downtown streets limit left-hand turns to nonpeak hours. Right-hand turns on a red light are allowed after coming to a full stop, unless otherwise noted. Weekday rush hours are from 7 to 9:30am and 3 to 6pm. Friday's crush of cars may start even earlier and will be especially busy on the Friday of a long weekend.

A double-decker local sightseeing bus

The city speed limit is 30 mph (50 km/h). Some intersections are monitored by police cameras. Seat belts are mandatory, as are helmets for motorcyclists.

The **British Columbia Automobile Association** (BCAA) offers assistance, maps, and guidebooks to members of the Canadian or American Automobile Association.

PARKING

Paid parking is available in Vancouver's numerous parking lots. Metered street parking is also available. Keep a variety of change on hand, including quarters and $1 coins. Credit cards are accepted for parking in many places. It may be less expensive to park in a lot and pay the day rate than to feed the meter throughout the day. Infractions ticketing is usually prompt and always expensive. Check posted street parking regulations; they may limit parking during rush hours or specify other parking regulations, such as a maximum of two hours' parking. Free street parking is generally available from 10pm to 6am. Again, check the posted parking regulations; they can vary. Some shopping malls and attractions offer free parking, although these are usually situated outside the downtown core.

TOWING

If your car is towed from a city street, contact **Busters Towing**. Its main impound yard is located near Science World on Industrial Avenue. If towed from a private lot, call the telephone number on the sign posted nearby.

An Aquabus ferry bringing passengers to Granville Island

DIRECTORY

USEFUL NUMBERS

Aquabus
Tel (604) 689-5858.
www.theaquabus.com

British Columbia Automobile Association
Tel (604) 268-5555; (604) 293-2222 for emergency road service.
www.bcaa.com

Busters Towing
Tel (604) 685-7246.
www.busterstowing.com

City of Vancouver Bicycle Hot Line
Tel (604) 871-6070.
www.vancouver.ca

False Creek Ferries
Tel (604) 684-7781.
www.granvilleislandferries.bc.ca

Tourism Vancouver Visitor Centre
200 Burrard St, plaza level.
Tel (604) 683-2000.
🕐 *mid-May–Sep: 8:30am–6pm daily; Oct–mid-May: 8:30am–5pm Mon–Sat.*
www.tourismvancouver.com

TransLink
Tel (604) 953-3333.
www.translink.ca

Walking Tours of Gastown
Tel (604) 683-5650 (Gastown Business Improvement Society).
www.gastown.org

West Coast Express
Tel (604) 488-8906.
www.westcoastexpress.com

VANCOUVER STREET FINDER

The key map below shows the area of Vancouver covered by the *Street Finder* maps, which can be found on the following pages. Map references for sights, hotels, restaurants, shops, and entertainment venues given throughout the Vancouver chapter of this guide refer to the grid on the maps. The first figure in the reference indicates which map to turn to (1 to 4); the letter and number that follow refer to the grid reference on that map.

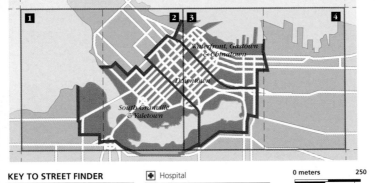

KEY TO STREET FINDER

- ■ Major sight
- ■ Minor sight
- ■ Station building
- 🚌 Bus station – long distance
- 🚇 SkyTrain
- 🅿 Parking
- ℹ Information
- ✚ Hospital
- 🚓 Police station
- ✝ Church
- ⊠ Post office
- ⚓ Ferry boarding point
- – – Ferry route
- ═ Railroad line
- → One-way street

0 meters   250

0 yards   250

SCALE OF MAPS 1–4

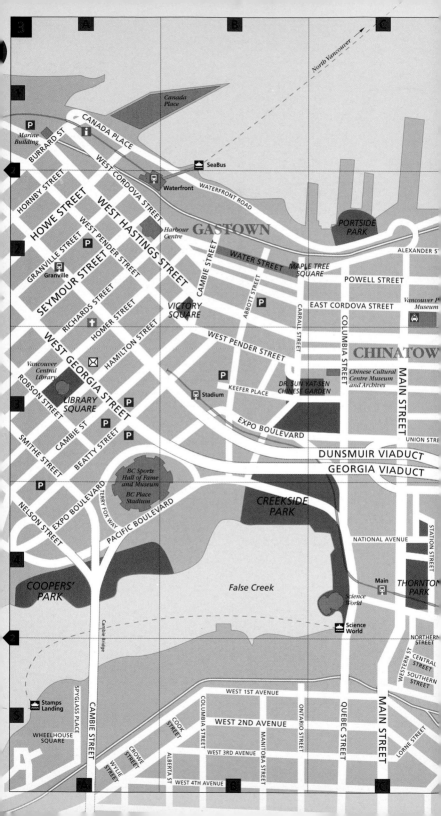

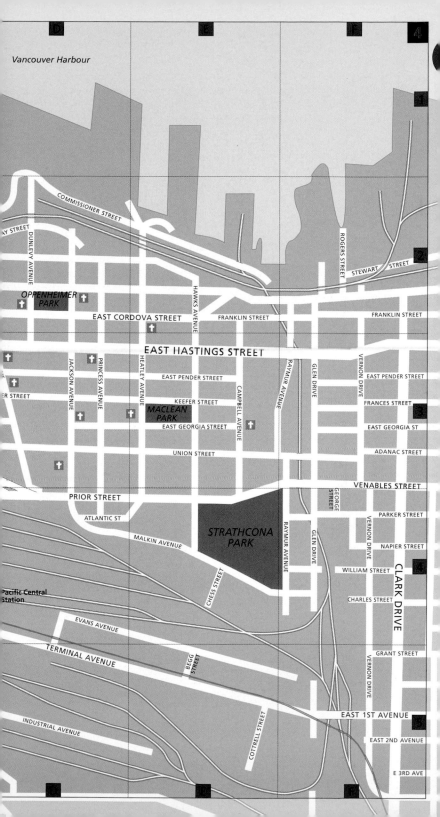

BRITISH COLUMBIA

British Columbia is one of Canada's most strikingly beautiful provinces. Tranquil islands grace its Pacific Ocean coastline while awe-inspiring mountain ranges on the mainland include the world-famous Rockies. Astounding natural vistas surround lively urban centers, from the large, modern cities of Vancouver and Victoria to small towns with historic pasts.

Thousands of years before the first Europeans arrived, the 366,254-sq-mile (948,600-sq-km) area that is now British Columbia was home to First Nations tribes. Today, reconstructions of their cedar longhouses and semi-subterranean pit houses may be seen in museums.

Spanish and British ships explored the province's 16,800-mile (27,000-km) coastline from 1774 onward. In 1792, Captain George Vancouver – for whom the province's largest city was later named – was impressed, describing "innumerable pleasing landscapes." British Columbia joined the confederation of Canada in 1871, and the Canadian Pacific Railway arrived in Vancouver in 1887, joining the new West Coast province to the already established eastern ones and bringing waves of new settlers. BC was built on logging, mining, and fishing, and while these industries have seen hard times over the years, they continue to support many communities today. Tourism, however, is now ranked second in the province's economy, after forestry.

British Columbia offers travelers an impressive array of breathtaking scenery and experiences. Vancouver Island's sandy beaches and rugged wilderness are a short drive or ferry ride from the urban pleasures of Victoria and of Vancouver, from which popular ski hills are only minutes away. Inland, the interior's many lakes provide glistening vistas and sunny playgrounds for water sports of all kinds. Nestled among the BC Rocky Mountains are historic mining towns, and provincial and national parks offering exciting winter skiing and summer hiking experiences. In the north, the Skeena River, the "river of mists," travels through ancient tribal lands, sprinkled with stunning First Nations totem poles. Prince Rupert is the port of call for the ferry to the remote, misty archipelago of Haida Gwaii, formerly known as the Queen Charlotte Islands.

The harbor in Masset on Graham Island, British Columbia

◁ **Detail of totem pole at Skidegate, a Haida community in Haida Gwaii (formerly the Queen Charlotte Islands)**

Exploring British Columbia

WILDLIFE VIEWING

Okanagan Valley sign

The exceptional beauty of British Columbia's coast, mountain ranges, forests, and lakes makes it a much-visited province. A wide variety of landscapes are to be found, from the northern Rockies with their bare peaks to the southern Okanagan Valley with its orchards and vineyards. To the west, Vancouver Island offers ancient rainforests and the impressive coastal scenery of the Pacific Rim National Park. Lying between the Pacific Ocean and the Coast Mountains, Vancouver is a stunningly attractive city, with good transportation links. The province's temperate climate means that BC has more species of plants and animals than anywhere else in the country. Millions of visitors come here every year, drawn by a range of outdoor activities.

SIGHTS AT A GLANCE

Atlin
Simpson Peak
2173m
Atlin Lake
Good Hope Lake
37
Meszah Peak
2164m
Dease Lake
Glenora
Mount Edziza
2787m
Mount Ratz
3136m
Meziadi Junction
37
THE HAZELTONS
CRUISE TO ALASKA
SMITHERS
30
Masset
28
16
PRINCE RUPERT
Kitim
Graham Island
HAIDA GWAII
Skidegate
29
Moresby Island
Princess Royal Island
Bella Bella
Queen Charlotte Sound
Port Hard

0 km   100

0 miles   100

SEE ALSO

Vancouver Island, British Columbia

KEY

- Highway
- Major road
- Minor road
- Main railroad
- Minor railroad
- International border
- State border
- △ Summit

Legislative Chamber in the provincial Parliament Buildings, Victoria

GETTING AROUND

Several major highways cross British Columbia: the Trans-Canada (Hwy 1), Crowsnest (Hwy 3), and Yellowhead (Hwy 16). The Coquihalla (Hwy 5) is a four-lane route between Hope and Kamloops. It is 45 miles (73 km) shorter than the Trans-Canada route. Hwy 97 links Dawson Creek with Whitehorse, in the Yukon. On Vancouver Island, Hwys 1, 4, and 19 are the main routes. VIA trains and Greyhound buses travel to many BC destinations.

Wooden waterwheel, Fort Steele Heritage Town

River

MUNCHO LAKE PROVINCIAL PARK 25

Liard

🏛🏚 24 **FORT NELSON**

Mount Roosevelt 2972m

Prophet River

Mount Lloyd George 2970m 97

ALASKA HIGHWAY

Sikanni Chief

Toad

Ituca Mountains

Hudson's Hope

Williston Lake 97 22 **DAWSON CREEK**

Chetwynd Tupper

FORT 23 **ST. JOHN**

Mackenzie

Tumbler Ridge

BRITISH COLUMBIA

Babine Lake Fort St. James

Fraser

Mount Sir Alexander 3274m

16 🏛 21 **PRINCE GEORGE**

McBride

Mount Robson 3954m

Nazko 97 16

Valemount

ahim Lake *Fraser Plateau* **WELLS GRAY PROVINCIAL PARK** 20

Mount Columbia 3747m

Monarch Mountain 3533m Williams Lake Clearwater 5 Mica Creek

YOHO NATIONAL PARK 19

Mount Waddington 4016m Clinton 97 **GLACIER NATIONAL PARK** 18 **KOOTENAY NATIONAL PARK** 17

Lillooet 1 Revelstoke **RADIUM HOT SPRINGS** 16

9 **KAMLOOPS** Invermere

99 **PURCELL MOUNTAINS** 15

WHISTLER 8 **OKANAGAN VALLEY** 12 10 **KELOWNA**

🏛 14 **FORT STEELE**

Powell River **SUMMERLAND** 11 Nelson Cranbrook Fernie

couver sland 19 Vancouver Hope 97 Castlegar 13

🏛 5 6 ✈ Abbotsford **THE KOOTENAYS**

NANAIMO 5 4 3 Osoyoos

7 2 **GULF ISLANDS**

PACIFIC RIM NPR 1 **CHEMAINUS**

BUTCHART GARDENS **VICTORIA** **COWICHAN DISTRICT**

Victoria ❶

Clock in the Bay Centre

A quiet city, Victoria has an old-fashioned atmosphere, one enhanced by the hanging flower baskets that decorate the streets. Established as a Hudson's Bay Company fur-trading post in 1843 by James Douglas, Victoria had its risqué moments during its Gold Rush years (1858–63), when thousands of prospectors drank in its saloons. Established as the capital of British Columbia in 1871, Victoria was soon outgrown by Vancouver. Today, this multicultural city is still BC's political center, as well as a popular attraction for visitors.

Historic buildings along Yates Street, typical of Victoria's Old Town

Parliament buildings illuminate the waters of the Inner Harbour

Exploring Victoria

Many of Victoria's attractions are downtown and in Old Town, which is bordered by Wharf, Humboldt, Douglas, and Fisgard Streets. Plaques on historic buildings, now housing funky shops and cafés, offer insight into this area that was, in the 1800s, Victoria's commercial center. Downtown stretches from Inner Harbour to Quadra, Belleville, and Herald Streets. Historic Fort Street is home to Antique Row. The visitors' center provides details on walking tours, including lantern and cemetery tours.

⚓ Inner Harbour
Foot of Government St.
Home to the Songhees, of the Coast Salish Nation, between 1858 and 1911, the Inner Harbour today is vibrant with boats, pedestrians strolling along the promenade, and street performers. Plaques along the walkway pay tribute to those who shaped the harbor's history. The promenade offers excellent views not only of the harbor but also of the Parliament Buildings and Empress Hotel, particularly in the reflecting sunlight of late afternoon.

Victoria's busy Inner Harbour at the foot of Government Street

For hotels and restaurants in this region see pp292–5 and pp311–13

SIGHTS AT A GLANCE

Bastion Square ②
The Bay Centre ⑥
Beacon Hill Park ⑮
Carr House ⑭
Centennial Square ⑤
Chinatown ④
Fairmont Empress Hotel ⑨
Helmcken House ⑩
Inner Harbour ①
Market Square ③
Parliament Buildings ⑬
Royal BC Museum ⑪
St. Andrew's Cathedral ⑦
Thunderbird Park ⑫
Victoria Bug Zoo ⑧

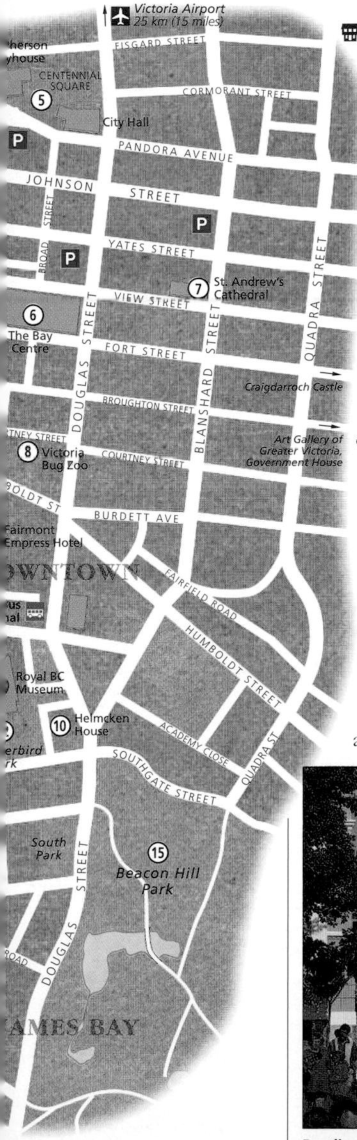

Key to Symbols *see back flap*

VISITORS' CHECKLIST

Road map 2 B5. 👥 *79,000.* ✈ *Victoria Airport, 15 miles (25 km) north of city.* 🚌 *Pacific Coach Lines, 700 Douglas St.* ⛴ *BC Ferries.* ℹ *812 Wharf St, (250) 953-2033.* 🎉 *JazzFest International (mid-Jun).* **www**.tourismvictoria.com

Bastion Square

Government St. ○ *daily.* ♿

This beautifully restored square faces Victoria's picturesque harbor and contains some of the city's oldest 19th-century buildings. What were once luxury hotels and offices, built during the boom era of the late 1800s, now house boutiques and gift shops. Restoration began in 1963 when it was discovered that the Hudson's Bay Company's fur-trading post Fort Victoria, established in 1843, once stood on this site. Today, this pedestrian square includes the MacDonald Block building, built in 1863 in Italianate style, with elegant cast-iron columns and arched windows. The old courthouse, built in 1889, houses the BC Maritime Museum. In summer, the square bustles with visitors and workers alike who come to lunch in one of the several courtyard cafés.

Bustling Bastion Square, dating back to the late 1880s

Decorative banners lining Market Square, Victoria

Market Square

560 Johnson St. ***Tel*** *(250) 386-2441.* ○ *10am–5pm daily.* ● *Dec 25.* ♿ *partial.*

Located two blocks north of Bastion Square on the corner of Johnson Street, Market Square boasts some of the finest Victorian saloon, hotel, and store façades in the city. Most of the buildings here date from the 1880s and 1890s, the boom period of the Klondike Gold Rush *(see p125)*. After decades of neglect, the area received a much-needed face-lift in 1975. Today, the square is a shoppers' paradise, with a variety of stores selling everything from books and jewelry to musical instruments and other arts and crafts. Concerts, festivals, and other events are held here throughout the year.

⌂ Chinatown

Bounded by Pandora Ave & Store, Government & Herald Sts.

Victoria's Chinatown, the oldest in Canada and once its largest, is now the country's smallest, yet its vegetable markets, curio shops, and restaurants provide hours' worth of exploration. The ornate **Gate of Harmonious Interest** (Fisgard and Government Streets) leads into the two-block-square area that was at one time home to Chinese railroad laborers and their families *(see p211)*.

Fan Tan Alley, possibly the world's narrowest street, was once filled with opium dens and gambling houses. Today, visitors will find an eclectic mix of shops here. From the alley, enter though the backdoor of **Chinatown Trading Co.** (551 Fisgard Street) to see artifacts from the district's earlier days, including those from a 19th-century gambling house.

The sunken knot garden behind City Hall at Centennial Square

❁ Centennial Square

Bounded by Fisgard, Douglas & Government Sts & Pandora Ave.

Created in 1963, Centennial Square is part of an effort to revitalize the city's downtown. Its centerpiece is a fountain with concrete "totems" adorned with mosaics by a local artist. Surrounding the public space are specialty shops, McPherson Playhouse – which opened in 1914 as the first Pantages Theatre and which has a beautiful baroque interior – a knot garden, and City Hall.

The Second Empire-style south wing of City Hall – its

The Second Empire-style City Hall, with its clock tower

red-brick façade and tin mansard roof exemplifying this style – was built in 1878. In 1880, a fire station was added, and in 1891, a northeast wing. The clock, installed in the tower (1890) in 1891, is still wound once a week. In 1963, the interior of City Hall was completely renovated and an International style west wing was added.

⌂ The Bay Centre

1150 Douglas St. **Tel** (250) 952-5680. ◯ 10am–7pm Mon–Wed & Sat, 10am–9pm Thu & Fri, 11am–6pm Sun. ♿ www.thebaycentre.ca

The Bay Centre sits behind the façades of several historic buildings on Government Street. The 1892 Driard Hotel was saved from demolition by a public campaign, as were the fronts of the 1910 Times Building and the 19th-century Lettice and Sears Building. Behind these and other elegant façades, more than 90 shops on four floors sell everything from fashion to handmade chocolates. In the atrium hangs a clock, its several faces displaying the time in various ports of the former British Empire.

⌂ St. Andrew's Cathedral

740 View St. **Tel** (250) 388-5571. ◯ daily. ✝ 8am Tue–Fri, 12:10pm Mon–Fri; 8am, 9:30am, 11am & 5pm Sun. ♿ www.standrewscathedral.com

Built in 1892, this is the oldest Roman Catholic church in the area. The Victorian Gothic-style cathedral made of stone, slate, and brick features a 175-ft- (53-m-) tall spire and beautiful stained-glass windows. Works of local First Nations artists were introduced during the 1980s renovations. The altar was designed by Charles Elliott, of the Coast Salish Nation; the candles on either side of the pulpit are decorated with Native designs.

St. Andrew's Cathedral, Victoria's first Roman Catholic church

⚘ Victoria Bug Zoo

631 Courtney St. **Tel** (250) 384-2847. ◯ 9am–5pm daily. ◯ Jan 1, Dec 25. ♿ www.bugzoo.bc.ca

Located one block north of the iconic Fairmont Empress Hotel, this unusual mini-zoo occupies only two rooms.

The central atrium in Victoria's Bay Centre, with its suspended clock

Here, visitors can get up close and personal with some of the world's most exotic insects. The Victoria Bug Zoo exhibits more than 50 species of insects, arachnids, and myriapoda; it also boasts the largest ant farm in Canada, comprising a colony of leaf-cutter ants. Visitors can wander around the zoo independently or join a free tour during which the knowledgeable guides share a series of fascinating facts on their charges. It is also possible to hold one of the zoo's friendly tarantulas, a surefire way to get over a fear of spiders. Also on display are some glow-in-the-dark scorpions. The small gift shop stocks pet tarantulas, insect-collecting kits, and even bug-infused lollipops.

The entranceway to the grand Fairmont Empress Hotel

🏨 Fairmont Empress Hotel

721 Government St.
Tel (250) 384-8111. ⬜ daily.
🚹 See **Where to Stay** p295.
www.fairmont.com
Completed in 1905 to a Francis Rattenbury design and built on what was once mud flats and the site of the city's unofficial dump, the Empress is one of Victoria's best-loved sights. Overlooking the Inner Harbour, the hotel dominates the city skyline with its ivy-covered Gothic splendor. You do not have to be a guest to experience the luxurious decor of the hotel's public bars and lounges, such as the Crystal Ballroom, with its Tiffany-glass dome. High tea, a

popular Empress tradition, is served daily. In front of the hotel stands a statue of Captain James Cook *(see p36)*, who, though he explored much of BC's coast, ironically never saw Victoria.

🏛 Helmcken House

10 Elliot Sq. **Tel** (250) 356-7226.
⬜ May–Oct: noon–4pm daily; Nov–Apr: call for hours. 📷 🚹 📷 📷
The home of Hudson's Bay Company employee Dr. John Sebastian Helmcken was built in 1852 and is one of the oldest surviving houses in British Columbia. The young doctor, who later helped negotiate BC's entry into the Dominion of Canada, built the house with his wife using Douglas firs felled in the surrounding forest. Built using the post-on-sill method popular in French Canada, it was the first residence outside the secure boundaries of Fort Victoria. A second section was added to the house in 1856, and a third in 1884.

Sign for Helmcken House

Wood-burning stove at the historic Helmcken House

Together, the additions reflect the change in construction methods in the second half of the 19th century. The simple but elegant dwelling contains many of the original furnishings, including the piano, which visitors are permitted to play. Other highlights include Dr. Helmcken's medical kit and equipment.

FROM FORT TO CAPITAL

James Douglas fell in love with Camosack, the area known to many now as Victoria, when he sailed into its harbor in 1842. As chief factor of the Hudson's Bay Company (HBC), he was there to establish a fur-trading post and fort, in part an effort to thwart American expansion into the region. Douglas was welcomed by the Lekwammen, ancestors of the Esquimalt and Songhee Nations. In 1843, Fort Camosack (later Fort Victoria) was established. By the end of the decade, the First Nations of the area had signed treaties, selling much of their land to the HBC. Small farms quickly sprung up, and the harbor was soon a busy port and a stopping-off point for prospectors in the 1858 gold rush. Victoria incorporated in 1862, four years later becoming capital of the Colony of British Columbia, the provincial capital once BC entered Confederation in 1871.

View of the growing community of Victoria, 1860

🍁 Thunderbird Park
Belleville & Douglas Sts.

This compact park, at the entrance to the Royal British Columbia Museum *(see pp252–3)*, is home to an imposing collection of plain and painted giant totem poles. During the summer, Native artists carve these handsome totems in the Thunderbird Park Carving Studio. The poles show and preserve the legends of many different First Nations of the Northwest Coast. Also in the park, the Kwakwaka'wakw big house, built in 1952, is a replica of a 19th-century big house in Fort Rupert.

Giant totem poles, a signature feature of Thunderbird Park

🏛 Parliament Buildings
501 Belleville St. **Tel** (250) 387-3046.
⬜ 9am–5pm daily. 🔴 Jan 1,
Dec 25. ♿ 📷

Facing the Inner Harbour, Victoria's many-domed Parliament Buildings are an impressive sight, particularly at night when the façades are

The spectacular main dome of the Parliament Buildings

illuminated by thousands of lights. This has been a tradition since 1956, though the buildings were first lit up as early as 1887, in celebration of Queen Victoria's diamond jubilee.

Designed by Francis Rattenbury in 1892, the buildings were completed in 1897, replacing the "Bird Cages," BC's first parliament buildings. (The carriage house on Superior Street behind the Parliament Buildings is the only remaining Bird Cage structure.) Rattenbury, a 25-year-old British architect who had arrived in British Columbia only the year before, won a national competition to design the buildings. He went on to design several of the province's landmarks, the Empress Hotel and Crystal Garden included.

The stone-and-marble buildings are home to the Provincial Legislature. The Legislative Chamber, where the assembly sits, is upstairs, off a small

The Legislative Chamber at Victoria's Parliament Buildings

gallery that boasts lovely stained-glass windows by William Morris. Visitors can view assembly sessions from the third-floor public galleries. A magnificent dome caps the nearby Lower and Upper Rotundas; the former, a perfect octagon, has a beautiful Italian mosaic floor.

British Columbia's history is depicted throughout the buildings. A statue of explorer Captain George Vancouver perches on top of the main dome. Inside, large murals painted during the Great Depression show scenes from BC history.

Carr House, where renowned artist Emily Carr lived as a child

🏛 Carr House
207 Government St. **Tel** (250) 383-5843. ⬜ May–Sep: 11am–4pm
Tue–Sat. 📷 ♿ 📷 📷
www.emilycarr.com

Emily Carr, one of Canada's best-known artists *(see p28)*, was born in 1871 in this attractive 1864 clapboard house.

Rooms are furnished in late 19th-century period style, with some original family pieces. Carr taught her first art classes to local children in the dining room. Carr's drawing of her father still sits on the mantel in the sitting room where, as an eight-year-old, she did her first sketches. Reproductions of Emily Carr's artwork hang in the Morning Room; the People's Gallery exhibits works of contemporary Canadian artists. The English garden showcases plants popular during the Victorian era.

🍁 Beacon Hill Park
Douglas St & Dallas Rd.
Tel (250) 361-0600. ⬜ daily. ♿
In the late 19th century, this delightful park was being used for stabling horses. In 1888, John Blair, a Scottish

A stately, centuries-old Garry oak tree in Beacon Hill Park

landscape gardener, redesigned the park to include two lakes and initiated extensive tree planting. Once a favorite haunt of artist Emily Carr *(see p28)*, this peaceful 184-acre (74.5-ha) park, the oldest and largest in Victoria, is now renowned for its lofty old trees (including the rare Garry oaks, some of which are more than 400 years old); stretches of wild camas lilies, once highly valued by the area's First Nations; picturesque duck ponds; and a cricket pitch that is more than 100 years old.

🏛 Art Gallery of Greater Victoria

1040 Moss St. *Tel (250) 384-4171.* 🔲 *10am–5pm Mon–Sat (to 9pm Thu), noon–5pm Sun & hols.* 🖼 ♿ 🖥 www.aggv.ca

This gallery's eclectic collection is housed in an impressive Victorian mansion east of the downtown area. Inside, fine wood moldings, original fireplaces, and tall ceilings provide a stately home for an array of exhibits, including a wide-ranging collection of Chinese and Japanese painting, ceramics, and pottery. The gallery also has the only authentic Shinto shrine in North America.

The collection of contemporary Canadian paintings includes those of famous local artist Emily Carr *(see p28)*. Executed between the 1900s and 1930s, Carr's paintings,

Art Gallery of Greater Victoria, shrine detail

with their haunting evocation of the stormy Northwest and the lives of Native peoples, are among the gallery's most popular exhibits. Carr's works, which include her writings, are rotated so that all pieces in the extensive collection can eventually be viewed.

♣ Craigdarroch Castle

1050 Joan Cres. *Tel (250) 592-5323.* 🔲 *10am–4:30pm daily.* ⬤ *major hols.* 🖼 🖥 www.thecastle.ca

Completed in 1890, Craigdarroch Castle, was the pet project of respected local coal millionaire Robert Dunsmuir, who built it for his wife in return for her leaving her native Scotland. Although not a real castle, the design of this large house was based on a castle in Ayrshire, Scotland, and mixes several architectural styles, including Gothic and Romanesque Revival.

When the castle was threatened with demolition in 1959, a group of local citizens successfully battled for its restoration. Today, the interior is a museum that offers an insight into the lifestyle of a wealthy entrepreneur.

The castle is noted for having one of the finest collections of Art Nouveau lead-glass windows in North America, and many of the rooms and hallways retain their patterned wood parquet floors and carved paneling in white oak, cedar, and mahogany. Every room is filled with opulent Victorian furnishings from the late

19th century and decorated in deep greens, pinks, and rusts. Several layers of the paint have been painstakingly removed from the drawing room ceiling to reveal the original stenciled and hand-painted decorations beneath, which include wonderfully detailed butterflies and lions.

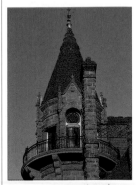

A tower at Craigdarroch Castle in the French Gothic style

🏛 Government House

1401 Rockland Ave. *Tel (250) 387-2080.* 🔲 *daily (gardens only).* ♿

The present Government House building was completed in 1959 after fire destroyed the 1903 structure, designed by Francis Rattenbury. The official residence of BC's lieutenant-governor, the house is closed to the public, but visitors can view 36 acres (14.6 ha) of stunning public gardens with lawns, ponds, an English country garden, and a Victorian rose garden. Marvelous views of the grounds can be enjoyed from Pearke's Peak, a mount formed from the rocky outcrops that surround the property and which contain rock gardens.

Government House, restored in 1959 with blue and pink granite

The Royal BC Museum

The Royal BC Museum tells the story of British Columbia through its natural history, geology, and peoples. The museum is regarded as one of the best in Canada for the striking way it presents its exhibits. The Natural History Gallery on the second floor contains a series of imaginative dioramas re-creating the sights, sounds, and even smells of areas such as the Pacific seashore, the ocean, and the rainforest. Every aspect of the region's history, including a reconstruction of an early 20th-century town, is presented on the third floor. Visitors can experience the street life of the time in a saloon and in a cinema showing silent films. The superb collection of Native art and culture includes a ceremonial Big House.

Third Floor

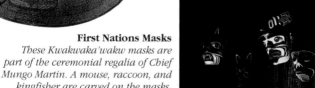

19th-Century Chinatown
As part of an 1875 street scene, this Chinese herbalist's store displays a variety of herbs used in traditional Chinese medicine.

★ **First Peoples Gallery**
Made from spruce root in the late 19th century, the art-work on this Haida hat depicts the crest of the mountain goat.

First Nations Masks
These Kwakwaka'wakw masks are part of the ceremonial regalia of Chief Mungo Martin. A mouse, raccoon, and kingfisher are carved on the masks.

KEY

- First Peoples Gallery
- Modern History Gallery
- Feature exhibit
- Natural History Gallery
- Newcombe Conference Hall
- National Geographic IMAX theater
- Nonexhibition space

Exterior of the Museum
The museum's main galleries opened in 1968. Previously the collections were displayed at several locations in the surrounding RBCM cultural precinct. The grounds include an archives building.

Modern History Gallery

*A variety of streets, stores,
and public buildings
are re-created in
this gallery. Here,
the Grand Hotel
stands on an
authentic wood-
cobbled street.*

VISITORS' CHECKLIST

675 Belleville St. **Tel** (250) 356-
7226. 5, 28, 30. 10am–
5pm daily (Jun–Sep: 10pm Fri & Sat).
Jan 1, Dec 25.
www.royalbcmuseum.bc.ca

Second
Floor

★ Natural History Gallery

*A full-size prehistoric tusked woolly
mammoth and dramatic glacial ice
wall are exhibited in lifelike dioramas
that re-create coastal forests since the
last ice age, and predict future
climate change scenarios.*

★ Coast Seashore Diorama

*This diorama features sound,
lighting, live sea creatures in
tidal pools, and realistic animals
such as this northern sea lion.*

MUSEUM GUIDE

*The main exhibits of the
museum are housed on
the second and third
floors. The Natural History
Gallery, on the second floor,
reconstructs a range of
environments in
displays including a
coastal rainforest to
a river delta. The
third floor has the First
Peoples and Modern
History galleries.*

STAR EXHIBITS

- ★ Coast Seashore
  Diorama

- ★ First Peoples
  Gallery

- ★ Natural History Gallery

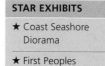

First
Floor

Main Entrance

Butchart Gardens ❷

800 Benvenuto Ave, Brentwood Bay, Vancouver Island. *Tel (250) 652-4422.* ◯ *9am daily; closing hrs vary by season.* 🈂 🔀 🖻 🍴 🔲
www.butchartgardens.com

These beautiful gardens were established in 1904

The lily pond in the formal Italian garden at Butchart Gardens

by Jennie Butchart, in the excavated quarry left behind by her husband's cement company. The site, home to thousands of rare plants, is arranged into distinct areas, including a formal Italian garden and a lovely rose garden. In summer, the gardens are illuminated and play host to evening jazz and classical music concerts. Fireworks displays are held on Saturday nights in July and August.

Cowichan District ❸

Vancouver Island. 🛈 *135 3rd St, Duncan, (250) 746-1099.*
www.cvrd.bc.ca

Cowichan District, on the south-central coast of Vancouver Island, consists of the Chemainus and Cowichan Valleys. Cowichan means "warm land" in the dialect of the Cowichan people, one of largest First Nations groups in BC. The main freshwater lake on the island, Lake Cowichan offers great opportunities for swimming, canoeing, and fishing. On the northern outskirts of Duncan lies the **BC Forest Discovery Centre**. Its displays include a replica logging camp. Duncan, "City of Totems," has over 40 magnificent totem poles. **Quw'utsun' Cultural Centre** shares the heritage of the Cowichan tribes through tours and events.

🏛 **BC Forest Discovery Centre**
2892 Drinkwater Rd, Duncan. *Tel (250) 715-1113.* ◯ *Apr–May: 10am–4pm Thu–Mon; Jun–Aug: 10am–5pm daily; Sep–mid-Oct: 10am–4:30pm daily.* ● *mid-Oct–Mar.* 🈂 🔀 🖻 🔲
www.bcforestmuseum.com

Pacific Rim National Park Reserve of Canada ❼

Three distinct areas make up this reserve: Long Beach, the West Coast Trail, and the Broken Group Islands. Together they occupy an 80-mile (130-km) strip of Vancouver Island's west coast. The park is a world-famous area for whale-watching. Long Beach offers a range of hiking trails. The most challenging hike is the 46-mile (75-km) West Coast Trail, accessible from May to September. The Broken Group Islands can be reached by boat only.

The Broken Group Islands
This archipelago of some 100 islands and islets is popular with kayakers and scuba divers.

Schooner Trail is one of nine scenic and easy-to-follow trails through the coastal temperate rainforest.

The Wickaninnish Centre has viewing platforms for whale-watching.

Tofino
LONG BEACH
Port Albion
Ucluelet
Bam

Long Beach
The rugged, windswept sands of Long Beach are renowned for their wild beauty, with crashing Pacific rollers, unbeatable surfing opportunities, rock pools filled with marine life, and scattered driftwood.

🏛 Quw'utsun' Cultural Centre
200 Cowichan Way, Duncan.
Tel (250) 746-8119. ☐ for groups
of 25 when pre-booked.
⦿ Oct–mid-Apr. ♿ 🖥 📷
www.quwutsun.ca

Chemainus ❹

Vancouver Island. 👥 4,000.
🛈 9796 Willow St, (250) 246-3944.
www.chemainus.bc.ca

When the local sawmill
closed in 1983, the picturesque town of Chemainus
transformed itself into a major
attraction with the painting
of giant murals that depict
the history of the region.
Local and international artists
continued the project, and
today, 37 murals appear on
specially built panels throughout the town, depicting
events in the region's past.

**Pleasure craft and fishing boats
moored in Nanaimo Harbour**

Nanaimo ❺

Road map 2 E4. 👥 79,000.
🛈 2290 Bowen Rd, (250) 756-0106.
www.tourismnanaimo.com

Originally the site of five
Coast Salish villages, Nanaimo
was established as a coal-
mining town in the 1850s.

Its Old City Quarter contains
many 19th-century buildings,
including the Nanaimo Court
House (31 Front Street),
designed in 1895 by Francis
Rattenbury. In the **Nanaimo
Museum**, the most intriguing
exhibit is a re-creation of
Nanaimo's 1950s Chinatown,
complete with wooden
sidewalks, a general store,
and an apothecary.

🏛 Nanaimo Museum
100 Museum Way. **Tel** (250) 753-
1821. ☐ Victoria Day–Labor Day:
10am–5pm daily; Labor Day–Victoria
Day: 10am–5pm Mon–Sat.
📷 ♿ 📷 🖥 by appt.
www.nanaimomuseum.ca

Gulf Islands ❻

Strait of Georgia. 🛈 (250) 754-
3500. **www**.gulfislandsguide.com

Their tranquility and natural
beauty draw visitors to the
Gulf Islands, where sightings of
eagles and turkey vultures are
common. Fishing charters and
kayak tours provide views of
otters, seals, and marine birds.
The largest and most populated
island, with about 10,000
residents, is **Saltspring**. In
summer, visitors stroll around
pretty Ganges Village. **Galiano**
has many hiking trails; **Mayne**'s
tiny century-old museum
recounts this island's history
as a stopping-off point for
Gold Rush miners and rum-
runners. **North** and **South
Pender Islands** are linked
by a wooden bridge. Relics
of a 5,000-year-old First
Nations settlement have
been found here. **Saturna**,
the smallest and most remote
of the islands, hosts a lamb
barbecue each Canada Day
(see p31). Visitors to **Gabriola**
can view Snuneymuxw First
Nations petroglyphs.

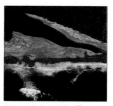

West Coast Trail
*Stunning scenery,
including moss-draped
rainforest, sea stacks,
and sea arches, is
typical of this trail.*

VISITORS' CHECKLIST

Hwy 4. **Tel** (250) 726-3500.
☐ daily. ♿ limited. 📷 Jun–Sep.

KEY

━ Major road

━ Minor road

-- West Coast Trail

─ National park boundary

─ River

🔺 Camping

🔀 Picnic area

🛈 Information

🔆 Viewpoint

At the Nitinat Narrows,
a short ferry ride trans-
ports hikers on the West
Coast Trail across this
pretty waterway.

0 km   10
0 miles   10

Port
Renfrew

**Kayaks at Otter Bay on
North Pender Island**

Whistler ⑧

Whistler Valley tour trolley

Mild pacific weather, reliable snow, and the greatest vertical rises of any ski runs in North America make Whistler one of the most popular winter sports destinations in the world. Visitors flock to the two side-by-side mountains of Whistler and Blackcomb, linked by the Peak 2 Peak Gondola, where activities include dog sledding, snowshoeing, and snowmobiling. In summer, hiking, mountain biking, canoeing, and horseback riding take place around the lakes and at nearby wilderness locations such as Garibaldi Provincial Park. Whistler co-hosted the 2010 Winter Olympic games with Vancouver.

One of a range of restaurant patios in Whistler Village

Blackcomb Peak

Blackcomb Mountain
The 7,992-ft- (2,436-m-) high Blackcomb Mountain has more than 100 marked trails and five alpine bowls, two of which are glaciers. Its longest run covers a 7-mile (11-km) stretch.

BLACKCOMB MOUNTAIN

The Rendezvous on Blackcomb Mountain
Snowboarders and skiers relax, refuel, and enjoy spectacular views at the Rendezvous restaurant and day lodge atop Blackcomb Mountain.

| 0 meters | 800 |
| 0 yards | 1000 |

★ Fairmont Chateau Whistler
The Fairmont Chateau Whistler (see p295) is as much a tourist attraction as it is a hotel, with its art-filled lobby, luxurious tapestries and chandeliers, and rooftop garden terrace.

STAR SIGHTS

★ Alta Lake

★ Fairmont Chateau Whistler

★ Whistler Village

For hotels and restaurants in this region see pp292–5 and pp311–13

Mountain biker in one of Whistler's many jump parks

VISITORS' CHECKLIST

Road map 2 B4. 🚡 *10,000.*
🚌 🚉 **i** *Tourism Whistler,
4230 Gateway Drive, Whistler,
(604) 932-3928 or (800) 944-
7853 (in Canada & US).*
🎿 🍴 🛍 🏨
www.whistler.com

Whistler Mountain
The 7,156-ft- (2,181-m-) high
Whistler Mountain has more
than 100 trails, and seven alpine
bowls, one of which is a glacier.
Its skiable terrain covers 4,757
acres (1,925 ha).

Whistler
Peak

*WHISTLER
MOUNTAIN*

Overlord
Glacier

*ALTA
LAKE*

★ Whistler Village
*A tranquil pond proves a restful
spot amid the bustle of Whistler
Village, where hotels, restaurants,
bars, and shops line the cobble-
stoned, car-free streets.*

★ Alta Lake
*Visitors come to this
1-mile- (1.6-km-) long
lake – surrounded by
forested mountains
and 80 ft (24.5 m)
at its deepest point –
to swim, kayak, sail-
board, and fish for
rainbow and Dolly
Varden trout. A
hiking trail en-
circles the lake.*

KEY

🍴	Restaurant
⛳	Golf course
🚣	Boating
🌤	Viewpoint
i	Information

Kamloops **9**

Road map 2 B4. **🏛** 87,000. **ℹ** 1290 W Trans-Canada Hwy, (250) 372-8000. **www**.tourismkamloops.com

Kamloops – which means "where the rivers meet" in the language of the Secwepemc, or Shuswap, people – is situated at the confluence of the North and South Thompson Rivers. Nestled amid mountains and lakes, the city offers hiking, biking, skiing, and golfing.

European settlement began here in 1812, with fur traders doing business with the Secwepemc. Remains of a 2,000-year-old village and re-created pit houses at the **Secwepemc Museum and Heritage Park** reflect the tribe's history.

US train robber Bill Miner arrived in Kamloops in 1904, on the run after committing a robbery. Kamloops and trains have been linked ever since. The restored 1912 Steam Locomotive No. 2141, one of the few remaining operational steam engines, leaves the historic CN station on a tour that harks back to the Wild West. A train ride can also be taken at **British Columbia Wildlife Park**, home to threatened animals.

Okanagan Valley wine

🏛 Secwepemc Museum and Heritage Park
200–355 Yellowhead Hwy. **Tel** (250) 828-9749. ◯ 8:30am–4:30pm daily. ● Labor Day–May: Sat & Sun. 📷 ✔ 🚻 🛗 ♿

🦌 British Columbia Wildlife Park
Hwy 1, 10.5 miles (17 km) E of Kamloops. **Tel** (250) 573-3242. ◯ 9:30am–5pm daily (to 9pm Jul–Aug; to 4pm Nov–Apr). 📷 ♿ 🛗 🚻 **www**.bczoo.org

Mission Hill Estate Winery in Westbank, near Kelowna

Kelowna **10**

Road map 2 B4. **🏛** 108,000. **ℹ** 544 Harvey Ave, (250) 861-3627. **www**.kelownachamber.org

Kelowna lies on the eastern shore of 56-mile- (80-km-) long Okanagan Lake. The Okanagan Valley's warm, dry climate has long attracted fruit growers, including Father Charles Pandosy, a French lay priest who arrived in 1859. Pandosy planted the area's first fruit trees at the Immaculate Conception Mission, the first non-Native settlement in the region. Today, the **Father Pandosy Mission** is a heritage site. Kelowna's peaches, apples, and cherries are plentiful, but its grapes make it the center of the largest and oldest wine-producing region in the province. Many of the Okanagan Valley's wineries are within a 30-minute drive of Kelowna. Wineries range from intimate to expansive; tours highlight grape-growing and harvesting methods. Orchard tours may include wagon rides

Vineyard in the Okanagan Valley sloping down to Okanagan Lake

and visits to petting zoos. Kelowna's lakefront parks and sandy beaches add to the enjoyment of fresh-fare restaurants. Okanagan Lake, and trails for hiking, biking, and horseback riding offer recreational activities. In winter, the powder snow here makes **Big White Ski Resort** (tel. 250/765-3101) a major draw for skiers.

🏛 Father Pandosy Mission
3685 Benvoulin Rd. **Tel** (250) 860-8369. ◯ Grounds: dawn–dusk daily; Buildings: Mar–Oct: 9am–5pm daily. 📷 donation.

Ripe peaches from the orchards of Summerland, Okanagan Valley

Summerland **11**

Road map 2 B4. **🏛** 11,000. **ℹ** 15600 Hwy 97, (250) 494-2686. **www**.summerlandchamber.com

Summerland has been synonymous with peaches since founder John Moore Robinson arrived in 1902 and persuaded farmers to turn to fruit growing. Today, its shops and town crier reflect an Old English theme.

The beautiful **Summerland Ornamental Gardens** overlook Okanagan Lake and Trout Creek Canyon. A viewpoint atop Giant's Head Mountain provides a lovely panorama.

Kettle Valley Railway, now a tourist attraction, operated here from 1915 to 1964. A 1924 Shay steam engine pulls two 1950 coaches and two open-air cars across the 238-ft- (73-m-) high Trout Creek Bridge.

🌺 Summerland Ornamental Gardens
4200 Hwy 97. **Tel** (250) 494-6385. ◯ 8am–sunset daily. 📷 ♿ 🚻

🚂 Kettle Valley Railway
18404 Bathville Rd. **Tel** (250) 494-8422. ◯ mid-May–mid-Oct: 10:30am & 1:30pm (days vary; call ahead). 📷 ♿ 🚻 **www**.kettlevalleyrail.org

Okanagan Valley Tour [12]

WINE ROUTE

Okanagan wine route

The Okanagan Valley is actually a series of valleys, linked by a string of lakes, that stretches for 155 miles (250 km) – from Osoyoos in the south to Sicamous in the north. The main towns here are connected by Highway 97, which passes through the desert landscape near Lake Osoyoos, and on to the lush green orchards and vineyards for which the valley is most noted. Mild winters and hot summers have made the Okanagan Valley one of Canada's favorite vacation destinations.

TIPS FOR DRIVERS

Tour length: *110 miles (176 km).*
Starting points: *On Hwy 97 from Vernon in the north, Osoyoos in the south.*
When to go: *Blossom and fruit festivals are held in spring and summer, when roadside stalls offer a cornucopia of fruit. Wine tours are available year-round.*

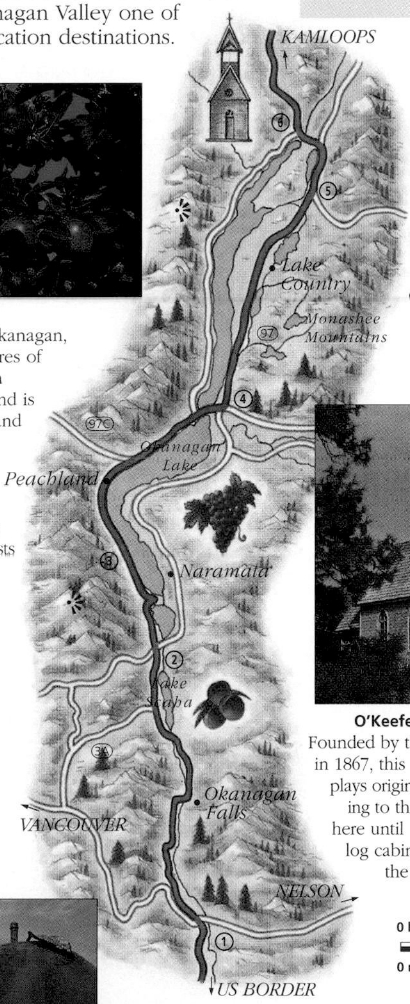
KAMLOOPS
Lake Country
Monashee Mountains
97
97C
Okanagan Lake
Peachland
Naramata
Lake Skaha
3A
Okanagan Falls
VANCOUVER
NELSON
US BORDER

Kelowna ④
The largest city in the Okanagan, Kelowna lies on the shores of Okanagan Lake between Penticton and Vernon, and is the center of the wine- and fruit-growing industries.

Summerland ③
This small but charming lakeside resort town boasts several 19th-century buildings and stunning views from the top of Giant's Head Mountain.

Penticton ②
This sunny lakeside town is known for the long Okanagan Beach, windsurfing, and local winery tours, as well as for its Peach Festival, held every August.

Vernon ⑤
Surrounded by farms and orchards, Vernon owes its lush look to the expansion of irrigation in 1908.

O'Keefe Historic Ranch ⑥
Founded by the O'Keefe family in 1867, this historic ranch displays original artifacts belonging to the family that lived here until 1977. The original log cabin remains, as does the church and store.

0 km 25
0 miles 25

Osoyoos ①
Visitors are drawn here by hot summers, the warm waters and sandy beaches of Lake Osoyoos, and the nearby pocket desert.

KEY

- Tour route
- Other road
- Viewpoint

The Kootenays ⑬

The Kootenays, named for the local Ktunaxa (Kutenai) Native tribe, is one of British Columbia's prettiest regions. Alpine-style towns are tucked amid the Columbia and Rocky Mountains in this southeast corner of the province. The area's three districts – East Kootenay, Central Kootenay, and Kootenay-Boundary – are geographically isolated from major urban centers, resulting in a slow pace that has encouraged the development of a healthy community of artisans and writers. Snow-capped peaks and glacial lakes can be accessed within a series of parks, where the plentiful powdery snow makes for excellent skiing. Throughout the area, world-famous natural hot springs well up; they can be enjoyed at several resorts. Glacier-fed Kootenay Lake, 90 miles (145 km) long, is famed for its superb fishing opportunities.

Hiking boots, a Kootenay must

Ainsworth Hot Springs
The temperature of these waters, which can be enjoyed in outdoor pools overlooking the mountains as well as in shallow natural pools in the nearby caves, averages 95°F (35°C).

Castlegar
Located at the confluence of the Kootenay and Columbia Rivers, Castlegar features a reconstructed Doukhobor village.

★ **Nelson**
With its heritage buildings, and large community of artists, Nelson is a lovely town in which to stroll. It is also a good base for hiking, skiing, and other outdoor activities.

For hotels and restaurants in this region see pp292–5 and pp311–13

★ Fernie

This scenic town lies in one of the Kootenays' most popular areas for snow sports. In the 1880s, Fernie was reputedly cursed by an Indian chief when he was betrayed by its founder. In 1964, the curse was officially lifted by a peace pipe-smoking ceremony.

VISITORS' CHECKLIST

Hwy 3. ☐ 225 Hall St, Nelson, (250) 352-3433. ☐ 2279 Cranbrook St N, Cranbrook, (250) 426-5914. ☐ 102 Hwy 3, Fernie, (250) 423-6868. ☐ all three offices: year-round: 9am–5pm Mon–Fri, Victoria Day–Labor Day: 10am–5pm Sat also. ✕ Cranbrook & Castlegar. ⛴ BC Ministry of Highways inland ferry service Kootenay Bay-Balfour, year-round, 6:30am–10:20pm daily; 35 mins; (250) 229-4215. **www**.th.gov.bc.ca **www**.hellobc.com

The Kootenay Bay–Balfour ferry, offering magnificent views of surrounding mountains from its decks

(95A)
Kimberley
Fort Steele
MOUNT FISHER
Cranbrook
Moyie Lake incial Park
MOYIE LAKE
Fernie
(3)
(3)
Crowsnest Highway
(93)

0 kilometers 25
0 miles 15

KEY

▬	Major road
▬	Minor road
⛴	Ferry
⛺	Camping
🌲	Picnic area
ℹ	Information
🌿	Viewpoint

STAR SIGHTS

★ Cranbrook

★ Fernie

★ Nelson

★ Cranbrook

Panoramic views can be enjoyed just a short hike from this town, which lies between the Rocky and Purcell Mountains. This land, where the Ktunaxa once camped, has excellent cross-country ski and hiking trails.

Exploring the Kootenays

Rushing rivers, deep lakes, and historic towns nestle among the sheer mountains of the Kootenays, a region at the southern end of the Canadian Rockies in the southeast corner of British Columbia. The Kootenays offer a wide range of outdoor activities, including heli-skiing, rock climbing, river rafting, and fly-fishing. Its horse ranches, ski lodges, and chartered houseboats offer visitors comfortable accommodation and opportunities for active and memorable vacations.

Nelson's pink-brick and marble City Hall, dating from 1902

Downhill skier on one of Fernie's spectacular ski runs

Fernie

Road map 2 C4. 🏠 *4,200.* 🚌
ℹ️ *102 Hwy 3, (250) 423-6868.*
www.tourismfernie.com

Fernie is an attractive, tree-lined town set amid the pointed peaks of Crowsnest Pass. The town owes its handsome appearance to a fire that razed it in 1908. All buildings constructed since are brick and stone. Among several historic buildings, the 1911 courthouse stands out as BC's only chateau-style courthouse.

Fernie boasts the best powder snow in the Rockies; the ski season runs from December to April. The Fernie Alpine Resort lifts can transport 12,300 skiers up the mountain every hour.

During the summer, magnificent mountain scenery can be enjoyed from a variety of hiking trails in Mount Fernie Provincial Park. Boat trips on the area's many lakes and rivers are popular, as is fishing. Helicopter sightseeing trips take visitors close to the mountains to see the formations and granite cliffs particular to this region of the Rockies.

Cranbrook

Road map 2 C4. 🏠 *19,000.* ✈️ 🚌
🏠 *2279 Cranbrook St N, (250) 426-5914.* **www.**cranbrookchamber.com

Cranbook, lying between the Purcell and Rocky Mountain ranges, is the largest town in southeast BC. A major transportation hub, it is within easy reach of spectacular scenery and boasts the highest density of grizzlies in the Rockies. These, along with the region's other wildlife, which includes elk, wolves, and cougars, may be spotted on the many trails in the area. Hikers should exercise caution (*see pp320–21*).

The Canadian Pacific Railway reached Cranbrook in 1898. The **Canadian Museum of Rail Travel** includes the magnificent Royal Alexandra Hall Café with its high decorative curved ceilings, and 12 restored luxury cars, including the 1929 Trans-Canada Limited.

🏛 **Canadian Museum of Rail Travel**
57 Van Horne St S. **Tel** *(250) 489-3918.* ⏰ *mid-Apr–Thanksgiving: 10am–6pm daily; Thanksgiving–mid-Apr: 10am–5pm Tue–Sat.*
📷 ♿ *partial.* 🎫 ℹ️

Nelson

Road map 2 C4. 🏠 *9,700.* 🚌
ℹ️ *225 Hall St, (250) 352-3433.*
www.discovernelson.com

One of the most attractive towns in southeastern British Columbia, Nelson overlooks Kootenay Lake. Established in the 1880s as a mining town, Nelson flourished with the arrival of the railroad in the 1890s, becoming a center for the transportation of ore and timber. Many of the town's public buildings and houses were constructed between 1895 and 1920. In 1979, a $3 million municipal renovation program helped restore the historic façades of the downtown buildings.

The town has a thriving cultural scene, with bookstores, art galleries, cafés, and craft shops. Visitors can enjoy the short ride on Car 23, a 1906 streetcar that operated here from 1924 to 1949. Restored in 1992, it now travels along Nelson's delightful waterfront.

The opulent dining car on a restored train at Cranbrook's rail museum

Exploring Nelson

Nelson's downtown, though hilly, is easily walkable. Over 350 historic buildings, from elegant mansions to elaborate commercial structures, give the city its unique style. Many of these restored buildings are part of Nelson's historic downtown walking tour. The visitors' center provides maps and guides for the tour.

🏛 Bank of Montreal

298 Baker St. ⚫ *bank & major hols.* ♿

When it opened in 1900, after a year under construction, the Bank of Montreal was considered one of the finest commercial buildings in the BC Interior. Its Italian influences include rounded window arches and detailed brickwork.

🏛 Mara-Barnard Block

421–431 Baker St. ♿

This elaborate High Victorian building, with unusual bay windows on the second floor, housed the first branch of the Royal Bank of Canada to open in BC, in 1897.

🏛 K.W.C. Block

488–498 Baker St. ♿

Built by three merchants, Kirkpatrick, Wilson, and Clements, in 1901, the K.W.C. Block is

the largest mercantile building in Nelson. The turret and window arches are noteworthy.

🏛 Houston Block

601–607 Baker St. ♿

Nelson's first mayor, John Houston, commissioned architect A.E. Hodgins to design the grand Houston Block, built in 1899, to house a bank.

🏛 Touchstones Nelson

502 Vernon St. **Tel** (250) 352-9813. ⭕ *10am–5pm daily (to 8pm Thu, to 4pm Sun).* ♿

Spokane pink brick and Kaslo marble make for a picturesque mixture of textures and patterns on the 1902 Post Office and Customs House, now a museum of art and history.

🏛 Nelson Court House

310 Ward St. **Tel** (250) 354-6165. ⭕ *year-round: 8:30am–4:30pm Mon–Fri.* ⚫ *major hols.* ♿

F.M. Rattenbury, designer of Victoria's Parliament Buildings (*see p250*), designed this fine example of Beaux Arts chateau architecture. Dating from 1909, it features a high pitched roof, towers, conical caps, gables, and paired windows,

Castlegar

Road map 2 C4. 🏘 *7,500.* ✈ 🚌
ℹ️ *1995 6th Ave, (250) 365-6313.*
www.castlegar.com

Located at the confluence of the Kootenay and Columbia Rivers, Castlegar is an angler's paradise. In the early 1900s, Doukhobors (Russian religious dissenters) fleeing persecution began arriving here. The **Doukhobor Discovery Centre** showcases the group's culture with displays of traditional clothes, and tools in a re-created village. Set in lovely grounds with river views and accessed via a 470-ft- (143-m-) long suspension bridge, **Zuckerberg Island Heritage Park** features a Lakes Salish pit house and Russian Orthodox chapel.

Statue of Tolstoy, Doukhobor Village

🏛 Doukhobor Discovery Centre

112 Heritage Way. **Tel** (250) 365-5327. ⭕ *May–Sep: 10am–5pm daily.* 🅿️ ♿

🏛 Zuckerberg Island Heritage Park

9th St at 7th Ave. **Tel** (250) 365-6440. ⭕ *Park: year-round; Chapel: May–Sep, call for hours.* 🅿️ by donation. 🚻 🚽

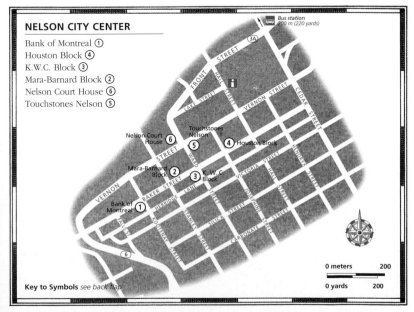

NELSON CITY CENTER

Bank of Montreal ①
Houston Block ④
K.W.C. Block ③
Mara-Barnard Block ②
Nelson Court House ⑥
Touchstones Nelson ⑤

Bus station
200 m (220 yards)

Touchstones Nelson

Nelson Court House ⑥ ⑤ ④ Houston Block

Mara-Barnard Block ② ③ K.W.C. Block

Bank of Montreal ①

⑥

0 meters 200
0 yards 200

Key to Symbols *see back flap*

19th-century barber's shop in Fort Steele Heritage Town

Fort Steele Heritage Town ⑭

Road map 2 C4. **Tel** (250) 426-7352.
◯ May–Jun & Sep–mid-Oct: 9:30am–5pm daily; Jul–Aug: 9:30am–6pm daily; mid-Oct–Apr: 10am–4pm daily.
🎦 👍 🄿 www.fortsteele.ca

Fort Steele is a re-creation of the mining supply town that was established at this site in 1864, when gold was discovered at Wild Horse Creek. Thousands of prospectors and entrepreneurs arrived by the Dewdney Trail, which linked the town of Hope to the gold fields. Originally called Galbraith's Ferry, the town was renamed after Samuel Steele, the North West Mounted Police superintendent who arrived in 1887 to restore peace between warring Ktunaxa Natives and European settlers. The town enjoyed a brief boom with the discovery of lead and silver, but the mainline railroad was routed through Cranbrook instead, and by the early 1900s, Fort Steele was a ghost town.

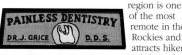

An historic dentist's sign in Fort Steele Heritage Town

Today, there are more than 60 reconstructed or restored buildings, staffed by guides in period costume, including the general store, livery stable, and North West Mounted Police officers' quarters, where personal items such as family photographs, swords, and uniforms create the illusion of recent occupation. Demonstrations of traditional crafts such as ice cream-making and quilting are also held here. "Living history" dramas and musical comedy shows staged in the Wild Horse Theater are inspired by the town's history, and tours at the nearby Wild Horse Creek Historic Site include a chance to pan for gold.

The Purcell Mountains ⑮

Road map 2 C4. 🛈 270 Kimberley Ave, Kimberley, (250) 427-3666.

The rugged and beautiful Purcell Mountains face the Rockies across the broad Columbia River Valley. The region is one of the most remote in the Rockies and attracts hikers and skiers from around the globe. A high range of granite spires, called the Bugaboos, also draws mountain climbers. In the north of the Purcell range, the Purcell Wilderness Conservancy – one of the range's few accessible areas – covers a vast 500,900 acres (202,709 ha).

From the nearby town of Invermere, it is possible to access the Earl Grey Pass Trail which extends 35 miles (56 km). It is named after

The Purcell Mountains, noted for remote rivers and forests

Earl Grey, Canada's Governor General from 1904 to 1911, who chose the Purcell range as the place to build a vacation cabin for his family, in 1912. The trail he traveled followed an established route used by the Kinbasket Natives of the Ktunaxa First Nations tribe. Today the trail is notoriously dangerous; bears, avalanches, and fallen trees are just some of the hazards hikers may encounter along the way. Hiking along it requires skill and experience and therefore should not be attempted by novice hikers.

Radium Hot Springs ⑯

Road map 2 C4. 🏔 625.
Tel (250) 347-9331.
www.radiumhotsprings.com

The town of Radium Hot Springs is famous for its mineral springs and is a good base for exploring nearby Kootenay National Park. In summer, flowerpots decorate motels along the highway through town, and the town has more visitors than residents. Many of the 1.2 million annual tourists come to bathe in the healing waters of the springs.

The nearby Columbia Valley Wetlands provide an important habitat for over 250 migratory waterfowl, such as Canada geese, great blue herons, and tundra swans. Fed by glacial waters, the Columbia River meanders through these extensive marshlands.

Fort Steele's Wasa Hotel, modeled on a popular 1904 East Kootenay resort

For hotels and restaurants in this region see pp292–5 and pp311–13

The dramatic peaks of the Rocky Mountains in Kootenay National Park

Kootenay National Park ⑰

Road map 2 C4. ▮ 7556 Main St E, Radium Hot Springs, (250) 347-9331. ◯ daily. **Visitors' center** ◯ late May–mid-Oct: 9am–5pm daily (late closing during Jul & Aug). ▨ ♿ ▯

Kootenay National Park covers 543 sq miles (1,406 sq km) of the most diverse terrain in the Rockies. Much of this scenery can be seen from the Kootenay Parkway (Hwy 93), which cuts through the park from north to south following the Vermilion and Kootenay Rivers. Most of the park's attractions can be seen from the many short trails that lead from the highway.

The road winds eastward through Sinclair Pass, where the high red walls of Sinclair Canyon, a limestone gorge, lead to the Sinclair Falls and the Redwall Fault. Here, rust-colored cliffs form a natural gateway across the highway.

Farther north, the magical Paint Pots, ocher and red pools formed from iron-rich mineral springs, are reached by a short trail from the road.

Glacier National Park ⑱

Road map 2 C4. ▮ Rogers Pass, (250) 837-7500. ◯ daily. ▨ ♿ ▯ www.pc.gc.ca

Glacier National Park covers 520 sq miles (1,350 sq km) of wilderness in the Selkirk Range of the Columbia Mountains. The park was established in 1886, and its growth was linked to the expansion of the railroad, which was routed through Rogers Pass in 1885. Today, one of the park's most accessible trails follows an abandoned railroad line. Other trails here offer visitors spectacular views of the park's 420 glaciers, including the Great Glacier, now known as the **Illecillewaet Glacier**.

Glacier National Park contains rainforests, glacial lakes, streams, and waterfalls. During winter, snow falls almost daily, totaling as much as 75 ft (23 m) per season. The threat of avalanches in the park is serious; skiers and climbers are always encouraged to obtain information about travel conditions before visiting.

The Rogers Pass line was eventually abandoned by the Canadian Pacific Railway because of the frequent avalanches, and a tunnel was built underneath it instead. The Trans-Canada Highway (Hwy 1) follows the route of the original rail line as it bisects the park en route to the lovely city of Revelstoke. From here, visitors may access the forests and jagged peaks of **Mount Revelstoke National Park**.

Illecillewaet Glacier, one of 420 glaciers in Glacier National Park

The ocher-colored Paint Pot pools in Kootenay National Park

HOT SPRINGS HAVENS

The geology of the Canadian Rockies has created numerous hot springs, formed naturally by groundwater seeping downward, coming into contact with hot rock 2–2.5 miles (3–4 km) below the earth's crust, and rising back to the surface at a very high temperature. The region's many hot springs resorts offer hot pools in the 100°F (38°C) range, as well as larger warm pools for swimming. The waters are rich in sulfates, calcium, and hydrogen sulfide and are said to benefit arthritis and rheumatism sufferers.

Roadside sign welcoming visitors to Radium Hot Springs

Yoho National Park ⑲

Inspired by the beauty of the area's mountains, lakes, waterfalls, and distinctive rock formations, this park was named Yoho for the Cree word meaning "awe and wonder." Yoho National Park lies on the western side of the Rockies range in British Columbia, north of Kootenay National Park. The park is ideal for climbing, hiking, canoeing, and cross-country skiing. It also is home to the Burgess Shale fossil beds, an extraordinary find of perfectly preserved marine creatures from the Cambrian period, over 500 million years ago. Access to the beds is by guided hike, limited to 15 people each trip.

Shooting star flower

WAPTA ICEFIELD

Emerald Lake
Emerald Lake Lodge provides facilities at this secluded spot in the middle of the park. The lake, named for the intense color of its waters, is a popular place for canoeing and walking.

Natural Bridge
Found in the center of the park, over the waters of Kicking Horse River, Natural Bridge is a rock bridge formed by centuries of erosion, which have worn a channel through solid rock. The bridge is a short drive from Highway 1.

VANCOUVER, GLACIER NATIONAL PARK

KEY

▬	Highway
▬	Major road
▬	River
▲	Campsite
⛽	Picnic area
ℹ	Information
✲	Viewpoint

Hoodoo Creek
Erosion created these mushroom-like towers of rock. A very steep 1-mile (1.6-km) ascent should be tackled only by fit bikers.

The Yoho Valley
is noted for its
stunning scenery,
which includes the
Takakkaw Falls.

VISITORS' CHECKLIST

Hwy 1. 🛈 Park Info Centre,
Field. **Tel** (250) 343-6783.
🚍 to Field. ◯ daily. ♿ 🍴
🅿 📷 🅰 www.pc.gc.ca

Takakkaw Falls
*Takakkaw means "it is
wonderful" in the language
of the local Native people, and
these, with a drop of 833 ft
(254 m), are among the most
impressive falls in Canada.
The falls can be accessed
along the Yoho Valley Road.*

CALGARY, BANFF
NATIONAL PARK

Burgess Shale was
declared a UN
World Heritage Site
so as to protect two
fossil beds. Guided
hikes here are by
reservation only.

Kicking Horse River
*This wild river rushes through Yoho along-
side the original 1880s railroad. Today
the tracks carry freight and the Rocky
Mountaineer tourist train (see p332).*

Lake O'Hara
*Shadowed by the majestic peaks of Mounts Victoria and Lefroy,
Lake O'Hara is astonishingly beautiful. Visitors wishing to use
the area's excellent hiking trails must book in advance, as
access is limited so as to protect this fragile environment.*

0 km   3
0 miles   3

Helmcken Falls, crowned by a rainbow, in Wells Gray Provincial Park

Wells Gray Provincial Park ⑳

Road map 2 B4. ▮ *425 E Yellowhead Hwy, Clearwater, (250) 674-2646.* ◯ *call for hrs.* **www.**wellsgray.ca

Wells Gray Provincial Park, in the Cariboo Mountains, is not only one of the largest but also one of the most beautiful wildernesses in British Columbia, offering wonders comparable to the Rockies in eastern BC. The park, established in 1939, is distinguished by alpine meadows, thundering waterfalls, and glacier-topped peaks that rise as high as 8,450 ft (2,575 m). The Canadian National Railroad and Highway 5 follow the Thompson River along the park's western edge, and both routes provide stunning views.

From the Clearwater Valley Road, off Highway 5, there are several trails, from easy walks to arduous overnight hikes in remote country. A short trail leads to spectacular 450-ft (137-m) **Helmcken Falls**, the fourth highest waterfall in Canada. Nearby Mushbowl Bridge provides the best view of the fast-moving Murtle River and the giant holes it has carved into the surrounding rock.

In late August and early September, Chinook salmon leap in futile attempts to continue upstream past the dramatic **Bailey's Chute**.

Four lakes located throughout the park provide excellent opportunities for canoeing and angling.

Prince George ㉑

Road map 2 B3. ▓ *77,700.* ▮ *1300 First Ave, (250) 562-3700.* **www.**tourismpg.com

The largest town in northern British Columbia, Prince George is a bustling supply-and-transportation center for the region. Two major highways pass through here: the Yellowhead (Hwy 16) and Highway 97, which becomes the Alaska Highway at Dawson Creek. Established in 1807 as Fort George, a fur-trading post at the confluence of the Nechako and Fraser Rivers, the town is well placed for exploring the province.

Prince George has all the facilities of a larger city, including its own symphony orchestra, several art galleries, and a university specializing in First Nations, environmental, and forestry studies.

Exploration Place lies on the site of the original fort, within the 65-acre (26-ha) Fort George Park. It contains a small collection of artifacts

from Native cultures, European pioneers, and early settlers of the region.

An important center for the lumber industry, the town of Prince George offers a range of free tours of local pulp mills, which take visitors through the process of wood production, from vast fields of young seedlings to hill-sized piles of planks and raw timber.

🏛 **Exploration Place**
333 Becott Pl. *Tel (250) 562-1612.* ◯ *Victoria Day–Thanksgiving: 10am–5pm daily; Thanksgiving–Victoria Day: 10am–5pm Wed–Sun.* ● *Jan 1, Dec 25 & 26.* 🅿🖥🛍👶♿ **www.**theexplorationplace.com

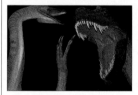

Dinosaur models on display at Exploration Place

Dawson Creek ㉒

Road map 2 B3. ▓ *11,000.* ▮ *900 Alaska Ave, (250) 782-9595.* **www.**tourismdawsoncreek.com

The formerly quiet town of Dawson Creek was transformed by the construction of the Alaska Highway, which began in 1942 and swelled the town's population from 600 to 10,000. Designated as historic Mile Zero on the road to Fairbanks, 1,486 miles (2,391 km) to

Former grain elevator turned art gallery in Dawson Creek

the north, the city recognizes this distinction with the **Mile Zero post** at 10th Street and 102nd Avenue. Located at the corner of Highway 97 and the Alaska Highway, the red-and-white 1931 **Northern Alberta Railway Station** is now a museum and information center. The 4-acre (1.6 ha) site includes the Mile Zero stone cairn marking the official start of the Alaska Highway. Next to the railway station is a 1948 grain elevator annex that is now an art gallery. The conversion of elevator to gallery involved the removal of 10 tons of grain dust. Shows include the work of local artists as well as major traveling collections. On Saturday mornings from May to October, a farmers' market held across from the stone cairn sells local produce and crafts.

The Mile Zero post at Dawson Creek

At **Walter Wright Pioneer Village**, restored buildings and farm machinery recreate the agricultural community of Dawson Creek before the highway was built.

🏛 **Walter Wright Pioneer Village**
1901 Alaska Hwy. *Tel* (250) 782-7144.
🕐 mid-May–Aug: 8:30am–9pm daily.
Sep–mid-May. 📷 donation. ♿

Fort St. John ㉓

Road map 2 B2. 👥 22,000.
ℹ 9523 100th St, (250) 785-3033.
www.fortstjohn.ca

The city of Fort St. John is located at Mile 47 of the Alaska Highway, among the rolling hills of the Peace River Valley. Fort St. John, originally one of six forts built in the area between 1794 and 1925, is the oldest non-Native settlement in British Columbia. At nearby Charlie Lake Cave, 10,000-year-old artifacts of the Paleo Indians have been found, making it the site of the earliest-known human activity in the province.

The area around Fort St. John is a unique ecosystem in which moose, deer, elk, and black bears abound. During the 1942 construction of the Alaska Highway, the town's population increased dramatically, from 800 to 6,000. When completed, the highway turned Fort St. John into a busy supply center catering to visitors to the area and supporting the agriculture industry in the surrounding countryside.

The town boomed in the 1950s, when oil was found here in what proved to be the largest oil field in BC. The city's pride in its industrial heritage is reflected in its **museum**, which has a 140-ft- (43-m-) high oil derrick at its entrance and exhibits telling the story of the local oil industry. Other attractions include a honey-processing plant, with one of the world's largest glass beehives. A popular seasonal activity is watching the northern lights, very visible here.

Fort Nelson ㉔

Road map 2 B2. 👥 4,800.
ℹ 5319 50th Ave S, (250) 774-2541.
www.tourismnorthernrockies.ca

Despite the growth of the oil, gas, and lumber industries in the 1960s and 1970s, Fort Nelson retains the atmosphere of a northern frontier town. Before the building of the Alaska Highway in the 1940s, Fort Nelson was an important stop en route to Yukon and Alaska, and until the 1950s it was without telephones, running water, or electricity. Fur trading was the main

The steaming waters of the Liard River Hot Springs, near Fort Nelson

activity until the energy boom; even today trappers continue to hunt beaver, wolf, and lynx, for both their fur and their meat.

This town at Mile 300 of the Alaska Highway has an air and bus service, a hospital, and good visitor facilities such as motels, restaurants, and gas stations. Local people are known for their friendliness, and during the busy summer months they run a program of free talks for visitors, describing life in the North.

The small **Fort Nelson Heritage Museum** displays photographs and artifacts that tell the story of the building of the Alaska Highway, and features a frontier-town general store and blacksmith's forge. The trapper's log cabin behind the museum is also worth visiting.

The region has over a dozen parks, including **Liard River Provincial Park**; its hot springs are open year round. The area is a world-class cross-country skiing destination.

Farmland alongside the Peace River near Fort St. John

The green waters of Muncho Lake framed by mountains in Muncho Lake Provincial Park

Muncho Lake Provincial Park ㉕

Road map 2 A1. **Tel** (250) 776-7000. ☐ May–Oct: daily. 🏕 to campsites.

One of three provincial parks that were established after the building of the Alaska Highway in 1942, Muncho Lake occupies the most scenic section of the road. The park encompasses the bare peaks of the northern Rockies, whose stark limestone slopes incorporate the faults, alluvial fans, and fantastic rock formations that are a testament to thousands of years of glacial erosion. Flash floods are common here.

The highway skirts the eastern shoreline of the 7.5-mile- (12-km-) long Muncho Lake before crossing the Liard River, where the Mackenzie Mountains begin. In early summer, passing motorists are likely to see moose grazing in wildflower meadows. The park's bogs are popular with botanists eager to see the rare yellow Lady's Slipper orchid. The roadside also attracts great numbers of goats, sheep, and caribou, which are drawn by deposits of sodium, known as mineral licks.

Visitors may stay in the park at one of its many campgrounds or lodges in order to explore its 218,480 acres (88,420 ha) of wilderness. The deep waters of Muncho Lake offer a good supply of trout for anglers. Narrated boat tours of the lake are offered by Double G Service (tel. 250/776-3411).

The Hazeltons ㉖

Road map 2 A3. 🏘 8,000. 🚹 4070 9th Ave, New Hazelton, (250) 842-6071. **www**.newhazelton.ca

In the 1860s, pioneer communities were established at the confluence of the Skeena and Bulkley Rivers, 180 miles (290 km) east of Prince Rupert. Today, three villages at this location – Old, New, and South Hazelton – are known collectively as the Hazeltons. The towns, named for the hazel bushes covering the region's river-carved terraces, lie near the cliffs of Mount Rocher Déboulé, which tower over the area at 3,300 ft (1,005 m).

All the Hazeltons are charming, particularly Old Hazelton (officially known as Hazelton Village), where the old-fashioned storefronts offer a reminder of the days when the town was a bustling river terminus. The Old Hazelton walking tour shows off remnants of a Victorian steam engine from early forestry days, Skeena River paddle-wheelers, the century-old St. Peter's Anglican Church, and the **Hazelton Pioneer Museum and Archives** in the library, which portrays the early days of the initial settlement.

The highlight of the area is the **'Ksan Historical Village**, a replica of a Northwest Coast-style Gitxsan village. Gitxsan First Nations people have lived in the area for thousands of years, particularly along the beautiful Skeena River valley. Their way of life was threatened by white settlers who arrived in the 1850s at Prince Rupert to work their way upriver to mine or farm, but the tribe has been recovering its traditions since the 1950s.

'Ksan totem poles at the 'Ksan Historical Village

Noted for their skill in creating carved and painted masks, totems, and canoes, Gitxsan elders are now schooling new generations in these skills at the 'Ksan village. Within the village complex are seven traditional longhouses, containing a carving school, totems, and a museum.

A 70-mile (113-km) self-guided driving tour winds through several First Nations villages, where one can see dozens of totem poles. Indeed, the Hazeltons are known as the "totem pole capital of the world." The area also abounds with recreational opportunities, including hiking and fishing.

🏛 Hazelton Pioneer Museum and Archives
4255 Government St, Hazelton. *Tel* (250) 842-5961.

🏛 'Ksan Historical Village
High Level Rd, Hazelton.
📍 *New Hazelton, (250) 842-5544.*
🕐 *Apr–Sep: 9am–5pm daily; Oct–Mar: 9:30am–4:30pm Mon–Fri.* 📷
♿ 🎫 🍴 📷 www.ksan.org

A main street in Smithers, against a backdrop of steep mountains

Smithers ㉗

Road map 2 A3. 🏘 6,000.
ℹ️ 1027 Aldous St, (250) 847-5072.
www.tourismsmithers.com

The picturesque town of Smithers, located in the center of the fertile Bulkley Valley, is surrounded by the panoramic scenery of local mountain ranges over which the snow-crested 8,599-ft (2,621-m) Hudson Bay Mountain presides. Smithers is a year-round outdoor center where

Babine Lake is recommended for its plentiful rainbow trout and char, and rafters on the challenging Bulkley River twist past pine-lined shores through a beautiful canyon. A bicycle ride or hike along the forested 8-mile (13-km) Perimeter Trail may offer sightings of moose, deer, and grouse, while grizzly and black bears, mountain goats, and caribou live higher on the slopes. In winter, downhill, cross-country, and telemark skiing are predominant. Hudson Bay Mountain resort (tel. 250/847-2058) features 18 runs and 1,750 ft (533 m) of vertical thrills. Snowmobiling and dog sledding are also popular.

Smithers' main street has an alpine theme, evident in the brick sidewalks, alpine-style storefronts, and *Alpenhorn Man*, a 7-ft (2-m) wooden statue of a man playing an alpenhorn. Colorful murals decorate the street, enhancing its shops and boutiques.

Prince Rupert ㉘

Road map 2 A3. 🏘 15,000.
ℹ️ 100 1st Ave W, (250) 624-5637.
www.visitprincerupert.com

Prince Rupert is the largest urban center on BC's northern coast. Located on Kaien Island, at the mouth of the Skeena River, the city is encircled by forests and mountains, and overlooks the fjord-studded coastline. The harbor, busy with cruise ships, ferries, and fishing boats, is the main access point for the rugged Haida Gwaii archipelago and Alaska.

A gift shop and gallery in Cow Bay, Prince Rupert

Like many of BC's major towns, Prince Rupert's development is linked to the growth of the railroad. Housed in the 1914 Grand Trunk Railroad Station, the **Kwinitsa Railway Museum** tells the story of businessman Charles Hay's big plans for the town, which were largely unfulfilled: he went down with the *Titanic* in 1912.

Tsimshian First Nations people were the area's first occupants; in the mid-19th century, the harbor was lined with their cedar houses and totems. The excellent **Museum of Northern British Columbia** focuses on Tsimshian history; tours showcase the culture over the past 10,000 years. In summer, a First Nations-led walking tour of nearby Laxspa'aws (Pike Island) provides information on five significant archaeological and village sites 1,800 years old.

🏛 Museum of Northern British Columbia
100 1st Ave W. **Tel** (250) 624-3207.
🕐 Jun–Aug: 9am–8pm daily (to 5pm Sun); Sep–May: 9am–5pm Mon–Sat.
🔴 Dec 25 & 26. 📷 ♿ 🎫 📷
www.museumofnorthernbc.com

One of the many renovated buildings by Prince Rupert's harbor

Haida Gwaii (Queen Charlotte Islands) ㉙

Balance Rock, Graham Island

Haida Gwaii, formerly known as the Queen Charlotte Islands, is an archipelago of about 150 islands, many with unique ecosystems. For thousands of years they have been home to the Haida Nation, a people renowned for their carvings and sculptures made of silver, gold, cedar, and argillite (a black, slate-like stone found only on these islands). The remote Gwaii Haanas National Park Reserve and Haida Heritage Site protects ancient Haida villages nestled amid lush cedar and hemlock rainforest, home to distinctive species such as dusky shrews and short-tailed weasels. Bald eagles nest along the coast, and in spring, hundreds of migrating gray whales can be seen. Haida Gwaii offers some of the West Coast's finest fishing, kayaking, hiking, scuba diving, and whale-watching.

Map labels:
LANGARA ISLAND
NADEN HARBOUR
Jalun River
Naden River
C Masse
Masse
EDEN LAKE
Sewall
MASSET INLET
Port Clements
GRAHAM ISLAND
Yellow
RENNELL SOUND
Qu Charlo
MORESBY ISLAND
M MO

Masset
The oldest fishing community in Haida Gwaii, Masset is popular with both anglers and tourists. Its Delkatla Wildlife Sanctuary, an intertidal wetland and birdwatcher's paradise, is refuge to more than 140 recorded species, including large flocks of migrating shorebirds. In the nearby Haida village of Old Masset, traditional jewelers, carvers, and weavers work in home studios.

STAR SIGHTS

★ Haida Heritage Centre

★ Naikoon Provincial Park

★ SGang Gwaay

Queen Charlotte City
This quaint fishing village, also known simply as Charlotte, is a good base from which to explore the islands and take an ecotour or a paddling trip in a Haida canoe. Its tiny downtown offers cafés, hotels, and shops.

For hotels and restaurants in this region see pp292–5 and pp311–13

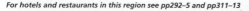

273

★ **Naikoon Provincial Park**
*Naikoon Provincial Park has breathtaking
views of Hecate Strait and Dixon Entrance. On
clear days, Alaska is visible from the north end.
Remnants of shipwrecks dot the park's 60 miles
(100 km) of broad sandy beach. Tow Hill, at
the park's north end, is an ancient volcano
with a massive basalt cliff.*

VISITORS' CHECKLIST

BC Ferries from Prince
Rupert, (888) 223-3779.
Gwaii Haanas National Park
Reserve & Haida Heritage Site,
(250) 559-8818. **www**.pc.gc.ca

KEY

▬	Paved road
▬	Dirt or four-wheel-drive road
▪ ▪	Hiking trail
△	Camping
▦	Picnic area
✈	Airport
⛴	Ferry
- -	Ferry route
☀	Viewpoint
ℹ	Information

Skidegate Inlet com-
prises the three com-
munities of Skidegate,
Queen Charlotte City,
and Sandspit, and is one
of the prime fishing
locations on the
islands. In the spring,
gray whales can be seen
resting and feeding here.

★ **Haida Heritage Centre**
*Haida Heritage Centre celebrates Haida
culture, past and present. Highlights here
include argillite and wood carvings,
totems dating to 1878, and Loos Taas,
a 49-ft- (150-m-) long canoe carved
by Haida artist Bill Reid.*

★ **SGang Gwaay (Ninstints)**
*A UNESCO World Heritage Site since
1981, this Haida village on Anthony
Island has more totems standing on
their original sites than any other Haida
village. Accessible by boat or plane only.*

Tow Hill

HECATE STRAIT

E RUPERT

koon
ional
k

Tlell

PRINCE RUPERT

kidegate

Sandspit

*LOUISE
ISLAND*

Ku'uuna
Llnagaay
(Skedans)

*IANU
AND*

Hlk'yah Llnagaay
(Windy Bay)

*LYELL
ISLAND*

Gwaii Haanas National Park
Reserve and Haida Heritage Site

*BURNABY
ISLAND*

SGang Gwaay
(Anthony Island)

*KUNGHIT
ISLAND*

0 kilometers	20
0 miles	10

Cruise to Alaska 30

Continuing a tradition that began in 1880, cruise ships ply the Inside Passage, a protected waterway that runs along the BC coast to the inlets of Alaska. The waters are calmer than those of the open Pacific Ocean, so that whales and porpoises are often sighted. The popular cruises, many of which are combined with shore excursions, attract over one million passengers a year.

The sails of Vancouver's Canada Place, starting point for cruises

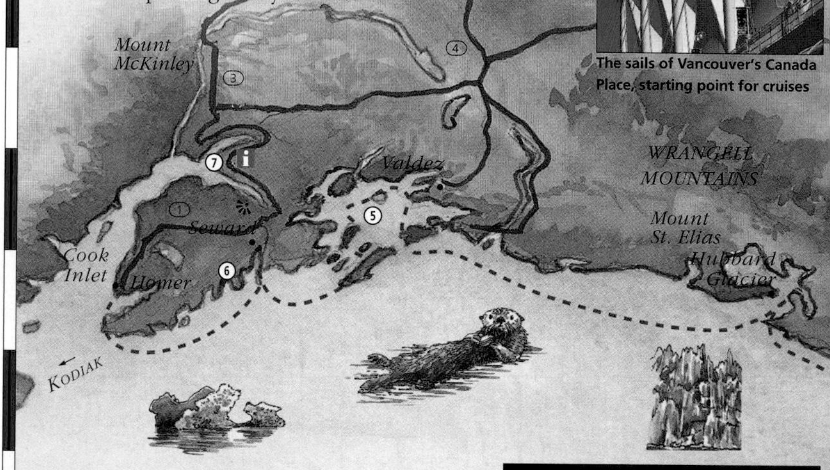
Mount McKinley
3
4
7
i
Valdez
1
Seward
5
6
Cook Inlet
Homer
Kodiak
WRANGELL MOUNTAINS
Mount St. Elias
Hubbard Glacier

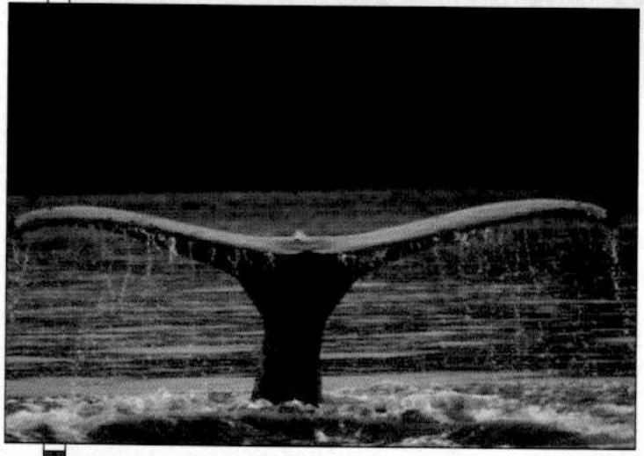

Kenai Fjords National Park 6

In the Seward region, the glacier-carved fjords of Kenai are home to whales, sea lions, and tufted puffins.

Prince William Sound 5

More than 20 active tidewater glaciers are to be found at the sound, with its 3,000 miles (4,830 km) of coastline. A horned puffin colony lives here year-round and up to 5,000 bald eagles summer here.

Anchorage 7

Fabulous views of the Chugach Mountains can be enjoyed from Anchorage, situated on a broad peninsula in Cook Inlet. The Alaska Native Heritage Center here displays historic tableaux illustrating the daily lives of the region's First Nations tribes.

0 kilometers 200

0 miles 150

KEY

- - Cruise route
— Major road
[i] Information
Viewpoint

Skagway ④

The boardwalk and false-fronted buildings of Skagway evoke the 19th century. The historic Klondike train, which steams through the cliff-hugging White Pass, starts here.

Whitehorse

Alaska Highway

③

④

Atlin Lake

③

Juneau ③

Alaska's capital is also its most beautiful city. Juneau is the gateway to the impressive 12-mile- (19-km-) long Mendenhall Glacier, which flows from the Juneau Icefield.

Gulf of Alaska

②

①

Prince Rupert

HAIDA GWAII (Queen Charlotte Islands)

Sitka ②

Czarist icons and Russian dancers remind visitors of Sitka's Russian heritage.

Bella Bella

Ketchikan ①

Colorful 19th-century buildings and boardwalks, Tlingit clan houses, a totem collection, and an eagle population make this town unforgettable.

VANCOUVER ISLAND

Vancouver

TRAVELERS' NEEDS

WHERE TO STAY

Whether you are looking for a relaxing oceanside inn, a small and welcoming bed-and-breakfast, a low-key hostel, a convenient motel, or a perfectly appointed hotel room in the heart of the city, the Pacific Northwest offers accommodation to suit every taste and budget. In addition to this wide range of options, rustic lodges and guest ranches, usually located outside towns and cities and near

Hotel sign in Bavarian-themed Leavenworth, Washington

scenic areas, provide lodgings and unforgettable outdoor experiences. For those who love to camp, the numerous state, provincial, and national parks throughout the region offer a choice of campsites including smaller sites for rough camping. In order to help you select a place to stay, the listings in *Choosing a Hotel,* on pages 282–95, recommend a variety of places, in all price ranges, each representing the best of its kind.

FINDING ACCOMMODATION

For accommodation in Oregon, **Travel Oregon** offers a handy online reservation service as well as a free publication called *Where to Stay in Oregon*. **Washington State Tourism** provides lodging and campground listings in its free booklet *Experience Washington,* which can be ordered by phone or downloaded from the Internet. **Tourism BC**'s *British Columbia Approved Accommodation* guide, available at no charge at tourist information centers, rates 800 BC government-inspected accommodations and campgrounds. Local bed-and-breakfast and inn agencies offer accommodation listings; check with the local visitors' center for details.

HOTELS

Hotels in the Pacific Northwest's major destinations are counted among the world's best. Luxury chains, such as the Four Seasons, Radisson, and Westin, as well as numerous independents, are generally located downtown. They usually offer stylish decor, an upscale restaurant, a spa, and valet parking. Reservations are recommended, especially if you plan to visit during a holiday or a popular festival or event *(see pp30–33).*

If you are looking for personalized guest services and luxurious amenities, you may wish to investigate boutique

hotels – small, exclusive, independently owned hotels, usually situated in city centers and resort destinations.

All the major mid-range hotel chains, including Best Western, Holiday Inn, and Marriott, can be found in the larger cities of the Pacific Northwest and often in smaller towns near popular destinations. These chains provide rooms that are not only affordable but also standardized: no matter where the hotel is located, they offer clean, reliable accommodations as well as facilities that typically include a hotel restaurant, a swimming pool, and a fitness center.

MOTELS

Motels offer much to travelers who are looking for simplicity and cleanliness. Most are located near busy highways and are a comfortable and inexpensive option as long as transportation into

the city is not an issue. Motels generally offer fewer amenities than hotels, although cable TV, private bathrooms, air conditioning, and ice and soda machines are standard. Reservations are usually not necessary.

BED-AND-BREAKFASTS AND INNS

The Pacific Northwest prides itself on its many welcoming and charming bed-and-breakfasts. Guestrooms are typically located in a large house in which the host also resides. Accommodations range from rooms in historic Victorian homes with beautiful gardens, situated in residential city neighborhoods, to rooms in rustic log homes near the mountains, and everything in between.

As the name suggests, guests are served breakfast, often buffet-style. When reserving, inquire about other meals as well; some bed-and-breakfasts

A charming bed-and-breakfast in Port Townsend, Washington

◁ **Recreational vehicles in Washington's Mount Rainier National Park**

also serve lunch and dinner. Most bed-and-breakfasts prohibit smoking, and some also have restrictions on children and pets.

The **Oregon** and the **Washington Bed and Breakfast Guilds** provide extensive information and listings detailing bed-and-breakfasts in these two states. For visitors to British Columbia, the **British Columbia Bed and Breakfast Innkeepers Guild** publishes a guide to accommodations that are approved by the agency. Like bed-and-breakfasts, inns come in all shapes and sizes, from small and rustic to large and luxurious.

Visitors to British Columbia may choose to stay at one of the province's numerous guest ranches, which include working cattle ranches. These properties offer a variety of activities, such as horseback riding and fishing, in a country setting, as well as the opportunity to participate in real ranch work. Visitors can choose from basic cabins, ski lodges, and luxury ranches featuring fireplaces, room service, air conditioning, hot tubs, and spa facilities. Contact the **BC Guest Ranchers' Association** for information.

HOSTELS

Hostels can be ideal for travelers on a budget. **Hostelling International** (HI) operates locations throughout the Pacific Northwest. HI memberships are available at a nominal fee (free for youths 18 years and younger) and entitle members to discounts on rooms, restaurant meals, car rentals, bus travel, airport shuttles, and more. Ask about other benefits at HI's regional offices.

A variety of accommodations are available: some hostels have kitchens, which are usually communal; many are dormitory-style with shared bathrooms. Calling ahead to reserve a space is advisable.

A variety of hostels are centrally located within the metropolitan Seattle and Portland areas. There are also hostels, both HI and those

The heritage Gatsby Mansion in Victoria, BC, now a bed-and-breakfast

unaffiliated to HI, throughout Oregon and Washington.

In British Columbia, hostels are to be found in Vancouver, Whistler, Vancouver Island, and at major destinations in the BC Interior. Hostel-style accommodation is also available at the YMCA and YWCA in Vancouver and, in summer, at several universities and colleges, including the University of British Columbia.

For an online directory of hostels worldwide, visit **www.hostels.com**.

CAMPGROUNDS

Throughout the Pacific Northwest, park facilities are basic – running water, flush or pit toilets, and a tenting area – although some sites have showers and running water. Privately owned tent, trailer, and recreational vehicle (RV) parks offer both simple sites with outhouses and full-service campgrounds with flush toilets, showers, electricity, and even playgrounds and games rooms.

In Oregon and Washington, some campgrounds accept reservations, whereas others are first come, first served. Campsites may be reserved up to a year in advance for certain weekends and holidays, such as July 4. Reservations for Oregon and Washington campsites can be made by contacting **Oregon State Parks** or **Washington State Parks**, or online at www.reserveamerica.com. Campgrounds at British Columbia's provincial and national parks fill up quickly.

Check the **BC Parks** website to determine which parks take reservations and reserve with **Discover Camping** by phone or online.

PRICES

With so many accommodation options, prices vary tremendously and depend on the season and availability. During peak tourist months, June to September, and public holidays, prices are higher in the city and at seaside or lakeside accommodations. The best deals at these locations are to be found in the off-season, October to April. Ski resorts are on an opposite schedule, which means that mountain accommodations in mid-summer are readily available and prices quite affordable.

It is best to stay in cities on weekends, when hotels have almost no business clientele, and to stay at bed-and-breakfasts outside cities or popular weekend destinations during the week, when prices often drop considerably. Be sure to inquire about package deals – many hotels offer discounts on tours and entrance to attractions, restaurant and store coupons, as well as free airport and city shuttle service.

Increasingly, hotels offer discounts on room rates when bookings are made over the Internet. Reserving a room with an Internet booking agency *(see p280)* can also result in savings, especially on last-minute deals. As well, many hotels offer discounts to members of auto clubs, and to students, and seniors, so it is always a good idea to inquire about these discounts when calling to reserve a room. Watch for hidden costs such as parking fees and single-occupancy surcharges.

Oregon's hotel tax varies from county to county. Hotel tax in Seattle is 15.6 percent but varies throughout the rest of Washington. In British Columbia, prices are subject to a 5 percent federal Goods and Services Tax (GST); a 7 percent provincial hotel tax on rooms in properties with four or more units; and in certain municipalities, an additional tax of up to 2 percent.

HOW TO BOOK

Reservations are recommended whatever the season, as festivals, conferences, and other events (see pp30–33) are held year-round throughout the Pacific Northwest. Campgrounds are especially popular during the summer, as are ski resorts in the winter. Most major hotels have toll-free reservation numbers and accept bookings by fax or Internet. Rooms can also be booked through Internet booking agencies, such as **Priceline. com** and **Expedia.com**.

If you have special requirements, such as a quiet room away from ice machines and elevators, make them known when you book your room. Reservations usually require a credit card number or a deposit the equivalent of one night's stay. Generally, refunds are made for cancellations if enough notice has been given; however, administration charges may apply. Notify the hotel if you expect to arrive later than 5pm or you may lose your reservations.

TRAVELERS WITH DISABILITIES

Hotels and motels in both the US and Canada are required by law to be wheelchair accessible, with

Sign in the Hotel de Haro lobby, Roche Harbor, San Juan Island

the exception of some in older buildings. The reality, however, is that this is not always the case. The vast majority of large private and chain hotels are equipped with the necessary facilities, including visual notification of the fire alarm and of incoming phone calls. Many also have suites designated specifically for people with disabilities. However, many of the older buildings and bed-and-breakfasts in the Pacific Northwest have narrow hallways that can obstruct wheelchairs and that are without ramps. As always, it is best to check in advance. In the US, the Society for Accessible Travel and Hospitality (see p327) provides travel tips and information about wheelchair access.

Many BC properties participate in the Access Canada program, which seeks to make traveling easier for seniors and people with

disabilities. Look for the Access Canada logo, which uses a numbered system from 1 to 4: 1 indicates accommodation suitable for active seniors and people with minor disabilities; 2, for seniors and people with moderate disabilities; 3, for people with advanced agility, hearing, mobility, and vision disabilities and independent wheelchair users; and 4, for those with severe disabilities.

TRAVELING WITH CHILDREN

Children are welcome in most hotels in the Pacific Northwest. Many hotels and motels offer family packages, services such as baby-sitting, and family games rooms. Call ahead to inquire about special rates and services for families and special accommodations for young children, such as cots, for which there is often a nominal fee of $10 to $15. It is advisable to inquire about a bed-and-breakfast's policy on accommodating children before booking a room.

BUSINESS TRAVELERS

Many hotels now provide travelers with access to fax machines and modems, and offer dual-line, direct-dial phone with voice mail, as well as fax and copier services. Larger hotels often maintain full-service business centers, which provide secretarial and courier services as well as Internet facilities.

The luxurious Fairmont Chateau Whistler, British Columbia

The Alaska Hotel in Dawson Creek, British Columbia, dating back to 1930

They may also have conference rooms that can be reserved in advance. If you plan to stay at an older property and wish to do business from there, make sure it has the facilities you require.

WHERE TO STAY IN PORTLAND

Most of the major hotel chains are represented in downtown Portland. They provide good bases for visitors who want to feel the pulse of the city and visit its museums and cultural attractions. Downtown hotels are also in close proximity to some of Portland's up-and-coming neighborhoods, such as the Pearl District. Most of the city's bed-and-breakfasts are located a bit farther afield.

WHERE TO STAY IN SEATTLE

Since Seattle's downtown is relatively small and many sights can be easily reached on foot, staying downtown is ideal for travelers. Accommodations in or near Pike Place Market are convenient for all the major shops and many rooms have stunning views of Elliott Bay and Puget Sound. Most of the major hotels are clustered together and are within walking distance of many of the city's best bars and restaurants. Pioneer Square and Belltown, two neighborhoods flanking downtown, on the south and north respectively, offer more affordable accommodations. Still central though just outside the downtown area, Capitol Hill and Queen Anne Hill offer comfortable accommodations in neighborhood surroundings.

WHERE TO STAY IN VANCOUVER

Most of Vancouver's hotels are clustered in the downtown shopping and business districts, although there are also several near the airport. Bed-and-breakfasts are located downtown as well as in residential neighborhoods such as Kitsilano or Shaughnessy. As in most major cities, prices are generally highest downtown.

One of several resort hotels in popular Lake Chelan, Washington

DIRECTORY

TOURIST OFFICES

Tourism BC
Tel (800) 435-5622.
www.hellobc.com

Travel Oregon
Tel (800) 547-7842.
www.traveloregon.com

Washington State Tourism
Tel (800) 544-1800.
www.experiencewa.com

BED-AND-BREAKFAST AND INN AGENCIES

BC Guest Ranchers' Association
Tel (877) 278-2922.
www.bcguestranches.com

British Columbia Bed and Breakfast Innkeepers Guild
www.bcsbestbnbs.com

Oregon Bed and Breakfast Guild
Tel (800) 944-6196.
www.obbg.org

Washington Bed and Breakfast Guild
Tel (800) 647-2918.
www.wbbg.com

HOSTELS

Hostelling International Canada
Tel (604) 684-7101.
www.hihostels.ca

Hostelling International Oregon Council
Tel (866) 447-3031.
www.portlandhostel.org

Hostelling International USA
www.hiusa.org

Hostels.com
www.hostels.com

CAMPGROUND RESERVATIONS

BC Parks
www.env.gov.bc.ca

Discover Camping
www.discovercamping.ca

Oregon State Parks
Tel (800) 452-5687.
www.oregonstateparks.org

Washington State Parks
Tel (888) 226-7688.
www.parks.wa.gov

RESERVATION AGENCIES

Expedia.com
www.expedia.com

Priceline.com
www.priceline.com

Choosing a Hotel

Hotels have been selected across a wide price range for facilities, good value, and location. All rooms have private bath, TV, air conditioning, and are wheelchair accessible unless otherwise indicated. Most have Internet access, and in some cases, fitness facilities may be offsite. The hotels are listed by area, and within these areas by price.

PRICE CATEGORIES
Price categories for all hotels are in US$ and are for a standard double room per night, inclusive of service charges, and any additional taxes:
US$ Under $100
US$$ $100–$150
US$$$ $150–$200
US$$$$ $200–$300
US$$$$$ Over $300

PORTLAND

DOWNTOWN Benson Hotel $$$
309 SW Broadway, 97205 **Tel** *(503) 228-2000* **Fax** *(503) 471-3920* **Rooms** *287*   **Map** *1 C4*

Built in 1912 by noted lumber baron and philanthropist Simon Benson, this stately hotel is filled with marble and polished Russian walnut details. Rooms are elegant and classically furnished; the sumptuous Presidential suite, host to every US president since Truman, is the height of luxury. **www.bensonhotel.com**

DOWNTOWN Governor Hotel $$$
614 SW 11th Ave., 97205 **Tel** *(503) 224-3400* **Fax** *(503) 241-2122* **Rooms** *100*   **Map** *1 B5*

On the National Register of Historic Places, this 1909 gem is full of Arts and Crafts details inside and out. The former lobby (now part of Jake's Grill) features historic murals depicting scenes from the Lewis and Clark expedition, and some of the elegantly furnished rooms offer fireplaces and balconies. **www.governorhotel.com**

DOWNTOWN Hilton Portland and Executive Tower $$$
921 SW 6th Ave., 97204 **Tel** *(503) 226-1611* **Fax** *(503) 220-2565* **Rooms** *782*   **Map** *1 C5*

This full-service hotel in the center of downtown is a favorite of business travelers, conventioneers, and tourists. Facilities include business and fitness centers, a magnificent pool area with glass ceiling, and a top-notch concierge. The surrounding blocks offer entertainment, dining, and shopping. **www.portland.hilton.com**

DOWNTOWN Paramount Hotel $$$
808 SW Taylor St., 97205 **Tel** *(503) 223-9900* **Fax** *(503) 223-7900* **Rooms** *154*   **Map** *1 B5*

From the impressive lobby to the spacious guestrooms outfitted with Biedermeier furnishings, this boutique hotel exudes a feeling of opulence. The most luxurious rooms have fireplaces, whirlpool baths, and private patios. The Dragonfish Café, on the ground floor, serves pan-Asian fusion cuisine. **www.portlandparamount.com**

DOWNTOWN Westin Portland $$$
750 SW Alder St., 97205 **Tel** *(503) 294-9000* **Fax** *(503) 241-9565* **Rooms** *205*   **Map** *1 C5*

One of Portland's most luxurious hotels, this member of the Westin chain offers luxurious rooms and superb service. Especially well equipped for business travelers, it has work desks with ergonomic chairs, wireless Internet, three meeting rooms, and a convenient central location. **www.starwoodhotels.com**

DOWNTOWN Heathman Hotel $$$$
1001 SW Broadway, 97205 **Tel** *(503) 241-4100* **Fax** *(503) 790-7110* **Rooms** *150*   **Map** *1 C5*

With its Old World charm and proximity to Portland's cultural district, this handsome 1927 institution is a magnet for visiting musicians and writers. Rooms feature city views and works by local artists. Amenities include a cozy library, an extensive movie collection, afternoon tea, and a first-rate restaurant and bar. **www.heathmanhotel.com**

DOWNTOWN Hotel Fifty $$$$
50 SW Morrison St., 97204 **Tel** *(503) 221-0711* **Fax** *(503) 484-1417* **Rooms** *140*   **Map** *2 D5*

Convenient to the freeway, MAX light rail, the convention center, and downtown shopping, this hotel has had a $7 million renovation and offers smart, comfortable rooms, many with city views. Its Willamette riverfront location makes it ideal for joggers and others who would like to enjoy Waterfront Park just across the street. **www.hotelfifty.com**

DOWNTOWN Hotel Lucia $$$$
400 SW Broadway, 97205 **Tel** *(503) 225-1717* **Fax** *(503) 225-1919* **Rooms** *128*   **Map** *1 C4*

With a sleek look, this stylish spot features high-tech touches, including high-speed wireless Internet, iPod recharging docks, and flatscreen televisions. Luxurious beds, a pillow menu, and pampering bath products contribute to the exceptional comfort. Acclaimed artwork lines the lobby and hallways. **www.hotellucia.com**

DOWNTOWN Hotel Monaco $$$$
506 SW Washington St., 97204 **Tel** *(503) 222-0001* **Fax** *(503) 222-0004* **Rooms** *221*   **Map** *1 C5*

Once the Lipman Wolfe Department Store, this renovated boutique hotel in a 1912 architectural gem boasts a large contemporary art collection and a plush, colorful decor inspired by Anglo-Chinois style. Located on transit lines in the heart of downtown, it offers convenient access to the entire city. **www.monaco-portland.com**

Key to Symbols *see back cover flap*

DOWNTOWN Hotel Vintage Plaza

422 SW Broadway, 97205 **Tel** *(503) 228-1212* **Fax** *(503) 228-3598* **Rooms** *117* — **Map** *1 C4*

With rooms named after Oregon wineries and vineyards, this handsome, centrally located hotel offers a complimentary wine reception every evening. Top-floor suites boast wall-to-floor conservatory windows with beautiful city views. The on-site Pazzo restaurant serves superb Italian cuisine. **www.vintageplaza.com**

DOWNTOWN The Nines

525 SW Morrison, Portland, 97204 **Tel** *(877) 229-9995* **Rooms** *331* — **Road Map** *1 C5*

This luxury hotel occupies the top nine floors of the landmark Meier & Frank building in downtown Portland. The lobby is decorated with contemporary work by local artists, a theme that extends to the sleek, tasteful rooms. This is a sophisticated hotel convenient for shopping. **www.thenines.com**

FARTHER AFIELD Ace Hotel

1022 SW Stark St., 97205 **Tel** *(503) 228-2277* **Fax** *(503) 228-2297* **Rooms** *79* — **Map** *1 B4*

After a complete renovation, the former Clyde Hotel has a mix of original 1912 details and a stylishly austere, modern look. Each guestroom in this hip, funky, totally original spot is one-of-a-kind; some have turntables (LPs are available for borrowing), and the hotel also rents bicycles free of charge. **www.acehotel.com**

FARTHER AFIELD Jupiter Hotel

800 E Burnside St., 97214 **Tel** *(503) 230-9200* **Fax** *(503) 230-8910* **Rooms** *81* — **Road Map** *1 A3*

Once a nondescript motor-court motel, this is one of the most fashionable hotels in Portland, with a bold, stylish look and posh amenities such as luxurious linens and fine toiletries. The on-site Doug Fir Restaurant and Lounge, open until 2:30am, is one of the city's top music venues. **www.jupiterhotel.com**

FARTHER AFIELD Kennedy School

5736 NE 33rd Ave., 97211 **Tel** *(503) 249-3983* **Fax** *(503) 288-6559* **Rooms** *35* — **Road Map** *1 A3*

This 1915 elementary school has been transformed into a B&B and entertainment complex. Whimsically decorated and furnished with antiques, classrooms-turned-guestrooms still have chalkboards and clocks, but now also have private bathrooms. Also on site are a movie theater, brewery, restaurant, and three bars. **www.mcmenamins.com**

FARTHER AFIELD Hotel deLuxe

729 SW 15th Ave., 97205 **Tel** *(503) 219-2094* **Fax** *(503) 219-2095* **Rooms** *130* — **Map** *1 A4*

Portland's much-loved old Mallory Hotel has a classic cinema theme that harks back to the Golden Era of Hollywood. It is sumptuously decorated in Art Deco style. Extras include a pillow menu, a doggie menu for your canine traveling companion, and a spiritual menu offering a choice of religious texts. **www.hoteldeluxeportland.com**

FARTHER AFIELD Inn at Northrup Station

2025 NW Northrup St., 97209 **Tel** *(503) 224-0543* **Fax** *(503) 273-2102* **Rooms** *70* — **Road Map** *1 A3*

In the heart of fashionable Northwest Portland, this old motel was transformed into a fun, psychedelically colored boutique hotel. Guest accommodations are all suites with full kitchens; many rooms have patios or balconies, and all guests can use the rooftop deck. A streetcar line is just steps away. **www.northrupstation.com**

FARTHER AFIELD Portland Marriott Downtown Waterfront

1401 SW Naito Parkway, 97201 **Tel** *(503) 226-7600* **Fax** *(503) 221-1789* **Rooms** *497* — **Road Map** *1 A3*

This riverside high-rise features modern facilities and a soothing white-on-white decor. Rooms are clean, plush, and comfortable; east-facing rooms offer magnificent views of the river and mountains. The center of downtown is nearby, and Waterfront Park lies just outside. **www.marriott.com**

FARTHER AFIELD Portland's White House Bed & Breakfast

1914 NE 22nd Ave., 97212 **Tel** *(503) 287-7131* **Fax** *(503) 249-1641* **Rooms** *8* — **Road Map** *1 A3*

Built by a lumber baron in 1911, this Greek Revival-style mansion, one of the grandest properties in the upscale Irvington neighborhood, bears a strong resemblance to its Washington, DC namesake. The place is handsomely appointed, with fine antiques and bathroom fixtures. **www.portlandswhitehouse.com**

FARTHER AFIELD The Lion and the Rose Victorian Bed & Breakfast

1810 NE 15th Ave., 97212 **Tel** *(503) 287-9245* **Fax** *(503) 287-9247* **Rooms** *6* — **Road Map** *1 A3*

This majestic 1906 Queen Anne-style mansion, listed on the National Register of Historic Places, offers six elegant guest rooms with private baths, cable TV, air conditioning, and wireless Internet. Located in the leafy, historic Irvington neighborhood, it's a short walk from restaurants, shops, and MAX light rail. **www.lionrose.com**

OREGON

ASHLAND Columbia Hotel

262 1/2 E Main St., 97520 **Tel** *(541) 482-3726* **Rooms** *24* — **Road Map** *1 A5*

An inexpensive, well-worn hotel, this homey spot in the center of Ashland is just a few minutes' walk from Shakespeare festival venues. Guestrooms are tidy and tastefully furnished, and skylights offer abundant natural light in the spacious lobby, where you can relax with coffee and the morning paper. **www.columbiahotel.com**

ASHLAND Ashland Springs Hotel ❄ [P] 🍴 👪 📺 [W] $$$$

212 E Main St., 97520 ***Tel*** *(541) 488-1700* ***Fax*** *(541) 488-1701* ***Rooms*** *70* ***Road Map*** *1 A5*

This nine-story landmark hotel, the tallest building between Portland and San Francisco when it was built in 1925, has been lovingly restored to its original elegance. Boasting a gorgeous lobby and rooms tastefully appointed with fine French fabrics, today it sets the standard for luxury in the region. **www.ashlandspringshotel.com**

ASTORIA Hotel Elliott ❄ [P] 👪 📺 [W] $$$$

357 12th St., 97103 ***Tel*** *(503) 325-2222* ***Fax*** *(503) 325-6868* ***Rooms*** *32* ***Road Map*** *1 A3*

Located in the heart of downtown and given a three-year, multi-million-dollar renovation, this is Astoria's top boutique hotel. The building retains many of its original 1924 details, while the facilities are fresh and luxurious: beds have thick duvets, goose-down pillows, and 440-count cotton sheets. **www.hotelelliott.com**

BAKER CITY Geiser Grand Hotel ❄ [P] 🍴 👪 📺 [W] $$

1996 Main St., 97814 ***Tel*** *(541) 523-1889* ***Fax*** *(541) 523-1800* ***Rooms*** *30* ***Road Map*** *1 C3*

This 1889 landmark was the finest hotel between Portland and Salt Lake City when it opened, and it still has little competition. Meticulously restored, it features mahogany millwork and a huge stained-glass skylight above the dining room. The restaurant is also among the best in the region. **www.geisergrand.com**

BEND McMenamin's Old St. Francis School [P] 🍴 👪 📺 [W] $$$

700 NW Bond St., 97701 ***Tel*** *(541) 382-5174* ***Fax*** *(541) 330-8561* ***Rooms*** *19* ***Road Map*** *1 B4*

Central Oregon's first parochial school now welcomes guests for food, drink, movies, and overnight stays. Rooms in the 1936 structure have private baths and all mod cons, while memorabilia from the school and community adorns the walls. Also on site are three pubs, four cottages, and a Turkish-style soaking pool. **www.mcmenamins.com**

BEND Seventh Mountain Resort ❄ [P] 🍴 🏊 👪 🏋 📺 [W] $$$

18575 SW Century Dr., 97702 ***Tel*** *(541) 382-8711* ***Fax*** *(541) 382-3517* ***Rooms*** *220* ***Road Map*** *1 B4*

Situated on the banks of the Deschutes River, this popular resort makes a fine base for skiers, rafters, anglers, and other outdoors-loving travelers. The homey, condo-style accommodations range from simple bedroom units to fully equipped suites, and amenities include heated pools, hot tubs, tennis courts, and hiking trails. **www.seventhmountain.com**

CANNON BEACH Cannon Beach Hotel [P] 🍴 👪 📺 [W] $$$

1116 S Hemlock St., 97110 ***Tel*** *(503) 436-1392* ***Fax*** *(503) 436-1396* ***Rooms*** *30* ***Road Map*** *1 A3*

Clad in weathered cedar shingles, this renovated 1910 loggers' boardinghouse offers all modern conveniences. Rooms have been individually decorated and some boast views of the Pacific Ocean. There is a restaurant off the lobby, and accommodation is also offered in three buildings close by. **www.cannonbeachhotel.com**

CANNON BEACH Stephanie Inn ❄ [P] 🍴 📺 [W] $$$$$

2740 S Pacific St., 97110 ***Tel*** *(503) 436-2221* ***Fax*** *(503) 436-9711* ***Rooms*** *50* ***Road Map*** *1 A3*

This romantic oceanside inn offers rooms with fireplaces, whirlpool tubs, and stunning views of Haystack Rock. Modern amenities include cordless phones and high-definition LCD televisions; breakfast buffet, wine, and hors d'oeuvres are included. The dining room offers Pacific Northwest cuisine for an additional charge. **www.stephanieinn.com**

CRATER LAKE NATIONAL PARK Crater Lake Lodge [P] 🍴 👪 📺 [W] $$$$

565 Rim Village Dr., 97604 ***Tel*** *(800) 774-2728* ***Fax*** *(541) 830-8514* ***Rooms*** *71* ***Road Map*** *1 B4*

Built in 1915, this grand lodge has been extensively renovated and sits in a spectacular location on the rim of Crater Lake. Built of native stone and wood, it offers claw-foot tubs in guest bathrooms, a massive fireplace in the Great Hall, and fine Northwest cuisine in the restaurant. Open May–Oct. **www.craterlakelodges.com**

EUGENE Campbell House [P] 🍴 👪 📺 [W] $$$

252 Pearl St., 97401 ***Tel*** *(541) 343-1119* ***Fax*** *(541) 343-2258* ***Rooms*** *18* ***Road Map*** *1 A4*

This handsome 1892 Victorian house is located on beautifully landscaped grounds high on a hillside in Eugene's historic Skinner Butte neighborhood. Sumptuously decorated rooms in three buildings – the main house, carriage house, and adjacent cottage – range from small yet comfortable to spacious. **www.campbellhouse.com**

EUGENE Excelsior Inn ❄ [P] 🍴 📺 [W] $$$

754 E 13th Ave., 97401 ***Tel*** *(541) 342-6963* ***Rooms*** *14* ***Road Map*** *1 A4*

Located close to the University of Oregon campus, this European-style bed-and-breakfast inn offers beautifully furnished rooms, each named after a different classical composer, with details such as hardwood floors, arched windows, and marble and tile baths. Complimentary full breakfast is included. **www.excelsiorinn.com**

GLENEDEN BEACH Salishan Spa & Golf Resort [P] 🍴 🏊 👪 🏋 📺 [W] $$$$

7760 N Hwy. 101, 97388 ***Tel*** *(541) 764-2371* ***Fax*** *(541) 764-3510* ***Rooms*** *205* ***Road Map*** *1 A3*

One of the Northwest's premier resorts, this complex is nestled on 350 quiet, wooded acres near Siletz Bay. In addition to full-service accommodations and spa treatments, it offers a renowned golf course, trails for hiking and birding, and the Oregon coast's most elegant dining, with a legendary wine cellar. **www.salishan.com**

HOOD RIVER Hood River Hotel ❄ [P] 🍴 👪 🏋 📺 [W] $$

102 Oak Ave., 97031 ***Tel*** *(541) 386-1900* ***Fax*** *(541) 386-6090* ***Rooms*** *41* ***Road Map*** *1 B3*

This charming and nicely restored 1913 hotel, located in the heart of downtown Hood River, offers views of the town on one side and of the Columbia River on the other. Guests can unwind by the fire in the cozy lobby and enjoy fine Pacific Northwest cuisine in the adjacent restaurant. **www.hoodriverhotel.com**

Key to Price Guide *see p282* **Key to Symbols** *see back cover flap*

IMNAHA Imnaha River Inn

73946 Rimrock Rd., 97842 **Tel** *(541) 577-6002* **Fax** *(541) 577-3070* **Rooms** *7*   **Road Map** *1 C3*

This superb log lodge nestled in the beautiful Imnaha River Canyon is an outdoor-lover's dream, providing easy access to hiking, hunting, fishing, rafting, and mountain-biking areas. Rooms are rustic but comfortable; all have views, and some have outside decks. Bathrooms are shared, but rooms have sinks. **www.imnahariverinn.com**

JACKSONVILLE Country House Inns

830 N 5th St., 97530 **Tel** *(800) 367-1942* **Rooms** *14*   **Road Map** *1 A4*

The rooms, suites, and cottages here are all located in historical homes dating from the 1860s, making this a very charming place to stay in central Jacksonville. Attractive gardens, an on-site bistro, and stylish, comfortable rooms are all part of the appeal. **www.countryhouseinns.com**

JACKSONVILLE Jacksonville Inn

175 E California St., 97530 **Tel** *(541) 899-1900* **Fax** *(541) 899-1373* **Rooms** *8*   **Road Map** *1 A4*

Located in the heart of downtown, this charming 1861 building dates back to Southern Oregon's Gold Rush era; specks of gold can still be seen in the mortar of the locally quarried sandstone walls in the dining area and lounge. Four cottages are also available, and the restaurant is renowned. **www.jacksonvilleinn.com**

JOSEPH Bronze Antler Bed & Breakfast

309 S Main St., 97846 **Tel** *(541) 432-0230* **Fax** *(541) 432-6219* **Rooms** *4*   **Road Map** *1 C3*

Built in 1925 and beautifully restored, this charming small B&B is the former Craftsman-style home of a local saw-mill supervisor. Period details include original woodwork, copper-plated hardware, and hand-stenciled wall designs. Cozy guestrooms enjoy mountain views. **www.bronzeantler.com**

LINCOLN CITY Ester Lee Motel

3803 SW Hwy. 101, 97367 **Tel** *(541) 996-3606* **Fax** *(541) 996-6743* **Rooms** *53*   **Road Map** *1 A3*

Pacific Coast views, along with wood-burning fireplaces and kitchens in most units, have earned this classic road-side motel and cottages a loyal following. Nearby are golf courses, shops, restaurants, and a casino, but the cozy, no-nonsense rooms are also good places for just watching the surf roll in. **www.esterlee.com**

MCMINNVILLE McMenamin's Hotel Oregon

310 NE Evans St., 97128 **Tel** *(503) 472-8427* **Fax** *(503) 435-3141* **Rooms** *42*   **Road Map** *1 A3*

This historic hotel in the heart of McMinnville is a popular stop for wine country tourists. Guests can choose among a variety of comfortable rooms, some with private baths. For food and drink, there is a speakeasy-style cellar bar, a first-floor pub, and a rooftop bar with great views. **www.mcmenamins.com**

MCMINNVILLE Youngberg Hill Vineyards and Inn

10660 SW Youngberg Hill Rd., 97128 **Tel** *(503) 472-2727* **Fax** *(503) 472-1313* **Rooms** *7*   **Road Map** *1 A3*

A winery and guesthouse in one, this imposing Craftsman-style inn sits high on a hill and overlooks the picturesque rolling vineyards of Pinot Noir and Pinot Gris. Luxurious rooms with en-suite baths have views of Mount Jefferson, Mount Hood, and the Coast Range. The property produces award-winning wines. **www.youngberghill.com**

MOUNT HOOD Timberline Lodge

27500 E Timberline Rd., 97028 **Tel** *(800) 547-1406* **Fax** *(503) 272-3710* **Rooms** *70*   **Road Map** *1 B3*

No other building symbolizes Oregon like the historic Timberline Lodge. The magnificent structure, famous from the exterior shots in the film "The Shining," was built in the 1930s by hundreds of craftspeople, and rich details abound. The lobby's massive stone fireplace is an attraction in itself. **www.timberlinelodge.com**

NEWPORT Sylvia Beach Hotel

267 NW Cliff St., 97365 **Tel** *(541) 265-5428* **Fax** *(541) 574-8204* **Rooms** *20*   **Road Map** *1 A3*

Housed in an old Craftsman-style building in the artsy Newport neighborhood of Nye Beach, this delightfully quirky hotel on the National Register of Historic Places is dedicated to book lovers. Each of the guestrooms is named after an author and decorated accordingly, and none has a television or phone. **www.sylviabeachhotel.com**

SALEM Salem Travelodge

1555 State St., 97301 **Tel** *(503) 581-2466* **Fax** *(503) 581-2811* **Rooms** *42*   **Road Map** *1 A3*

Enjoying a quiet location close to all of the capital's major sites, this motel offers basic, affordable accommodation for business and leisure travelers. Rooms have all the standard amenities; some have kitchenettes. High-speed Wi-Fi and Continental breakfast are complimentary. There is an outdoor heated pool. **www.travelodge.com**

SEASIDE Gilbert Inn

341 Beach Dr., 97138 **Tel** *(503) 738-9770* **Fax** *(503) 717-1070* **Rooms** *10*   **Road Map** *1 A3*

Just a half-block from the Pacific and a block from Broadway, Seaside's main street, this charming, nicely maintained Queen Anne-style B&B offers guests period elegance. Original tongue-and-groove fir paneling covers the walls and ceiling, and the innkeepers' family heirlooms are part of the Victorian decor. **www.gilbertinn.com**

STEAMBOAT Steamboat Inn

42705 N Umpqua Hwy., 97447 **Tel** *(541) 498-2230* **Fax** *(541) 498-2411* **Rooms** *20*   **Road Map** *1 A4*

A complex of suites, cabins, cottages, and houses, this retreat on a remote stretch of river is among Oregon's most renowned lodgings. Fly-fisherman come from all over to try this storied part of the Umpqua River, and the inn is also one of the state's top dining destinations. **www.thesteamboatinn.com**

SUNRIVER Sunriver Resort
🖼 🅿 🍴 ♨ 🚶 📺 🗐 Ⓦ $$$$
17600 Center Dr., 97707 **Tel** *(800) 801-8765* **Fax** *(541) 593-5458* **Rooms** *600*   **Road Map** *1 B4*

This vast, full-service resort provides all the elements of a rejuvenating getaway in the Cascade foothills south of Bend. Accommodations range from luxurious lodge suites to private condos, and surrounding them are such amenities as four golf courses, six restaurants, four swimming pools, and miles of biking trails. **www.sunriver-resort.com**

TROUTDALE McMenamin's Edgefield
🅿 🍴 🚶 🗐 Ⓦ $$
2126 SW Halsey St., 97060 **Tel** *(503) 669-8610* **Fax** *(503) 665-4209* **Rooms** *114*   **Road Map** *1 A4*

Built in 1911, this Georgian Revival-style manor served for decades as the Multnomah County Poor Farm; it is now the crown jewel of the McMenamin's empire of hotels, breweries, and pubs. In addition to its many guestrooms, the property includes a brewery, winery, distillery, movie theater, pool hall, and more. **www.mcmenamins.com**

WALLOWA LAKE Wallowa Lake Lodge
🅿 🍴 🚶 🗐 Ⓦ $$
60060 Wallowa Lake Hwy., 97846 **Tel** *(541) 432-9821* **Fax** *(541) 432-4885* **Rooms** *30*   **Road Map** *1 C3*

This handsome converted hunting lodge, built in 1923, offers rooms both in its main building and in eight cabins set over eight acres of lakeside property. Lodge rooms feature antique furnishings, Oriental carpets, and lake views through tall Ponderosa pines; the 1950s cabins have stone fireplaces and kitchens. **www.wallowalake.com**

WARM SPRINGS Kah-Nee-Tah Resort and Casino
🖼 🅿 🍴 ♨ 🚶 📺 🗐 Ⓦ $$$
6823 Hwy. 8, 97761 **Tel** *(541) 553-1112* **Fax** *(541) 553-1071* **Rooms** *139*   **Road Map** *1 B3*

With 300 days of sunshine annually, this is a beloved resort for Oregonians. The modern, arrow-shaped lodge draws countless visitors to the Confederated Tribes of Warm Springs Reservation for relaxing, dining, spa treatments, and gaming. There is golfing, hiking, horseback riding, and kayaking in the Warm Springs River. **www.kahneeta.com**

SEATTLE

PIKE PLACE MARKET AND THE WATERFRONT Pensione Nichols
🗐 $$$
1923 1st Ave., 98101 **Tel** *(206) 441-7125* **Fax** *(206) 441-7125* **Rooms** *12*   **Map** *3 C1*

Conveniently sited in Pike Place Market, this unique, European-style B&B offers simple, eclectically furnished rooms at fair prices. Smaller rooms share baths, and some have downtown views; the two spacious suites have private baths, full kitchens, and balconies with views of Puget Sound and the Olympic Mountains. **www.pensionenichols.com**

PIKE PLACE MARKET AND THE WATERFRONT The Edgewater
🖼 🅿 🍴 🚶 📺 🗐 Ⓦ $$$$$
2411 Alaskan Way, 98121 **Tel** *(206) 728-7000* **Fax** *(206) 441-4119* **Rooms** *223*   **Map** *3 A1*

For waterfront lodging, this place is hard to beat: it sits right on a pier, and half the rooms offer terrific views. Inside, it feels like a plush lodge as much as a city hotel, with knotty-pine furniture and river-rock fireplaces. The top-notch restaurant offers outdoor dining. **www.edgewaterhotel.com**

PIKE PLACE MARKET AND THE WATERFRONT Inn at the Market
🖼 🅿 🍴 🚶 🗐 Ⓦ $$$$$
86 Pine St., 98101 **Tel** *(206) 443-3600* **Fax** *(206) 448-0631* **Rooms** *70*   **Map** *3 C1*

Set in a landscaped courtyard off Pike Place Market, this lovely hotel offers rooms with stunning views of Elliott Bay from floor-to-ceiling bay windows. The inn's three restaurants include Campagne and Café Campagne *(see p303)*, serving superb French cuisine. The rooftop deck is a spectacular spot in dry weather. **www.innatthemarket.com**

SEATTLE CENTER AND BELLTOWN Inn at Queen Anne
🅿 🗐 Ⓦ $$$
505 1st Ave. N, 98109 **Tel** *(206) 282-7357* **Fax** *(206) 217-9719* **Rooms** *68*   **Map** *1 B3*

A stone's throw from KeyArena, this converted 1928 apartment building is convenient to both Seattle Center and downtown. Rooms are decorated simply, with Mission-style furnishings and earth-tone textiles; they also include kitchenettes. **www.innatqueenanne.com**

SEATTLE CENTER AND BELLTOWN MarQueen Hotel
🅿 🍴 🚶 📺 🗐 Ⓦ $$$
600 Queen Anne Ave. N, 98109 **Tel** *(206) 282-7407* **Fax** *(206) 283-1499* **Rooms** *58*   **Map** *1 B3*

Built in 1918 as an engineering school, this quaint small hotel is close to the McCaw Opera House and other performance venues at Seattle Center. All of the tastefully appointed rooms have kitchens, hardwood floors with area rugs, and upscale toiletries and robes. Salon and spa services are also available. **www.marqueen.com**

FARTHER AFIELD Ace Hotel
🅿 🚶 🗐 Ⓦ $$
2423 1st Ave., 98121 **Tel** *(206) 448-4721* **Fax** *(206) 374-0745* **Rooms** *28*   **Map** *1 C5*

Chic white-on-white decor and friendly service are the hallmarks of this modern, minimalist Belltown hotel, which is popular with artists and musicians. Rooms in the updated old rooming house have high ceilings and low platform beds with army-surplus blankets; half share baths. Complimentary Continental breakfast. **www.acehotel.com**

FARTHER AFIELD Gaslight Inn
♨ Ⓦ $$
1727 15th Ave., 98122 **Tel** *(206) 325-3654* **Fax** *(206) 328-4803* **Rooms** *8*   **Road Map** *1 A2*

On the quieter east side of Capitol Hill, this beautifully restored inn dating from 1906 has a wealth of fine details and ample public space for displaying its stunning collection of Northwest art. Rooms are furnished with antiques; each is different, and may include a fireplace, private deck, or private garden. **www.gaslight-inn.com**

Key to Price Guide *see p282* **Key to Symbols** *see back cover flap*

FARTHER AFIELD Chambered Nautilus Bed & Breakfast Inn
P 🖿 W $$$

5005 22nd Ave. NE, 98105 **Tel** *(206) 522-2536* **Fax** *(206) 528-0898* **Rooms** *10*   **Road Map** *1 A2*

This stately 1915 Georgian Colonial home is set on a peaceful hill a short walk from the University of Washington campus. The antiques-filled rooms have cozy robes, bottled water, and private baths; some have fireplaces, porches, and kitchens. Hearty three-course breakfasts and fresh-roasted coffee are available. **www.chamberednautilus.com**

FARTHER AFIELD Executive Hotel Pacific
🖼 **P** 🍴 🛎 🖿 W $$$

400 Spring St., 98104 **Tel** *(206) 623-3900* **Fax** *(206) 623-2059* **Rooms** *160*   **Map** *4 D2*

A $4 million renovation has spruced up this 1928 classic hotel. Rooms are on the small side, but are stylish and comfortable, with sparkling tiled bathrooms. The on-site Jasmine restaurant serves pan-Asian fusion cuisine, and the hotel's central downtown location is superb, with many attractions close by. **www.executivehotels.net**

FARTHER AFIELD Hotel Max
🖼 **P** 🍴 🛎 🖿 W $$$

620 Stewart St., 98101 **Tel** *(206) 728-6299* **Fax** *(206) 443-5754* **Rooms** *165*   **Map** *2 D5*

This 1920s-era hotel has been dramatically updated with striking, saturated colors and a huge collection of contemporary Northwest art. Beds feature fine linens, and guests can choose from a pillow menu and spiritual menu offering a choice of religious text. **www.hotelmaxseattle.com**

FARTHER AFIELD Inn at Virginia Mason
🖼 **P** 🍴 🖿 W $$$

1006 Spring St., 98104 **Tel** *(206) 583-6453* **Fax** *(206) 223-6771* **Rooms** *79*   **Map** *4 E1*

In a quiet neighborhood uphill from downtown, this elegantly converted apartment building serves business and leisure travelers as well as patients and doctors visiting the adjacent hospital. Rooms combine period charm with modern amenities, and two larger suites feature fireplaces and views of the city. **www.innatvirginiamason.com**

FARTHER AFIELD Mayflower Park Hotel
🖼 **P** 🍴 🛎 🖿 W $$$

405 Olive Way, 98101 **Tel** *(206) 623-8700* **Fax** *(206) 382-6996* **Rooms** *160*   **Map** *2 D5*

One of the last of Seattle's independently owned classic hotels, this refurbished 1927 property is ideally located for shoppers. It opens directly into the upscale Westlake Center mall, and is just a block away from the flagship Nordstrom's and Macy's. The on-site Andaluca restaurant serves fine Mediterranean cuisine. **www.mayflowerpark.com**

FARTHER AFIELD Roosevelt Hotel
🖼 **P** 🍴 🏃 🛎 🖿 W $$$

1531 7th Ave., 98101 **Tel** *(206) 621-1200* **Fax** *(206) 233-0335* **Rooms** *151*   **Map** *4 D1*

Like most of downtown Seattle's refurbished 1920s hotels, this classic high-rise offers small but nicely appointed rooms with bathrooms to match. Its central location is convenient for shopping, the convention center, and the monorail to Seattle center. The attached Von's Roast House serves hearty American fare. **www.roosevelthotel.com**

FARTHER AFIELD Grand Hyatt Seattle
🖼 **P** 🍴 🏃 🛎 🖿 W $$$$

721 Pine St., 98101 **Tel** *(206) 774-1234* **Fax** *(206) 774-6120* **Rooms** *425*   **Road Map** *1 A2*

This large luxury hotel is sleek and stylish, but also designed to appeal to high-tech professionals. In addition to large bathrooms and views of the city, it offers wireless Internet, multiple telephones, electronic blackout drapes, and in-room safes large enough to store a laptop. **www.grandseattle.hyatt.com**

FARTHER AFIELD Hotel Deca
🖼 **P** 🍴 🛎 🖿 W $$$$

4507 Brooklyn Ave. NE, 98105 **Tel** *(206) 634-2000* **Fax** *(206) 547-6029* **Rooms** *158*   **Road Map** *1 A2*

This Art Deco-style property is conveniently located for the University of Washington just two blocks away. Decorated with a bold, colorful scheme, it offers clean rooms and dining at the excellent District Lounge restaurant. Rooms on upper floors have terrific views. **www.hoteldeca.com**

FARTHER AFIELD Hotel Monaco
🖼 **P** 🍴 🏃 🛎 🖿 W $$$$

1101 4th Ave., 98101 **Tel** *(206) 621-1770* **Fax** *(206) 621-7779* **Rooms** *189*   **Map** *3 C2*

Upbeat, playful Mediterranean decor – think bold stripes, sumptuous fabrics, and a marine-themed mural – and excellent service draw artists and young business professionals to this top-rated, centrally located hotel. Rates include a nightly wine tasting and even a pet goldfish to keep for the duration of your stay. **www.monaco-seattle.com**

FARTHER AFIELD Inn at Harbor Steps
🖼 **P** 🏊 🏃 🛎 🖿 W $$$$

1221 1st Ave., 98101 **Tel** *(206) 748-0973* **Fax** *(206) 748-0533* **Rooms** *28*   **Map** *3 C2*

This boutique hotel at the base of a modern residential high-rise boasts an unsurpassed location for both business and leisure travelers, with all of downtown, Pioneer Square, the waterfront, and Pike Place Market in easy walking distance. Rooms are bright, cozy, and spacious, most with garden views and fireplaces. **www.innatharborsteps.com**

FARTHER AFIELD Sorrento Hotel
🖼 **P** 🍴 🏃 🛎 🖿 W $$$$

900 Madison St., 98104 **Tel** *(206) 622-6400* **Fax** *(206) 343-6155* **Rooms** *76*   **Map** *4 E1*

High above downtown on First Hill, this elegant classic offers some of Seattle's finest accommodation, exceptional service, and great views from west-facing rooms. Each of the rooms is one-of-a-kind, but each features Italian marble bathrooms and a wealth of creature comforts. **www.hotelsorrento.com**

FARTHER AFIELD Westin Seattle
🖼 **P** 🍴 🏊 🏃 🛎 🖿 W $$$$

1900 5th Ave., 98101 **Tel** *(206) 728-1000* **Fax** *(206) 728-2259* **Rooms** *891*   **Map** *2 D5*

The twin cylindrical towers of this vast hotel are prominent features of the Seattle skyline. Large, modern rooms offer unbeatable views of the city, Lake Union, Puget Sound, and the Olympic and Cascade mountains. Coldwater Bar & Grill, one of two attached restaurants, offers innovative Northwest cuisine. **www.starwoodhotels.com**

FARTHER AFIELD W Seattle
1112 4th Ave., 98101 **Tel** *(206) 264-6000* **Fax** *(206) 264-6100* **Rooms** *429*　　　　　**Map** *4 D2*

Crowned by a distinctive steel-and-mesh pyramid on its rooftop, this chic modern hotel draws fashionable visitors. With stylish, retro-minimalist decor, the rooms offer deluxe amenities. The 24th-floor suite is the ultimate in lavish; even the whirlpool bath has stunning city views. **www.whotels.com**

FARTHER AFIELD Alexis Hotel
1007 1st Ave., 98104 **Tel** *(206) 624-4844* **Fax** *(206) 621-9009* **Rooms** *121*　　　　　**Map** *3 C2*

This handsome boutique hotel, a landmark on the National Register of Historic Places, boasts luxurious Northwest-inspired decor and celebrated service. The hotel's guestrooms and public spaces, which have been given a $10 million renovation, are showcases for works by local artists. An Aveda spa is on-site. **www.alexishotel.com**

FARTHER AFIELD Fairmont Olympic Hotel
411 University St., 98101 **Tel** *(206) 621-1700* **Fax** *(206) 682-9633* **Rooms** *450*　　　　　**Map** *4 D1*

Possibly the grandest property in Seattle, modeled on an Italian Renaissance palazzo. The lobby, rich in marble and plush carpets, is worth a visit even if you are not staying here. Room decor is understated and refined, and service is top-notch. Facilities include a full-service health club and pool. **www.fairmont.com**

WASHINGTON

BELLINGHAM Chrysalis Inn & Spa
804 10th St., 98225 **Tel** *(360) 756-1005* **Fax** *(360) 647-0342* **Rooms** *43*　　　　　**Road Map** *1 A1*

Overlooking Bellingham Bay, this is Bellingham's finest hotel. The decor is warm and modern, with plenty of exposed wood, slate, and earth tones; there is a full-service spa and a romantic Mediterranean-style wine bar on the premises. A railroad runs below, but noise is infrequent and earplugs are provided. **www.thechrysalisinn.com**

CHELAN Campbell's Resort
104 W Woodin Ave., 98816 **Tel** *(509) 682-2561* **Fax** *(509) 682-2177* **Rooms** *170*　　　　　**Road Map** *1 B2*

With a prime beachfront location, this long-time local favorite offers a host of on-site amenities including spa, conference facilities, outdoor heated pool, and beach bar. All of the spacious rooms include a balcony or a patio, and some have fireplaces and kitchens. There is even a boat moorage for water arrivals. **www.campbellsresort.com**

DEER HARBOR Inn on Orcas Island
114 Channel Rd., 98243 **Tel** *(360) 376-5227* **Fax** *(360) 376-5228* **Rooms** *8*　　　　　**Road Map** *1 A1*

A New England-style structure located in a marsh-side setting close to Deer Harbor, this quiet retreat offers a variety of rooms in the main house, a carriage house, and a waterside cottage. All rooms have water views, and the inn is ideal for bird-watchers. Children under 18 are not allowed. **www.theinnonorcasisland.com**

EASTSOUND Orcas Suites at Rosario
1600 Rosario Rd., 98245 **Tel** *(360) 376-6262* **Rooms** *116*　　　　　**Road Map** *1 A1*

Located on a hillside of the beautiful Orcas Island, these suites offer views of Cascade Bay from every window and balcony. One and two bedroom suites are available, some with kitchens. All rooms are tastefully decorated. **www.orcassuites.com**

EASTSOUND Turtleback Farm Inn
1981 Crow Valley Rd., 98245 **Tel** *(360) 376-4914* **Fax** *(360) 376-5329* **Rooms** *11*　　　　　**Road Map** *1 A1*

Set in lush grounds overlooking its own duck pond, this converted late 19th-century farmhouse is a popular retreat. Rooms are furnished with antiques and decorated with floral fabrics, and all have private baths – many have claw-foot tubs and private decks. There is a lovely fireplace in the living room. **www.turlebackinn.com**

ELLENSBURG Inn at Goose Creek
1720 Canyon Rd., 98926 **Tel** *(509) 962-8030* **Fax** *(509) 962-8031* **Rooms** *10*　　　　　**Road Map** *1 B2*

Not much to look at on the outside, but this bed and breakfast inn located just off Interstate 90 offers ten whimsically and lavishly decorated rooms, each with its own unique theme. One is dedicated to honeymoons and anniversaries; others have Christmas, rose garden, sports, and Ellensburg rodeo motifs. **www.innatgoosecreek.com**

FORKS Kalaloch Lodge
157151 Hwy. 101, 98331 **Tel** *(866) 297-7367* **Fax** *(360) 962-3391* **Rooms** *64*　　　　　**Road Map** *1 A2*

Perched on a bluff overlooking the Pacific Ocean, this shingled 1953 lodge is an Olympic National Park favorite, so make reservations well in advance. Accommodations include lodge rooms as well as dozens of rustic cabins, many of which feature Franklin-style wood-burning stoves. **www.olympicnationalparks.com**

FRIDAY HARBOR Friday Harbor House
130 West St., 98250 **Tel** *(360) 378-8455* **Fax** *(360) 378-8453* **Rooms** *23*　　　　　**Road Map** *1 A1*

Walking distance from the Friday Harbor ferry terminal, this intimate boutique hotel is an ideal romantic getaway. Rooms in tranquil earth tones offer views of the harbor and beyond, plus fireplaces and whirlpool baths; most have decks or balconies. The restaurant has some of the Islands' best Northwest cuisine. **www.fridayharborhouse.com**

LEAVENWORTH Haus Rohrbach Pension

12882 Ranger Rd., 98826 **Tel** *(509) 548-7024* **Fax** *(509) 548-5038* **Rooms** *10*   **Road Map** *1 B2*

Overlooking the town and valley, this Alpine-style pension has ten whimsically named rooms, most with private baths and balconies offering mountain and valley views. Guests can swim in the pool and sunbathe in summer, and use the spa year-round. Rates include a hearty full breakfast. **www.hausrohrbach.com**

LEAVENWORTH Hotel Pension Anna

926 Commercial St., 98826 **Tel** *(509) 548-6273* **Fax** *(509) 548-4656* **Rooms** *16*   **Road Map** *1 B2*

This delightful German-style inn has rooms and suites with imported furniture from Austria and Germany; all have private baths. The most luxurious suite occupies part of an adjacent renovated church, complete with soaring ceilings and two twin beds in the old choir loft. Rates include a full German-style breakfast. **www.pensionanna.com**

MT. RAINIER NATIONAL PARK National Park Inn

Mount Rainier National Park, 98304 **Tel** *(360) 569-2275* **Fax** *(360) 569-2770* **Rooms** *25*   **Road Map** *1 B2*

The smaller of Mt. Rainier National Park's two lodges, this 1920s inn in Longmire, at the southwest corner of the park, is a rustic retreat with charming but basic rooms. Open year-round, it attracts hikers and climbers in the summer and snowshoers and cross-country skiers in the winter. **www.mtrainierguestservices.com**

MT. RAINIER NATIONAL PARK Paradise Inn

Mount Rainier National Park, 98304 **Tel** *(360) 569-2270* **Fax** *(360) 569-2770* **Rooms** *121*   **Road Map** *1 B2*

Built in 1916 and opened after an extensive renovation, this shingled structure is a classic national park lodge, with lofty cathedral ceilings, massive exposed beams, and decorative woodwork dating to the inn's earliest years. Many rooms offer stunning mountain views, and access to hiking trails is just outside. **www.mtrainierguestservices.com**

NAHCOTTA Moby Dick Hotel

25814 Sandridge Rd., 98637 **Tel** *(360) 665-4543* **Fax** *(360) 665-6887* **Rooms** *10*   **Road Map** *1 A2*

Located in a placid setting near the north end of Long Beach peninsula, this 1930s hotel is thoroughly charming in a funky, bohemian style. Inside this quiet retreat are cozy rooms and ample public space; outside are large gardens, a Japanese-style sauna, a spacious yurt, and an oyster farm. **www.mobydickhotel.com**

OLYMPIA Lighthouse Bungalow

1215 E Bay Dr., 98506 **Tel** *(360) 754-0389* **Rooms** *2*   **Road Map** *1 A2*

This charming old bungalow on the shores of Puget Sound is perfect for families and groups, with two well-appointed units including kitchens for self-catering. The upper deck offers four bedrooms and baths, two fireplaces, wood floors, and space enough for eight guests; the lower sleeps up to four. **www.lighthousebungalow.com**

PORT ANGELES Downtown Hotel

101 1/2 E Front St., 98362 **Tel** *(360) 565-1125* **Rooms** *17*   **Road Map** *1 A2*

This small European-style hotel occupies two floors above ground-level retail businesses in the heart of downtown. Modestly but nicely appointed lodging, convenient for travelers taking the ferry to Victoria. Some rooms share baths; some have kitchens and views of the Olympic Mountains. **www.portangelesdowntownhotel.com**

PORT ANGELES Lake Crescent Lodge

416 Lake Crescent Rd., 98363 **Tel** *(360) 928-3211* **Fax** *(360) 928-3253* **Rooms** *52*   **Road Map** *1 A2*

Set in a secluded spot on the shore of the fjord-like Lake Crescent, this lodge makes a fine base for exploring the northern reaches of the Olympic National Park. Guests can choose among rooms in the 1916 main building or the many adjacent cottages. The lodge is closed in winter. **www.lakecrescentlodge.com**

QUINAULT Lake Quinault Lodge

345 South Shore Rd., 98575 **Tel** *(360) 288-2900* **Fax** *(360) 288-2901* **Rooms** *92*   **Road Map** *1 A2*

This grand 1926 lodge sits by the rainforest above the shore of Lake Quinault, in the remote southwestern corner of Olympic National Park. It offers old-style comfort, with few televisions and phones, but the rooms are comfortable, the views excellent, and the food worth a visit on its own. **www.visitlakequinault.com**

ROCHE HARBOR Roche Harbor Village

248 Reuben Memorial Dr., 98250 **Tel** *(360) 378-2155* **Fax** *(360) 378-6809* **Rooms** *78*   **Road Map** *1 A1*

Lodging in this San Juan Island complex includes the Hotel de Haro, a charming 1886 hotel where former US president Teddy Roosevelt once stayed; the McMillin suites, offering luxury rooms; and the company town cottages, former homes of the families of men who used to work the local lime kilns. **www.rocheharbor.com**

SEAVIEW Shelburne Inn

4415 Pacific Way, 98644 **Tel** *(360) 642-2442* **Fax** *(360) 642-8904* **Rooms** *15*   **Road Map** *1 A2*

This celebrated spot was built in 1896 as a retreat for visitors from Portland and has been a landmark inn ever since. All of the antiques-furnished rooms have private baths; most have private decks. Gourmet breakfast is included, and the inn's Shoalwater Restaurant is among the best in the region. **www.theshelburneinn.com**

SNOQUALMIE Salish Lodge

6501 Railroad Ave., 98065 **Tel** *(425) 888-2556* **Fax** *(425) 888-2420* **Rooms** *89*   **Road Map** *1 B2*

Perched above the thundering Snoqualmie Falls, this lodge occupies one of the state's most spectacular locations. Luxury and romance are paramount here; every room is equipped with a whirlpool tub, wood-burning fireplace, and featherbed. The internationally acclaimed spa sets the standard for comfort and relaxation. **www.salishlodge.com**

SPOKANE The Davenport Hotel $$$

10 S Post St., 99201 **Tel** *(509) 455-8888* **Fax** *(509) 624-4455* **Rooms** *284*   **Road Map** *1 C2*

Built in 1914, this historic hotel was among the nation's finest when it first opened its doors, and has been returned to its former glory. The lobby and the "Hall of the Doges" ballroom are jaw-droppingly ornate, and the guestrooms, while not as spectacular, are elegant and comfortable. **www.thedavenporthotel.com**

STEHEKIN Stehekin Landing Resort $$

1 Stehekin Landing, 98816 **Tel** *(509) 682-4494* **Fax** *(509) 856-2579* **Rooms** *28*   **Road Map** *1 A1*

Hidden in the North Cascades on Lake Chelan, this year-round lodge is accessible by ferry, float plane, or hiking trail only. There are no roads or televisions, and just a single pay phone in this tranquil area. Comfortably appointed rooms offer forest and lake views. **www.stehekinlanding.com**

STEVENSON Skamania Lodge $$$$

1131 SW Skamania Lodge Way, 98648 **Tel** *(509) 427-7700* **Fax** *(509) 427-2547* **Rooms** *254*   **Road Map** *1 B3*

With unsurpassed views of the Columbia Gorge, best seen from the Washington side of the river, this modern version of the grand lodges of the past attracts golfers with its acclaimed 18-hole course, as well as windsurfers, mountain bikers, and hikers. The Cascade Room restaurant serves fine Northwest cuisine. **www.skamania.com**

TACOMA Chinaberry Hill $$$

302 Tacoma Ave. N, 98403 **Tel** *(253) 272-1282* **Fax** *(253) 272-1335* **Rooms** *6*   **Road Map** *1 A2*

Located high above Tacoma, this handsome Victorian hotel seems a world away from the city below. Rooms in the main house and adjacent carriage house are spacious and luxurious; the beautifully landscaped grounds and wide wrap-around porch are perfect for watching ships go by on Commencement Bay. **www.chinaberryhill.com**

TACOMA Hotel Murano $$$

1320 Broadway Plaza, 98402 **Tel** *(253) 238-8000* **Fax** *(253) 591-4105* **Rooms** *320*   **Road Map** *1 A2*

In a city renowned for its glass-blowing tradition, Hotel Murano showcases glass sculpture and contemporary art in its public spaces. This extremely hip and stylish hotel gets all the details right. Rooms are spacious and modern, and the hotel is in the heart of downtown. **www.hotelmuranotacoma.com**

TACOMA Silver Cloud Inn $$$

2317 N Ruston Way, 98402 **Tel** *(253) 272-1300* **Fax** *(253) 274-9176* **Rooms** *90*   **Road Map** *1 A2*

This outpost of a Northwest chain claims a prime location, on a pier extending into Commencement Bay from the bustling waterfront. Every room offers a bay view, microwave, and refrigerator, and some have whirlpool tubs. Several of Tacoma's best restaurants are within easy walking distance. **www.silvercloud.com**

WALLA WALLA Marcus Whitman Hotel $$$

6 W Rose St., 99362 **Tel** *(866) 826-9422* **Fax** *(509) 524-1747* **Rooms** *91*   **Road Map** *1 C3*

This 1928 high-rise is once again a focal point of downtown Walla Walla, providing both fine accommodation and fine dining in the heart of Washington's wine country. Guestrooms are divided between the original tower and a newer addition; the tower suites are the nicest rooms in town. **www.marcuswhitmanhotel.com**

WALLA WALLA Inn at Abeja $$$$

2014 Mill Creek Rd., 99362 **Tel** *(509) 522-1234* **Fax** *(509) 529-3292* **Rooms** *6*   **Road Map** *1 C3*

This meticulously restored farmstead east of Walla Walla is home to both a winery and the region's most sophisticated hotel. Three original cottages, the old carriage house, and a barn now provide six immaculate suites with fine furnishings. Wine touring from here is popular. **www.abeja.net**

WOODINVILLE Willows Lodge $$$$

14580 NE 145 St., 98072 **Tel** *(425) 424-3900* **Fax** *(425) 424-2585* **Rooms** *84*   **Road Map** *1 C3*

Just 20 minutes outside Seattle on five landscaped acres beside the Sammamish River in western Washington's wine country, this luxury resort is modeled after bygone Northwest lodges. Accommodations are first-rate, but the main attraction is culinary, with the Barking Frog and legendary Herbfarm restaurants on-site. **www.willowslodge.com**

YAKIMA A Touch of Europe Bed & Breakfast $$

220 N 16th Ave., 98902 **Tel** *(509) 454-9775* **Fax** *(509) 452-1303* **Rooms** *2*   **Road Map** *1 B2*

This gracious Queen Anne-style house on a hilltop corner in Yakima provides sophisticated and romantic accommodation with Old World charm. With advance notice and for an extra charge, the chef/owner serves superb meals, from high tea to seven-course dinners, the equal of any restaurant meal in the city. **www.winesnw.com**

YAKIMA Birchfield Manor Country Inn $$

2018 Birchfield Rd., 98901 **Tel** *(509) 452-1960* **Fax** *(509) 452-2334* **Rooms** *11*   **Road Map** *1 B2*

Just 4 miles (3.2 km) outside Yakima, this 1910 farmhouse offers elegant rooms furnished with antiques in both the manor house and guest cottage (manor rooms have no phone or TV). Thursday through Saturday, the dining room is one of the Yakima Valley's finest restaurants, with an award-winning wine list. **www.birchfieldmanor.com**

YAKIMA Oxford Inn $$

1603 E Yakima Ave., 98901 **Tel** *(509) 457-4444* **Fax** *(509) 453-7593* **Rooms** *92*   **Road Map** *1 B2*

Surprisingly nice for a budget hotel, this spot on the western edge of Washington's wine country has spacious rooms, an outdoor pool, and an exercise room. Best of all is the Yakima River just outside; guests can stroll the riverside paths or just take in the view from their balconies. **www.oxfordinnyakima.com**

Key to Price Guide *see p282* **Key to Symbols** *see back cover flap*

VANCOUVER

WATERFRONT, GASTOWN, AND CHINATOWN Days Inn Downtown  $$$$
921 W Pender St., V6C 1M2 **Tel** *(604) 681-4335 or (877) 681-4335* **Fax** *(604) 681-7808* **Rooms** *85* **Map** *3 A2*

Providing spotless, nicely appointed rooms with cheerful color schemes, this hotel's central location and handy services, such as a complimentary shuttle to downtown locations make it a popular choice. Upgrade from a Standard Double to a Deluxe Queen for more room. **www.daysinnvancouver.com**

WATERFRONT, GASTOWN, AND CHINATOWN Delta Vancouver Suites $$$$
550 W Hastings St., V6B 1L6 **Tel** *(604) 689-8188 or (888) 890-3222* **Fax** *(604) 605-8881* **Rooms** *225* **Map** *3 A2*

Geared mainly to business travelers, guestrooms are outfitted with two phone lines, personalized voice mail, and a work desk. Each room has a living area separated from the bedroom. The hotel is convenient for all downtown facilities and discounted weekend rates are available online. **www.deltahotels.com**

WATERFRONT, GASTOWN, AND CHINATOWN Fairmont Waterfront $$$$$
900 Canada Place Way, V6C 3L5 **Tel** *(604) 691-1991 or (800) 257-7544* **Fax** *(604) 691-1999* **Rooms** *489* **Map** *3 A1*

This harborfront property, a modern glass-and-steel building tempered by terraced gardens, offers luxurious rooms, many with majestic views of the mountains. Spacious rooms are filled with modern amenities, as well as luxuries such as bathrobes and remote checkout. A walkway links the hotel to cruise ship terminals. **www.fairmont.com**

WATERFRONT, GASTOWN, AND CHINATOWN Pan Pacific Vancouver $$$$$
999 Canada Pl., V6C 3B5 **Tel** *(604) 662-8111 or (877) 324-4856* **Fax** *(604) 685-8690* **Rooms** *504* **Map** *4 A1*

Part of the iconic Canada Place, this prestigious hotel shares a spectacular harbor frontage with the Vancouver Convention Centre and cruise ship terminals. The beautifully appointed rooms have marble bathrooms and stunning views. Also home to the Five Sails Restaurant. **www.panpacific.com**

DOWNTOWN HI Vancouver Downtown $
1114 Burnaby St., V6E 1P1 **Tel** *(604) 684-4565 or (888) 203-4302* **Fax** *(604) 684-4540* **Rooms** *223 beds* **Map** *2 E3*

One of two centrally located Hostelling International properties, this features a large kitchen, library filled with local literature, games room, travel agency, and bike hire. A shuttle runs between the two downtown hostels and Jericho Beach, where a beachside hostel is popular with young travelers looking to escape the city. **www.hihostels.ca**

DOWNTOWN Victorian Hotel $$
514 Homer St., V6B 2V6 **Tel** *(604) 681-6369 or (877) 681-6369* **Fax** *(604) 681-8776* **Rooms** *49* **Map** *3 A2*

Constructed after the great fire of 1898, this three-story hotel is a good choice for budget travelers looking for something a little more private than staying in a hostel. Rooms are adequate, although many share bathrooms. All rooms have a sink and the en-suite rooms have bay windows. **www.victorianhotel.ca**

DOWNTOWN Hampton Inn & Suites $$$$
111 Robson St., V6B 2A8 **Tel** *(604) 602-1008 or (877) 602-1008* **Fax** *(604) 602-1007* **Rooms** *132* **Map** *3 A3*

This smart, modern hotel is well appointed with guestroom facilities such as umbrellas, safes, and complimentary bottled water. Some of its rooms provide views of False Creek, as does the rooftop Jacuzzi. Rates include a light break-fast at the in-house restaurant, where tables spill out onto busy Robson Street. **www.hamptoninnvancouver.com**

DOWNTOWN Sutton Place Hotel $$$$
845 Burrard St., V6Z 2K6 **Tel** *(604) 682-5511 or (866) 378-8866* **Fax** *(604) 682-5513* **Rooms** *397* **Map** *2 F2*

Generally regarded as one of North America's finest hotels, European touches lend charm to this lavishly appointed property, offering plush rooms with kingsize beds and a popular restaurant, Fleuri *(see p309)*. Twice-daily maid service and fresh in-room flowers add to the charm. A spa and health center are also on-site. **www.suttonplace.com**

DOWNTOWN Fairmont Hotel Vancouver $$$$$
900 W Georgia St., V6C 2W6 **Tel** *(604) 684-3131 or (800) 257-7544* **Fax** *(604) 662-1929* **Rooms** *556* **Map** *2 F2*

Easily identified by its oxidized copper roof, this landmark railroad hotel prides itself on its reputation for excellent service and sophistication, as well as the award-winning Griffins restaurant. Over $70 million was spent on restoring this 1939 hotel in the 1990s, and it shows throughout public areas and guestrooms. **www.fairmont.com**

DOWNTOWN Wedgewood Hotel & Spa $$$$$
845 Hornby St., V62 1V1 **Tel** *(604) 689-7777 or (800) 663-0666* **Fax** *(604) 608-5348* **Rooms** *83* **Map** *2 F2*

This boutique hotel combines elegance and intimacy, with antiques and original artwork. Its tastefully decorated rooms and attentive service add to the refined ambience. For a splurge, reserve a Penthouse Suite with French doors to a private garden terrace. A luxurious spa and upscale restaurant are also onsite. **www.wedgewoodhotel.com**

GRANVILLE SOUTH AND YALETOWN Samesun Vancouver $
1018 Granville St., V62 1L5 **Tel** *(604) 682-8226 or (877) 972-6378* **Fax** *(604) 682-8240* **Rooms** *220 beds* **Map** *2 F3*

This is the best of Vancouver's privately owned backpacker lodges. Located close to the entertainment district and within walking distance of the waterfront, dormitories are on the small side, but the interior has colorful decor and communal facilities are well kept. The rooftop patio is a welcome bonus. **www.samesun.com**

GRANVILLE SOUTH AND YALETOWN Howard Johnson Vancouver $$$

1176 Granville St., V6Z 1L8 **Tel** *(604) 688-8701* **Fax** *(604) 688-8335* **Rooms** *110*   **Map** *2 F3*

A popular choice, this establishment is one of the least expensive of the centrally located hotel chains. Standard rooms have double beds, or upgrade to a spacious Junior Suite for a few dollars extra. Rates include a daily newspaper and passes to a local fitness club. Designated parking is at an adjacent lot. **www.hojovancouver.com**

GRANVILLE SOUTH AND YALETOWN Opus Hotel $$$$

322 Davie St., V6B 5Z6 **Tel** *(604) 642-6787 or (866) 642-6787* **Fax** *(604) 642-6780* **Rooms** *96*   **Map** *2 F4*

This hip Yaletown hotel exudes sophistication and opulence. The dramatically structured guestrooms are defined by five lifestyle-inspired design schemes, from traditionalist to minimalist to ultra-modern. Typical of the edgy design are rooms with bathrooms overlooking the street below. Trendy on-site bar and restaurant. **www.opushotel.com**

FARTHER AFIELD Grouse Inn $$

1633 Capilano Rd., Vancouver, V7P 3B3 **Tel** *(604) 988-7101* **Fax** *(604) 988-7102* **Rooms** *80*   **Road Map** *1 A1*

A family-friendly motel with an adventure playground and outdoor heated pool. This comfortable inn is near the Lions Gate Bridge, with easy access to both downtown and North Shore attractions. The two-bedroom suites with full kitchens are perfect for families. Rates include a light breakfast. **www.grouseinn.com**

FARTHER AFIELD Pacific Spirit Guest House $$

4080 W 35th Ave., Vancouver, V6N 2P3 **Tel** *(604) 261-6837 or (866) 768-6837* **Rooms** *2*   **Road Map** *1 A1*

In a quiet residential area and across the road from the wilderness of Pacific Spirit Regional Park, this welcoming bed-and-breakfast has a communal area filled with local literature. One room has pleasant garden views while the other features a king bed. Rates include a generously portioned cooked breakfast. **www.vanbb.com**

FARTHER AFIELD Best Western Sands by the Sea $$$

1755 Davie St., Vancouver, V6G 1W5 **Tel** *(604) 682-1831* **Fax** *(604) 682-3546* **Rooms** *120*   **Map** *2 D2*

In walking distance of the beach at English Bay and the shopping precinct along Denman Street, this low-key hotel offers standard rooms with either mountain or water views. The on-site bar also has sweeping harbor views, while the restaurant offers a wide-ranging menu to suit all tastes. **www.bestwesternsandshotelvancouver.com**

FARTHER AFIELD Sylvia Hotel $$$

1154 Gilford St., Vancouver, V6G 2P6 **Tel** *(604) 681-9321* **Fax** *(604) 682-3551* **Rooms** *120*   **Map** *1 C1*

Built in 1912, this landmark brick and terra-cotta former apartment building by English Bay is a designated heritage structure, distinctive for the Virginia creeper ivy covering its exterior. The dark wood details and the plainly furnished rooms would appear to have seen better days. The larger rooms have small kitchens. **www.sylviahotel.com**

FARTHER AFIELD Thistle Down House $$$

3910 Capilano Rd., N Vancouver, V7R 4J2 **Tel** *(604) 986-7173* **Fax** *(604) 980-2939* **Rooms** *5*   **Road Map** *1 A1*

A 1920s, Craftsman-style heritage home, this quaint bed-and-breakfast is filled with handcrafted furnishings and surrounded by a lovely garden. The rate includes afternoon tea, which can be enjoyed beside an open fire or in the well-tended garden, and a gourmet breakfast. **www.thistle-down.com**

FARTHER AFIELD Granville Island Hotel $$$$

1253 Johnston St., V6H 3K9 **Tel** *(604) 683-7373 or (800) 663-1840* **Fax** *(604) 683-3061* **Rooms** *85*   **Map** *2 E5*

A deluxe yet casual boutique hotel matched in ambience to bustling Granville Island, this property has spacious, welcoming rooms, some with wooden beams and Persian rugs. Island attractions are in walking distance, or catch a ferry downtown, go kayaking from the marina, or try the beer brewed in-house. **www.granvilleislandhotel.com**

FARTHER AFIELD O Canada' House $$$$

1114 Barclay St., Vancouver, V6E 1H1 **Tel** *(604) 688-0555* **Fax** *(604) 488-0556* **Rooms** *7*   **Road Map** *1 A1*

The national anthem "O Canada" was written in this restored house built in 1897 for a prominent banker. It has since been converted to a Victorian-style B&B with wrap-around porch and English garden. Enjoy gourmet breakfasts and the hosts' attentive service, as well as a prime West End location. **www.ocanadahouse.com**

FARTHER AFIELD Fairmont Vancouver Airport $$$$$

3111 Grant McConachie Way, Richmond, V7B 1X9 **Tel** *(604) 207-5200* **Rooms** *392*   **Road Map** *1 A1*

Located in Vancouver International Airport, this modern hotel offers deluxe, soundproof rooms, remote-controlled dark curtains (perfect for jet-lagged travelers), spa services, and various dining options. Departing passengers have the convenience of checking in for flights as they check out of the hotel. **www.fairmont.com**

BRITISH COLUMBIA

CLEARWATER Helmcken Falls Lodge $$$

6664 Clearwater Valley Rd., V0E 1N0 **Tel** *(250) 674-3657* **Fax** *(250) 674-2971* **Rooms** *21*   **Road Map** *2 B4*

Originally a lodge for hunting and fishing tours, this complex at the Wells Gray Provincial Park entrance has grown to include various rustic accommodation options. The lodge, with basic rooms, is surrounded by cabins. Activities include horseback riding, canoeing, and guided hikes. Closed Apr, mid-Oct–mid-Dec. **www.helmckenfalls.com**

Key to Price Guide *see p282* **Key to Symbols** *see back cover flap*

CRANBROOK Kootenay Country Inn

P 🕴 📖 W $$

1111 Cranbrook St., V1C 3S4 **Tel** *(250) 426-2296* **Fax** *(250) 426-3533* **Rooms** *36*   **Road Map** *2 C4*

Located along the main commercial strip, this motel is also within walking distance of downtown. A combination of modest prices, comfort, and country-style decor make it a popular choice. On-site facilities include indoor whirlpool, sauna, and laundry. **www.kootenaycountryinn.com**

DAWSON CREEK The Alaska Hotel

P 🍴 $

10209 10th St., V1G 3T5 **Tel** *(250) 782-7998* **Fax** *(250) 782-6277* **Rooms** *14*   **Road Map** *2 B3*

At the heart of Dawson Creek, right by Mile 0, stands the historic Alaska Hotel, with its old-world charm and Gold Rush-era façade. Rooms are basic, with shared bathrooms; there's a pub on the first floor with live music nightly, and next door is the Alaska Café, a local landmark and popular stopping point for tourists. **www.alaskahotel.com**

FERNIE Griz Inn

🛗 P 🍴 � W $$

5369 Ski Hill Rd., V0B 1M6 **Tel** *(800) 661-0118* **Fax** *(250) 423-9287* **Rooms** *45*   **Road Map** *2 C4*

You can stay within walking distance of town, but a more enjoyable option is this alpine-themed inn at the base of the local alpine resort. Winter is high season, meaning discounted rates and minimal crowds through summer. Hike and mountain bike from the lodge, then relax in the outdoor hot tub. **www.grizinn.com**

FORT ST. JOHN Quality Inn Northern Grand

🛗 P 🍴 � 🕴 W $$$

9830 100th Ave., V1J 1Y5 **Tel** *(250) 787-0521* **Fax** *(250) 787-2648* **Rooms** *125*   **Road Map** *2 B2*

One of the best motel accommodations along the Alaska Highway. Spacious, comfortable rooms are decorated in smart colors and filled with amenities including coffeemakers, hairdryers, and heated bathroom floors. Upgrade to an Executive Suite and enjoy a Jacuzzi tub, stereo system, and a brass bed. **www.qualityinnnortherngrand.com**

GALIANO ISLAND Galiano Inn

P 🍴 W $$$$

134 Madrona Dr., V0N 1P0 **Tel** *(250) 539-3388 or (877) 530-3939* **Fax** *(250) 539-3338*   **Road Map** *2 B4*

Overlooking the bay where the local ferry docks, this upscale inn features a restaurant with tables that spill out onto a waterfront terrace and a spa where many of the treatments can be taken outdoors. The guestrooms all have balconies with water views and are filled with European-style charm. **www.galianoinn.com**

GIBSONS Bonniebrook Lodge

P 🍴 🕴 📖 W $$$$

1532 Ocean Beach Esplanade, V0N 1V5 **Tel** *(604) 886-2887* **Fax** *(604) 886-9241* **Rooms** *7*   **Road Map** *2 B4*

In a 1920s heritage building in Gibsons on the Sunshine Coast, a 40-minute ferry ride from West Vancouver, this hotel has spectacular views and luxuriously appointed suites, with gas fireplaces and jetted tubs. The on-site restaurant serves organic food. Guests can enjoy a private beach just across the road. **www.bonniebrook.com**

GLACIER NATIONAL PARK Glacier Park Lodge

🛗 P 🍴 W $$

The Summit, Trans-Canada Hwy, Rogers Pass., V0E 2S0 **Tel** *(250) 837-2126* **Rooms** *50*   **Road Map** *2 C4*

Designer-decorated rooms and modern amenities are found in this spacious lodge. Enjoy superb views of the Selkirk Mountains and the Asulkan Glacier from the comfort of the dining room or lounge. The lodge is within walking distance of the park visitor center and its interesting history displays. **www.glacierparklodge.ca**

GOLDEN Kicking Horse River Lodge

P 🍴 W $$

801 9th St. N., V0A 1H2 **Tel** *(250) 439-1112 or (877) 547-5266* **Fax** *(250) 439-3992* **Rooms** *17* **Road Map** *2 C4*

An impressive polished log building overlooking the Kicking Horse River, this lodge caters to backpackers with dorm rooms and to travelers looking for more privacy with double rooms. The construction may be traditional, but the facilities are modern, including Wi-Fi and large-screen TV. The on-site cafe has riverside seating. **www.khrl.com**

HARRISON HOT SPRINGS Harrison Hot Springs Resort & Spa

🛗 P 🍴 �swim 🕴 🕴 W $$$$

100 Esplanade Ave., V0M 1K0 **Tel** *(604) 796-2244* **Fax** *(604) 796-3682* **Rooms** *337*   **Road Map** *2 B4*

The reason to stay at this hotel is to soak in the resort's massive mineral springs pool complex, which includes a family-friendly outdoor pool. It is also handy for the beach, and encourages pampering with its own spa, steam room, and sauna. Guestrooms have been revamped and are spacious and comfortable. **www.harrisonresort.com**

KAMLOOPS Plaza Heritage Hotel

🛗 P 🍴 W $$

405 Victoria St., V2C 2A9 **Tel** *(250) 377-8075 or (877) 977-5292* **Fax** *(250) 377-8076* **Rooms** *67* **Road Map** *2 B4*

Beautifully restored to a 1920s heritage style, rooms in this six-story downtown hotel are uniquely decorated, retaining the elegance of the original furnishings and fixtures. A beer-and-wine shop is on-site, as is a restaurant hosting an inexpensive Sunday brunch. Golf packages at local courses are an excellent deal. **www.plazaheritagehotel.com**

KELOWNA Manteo Resort

🛗 P 🍴 �swim 🕴 🕴 📖 W $$$$

3762 Lakeshore Rd., V1W 3L4 **Tel** *(250) 860-1031* **Fax** *(250) 860-1041* **Rooms** *102*   **Road Map** *2 B4*

The emphasis is on recreation at this lakefront resort – rent a boat from the marina, relax on the beach, swim in one of three pools, watch the latest releases in the movie theater, or try your hand at tennis. Modern rooms in varying configurations suit all travelers, including large families. **www.manteo.com**

KOOTENAY NATIONAL PARK Kootenay Park Lodge

P 🍴 🕴 $$

Vermilion Crossing, Hwy. 93, T1L 1B3 **Tel** *(403) 762-9196* **Fax** *(403) 283-7482* **Rooms** *12*   **Road Map** *2 C4*

Built by the Canadian Pacific Railway in 1923, these simple log cabins range in size from studios to those with full kitchens. A restaurant is in the main lodge while the complex also holds an official Parks Canada information center, a gift shop, and a gas station. Open mid-May to September. **www.kootenayparklodge.com**

MALAHAT Prancing Horse Retreat

573 Ebadora Lane, V0R 2L0 **Tel** *(250) 743-9378* **Fax** *(250) 743-9372* **Rooms** *7*   **Road Map** *2 B5*

Set high up along the Malahat highway and surrounded by forest, this charming Victorian retreat offers classy guestrooms, some with soaker tubs, fireplaces, and private decks overlooking the Finlayson Arm. Gourmet breakfasts, huge arbutus trees, multitiered decks, and a gazebo are all additional benefits. **www.prancinghorse.com**

MAYNE ISLAND Ocean Wood Resort

630 Dinner Bay Rd., V0N 2J0 **Tel** *(250) 539-5074* **Fax** *(250) 539-3002* **Rooms** *12*   **Road Map** *2 B5*

Hidden among trees on 10 acres (4 ha) of waterfront, this island getaway comes with charming rooms and cozy chairs by the fireplace. Breakfast and afternoon tea are included, and there is licensed, gourmet dining on-site. A path leads through the garden to the ocean. **www.oceanwood.com**

NANAIMO Buccaneer Inn

1577 Stewart Ave., V9S 4E3 **Tel** *(250) 753-1246* **Fax** *(250) 753-0507* **Rooms** *14*   **Road Map** *2 B4*

At first glance, the Buccaneer looks no different to the dozens of other motels around Nanaimo, but it provides excellent value and the spacious rooms are filled with amenities. A nautical theme and well-manicured grounds with barbecue area add to the appeal. This motel is particularly popular with scuba divers. **www.buccaneerinn.com**

NELSON Dancing Bear Inn

171 Baker St., V1L 4H1 **Tel** *(877) 352-7573* **Fax** *(250) 352-9818* **Rooms** *26 beds*   **Road Map** *2 C4*

One of the Pacific Northwest's finest backpacker lodges, the Dancing Bear Inn is a beautifully restored building on Nelson's main street. The inn offers comfortable accommodation in dorms and double rooms, a welcoming lounge area with a TV and Internet access, a modern kitchen, a laundry, and friendly hosts. **www.dancingbearinn.com**

PARKSVILLE Tigh-Na-Mara

1155 Resort Dr., V9P 2E5 **Tel** *(250) 248-2072* **Fax** *(250) 248-4140* **Rooms** *192*   **Road Map** *2 B4*

This, British Columbia's largest spa resort, provides a variety of lodgings: log cottages, ocean-view condos, or studios. While parents are drawn to the resort by relaxing massages, caviar facials, and hot pools, it is swimming and digging for clams on the adjacent beach that keeps children occupied. **www.tigh-na-mara.com**

PENTICTON Naramata Heritage Inn & Spa

3625 1st St., Naramata, V0H 1N0 **Tel** *(250) 496-6808* **Fax** *(250) 496-5001* **Rooms** *12*   **Road Map** *2 B4*

Dating to 1908, this elegant lakeside hotel is in the small village of Naramata, north of Penticton. The elegant rooms are filled with historic charm, yet come with modern touches like heated bathroom floors and a patio or balcony furnished with wrought-iron furniture. **www.naramatainn.com**

PRINCE GEORGE Esther's Inn

1151 Commercial Cres., V2M 6W6 **Tel** *(250) 562-4131* **Fax** *(250) 562-4145* **Rooms** *118*   **Road Map** *2 B3*

A slice of tropical life in the north. This South Seas-themed property offers spotless guestrooms; suites open onto two indoor garden courtyards. The tropical theme is further enhanced by hot tubs, lush plants, and an indoor swimming pool and waterslide complex. A business center and laundry are also on-site. **www.esthersinn.com**

PRINCE RUPERT Eagle Bluff Bed & Breakfast

201 Cow Bay Rd., V8J 1K4 **Tel** *(250) 627-4955* **Fax** *(250) 627-7945* **Rooms** *5*   **Road Map** *2 A3*

Eagle Bluff is built over the water at Cow Bay, a tourist precinct that has risen from a rowdy fishing port. Most rooms share bathrooms, but the top-floor suite has an en-suite bathroom and water views. A hearty breakfast is included in the rates while dinner can be enjoyed at surrounding restaurants. **www.eaglebluff.ca**

QUEEN CHARLOTTE CITY Dorothy and Mike's Guesthouse

3127 2nd Ave., V0T 1S0 **Tel** *(250) 559-8439* **Fax** *(250) 559-8439* **Rooms** *8*   **Road Map** *2 A4*

The hosts of this centrally located lodging, long-time residents of the islands, provide a library on the native Haida culture and wildlife. Rooms and suites are cozy, including one with a private deck and water views. Rates include a cooked breakfast. Guests can rent bikes or an economical Smart Car. **www.qcislands.net/doromike**

RADIUM HOT SPRINGS Radium Resort

8100 Golf Course Rd., V0A 1M0 **Tel** *(250) 347-9311* **Fax** *(250) 347-6299* **Rooms** *118*   **Road Map** *2 C4*

This all-season resort affords spectacular views of the surrounding Rocky and Purcell mountain ranges while offering myriad recreational activities: two golf courses, tennis, squash, hiking, biking, and more. Lodging options include standard hotel rooms, self-contained condos, and multi-room villas with barbecues. **www.radiumresort.com**

SALT SPRING ISLAND Anne's Oceanfront Hideaway B&B

168 Simson Rd., V8K 1E2 **Tel** *(250) 537-0851 or (888) 474-2663* **Fax** *(250) 537-0861* **Rooms** *4*   **Road Map** *2 B4*

A relaxing spot, with stylishly appointed rooms, each with fireplace, reclining chairs, TV/DVD combination, wireless Internet, and bathroom with hydro-massage tub. The ocean view from the outside hot tub is stunning. Rates include a multi-course breakfast with bakery items that are prepared in-house. **www.annesoceanfront.com**

SMITHERS Hudson Bay Lodge

3251 E Hwy 16., V0J 2N0 **Tel** *(250) 847-4581 or (800) 663-5040* **Fax** *(250) 847-4878* **Rooms** *96* **Road Map** *2 A4*

This family-owned, full-service hotel is set at the base of Hudson Bay Mountain and within walking distance of downtown Smithers. The Tudor exterior hides alpine-style interior decor and nicely appointed rooms with large bathrooms. Facilities include a laundry, hot tub, and pub. Rates include airport transfer. **www.hudsonbaylodge.com**

Key to Price Guide *see p282* **Key to Symbols** *see back cover flap*

SOOKE Sooke Harbour House
P ⅰ ᴡ $\$\$\$\$\$$

1528 Whiffen Spit Rd., V0S 1N0 **Tel** *(250) 642-3421* **Fax** *(250) 642-6989* **Rooms** *28* **Road Map** *2 B5*

A picturesque country-style inn by the sea combining a hotel, fine-dining restaurant *(see p312)*, spa, and art gallery. Each luxurious, individually designed room has a private balcony with ocean views, original artwork, and fireplace. Meal and accommodation packages provide value. Complimentary breakfast. **www.sookeharbourhouse.com**

TOFINO Middle Beach Lodge
P ⅰ ᴡ $\$\$\$$

400 Mackenzie Beach Rd., V0R 2Z0 **Tel** *(250) 725-2900* **Fax** *(250) 725-2901* **Rooms** *64* **Road Map** *2 A4*

The unique assortment of accommodation this property offers – a beach lodge, a headland lodge, or self-contained cabins – strives to offer a true Pacific Northwest experience, with timbered buildings furnished with rustic pieces and stone fireplaces. The adults-only rooms in the Lodge at the Beach provide the best value. **www.middlebeach.com**

TOFINO Wickaninnish Inn
P ⅰ 🏊 📺 🍽 ᴡ $\$\$\$\$\$$

500 Osprey Lane, Chesterman Beach, V0R 2Z0 **Tel** *(250) 725-3100* **Fax** *(250) 725-3110* **Rooms** *75* **Road Map** *2 A4*

The original Tofino luxury oceanfront property, Wickaninnish Inn boasts panoramic views of the ocean and nearby islands from its perch at the tip of a rocky promontory. The spacious rooms have floor-to-ceiling windows and super-comfortable beds. Pointe Restaurant dishes up local cuisine with magnificent ocean views. **www.wickinn.com**

VICTORIA Spinnakers Gastro Brewpub & Guesthouses
P ⅰ ᴡ $\$\$\$$

308 Catherine St., V9A 3S8 **Tel** *(250) 386-2739* **Fax** *(250) 384-3246* **Rooms** *10* **Road Map** *2 B5*

Overlooking Victoria's Inner Harbour, Spinnakers is in a great location, with a walkway just outside that leads downtown. Some of the suites have fireplaces and jetted tubs. All include a fresh breakfast basket and newspaper in the mornings. The in-house pub is very inviting and brews its own award-winning beers. **www.spinnakers.com**

VICTORIA Abigail's Hotel
P 🍽 ᴡ $\$\$\$\$$

906 McClure St., V8V 3E7 **Tel** *(250) 388-5363* **Fax** *(250) 388-7787* **Rooms** *23* **Road Map** *2 B5*

This charming inn epitomizes Old World charm with heritage Tudor architecture, English gardens, and old-fashioned hospitality. Some rooms have wood-burning fireplaces and Jacuzzi tubs; spa services are available. Enjoy complimentary gourmet breakfast in the large dining room and evening hors d'oeuvres in the library. **www.abigailshotel.com**

VICTORIA Gatsby Mansion Inn
P ⅰ ᴡ $\$\$\$\$$

309 Belleville St., V8V 1X2 **Tel** *(250) 388-9191* **Rooms** *20* **Road Map** *2 B5*

This handsome, early 20th-century inn offers bed-and-breakfast in elegant surroundings that feature stained-glass windows, crystal chandeliers, stone fireplaces, and frescoed ceilings. There is a choice of topiary, rose garden, or harbor views from the beautifully furnished rooms. Breakfast and afternoon tea included. **www.gatsbymansion.com**

VICTORIA Oswego Hotel
🛗 P ⅰ 📺 🍽 ᴡ $\$\$\$\$$

500 Oswego St., V8V 5C1 **Tel** *(250) 294-7500 or (877) 767-9346* **Fax** *(250) 294-7509* **Rooms** *80* **Road Map** *2 B5*

The contemporary Oswego is very different from Victoria's traditional hotels. Within walking distance of the Inner Harbour, the guestrooms have a slick West Coast feel and each has a full kitchen with stainless-steel appliances. Upper-floor rooms have water views, as do both two-bedroom Penthouse Suites. **www.oswegovictoria.com**

VICTORIA Fairmont Empress
🛗 P ⅰ 🏊 📺 ᴡ $\$\$\$\$\$$

721 Government St., V8W 1W5 **Tel** *(250) 384-8111* **Fax** *(250) 389-2747* **Rooms** *477* **Road Map** *2 B5*

A 1989 renovation restored this ivy-covered Inner Harbour landmark to its early 19th-century grandeur. The "grand duchess" of the Fairmont group is famed for its afternoon tea service. Its guestrooms are sumptuously appointed in period furnishings, although standard rooms are on the small side by modern standards. **www.fairmont.com**

WHISTLER Riverside RV Resort
P ⅰ 🎿 $\$\$\$$

8018 Mons Rd., V0N 1B8 **Tel** *(604) 905-5533* **Fax** *(604) 905-5539* **Rooms** *14* **Road Map** *2 B4*

This cluster of cabins is a good alternative to Whistler's large hotels. The peeled log cabins ooze charm and each comes with a full kitchen. The on-site café opens early for breakfast, after which you can walk or bike along paved trails to the local swimming lake or Village Centre. **www.whistlercamping.com**

WHISTLER Westin Resort & Spa
🛗 P ⅰ 🏊 📺 🍽 ᴡ $\$\$\$\$$

4090 Whistler Way, V0N 1B4 **Tel** *(604) 905-5000* **Fax** *(604) 905-5640* **Rooms** *419* **Road Map** *2 B4*

This upmarket resort is built with indigenous materials in the West Coast rustic chic style. It is located right on the mountainside, close to shops and ski lifts. The rooms are spacious and filled with all mod cons, including kitchens with stainless steel appliances, connected work desks, and deep soaker tubs. **www.westinwhistler.com**

WHISTLER Fairmont Chateau Whistler
🛗 P ⅰ 🏊 📺 🍽 ᴡ $\$\$\$\$\$$

4599 Chateau Blvd., V0N 1B4 **Tel** *(604) 938-8000* **Fax** *(604) 938-2291* **Rooms** *550* **Road Map** *2 B4*

The lobby's rich carpeting, First Nations art, and goldleaf domed ceiling convey an air of easy grandeur, reinforced by the luxurious rooms and suites. Guests pamper themselves in the Vida spa or in the restaurant's private wine room. The hotel's golf course is one of the finest in the valley. **www.fairmont.com**

YOHO NATIONAL PARK Cathedral Mountain Lodge
P ⅰ $\$\$\$\$\$$

Yoho Valley Rd., V0A 1G0 **Tel** *(866) 619-6442* **Fax** *(250) 343-6424* **Rooms** *31* **Road Map** *2 C4*

These beautiful log cabins along the Kicking Horse River are surrounded by towering mountains. Each has a log bed topped by a down duvet, wood or gas fireplace, bathroom with soaker tub and bathrobes, and private deck. Rates include a Continental breakfast. The on-site restaurant is recommended for dinner. **www.cathedralmountain.com**

WHERE TO EAT

The Pacific Northwest is known for its large number of coffee bars as well as the vast range of fresh local seafood it has to offer, from wild salmon to oysters, clams, and crab. Portland, Seattle, and Vancouver are all in the midst of a culinary revolution – small neighborhood, chef-owned restaurants are popping up on every block, showcasing

Emblem of Starbucks, the coffee bar chain

a broad array of fare and adding depth to the choices. Visitors can find a terrific French bistro neighbored by an affordable Thai noodle house and a mid-range Mediterranean seafood restaurant. Farm-fresh, local flavors mark the ingenious creations of the region's finest restaurants. Other eateries boast down-to-earth fare with the same freshness.

PACIFIC NORTHWEST CUISINE

Increasingly, Pacific Northwest restaurants offer menus that highlight local produce, of which there is a wide variety. Oregon's climate is particularly conducive to growing wild mushrooms. Washington is perhaps best known for its apples, though it also grows many types of berries. In British Columbia, tree fruits, including apples, pears, peaches, cherries, and plums, often feature in its cuisine. Pacific Northwest grapes and wineries are celebrated as some of the best in the world, so it is no surprise that many wine bars are also opening throughout the region.

Seafood is very much the focus of Pacific Northwest cuisine. On just about every menu and in just about every type of restaurant, salmon, halibut, crab, mussels, clams,

Microbrewed beers of the Pacific Northwest

and oysters are on offer, whether in the form of cakes, chowder, or fish and chips. Smoked salmon, which has its origins in Native customs, is ubiquitous. Oysters are gaining in popularity not only on the local but also the national level. With so many varieties to choose from, making a meal of several types of oysters on the half shell while sipping a local beer at one of the many oyster bars is a popular pastime of locals and visitors alike.

Eating healthily in the region's restaurants is easy. Low-fat dishes are staples on most menus, as are vegetarian options, ranging from salads and wraps to Mongolian grills and Buddhist banquets. Native cuisine, using local ingredients such as seaweed, fern shoots, wild berries, oolichan (a small silvery fish), and caribou, can also be enjoyed, and is sometimes combined with traditional Native song and dance performances in an authentic setting.

Ivans, offering clams and other seafood to Seattle

TYPES OF RESTAURANTS

Eating establishments in the Pacific Northwest run the gamut, from five-star gourmet restaurants, bistros, and pubs to noodle houses and sushi bars to fast food and take-out. Coffee shops, bagel and bake shops, and ice-cream stores are all also easy to find.

Ethnic restaurants – French, Italian, Hungarian, Greek, Indian, and Caribbean to mention a few – are thriving and have given rise to a fusion cuisine unique to the West Coast. Asian restaurants are plentiful; there is usually at least one Thai and Japanese restaurant in every neighborhood. Sushi bars here are good as well, since the fish is so varied and fresh. Dining on authentic Japanese, Korean, Chinese, or Thai food in the Chinatown or International District found in all the major cities of the Pacific Northwest is inexpensive. Many Chinese restaurants serve *dim sum*, a traditional Chinese brunch.

ALCOHOL AND SMOKING

Smoking is banned in all indoor public places in British Columbia. Washington has banned smoking statewide

One of the many cafés in Seattle with both indoor and outdoor seating

in all public places and in places of employment. In Oregon it has similarly been banned in workplaces, bars, and restaurants.

Alcohol is available only in licensed establishments. Dining in taverns or certain parts of restaurants may be restricted. When they plan to order alcohol in any establishment, diners should always bring a valid form of picture identification, such as a driver's license or passport, as waitpersons are required by law to check the age of patrons who order alcohol. The legal drinking age in Washington and Oregon is 21, in British Columbia, 19.

HOURS

Coffee shops and restaurants serving full breakfasts open at 6 or 7am. With one on just about every downtown street corner, coffee shops are the best bet for a toasted bagel or pastry and a cup of coffee in the morning. Breakfast, which generally consists of some combination of pancakes, toast, eggs, omelets, sausages, and bacon, is typically served until 11am. On Sundays, brunch is served between 8am and 2pm at many restaurants that are not open for breakfast during the week.

Lunch hours are usually between 11:30am and 3pm. In the cities, many of the more upscale restaurants offer lunches that mirror the dinner menu in every aspect

The elegant Tea Court at The Heathman Restaurant in Portland

Mo's Seafood Restaurant, Newport, Oregon, serving the catch of the day

but price, making the midday meal a smart choice for travelers who want to dine at the best restaurants while on a budget. Dinner hours generally run from 5pm to 9 or 10pm, later in busier areas and on weekends. Some exclusive restaurants open for dinner only. Almost all restaurants are open on Fridays and Saturdays, but it is not uncommon for them to be closed on Sundays and Mondays. Check in advance with each establishment for specific times.

Sign at Granville Island, Vancouver

RESERVATIONS

Reservations are needed for the better or more popular restaurants and some will only accept reservations for parties of six or more. However, most restaurants do not require reservations. If booking more than a day in advance, confirm the booking on the day of your reservation.

PRICES

Dinner entrées in Oregon and Washington cost between $9 and $16 at casual restaurants; between $17 and $40 at fine-dining establishments. Taxes on foods and alcoholic beverages in Oregon and Washington vary from county to county; in the Seattle area, it is 10 percent. In BC, dinner entrées range from CAN $12 to $20 at casual spots, from CAN $25 to $40 at the more exclusive restaurants. Restaurant meals are not subject to the 7 percent tax. Lunch costs from CAN $7 to $20, breakfast CAN $5 to $12. Alcoholic drinks are subject to a tax of 10 percent.

PAYING AND TIPPING

Nearly all restaurants accept major credit cards. Traveler's checks in US or Canadian currency are accepted with appropriate identification. Personal checks are usually not welcome.

At any sit-down restaurant with a waitperson, it is customary to tip 15 to 20 percent of the price of the meal, before tax. As a general rule, tipping 15 percent is about average; a 20 percent tip is generally given when service has been exceptionally good. When paying for the meal with a credit card, the tip amount can be added on the credit card slip. At coffee bars or cafeteria-style restaurants, a tip jar is often located near the cash register.

DRESS CODES

The Pacific Northwest is, in general, a casual place. At most city restaurants, business-casual is appropriate: khakis and button-down shirts for men; a sweater or blouse and pants or skirt for women. Outside the cities, dress is often more casual, and most restaurants do not have dress codes. Usually, the more exclusive the restaurant, the more formal it is.

CHILDREN

Well-behaved children are welcome at most restaurants and many establishments cater especially to families with children. High chairs and booster seats are often available, as is a special kid's menu or portions.

Choosing a Restaurant

Restaurants have been chosen across a wide price range for their value, good food, atmosphere, and location. The chart below highlights some of the factors that may influence your choice of where to eat. Restaurants are listed by area, and within these areas by price. Map references refer to Street Finder maps and the road map inside the back flap.

PRICE CATEGORIES
Prices are in US$ and are for a three-course meal for one, half a bottle of house wine, and all unavoidable extra charges such as sales tax and service.
US[$] Under $30
US[$][$] $30–$45
US[$][$][$] $45–$60
US[$][$][$][$] $60–$80
US[$][$][$][$][$] Over $80

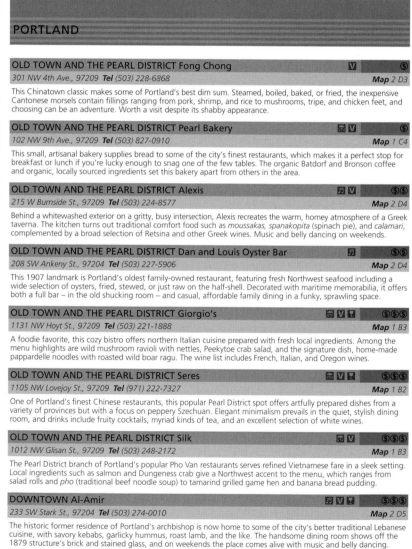

PORTLAND

OLD TOWN AND THE PEARL DISTRICT Fong Chong [V] [$]
301 NW 4th Ave., 97209 ***Tel*** *(503) 228-6868* ***Map*** *2 D3*

This Chinatown classic makes some of Portland's best dim sum. Steamed, boiled, baked, or fried, the inexpensive Cantonese morsels contain fillings ranging from pork, shrimp, and rice to mushrooms, tripe, and chicken feet, and choosing can be an adventure. Worth a visit despite its shabby appearance.

OLD TOWN AND THE PEARL DISTRICT Pearl Bakery ⛱ [V] [$]
102 NW 9th Ave., 97209 ***Tel*** *(503) 827-0910* ***Map*** *1 C4*

This small, artisanal bakery supplies bread to some of the city's finest restaurants, which makes it a perfect stop for breakfast or lunch if you're lucky enough to snag one of the few tables. The organic Batdorf and Bronson coffee and organic, locally sourced ingredients set this bakery apart from others in the area.

OLD TOWN AND THE PEARL DISTRICT Alexis ♫ [V] [$][$]
215 W Burnside St., 97209 ***Tel*** *(503) 224-8577* ***Map*** *2 D4*

Behind a whitewashed exterior on a gritty, busy intersection, Alexis recreates the warm, homey atmosphere of a Greek taverna. The kitchen turns out traditional comfort food such as *moussakas, spanakopita* (spinach pie), and *calamari*, complemented by a broad selection of Retsina and other Greek wines. Music and belly dancing on weekends.

OLD TOWN AND THE PEARL DISTRICT Dan and Louis Oyster Bar ♫ [$][$]
208 SW Ankeny St., 97204 ***Tel*** *(503) 227-5906* ***Map*** *2 D4*

This 1907 landmark is Portland's oldest family-owned restaurant, featuring fresh Northwest seafood including a wide selection of oysters, fried, stewed, or just raw on the half-shell. Decorated with maritime memorabilia, it offers both a full bar – in the old shucking room – and casual, affordable family dining in a funky, sprawling space.

OLD TOWN AND THE PEARL DISTRICT Giorgio's ⛱ [V] 🍷 [$][$][$]
1131 NW Hoyt St., 97209 ***Tel*** *(503) 221-1888* ***Map*** *1 B3*

A foodie favorite, this cozy bistro offers northern Italian cuisine prepared with fresh local ingredients. Among the menu highlights are wild mushroom ravioli with nettles, Peekytoe crab salad, and the signature dish, home-made pappardelle noodles with roasted wild boar ragu. The wine list includes French, Italian, and Oregon wines.

OLD TOWN AND THE PEARL DISTRICT Seres ⛱ [V] 🍷 [$][$][$]
1105 NW Lovejoy St., 97209 ***Tel*** *(971) 222-7327* ***Map*** *1 B2*

One of Portland's finest Chinese restaurants, this popular Pearl District spot offers artfully prepared dishes from a variety of provinces but with a focus on peppery Szechuan. Elegant minimalism prevails in the quiet, stylish dining room, and drinks include fruity cocktails, myriad kinds of tea, and an excellent selection of white wines.

OLD TOWN AND THE PEARL DISTRICT Silk ⛱ [V] [$][$][$]
1012 NW Glisan St., 97209 ***Tel*** *(503) 248-2172* ***Map*** *1 B3*

The Pearl District branch of Portland's popular Pho Van restaurants serves refined Vietnamese fare in a sleek setting. Local ingredients such as salmon and Dungeness crab give a Northwest accent to the menu, which ranges from salad rolls and *pho* (traditional beef noodle soup) to tamarind grilled game hen and banana bread pudding.

DOWNTOWN Al-Amir ♫ [V] 🍷 [$][$][$]
233 SW Stark St., 97204 ***Tel*** *(503) 274-0010* ***Map*** *2 D5*

The historic former residence of Portland's archbishop is now home to some of the city's better traditional Lebanese cuisine, with savory kebabs, garlicky hummus, roast lamb, and the like. The handsome dining room shows off the 1879 structure's brick and stained glass, and on weekends the place comes alive with music and belly dancing.

DOWNTOWN The Heathman Restaurant ♫ ⛱ [V] 🍷 [$][$][$][$]
1001 SW Broadway, 97205 ***Tel*** *(503) 790-7752* ***Map*** *1 C5*

Normandy meets the Northwest in the cooking of award-winning chef Philippe Boulot, whose menus follow the seasons in search of the freshest, finest ingredients. Standout dishes may include pistachio-stuffed rabbit leg, Pekin duck a l'orange, and for breakfast, smoked salmon hash. France and Oregon dominate the extensive wine list.

Key to Symbols *see back cover flap*

DOWNTOWN Higgins Restaurant $$$$
1239 SW Broadway, 97205 Tel (503) 222-9070 **Map** *3 B1*

A light-filled, multi-level space inspired by classic Parisian bistros, chef Greg Higgins' landmark restaurant is a shrine to seasonal, sustainable cuisine. The menu features inventive preparations of produce, meats, and fish from local farms, ranches, and waters, and the wine list has a strong Northwest focus.

DOWNTOWN Jake's Famous Crawfish $$$$
401 SW 12th Ave., 97205 Tel (503) 226-1419 **Map** *1 B4*

A Portland institution and tourist destination, this 1892 fish house boasts nearly three dozen kinds of fresh fish and seafood daily. The menu offers them steamed, stuffed, seared, sautéed, and sauced, but you can get most things simply grilled, often the best. Polished paneling, old artwork, and crisply attired waiters create a clubby atmosphere.

FARTHER AFIELD Genies Café $
1101 SE Division St., 97202 Tel (503) 445-9777 **Road Map** *1 A3*

More than most breakfast and lunch spots, Genies is devoted to seasonal, sustainable cuisine, so the ever-changing menu may feature such items as a morel scramble or sausage frittata with fiddleheads and nettles. Several fine versions of eggs Benedict and classic sandwiches are available year-round.

FARTHER AFIELD Hopworks Urban Brewery $
2944 SE Powell Blvd., 97202 Tel (503) 232-4677 **Road Map** *1 A3*

This friendly establishment is located in a converted tractor showroom, which gives it an industrial, though cozy, atmosphere. Determined to be as carbon-neutral as possible, Hopworks uses mainly organic, local ingredients in both its beers and its food. Try the seven-grain stout with the Backyard BBQ pizza.

FARTHER AFIELD La Sirenita $
2817 NE Alberta St., 97211 Tel (503) 335-8283 **Road Map** *1 A3*

Of the many taquerias – no-nonsense joints serving Mexican and Tex-Mex fast food such as tacos and burritos all over Portland – this one has cultivated perhaps the widest following. You can get hefty, meaty burritos here for under $4, as well as some finer fare such as seafood-laden soup and shrimp cocktail.

FARTHER AFIELD Pause Kitchen and Bar $
5101 N Interstate Ave., 97217 Tel (971) 230-0705 **Road Map** *1 A3*

A neighborhood joint with a family-friendly atmosphere and prices, as well as a late-night hangout with a decent selection of wines and beers. More than most pubs, Pause is dedicated to the virtues of good food with home-made charcuterie, confit, and pickles featuring prominently on the menu.

FARTHER AFIELD Saburo's Sushi House $
1667 SE Bybee Blvd., 97202 Tel (503) 236-4237 **Road Map** *1 A3*

This tiny sushi spot in the Westmoreland neighborhood is always packed with fresh-fish fans, and long waits are common. In addition to the large servings of sushi, signature dishes include broiled *hamachi* (yellowtail) collar and creamy scallops. For those who prefer cooked fish, traditional dishes such as tempura and teriyaki are available.

FARTHER AFIELD Apizza Scholls $$
4741 SE Hawthorne Blvd., 97215 Tel (503) 233-1286 **Road Map** *1 A3*

Widely considered Portland's pizza mecca, this wildly popular spot is devoted to classic New York-style pies, with crackly crust made from slow-fermented dough and cooked at nearly 900 degrees. The kitchen is uncompromising, service can be brusque, and the place closes early if the dough runs out, but devoted crowds remain undeterred.

FARTHER AFIELD Bernie's Southern Bistro $$
2904 NE Alberta St., 97211 Tel (503) 282-9864 **Road Map** *1 A3*

Southern classics are the focus at this handsome, roomy restaurant on bustling Alberta Street. Along with such dishes as fried green tomatoes, buttermilk fried chicken, blackened catfish, and bourbon barbecued ribs, Bernie's also offers a wide selection of boutique bourbons and some of Portland's finest patio dining in summer.

FARTHER AFIELD Caffe Mingo $$
807 NW 21st Ave., 97209 Tel (503) 226-4646 **Road Map** *1 A3*

Cramped, crowded, and convivial, this Northwest trattoria puts gusto and finesse in perfect balance. Once you've endured the almost inevitable wait, enjoy such dishes as bruschetta with wild mushrooms, signature penne with chianti- and espresso-braised beef, and panna cotta with fresh fruit. Some excellent Italian wines.

FARTHER AFIELD Delta Café $$
4607 SE Woodstock Blvd., 97206 Tel (503) 771-3101 **Road Map** *1 A3*

Hearty cooking of the Deep South in Southeast Portland, where you'll rub elbows with students from nearby Reed College and assorted hipsters. Fried chicken, blackened catfish, jambalaya, pork ribs, and collard greens are menu highlights. Be prepared for crowds, noise, huge portions, and loads of cheap beer.

FARTHER AFIELD Esparza's Tex-Mex Café $$
2725 SE Ankeny St., 97214 Tel (503) 234-7909 **Road Map** *1 A3*

Boxy, brightly colored, and adorned with kitsch, this is the city's top destination for the Tejano food of the US southern border. Under the watchful eyes of lit-up longhorn skulls, you can sink your teeth into myriad delicious meats, from beef brisket and shredded pork to ostrich, calf brains, and venison tongue.

FARTHER AFIELD Lemongrass

1705 NE Couch St., 97232 **Tel** *(503) 231-5780*   **Road Map** *1 A3*

A pioneer in Portland Thai cuisine, this quietly elegant spot offers a modest menu of vividly flavorful Thai dishes including succulent fish cakes, savory Thai noodles, and several hand-crushed curries. The service here can be slow on busy nights, but the superlative food is worth the wait. Cash only.

FARTHER AFIELD Navarre

10 NE 28th Ave., 97232 **Tel** *(503) 232-3555*   **Road Map** *1 A3*

A tapas-style restaurant and wine bar, with inventive Spanish, Italian, and French cuisine. Navarre is a partner in a community-sustained agriculture program, so the menu's abundant produce is farm-fresh and constantly changing. The wine list, among the city's best, is as eclectic and carefully thought out as the menu.

FARTHER AFIELD Podnah's Pit Barbecue

1625 NE Killingsworth St., 97211 **Tel** *(503) 281-3700*   **Road Map** *1 A3*

Slow-smoked Texas barbecue with a cult following. The dining room is decidedly no-frills, but the moist, tender meats from the oak-fired smoker keep the place packed. Main attractions include brisket, lamb spare ribs, prime rib, and pulled pork sandwiches. A small selection of wines and microbrews complement the meaty fare.

FARTHER AFIELD Savoy Tavern & Bistro

2500 SE Clinton St., 97202 **Tel** *(503) 808-9999*   **Road Map** *1 A3*

The classic midwestern supper club, reimagined. The menu is based on Wisconsin cuisine at this popular Southeast Portland spot. Choices include fried cheese curds, iceberg lettuce salad, pan-fried trout, and Chicken Kiev. Retro food, done with a sure hand, in a retro atmosphere outfitted with mid-century furnishings.

FARTHER AFIELD Gino's Restaurant and Bar

8057 SE 13th Ave., 97202 **Tel** *(503) 233-4613*   **Road Map** *1 A3*

Housed in a 100-year-old building (the sign for the bygone Leipzig Tavern still hangs outside) with a massive wooden bar, this Sellwood trattoria is a favorite among the city's Italian restaurants. Devoted patrons come for huge, extra-garlicky Caesar salads, steamed clams and mussels, superb pastas, and a well-chosen, reasonably-priced wine list.

FARTHER AFIELD Le Bistro Montage

301 SE Morrison St., 97214 **Tel** *(503) 234-1324*   **Road Map** *1 A3*

Situated in an up-and-coming industrial area, Le Bistro Montage is packed with hipsters, students, and professionals until the early hours of the morning. The jambalayas are spicy and generous, and include a few exotic options such as catfish and alligator. The staff will gladly wrap any leftovers in a foil-sculpted masterpiece. Closed Mon lunch.

FARTHER AFIELD Natural Selection

3033 NE Alberta St., 97211 **Tel** *(503) 288-5883*   **Road Map** *1 A3*

With its modern rustic decor, Natural Selection offers vegan and vegetarian dishes that highlight the flavors of the Mediterranean. Chef Aaron Woo creates wonderful combinations such as polenta with lobster mushrooms, and gluten-free lemon macadamia cake. Reservations recommended. Open for dinner only Wed–Sat.

FARTHER AFIELD Nostrana

1401 SE Morrison St., 97214 **Tel** *(503) 234-2427*   **Road Map** *1 A3*

Food fanatics flock to Nostrana for Italian dishes made with obsessive attention to detail. Pizzas from a massive, wood-fired oven are the centerpiece; served uncut in traditional Italian style, they are simple and full of flavor. Other items on the ever-changing menu may include sausage-stuffed cardoons and dandelion salad with duck prosciutto.

FARTHER AFIELD Toji Korean Grill House

4615 SE Hawthorne Blvd., 97215 **Tel** *(503) 232-8998*   **Road Map** *1 A3*

Tables at this elegant restaurant are equipped with grills, and the offerings include exquisite meats, seafood, and vegetables for you to cook up yourself or with the assistance of the staff. Varieties of *kimchi*, soups, and noodle dishes are among the excellent traditional non-grilled items, and the drinks list offers Asian beers, sake, and Korean wines.

FARTHER AFIELD Paley's Place

1204 NW 21st Ave., 97209 **Tel** *(503) 243-2403*   **Road Map** *1 A3*

Chef Vitaly Paley is one of Portland's star chefs, and his intimate eatery, located in a Victorian house in a historic neighborhood, is a shrine of Northwest cuisine. Highlights include citrus-cured salmon with crème fraîche and caviar, spit-roasted suckling lamb, corn and Dungeness crab risotto, and arguably the best burger in the city.

OREGON

ASHLAND Alex's Plaza Restaurant and Bar

35 N Main St., 97520 **Tel** *(541) 482-8818*   **Road Map** *1 A5*

Located in a historic creekside building in the heart of Ashland, Alex's is a comfortable, light-filled place with hearty comfort food served indoors by the fireplace, at the casual bar, or outside on the deck, complete with views. Pasta dishes, fish specials, and small tapas-style plates to share are all made with local ingredients whenever possible.

ASHLAND Peerless Restaurant

265 4th St., 97520 **Tel** *(541) 488-6067* **Road Map** *1 A5*

This lovely spot, set in a handsomely restored hotel on the National Register of Historic Places, offers creative Northwest cuisine and a dedication to sustainability. Fresh local meats, produce, and artisanal cheese from local dairies make up the menu, while an award-winning wine list and a gorgeous garden enhance the experience.

ASTORIA Wet Dog Café

144 11th St., 97103 **Tel** *(503) 325-6975* **Road Map** *1 A3*

Housed in a huge old warehouse on the Columbia River Waterfront, Astoria's first brewpub is the restaurant of Astoria (formerly Pacific Rim) Brewing. Several craft brews are on tap along with a full bar, and the food is typical pub fare: fish and chips, burgers and the like, with ribs on Fridays. Weekend nights heat up with live music.

ASTORIA Columbian Café

1114 Marine Dr., 97103 **Tel** *(503) 325-2233* **Road Map** *1 A3*

Cramped and funky, this hole-in-the-wall diner is an Astoria institution. From the excellent hearty breakfasts to dinner, there is always good vegetarian fare as well as meats and seafood. Crêpes are a specialty, and among the condiments are Uriah's St. Diablo jellies (in red pepper, jalapeño, and garlic flavors); you will want to buy a few jars to go.

BAKER CITY Baker City Café

1840 Main St., 97814 **Tel** *(541) 523-6099* **Road Map** *1 C3*

This casual eatery offers a fun, friendly environment, and Italian-American café standard fare such as pizzas, pastas, and salads in huge portions. With modest prices and a wide variety of menu options for kids, it is a popular choice for local families and visitors alike.

BAKER CITY Geiser Grill

1996 Main St., 97814 **Tel** *(541) 523-1889* **Road Map** *1 C3*

One of Oregon's finest restaurants east of the Cascades. The ambiance in the historic Geiser Grand Hotel is stately and striking, with crystal chandeliers, crisp linens, abundant wood trim, and a huge, original stained-glass skylight. Among the specialties are mesquite-smoked prime rib, Pacific salmon, and, for breakfast, smoked corn beef hash.

BEND Deschutes Brewery and Public House

1044 NW Bond St., 97701 **Tel** *(541) 382-9242* **Road Map** *1 B4*

Award-winning Deschutes Brewery is one of the West's top beer producers, with popular brews like Mirror Pond Pale Ale and Black Butte Porter. The brewpub fare is better than most, with hearty specialty sandwiches and home-made sausage, bread, and mustard. Meat for the burgers comes from animals raised on the brewery's spent grain and hops.

BEND Zydeco Kitchen & Cocktails

919 Bond St., 97701 **Tel** *(541) 312-2899* **Road Map** *1 B4*

Top-notch service and mostly organic ingredients combine to make Zydeco one of Bend's best restaurants. The large menu features a range of Cajun-inspired staples – including barbecued ribs, jambalaya, and corn fritters – and some unusual entrées such as the Creole smoked tofu. The Key Lime Pie is also excellent. Closed Sat & Sun lunch.

CANNON BEACH Mo's at Tolovana

195 Warren Way, 97145 **Tel** *503 436-1111* **Road Map** *1 A3*

Mo's restaurants are Oregon coast classics, serving basic seafood such as rich clam chowder and fish and chips in family-friendly locations. The Tolovana branch serves the usual Mo's fare in a stunning location, with views of waves lapping the shore and Haystack Rock in the distance. Touristy, but for good reason.

CANNON BEACH The Bistro

263 N Hemlock St., 97145 **Tel** *(503) 436-2661* **Road Map** *1 A3*

A tiny, intimate eatery tucked away down a brick path, this cozy spot is a little pocket of French country on the Pacific. The kitchen serves superb fish and seafood dishes – seafood stew, pan-fried oysters, crab cakes, baked salmon – often with a Mediterranean accent. The place regularly fills up, so reservations are highly recommended.

CARLTON Cuvée

214 W Main St., 97111 **Tel** *(503) 852-6555* **Road Map** *1 A3*

In one of the more charming small towns of Oregon's wine country, this refined restaurant offers traditional French country fare to accompany the wines of the local vineyards. Alsace-born Gilbert Henry's menu is strong on seafood, with excellent versions of bouillabaisse and Coquilles St. Jacques, but also includes such delicacies as *escargot*.

DAYTON Joel Palmer House

600 Ferry St., 97114 **Tel** *(503) 864-2995* **Road Map** *1 A3*

Set in a historic Antebellum mansion on Dayton's main street, the Joel Palmer House is a top wine country destination. Chef Christopher Czarnecki specializes in mushrooms, which make appearances in his menu in porcini sauces, the pâté with truffle and chanterelles, and the exquisite three-mushroom tart. The wine list is Pinot Noir heaven.

DUNDEE Tina's

760 Hwy. 99W, 97115 **Tel** *(503) 538-8880* **Road Map** *1 A3*

This intimate spot is renowned as a pioneer in wine country fine dining. The French-Northwest menu focuses on seasonal, regional ingredients treated with simplicity and elegance – braised rabbit, and goat's cheese soufflé are amongst the dishes on offer. The terrific wine list reads like an Oregon winemakers' Hall of Fame.

EUGENE Taqueria Mi Tierra
68 Blair St., 97402 **Tel** *(541) 743-0779* Ⓥ Ⓢ

Road Map *1 A4*

Come to this family-run hole-in-the-wall taqueria for authentic Mexican flavors. On the menu are weekly specials, combo plates for under $6, and a variety of fresh salsas. The same family also owns the Mexican grocery store next door, where you can stock up on baked goods or the necessary items for your own taco-based dinner.

EUGENE Beppe & Gianni's Trattoria
1646 E 19th Ave., 97403 **Tel** *(541) 683-6661* ⒶⓋ🍽 ⓈⓈⓈ

Road Map *1 A4*

Eugene's top Italian restaurant serves a variety of expertly executed pastas alongside meat and fish dishes, with fine fresh produce incorporated throughout. The magnificent Italian wine list is worth a visit in itself. Located in a handsome craftsman-style house, the restaurant also features a deck for alfresco dining during the summer.

EUGENE Oregon Electric Station
27 E 5th Ave., 97401 **Tel** *(541) 485-4444* 🎵ⒶⓋ🍽 ⓈⓈⓈⓈ

Road Map *1 A4*

Housed in the beautiful 1912 depot of a long-defunct electric railroad, this charming restaurant serves top-notch steak, fish, and pasta dishes complemented by over 250 wines. Guests can dine in the high-ceilinged depot, in one of several lounges, aboard antique train cars, or outside on the broad patio.

GLENEDEN BEACH The Prime Steakhouse
7760 N Hwy. 101, 97388 **Tel** *(800) 452-2300* Ⓥ🍽 ⓈⓈⓈⓈⓈ

Road Map *1 A3*

One of the finest restaurants on the exclusive Salishan Spa & Golf Resort, The Prime Steakhouse has a decades-long reputation as one of the best places to eat in the Northwest. Regional delicacies are prepared with expert hands. The wine cellar is legendary; among the largest in the region, it includes an unrivaled collection of Oregon wine.

GOVERNMENT CAMP Huckleberry Inn
88611 E Government Camp Loop, 97028 **Tel** *(503) 272-3325* Ⓥ Ⓢ

Road Map *1 B3*

In a mountainside village on the road from Portland over Mount Hood, the rustic Huckleberry Inn offers 24-hour dining in a family-style restaurant, plus an adjoining steakhouse open on weekends during ski season. Burgers, sandwiches, and breakfast favorites dominate the menu, and a slice of huckleberry pie with coffee is de rigueur.

HOOD RIVER Full Sail Brewing Company
506 Columbia St., 97031 **Tel** *(541) 386-2247* 🎵ⒶⓋ ⓈⓈ

Road Map *1 B3*

After a day of windsurfing, the pub of the popular Full Sail brewery is an ideal spot to kick back, take in the Columbia River breeze, and sample a range of tasty craft brews. You can snack on small plates, sandwiches, and salads, or tuck into a rib-eye steak or hearty halibut and chips.

HOOD RIVER Celilo
16 Oak St., 97031 **Tel** *(541) 386-5710* Ⓥ🍽 ⓈⓈⓈ

Road Map *1 B3*

Hood River's most stylish restaurant is this sleek, modern interpretation of a timbered lodge. Driven by a devotion to using fresh and local ingredients, the kitchen turns out delicious dishes that change with the seasons. Home-made pastas are a strong point, as are seafood preparations such as skillet-roasted mussels and rich seafood risotto.

HOOD RIVER Mount Hood Railroad Dinner Train
110 Railroad Ave., 97031 **Tel** *(541) 386-3556* 🍴Ⓥ🍽 ⓈⓈⓈⓈⓈ

Road Map *1 B3*

Saturday-dinner and Sunday-brunch menus are offered aboard four-hour rail excursions through the beautiful land-scape south of the Columbia River, with magnificent views of Mount Hood and Mount Adams. Passengers can enjoy classic dishes like prime rib and eggs Benedict in restored dining cars with roomy booths and large windows.

JOSEPH Embers Brewhouse
204 N Main St., 97846 **Tel** *(541) 432-2739* ⒶⓋ Ⓢ

Road Map *1 C3*

This popular, casual brewhouse offers 17 regional craft brews, along with appetizers, sandwiches, burgers, pizzas, and calzones. In good weather, guests can eat, drink, and take in the crisp mountain air on a large deck with views of the beautiful Wallowa Valley.

JOSEPH Outlaw Restaurant and Saloon
108 N Main St., 97846 **Tel** *(541) 432-4321* ⒶⓋ Ⓢ

Road Map *1 C3*

The menu in this relaxed, family-friendly spot includes such tried-and-tested American standards as steaks, pastas, burgers, and seafood dishes. Kids will appreciate the in-house ice-cream bar; a variety of other desserts are also available. With plenty of space for outside dining, it is a great summer spot.

LINCOLN CITY Blackfish Café
2733 NW Hwy. 101, 97367 **Tel** *(541) 996-1007* Ⓥ🍽 ⓈⓈ

Road Map *1 A3*

Chef/owner Rob Pounding, one of the best chefs in the Northwest, maintains close relationships with fishermen, growers, and foragers to obtain the freshest ingredients possible, then combines them in simple, imaginative dishes that allow the flavors to sing. All manner of seafood dominates the ever-changing and reasonably priced menu.

MCMINNVILLE Nick's Italian Café
521 NE 3rd St., 97128 **Tel** *(503) 434-4471* 🍴🎵Ⓥ🍽 ⓈⓈⓈ

Road Map *1 A3*

A wine-country landmark in a former osda fountain, chef Nick Peirano's place draws diners from across the North-west for hearty, multi-course, fixed-menu dinners. A typical dish might be Dungeness crab lasagna, braised rabbit, or grilled salmon, plus Nick's signature minestrone. The wine list attests to a close relationship with local vintners.

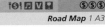

Key to Price Guide *see p298* **Key to Symbols** *see back cover flap*

NEWPORT April's at Nye Beach

$ $ $

749 NW Third St., 97365 **Tel** (541) 265-6855

Road Map 1 A3

The Pacific meets the Mediterranean in the artsy, historic Newport neighborhood of Nye Beach. This cozy café offers ocean views and fine, creatively conceived Northwest cuisine with an Italian accent, accompanied by well selected and affordable wines. Do not miss the fish soup and other seafood, but save room for the excellent desserts.

OTIS Otis Café

$

1259 Salmon River Hwy., 97368 **Tel** (541) 994-2813

Road Map 1 A3

An obligatory stop if you are headed to the coast on the Salmon River Highway, this little roadside café is open all day but is especially renowned for its enormous, delicious breakfasts. Try the hash browns topped with cheddar, huge home-made cinnamon rolls, or marionberry pie, and grab a loaf of bread (molasses or sourdough) to go.

PACIFIC CITY Pelican Pub and Brewery

$ $

33180 Cape Kiwanda Dr., 97135 **Tel** (503) 965-7007

Road Map 1 A3

This craft brewery boasts numerous awards and, with its position at the foot of Cape Kiwanda's sandstone bluffs, possibly the most stunning location of any Northwest brewery. Open for three meals a day, the pub's menu is more sophisticated than most and includes ginger-glazed salmon, mahi-mahi fish and chips, and crab-cake eggs Benedict.

SALEM La Capitale Brasserie

$ $ $

508 State St., 97301 **Tel** (503) 585-1975

Road Map 1 A3

Housed in a historic building in downtown Salem, this upscale yet casual French restaurant focuses on local ingredients and fine wines. On the menu are perfect *pommes frites* and creative combinations – such as the line-caught Oregon ling cod with Mt. Hood morels. Their home-made charcuterie plates are also worth a try. Closed Sun.

SEATTLE

PIKE PLACE MARKET AND THE WATERFRONT Athenian Inn

$ $

1517 Pike Pl., 98101 **Tel** (206) 624-7166

Map 3 C1

More renowned for its view and its appearance in the movie *Sleepless in Seattle* than for the food itself, this beloved, well-worn old-timer in Pike Place Market offers friendly service along with an extensive menu of American fare and microbrews. The menu leans toward seafood, with oyster omelets, mussel soup, grilled fish, and salmon and chips.

PIKE PLACE MARKET AND THE WATERFRONT Tango Restaurant & Lounge

$ $

1100 Pike St., 98101 **Tel** (206) 583-0382

Map 3 C1

Diners will find attentive and friendly service at this Capitol Hill tapas bar located in a 1908 brick building. Start with the shrimp ceviche, try a few hot tapas, share a bowl of paella, and top it all off with Tango's famous chocolate diablo cake – possibly Seattle's best dessert. Open daily for dinner only.

PIKE PLACE MARKET AND THE WATERFRONT Le Pichet

$ $ $

1933 1st Ave., 98101 **Tel** (206) 256-1499

Map 3 C1

This crowded bistro is as close as Seattle comes to a little piece of Paris, right down to the zinc bar. Highlights include *escargots*, lamb-garlic sausage, and a terrific roasted chicken with apples and potatoes. The wine list is worth a long exploration, and the place is open in the morning for coffee and pastry and at lunch for charcuterie.

PIKE PLACE MARKET AND THE WATERFRONT The Pink Door

1919 Post Alley, 98101 **Tel** (206) 443-3241

Map 3 B1

Decorated in what its owner calls "Italian garage sale-style," this lively and unique trattoria serves hearty, rustic Italian-American fare. Its commitment to the organic and sustainable extends to the excellent West Coast and Italian wine list, which features several selections from organic and biodynamic producers. The free nightly cabaret is wild.

PIKE PLACE MARKET AND THE WATERFRONT Shea's Lounge

$ $ $

94 Pike St. #34, 98101 **Tel** (206) 467-9990

Map 3 C1

The stylish but more casual counterpart to the adjacent Chez Shea. The menu features luxurious dishes made with top-quality local and seasonal ingredients. Look for such delicacies as salmon tartare, duck carpaccio, tenderloin of beef roulade, and leek and morel crêpes.

PIKE PLACE MARKET AND THE WATERFRONT Café Campagne

$ $ $ $

1600 Post Alley, 98101 **Tel** (206) 728-2233

Map 3 B1

Sister restaurant to the more formal and expensive Campagne upstairs, this café is a snug, convivial spot for enjoying deftly prepared French fare. The menu is full of bistro classics such as *oeufs en meurette* (poached eggs on croutons with wine and foie gras sauce), croque monsieur, country pâté, and magnificent steak frites.

PIKE PLACE MARKET AND THE WATERFRONT Etta's Seafood

$ $ $ $

2020 Western Ave., 98121 **Tel** (206) 443-6000

Map 3 B1

The most seafood-focused of Tom Douglas's 12 restaurants, this chic spot just a stroll from the market boasts dramatic decor and a buzzing crowd. Tuna, salmon, halibut, and crab are highlights, with items such as Kobe beef and Oregon quail to appease landlocked palates. Do not miss the signature crab cakes.

PIKE PLACE MARKET AND THE WATERFRONT Ivar's Acres of Clams ⛱ [V] 🍷 $$$$

1001 Alaskan Way, 98104 ***Tel*** *(206) 624-6852* ***Map*** *3 C2*

A venerable Seattle institution, this popular waterfront spot offers terrific crab, clam, oyster, and salmon dishes, as well as the classic fish and chips they've been serving since 1938. You can watch the ferries gliding by out the window, and many diners like to sit outside on the dock and feed the seagulls their spare French fries.

PIKE PLACE MARKET AND THE WATERFRONT Matt's in the Market [V] 🍷 $$$$

94 Pike St. #32, 98101 ***Tel*** *(206) 467-7909* ***Map*** *3 C1*

The city's favorite little gourmet establishment, tucked into the Corner Market Building, expanded into the adjoining space in 2007, but has kept its close, convivial atmosphere. The mercurial kitchen applies a variety of influences to whatever is fresh at the moment to create an ever-changing, always interesting menu. Smoked catfish is a specialty.

PIKE PLACE MARKET AND THE WATERFRONT Place Pigalle ⛱ [V] 🍷 $$$$

81 Pike St., 98101 ***Tel*** *(206) 624-1756* ***Map*** *3 C1*

A former fisherman's tavern, this quiet little nook of Pike Place Market is the perfect spot for a romantic evening. In classic bistro style, it presents Pacific Northwest cuisine with Continental and Southwestern influences, award-winning seafood dishes, and other imaginative creations. Ask for a window table and enjoy gorgeous views.

PIONEER SQUARE AND DOWNTOWN Salumi 🍴 [V] 🍷 $

309 3rd Ave. S, 98104 ***Tel*** *(206) 621-8772* ***Map*** *4 D3*

Armandino Batali's tiny Pioneer Square lunch spot is mecca to legions who regularly pack the place for authentic, intensely flavorful Italian sausages. Salumi sells retail salami and other cured meat products, and serves a small menu of sandwiches, soups, and pastas as well. Open only Tue–Fri, and there is almost always a wait.

SEATTLE CENTER AND BELLTOWN Farestart [V] $

700 Virginia St., 98101 ***Tel*** *(206) 267-7601* ***Map*** *2 D5*

In addition to offering good American fare, Farestart serves an important social function, providing culinary training and a placement program for the homeless and other disadvantaged individuals. Open for lunch Monday to Friday and for dinner on Thursdays (6–8pm), often with a celebrity chef. Try the field roast sandwich, a vegetarian burger.

SEATTLE CENTER AND BELLTOWN Pagliacci Pizzeria [V] $

550 Queen Anne Ave. N, 98109 ***Tel*** *(206) 285-1232* ***Map*** *1 B3*

One of Seattle's most popular pizzerias. The kitchen here sticks to traditional New York cooking, with a thin and tangy crust. Toppings range from classic combinations such as the margherita (tomato, mozzerella, and basil) to spinach and chicken to spicy pepperoni made by Seattle's artisan sausage-maker Salumi.

SEATTLE CENTER AND BELLTOWN Sam's Sushi [V] $

521 Queen Anne Ave. N, 98109 ***Tel*** *(206) 282-4612* ***Map*** *1 B3*

This simple, no-nonsense Japanese spot serves decent sushi, *gyoza* (fried dumplings), teriyaki, and other traditional favorites. The owner maintains a casual atmosphere, with sports on the TV, comfortable seating, and reliable and affordable fare that attracts a loyal host of regulars.

SEATTLE CENTER AND BELLTOWN Peso's Kitchen & Lounge [V] $$

605 Queen Anne Ave. N, 98109 ***Tel*** *(206) 283-9353* ***Map*** *1 B3*

With a luridly red ceiling and kitschy bullfight artwork, this bustling Mexican spot is a fun and funky scene. The menu includes traditional fare such as *carne asada* (broiled flank steak) and grilled prawns, and the heat can be enhanced with fiery habañero sauce. Award-winning margaritas flow freely during happy hour at the adjacent lounge.

SEATTLE CENTER AND BELLTOWN Dahlia Lounge [V] 🍷 $$$

2001 4th Ave., 98121 ***Tel*** *(206) 682-4142* ***Map*** *2 D5*

Constantly redefining Pacific Northwest cuisine, Seattle's celebrity chef and restaurateur serves sophisticated fare in his smart, crimson-colored dining room. The menu changes daily, but offerings may include rotisseried Peking duck, grilled King Salmon, and hanger steak with caraway spaetzle and gruyère.

SEATTLE CENTER AND BELLTOWN Shiro's [V] 🍷 $$$

2401 2nd Ave., 98121 ***Tel*** *(206) 443-9844* ***Map*** *1 C5*

Possibly the finest sushi in a seafood-saturated city; it doesn't get fresher than this. In a spare, intimate space, sushi master Shiro Kashiba serves a repertoire of familiar cuts and special rolls, plus other seafood specialties including fired softshell crab, monkfish liver pate, broiled blackcod, and sea urchin tempura.

FARTHER AFIELD Beth's Café $

7311 Aurora Ave. N, 98103 ***Tel*** *(206) 782-5588* ***Road Map*** *1 A2*

A legendary dive for half a century, this 24-hour spot serves monstrous breakfasts and other greasy-spoon classics to both the early-morning and the late-night crowd. Omelets come in 6- and 12-egg versions with huge helpings of hash browns. There is a lunch menu, too, with sandwiches, salads, and burgers, including a half-pound version.

FARTHER AFIELD House of Hong 🍴 [V] $

409 8th Ave. S, 98104 ***Tel*** *(206) 622-7997* ***Road Map*** *1 A2*

During the day, this is the spot for Seattle's best dim sum. Carts speed by in the vast dining room with dozens of different kinds of dumplings, wonton, buns, rolls, and other Cantonese treats, from deep-fried spiced calamari to mango pudding. At night, the menu changes to Hunan and Szechuan dishes.

FARTHER AFIELD Kauai Family Restaurant

6324 6th Ave. S, 98108 **Tel** *(206) 762-3469*   **Road Map** *1 A2*

Well off the beaten track in the industrial neighborhood of Georgetown, this diner offers one of the city's few authentic Hawaiian eats. Kauai-born Peter Buza and family serve such island classics as kalua pork, lomi salmon, ahi poke, and spam *musubi* (a sushi-like snack of spam on rice wrapped in seaweed), plus burgers, BLTs, and the like.

FARTHER AFIELD Café Flora

2901 E Madison St., 98112 **Tel** *(206) 325-9100*   **Road Map** *1 A2*

This airy Madison Valley restaurant celebrates the possibilities of vegetarian cooking with the seasonal bounty of the Northwest. Look for coconut-breaded tofu with sweet chili sauce, inventive pizzas, and the portabella Wellington, in puff pastry with leeks and mushroom-pecan pâté. The wine list is eclectic and well-chosen.

FARTHER AFIELD Dinette

1545 E Olive Way, 98122 **Tel** *(206) 328-2282*   **Road Map** *1 A2*

A charming little restaurant on Capitol Hill, Dinette serves rustic European fare with a flair. Their toasts, with creamy gorgonzola and walnuts, or chicken liver mousse with peppers, are great for lighter appetites, while the fish of the day or steaks are more substantial. The restaurant has a soothing, calm atmosphere.

FARTHER AFIELD Palace Kitchen

2030 5th Ave., 98121 **Tel** *(206) 448-2001*   **Road Map** *1 A2*

Part of chef Tom Douglas's empire, this stylish restaurant and bar under the monorail specializes in grilled meats, seafood, and hearty American fare. Menu highlights include local mussels with chorizo, a selection of artisanal cheeses, and a burger widely regarded as Seattle's best. After 10pm, omelets can also be ordered for late-night breakfast.

FARTHER AFIELD Ray's Boathouse

6049 Seaview Ave. NW, 98107 **Tel** *(206) 789-3770*   **Road Map** *1 A2*

Once a boat rental and bait shop with a coffeehouse on the side, Ray's is now a Seattle icon and one of the top seafood restaurants in the country. Upstairs is a lively and casual lounge; downstairs is formal and sedate. On both floors you can enjoy unfussy preparations of spectacularly fresh fish while you take in the gorgeous view.

FARTHER AFIELD Wild Ginger

1401 3rd Ave., 98101 **Tel** *(206) 623-4450*   **Road Map** *1 A2*

This pan-Asian fusion restaurant is hugely popular. In a sleek, stylish setting, devoted customers enjoy such delicacies as wild ginger fragrant duck, seven flavor beef, and Dungeness crab served seasonally in any one of five different preparations. The satay bar offers grilled items including scallops and boar. There's also a substantial vegetarian menu.

FARTHER AFIELD Elliott's Oyster House

1201 Alaskan Way, 98101 **Tel** *(206) 623-4340*   **Road Map** *1 A2*

Tourists and locals rub elbows at this busy, convivial seafood house at the heart of Seattle's downtown waterfront. The focal point of the teak- and copper-accented interior is the 21-ft- (7-m-) long oyster bar, where guests can order from as many as 20 different varieties of oyster. King Salmon and Dungeness crab are also specialties.

FARTHER AFIELD Flying Fish

300 Westlake Ave. N, 98121 **Tel** *(206) 728-8595*   **Road Map** *1 A2*

The Asian-influenced menu at this hip, upscale spot offers a dazzling array of fish and seafood. Small plates may include Thai crab cake and seared scallops with pineapple hollandaise; large plates include black cod marinated in sake and seafood hot pot with Thai yellow curry. An abbreviated menu and well-stocked bar fuel the late-night scene.

FARTHER AFIELD Serafina

2043 Eastlake Ave. E, 98102 **Tel** *(206) 323-0807*   **Road Map** *1 A2*

This intimate, out-of-the-way spot in the Eastlake neighborhood serves honest Italian country fare in a warm, rustic setting. Local, seasonal products are the foundation of the menu; try mussels simmered with smoked tomatoes and harissa, sweet pea and ricotta ravioli tossed with herbs, and the signature *melanzanes* (baked eggplant with ricotta).

FARTHER AFIELD Canlis

2576 Aurora Ave. N, 98109 **Tel** *(206) 283-3313*   **Road Map** *1 A2*

In the vanguard of Seattle fine dining since 1950, this special occasion favorite features terrific Lake Union views and fabulous seafood and steaks, as well as an excellent wine list with over 2000 selections. The interior reflects nature, live music accompanies diners, and the atmosphere is formal – no jeans or similarly casual dress.

FARTHER AFIELD Crush

2319 E Madison St., 98112 **Tel** *(206) 302-7874*   **Road Map** *1 A2*

In a Tudor house remodeled with a sleek, chic interior, chef Jason Wilson creates delicious modern Northwest cuisine devoted to the seasonal and sustainable. The menu is ever-changing, but intriguing, nicely balanced combinations are the rule such as seared scallops with persimmon and black cod with Syrah sauce. Bold and extravagant wine list.

FARTHER AFIELD The Herbfarm

14590 NE 145th St., 98072 **Tel** *(206) 485-5300*   **Road Map** *1 A2*

The Northwest's most extravagant dining experience, known to gastronomes around the world. Chef Jerry Traunfeld prepares nine-course dinners from the farm's own produce and from the ingredients of local growers; liberally enhanced with herbs and beautifully presented, each dish is also paired with a wine from the 24,000-bottle cellar.

FARTHER AFIELD Metropolitan Grill

820 2nd Ave., 98104 **Tel** *(206) 624-3287*   **Road Map** *1 A2*

Long an establishment for Seattle's power brokers, this handsome, luxurious steakhouse is a warm and sophisticated setting for enjoying the best beef in the city. "The Met" also offers a dizzying array of premium vodkas and gins for martinis, and the voluminous wine list specializes in big West Coast reds.

FARTHER AFIELD Rover's

2808 E Madison St., 98112 **Tel** *(206) 325-7442*   **Road Map** *1 A2*

One of Seattle's very finest restaurants. French chef Thierry Rautureau has brought his French classical training to the Northwest with exquisite results. You can choose à la carte options or one of three fixed tasting menus, including one which features some of the best, most refined vegetarian food in the region.

WASHINGTON

ASHFORD Alexander's Country Inn

37515 State Rd. 706 E, 98304 **Tel** *(800) 654-7615*   **Road Map** *1 B2*

Opened in 1912 and located just a mile from Mt. Rainier National Park, this classic inn offers both elegant accommodation and some of the best food in the area. Fresh steelhead trout from the ice-cold, on-site pond headlines a menu of fish and seafood, steaks, and pasta. Desserts include home-made wild blackberry pie.

BELLINGHAM The Oyster Bar

2578 Chuckanut Dr., 98232 **Tel** *(360) 766-6185*   **Road Map** *1 A1*

A venerable institution dating back to the 1920s, this lodge-like restaurant boasts stellar seafood and jaw-dropping views of the San Juan Islands. As the name suggests, a variety of local oysters leads the menu, which also offers such options as crab cakes, steamed mussels, bouillabaisse, wild mushroom ravioli, and a daily game special.

CHELAN Cantina Caverna

114 N Emerson St., 98816 **Tel** *(509) 682-5553*   **Road Map** *1 B2*

This local favorite features a long menu of Latin and Mexican fare, such as tacos and burritos, plus many seafood specialties including *arroz con mariscos* (shrimp with rice), and beer-battered steamed clams. The *carne asada* and mustache burger (with pulled pork on top) are popular.

CHELAN Local Myth Pizza

122 S Emerson St., 98816 **Tel** *(509) 682-2914*   **Road Map** *1 B2*

A step up from the usual pizza joint, this funky little pizzeria is always busy in the summer, when locals and tourists pack the resort community of Chelan. Pizzas are thin, with delicious gourmet toppings that include prosciutto, walnuts, and creamy leek sauce. Gluten-free pizzas are also available, as is an extensive drinks menu. Closed Sun lunch.

EASTSOUND Rose's Bakery & Cafe

382 Prune Alley, Eastsound, 98245 **Tel** *(360) 376-5805*   **Road Map** *1 A1*

One of the most popular lunch spots on Orcas Island, Rose's serves a delicious range of salads, sandwiches, thin-crust pizzas and pestos made with organic and locally sourced ingredients wherever possible. The fire-roasted vegetables with pasta and Mediterranean lamb meatloaf sandwiches are a couple of customer favorites.

ELLENSBURG Valley Café

105 W 3rd Ave., 98926 **Tel** *(509) 925-3050*   **Road Map** *1 B2*

Located in the heart of Washington's cowboy country, this charming Art Deco bistro is a gem. The decor is genuine 1930s diner, and the menu of superb dishes made from locally raised meats and produce is enticing; do not miss the local lamb. For those interested in exploring Washington wines, Valley Café has a terrific selection.

FRIDAY HARBOR Duck Soup Inn

50 Duck Soup Lane, 98250 **Tel** *(360) 378-4878*   **Road Map** *1 A1*

In a placid setting by a pond in the woods of San Juan Island, this elegant country restaurant is cozy and romantic, with a fieldstone fireplace. Cuisine is innovative, seasonal Northwest; meat, seafood, herbs, and flowers are local, but the inspiration comes from everywhere. Menus may include scallop sashimi, tandoori quail, or North African lamb tagine.

FRIDAY HARBOR The Place Bar & Grill

1 Spring St., 98250 **Tel** *(360) 378-8707*   **Road Map** *1 A1*

Close to the ferry dock, this small, sophisticated waterfront spot offers exquisite Asian-inflected meals with lovely harbor views. Among the highlights of the menu are the Pacific Rim bouillabaisse with coconut milk and jasmine rice, New Zealand lamb chops with an Indonesian accent, and a mushroom and vegetable stir-fry called "Evil Jungle Prince."

LEAVENWORTH Andreas Keller

829 Front St., 98826 **Tel** *(509) 548-6000*   **Road Map** *1 B2*

This casual, traditional Bavarian-style eatery serves hearty wursts, schnitzel, weinkraut, and other German fare, including rotisserie-broiled pork hock and chicken. Live accordion music adds to the fun atmosphere, and kids are welcome. The wine list is modest and well priced, and the beer list features nearly 20 Bavarian brews.

Key to Price Guide *see p298* **Key to Symbols** *see back cover flap*

LEAVENWORTH Café Mozart

829 Front St., 98826 **Tel** *(509) 548-0600*   **Road Map** 1 B2

Upstairs from Andreas Keller, this elegant spot serves refined Middle-European fare accompanied on weekends by live harp music. The menu features pork, veal, and chicken schnitzels, sauerbraten, and spaetzle, along with roast duck and other hearty dishes. US and European wine list with Washington and Germany especially well represented.

LOPEZ VILLAGE Bay Café

9 Old Post Rd., 98261 **Tel** *(509) 468-3700*   **Road Map** 1 A1

A magnet for epicures from all over the San Juan Islands, with magnificent waterfront views and food to match. Flavor combinations are unusual with dishes drawing on far-flung influences, as in the Malaysian-style seafood curry and rack of lamb with mint-cilantro-basil salsa verde. Dishes are often delightfully garnished with edible flowers.

MAZAMA Freestone Inn

31 Early Winters Dr., 98833 **Tel** *(509) 996-3906*   **Road Map** 1 B2

The mountain views and massive stone hearth are as memorable as the food at this luxury lakeside inn in the North Cascades. The seasonal menu may feature such creative dishes as miso-grilled filet mignon with wasabi mashed potatoes, lemongrass-cured pork tenderloin, or salmon basted with molasses and bourbon.

NAHCOTTA Arrowleaf Bistro

253 Riverside Ave., Winthrop 98862 **Tel** *(509) 996-3919*   **Road Map** 1 B1

This intimate bistro serves locally inspired cuisine with a French twist, using fresh, local, and organic ingredients. Wild mushroom sauté, free-range veal *osso bucco*, and trout *en papillote* are typical of the dishes served. The bistro is located on a main road in Wunthrop, but outdoor seating is available with riverside views.

OLYMPIA The Spar Café

114 4th Ave. E, 98501 **Tel** *(360) 357-6444*   **Road Map** 1 A2

Bought and renovated in 2007 by Portland's McMenamin's chain, the Spar, opened in 1935, has kept its old-time, blue-collar feel. In a handsome, heavily wood-trimmed dining room guests can tuck into burgers, pizzas, salads, and Spar classics like Olympic oyster stew and the "4th Avenue Mess" breakfast. Ales are brewed on the premises.

PORT TOWNSEND Khu Larb Thai

225 Adams St., 98368 **Tel** *(360) 385-5023*   **Road Map** 1 A2

In the heart of historic downtown, this was the first Thai restaurant on the Olympic peninsula and still the standard-bearer. The long menu is particularly strong on seafood and vegetarian dishes, such as mussels with curry paste and stir-fried vegetables with bamboo shoots and Thai basil. Food is served as searingly spicy as you like.

PORT TOWNSEND Silverwater Café

237 Taylor St., 98368 **Tel** *(360) 385-6448*   **Road Map** 1 A2

Using the best of locally harvested products, the kitchen at this airy, mellow spot prepares creative Northwest cuisine with occasional Mediterranean and Asian accents. Outstanding soups and seafood dishes, including ahi with lavender pepper, and prawns with cilantro-ginger-lime butter, are highlights. The Silverwater also sells its own line of spices.

SEAVIEW The Depot Restaurant

1208 38th Pl. & L St., 98644 **Tel** *(360) 642-7880*   **Road Map** 1 A2

As the name suggests, The Depot is housed in a former railroad depot from 1905. Patrons can choose to dine in the casual, intimate interior and the heated outdoor patio. On the menu are elegant entrées (try the sea scallops with mango purée) and comfort food with a unique twist, such as the crab mac and cheese. Open daily for dinner only.

SPOKANE Steam Plant Grill

159 S Lincoln St., 99201 **Tel** *(509) 777-3900*   **Road Map** 1 C2

As the name suggests, this stylish grill is in the striking, unusual location of an old steam and electric plant, complete with towering smokestacks. The scene is vibrant, with power lunches and a bustling bar after work. The menu includes sandwiches, pastas, and creative meat and fish preparations. Coeur d'Alene beers are brewed on the premises.

SPOKANE Wild Sage American Bistro

916 W 2nd Ave., 99201 **Tel** *(509) 456-7575*   **Road Map** 1 C2

Spokane has yet to develop a reputation for fine dining, but the elegant Wild Sage is an auspicious start. This bistro with three separate dining areas serves quality American fare, creatively presented. Some of the top choices include white Cheddar fondue, Brandt Farm steak, and coconut cream layer cake. Open daily for dinner only.

TACOMA Café Divino

2112 N 30th St., 98403 **Tel** *(253) 779-4226*   **Road Map** 1 A2

In historic Old Town Tacoma, a quiet business district abutting Commencement Bay, this is a friendly, unpretentious little spot two blocks from the waterfront. Casual and convivial, it serves a loosely Italian menu ranging from lasagna and *cannelloni* to smoked salmon *quesadillas*, baked brie with pears, and a crab-laden sandwich on focaccia.

TOPPENISH Heritage Inn

100 Spiel-Yi Loop, 98948 **Tel** *(509) 865-2551*   **Road Map** 1 B2

Part of the Yakima Nation Cultural Heritage Center, this unusual restaurant offers American and Native American dishes. Fare may include buffalo steaks and stew, salmon stew, salmon with huckleberry sauce, and huckleberry pie. The menu also includes more familiar items such as teriyaki chicken, crab cakes, and prime rib.

VANCOUVER Beaches Restaurant & Bar ⛱ [V] $$$

1919 SE Columbia River Dr., 98661 ***Tel*** *(360) 699-1592* ***Road Map*** *1 A1*

Fun and family-friendly, this popular beach-themed spot on the north shore of the Columbia River offers steak, seafood, chicken, pasta, and pizza. Among the menu favorites are big salads with chicken and seafood, pizzas from the wood-fired oven, and an extravagant seafood boil. There are fine river views, especially at sunset.

VANCOUVER Hudson's [V] 🍷 $$$

7801 NE Greenwood Dr., 98662 ***Tel*** *(360) 816-6100* ***Road Map*** *1 A1*

In a landscape dominated by chain eateries, Hudson's is a bright spot. Located in the faux-rustic, upscale Heathman Lodge, it offers Northwest seasonal comfort food; most of it is a carnivore's delight – venison, pork prime rib, beef tenderloin, and *osso bucco* are highlights. The wine list is devoted to Washington, Oregon, and California wineries.

WALLA WALLA Olive Marketplace & Café ♫ ⛱ [V] 🍷 $

21 E Main St., 99362 ***Tel*** *(509) 525-0200* ***Road Map*** *1 C3*

Occupying three red-brick storefronts on Main Street, this deli is a great spot for healthy, hearty breakfasts and lunches such as eggs Benedict, cheese blintzes, and hot and cold sandwiches. Also a gourmet grocery with a huge inventory of everything from vinegars and jams to cheeses and bottled sauces, and a full-service bakery.

WALLA WALLA Brasserie Four ♫ ⛱ [V] $$

4 E Main St., 99632 ***Tel*** *(509) 529-2011* ***Road Map*** *1 C3*

With its high ceilings, minimalist decor and casual atmosphere, Brasserie Four's patrons focus on the food. Unusual pizzas (duck or *legume* pizza, for example), tasty French onion soup, wonderful mussels, quiches, and salads are found on the French-inspired menu. The Sunday brunch is popular.

WALLA WALLA Whitehouse-Crawford [V] 🍷 $$$$

55 W Cherry St., 99362 ***Tel*** *(509) 525-2222* ***Road Map*** *1 C3*

In a converted sawmill shared with the barrel room of Seven Hills Winery, this elegant restaurant has helped to transform Walla Walla's culinary culture. Part of an exodus from Seattle's best restaurants, chef Jamie Guerin follows the seasons with his menu and draws heavily on local producers for his ingredients. Even the burgers are first-class.

YAKIMA Café Mélange [V] 🍷 $$$

7 N Front St., 98901 ***Tel*** *(509) 453-0571* ***Road Map*** *1 B2*

Small and understated, and a longtime Yakima favorite. Situated in the North Front Street Historical District, Café Mélange offers a variety of pasta dishes as well as hearty entrées such as beef tenderloin with shiitake mushrooms, veal marsala, and roast duck with marionberry port sauce. The superb wine list features many local producers.

YAKIMA Birchfield Manor Restaurant 🍴 [V] 🍷 $$$$

2018 Birchfield Rd., 98901 ***Tel*** *(509) 452-1960* ***Road Map*** *1 B2*

This stately 1910 farmhouse is home to both luxurious accommodations and luxurious dining. King salmon in puff pastry with Chardonnay sauce is the house specialty; other entrée options on the five-course fixed menu include wild mushroom risotto and roasted rack of lamb with Cabernet sauce. Impressive wine collection.

VANCOUVER

WATERFRONT, GASTOWN, AND CHINATOWN Hon's Wun Tun House [V] $

268 Keefer St., V6A 1X5 ***Tel*** *(604) 688-0871* ***Map*** *3 C3*

Enjoy inexpensive, satisfying food at this large restaurant specializing in Cantonese dishes. The dim sum is extremely popular with the lunchtime crowd. In the evening it is potstickers (steamed dumplings fried on one side) and noodles that are most requested. There are many vegetarian choices as well as exotic meats for the brave.

WATERFRONT, GASTOWN, AND CHINATOWN Kitanoya Guu [V] $

105–375 Water St., V6B 5C6 ***Tel*** *(604) 685-8682* ***Map*** *3 B2*

An informal, energetic Japanese restaurant. Known in Japan as izakaya-style dining, it is similar to a North American neighborhood pub, but instead of wings and nachos, choices include banana tempura, deep-fried brie and mango sauce, and tuna with avocado rolls. It is popular with the young Japanese community and gets noisy later in the evening.

WATERFRONT, GASTOWN, AND CHINATOWN Floata Seafood Restaurant 🍴 [V] $$$

400-180 Keefer St., V6A 4E7 ***Tel*** *(604) 602-0368* ***Map*** *3 C3*

There is plenty of room in this 1,000-seat Chinese restaurant, the largest in Canada. The restaurant is busiest during lunch for dim sum, comprising bite-sized Chinese delicacies wheeled to your table. The emphasis at both lunch and dinner is on seafood, but highlights also include barbecued Peking duck and the dessert buffet bar.

WATERFRONT, GASTOWN, AND CHINATOWN Steamworks Brewing Company ⛱ [V] $$$

375 Water St., V6B 5C6 ***Tel*** *(604) 689-2739* ***Map*** *3 B2*

Housed on two floors of a stone building on the edge of Gastown, this popular spot is best known for its beers which are brewed in-house using underground steam lines as part of the brewing process. The food is also good – beer soup, grilled halibut with ginger curry cream sauce, and seafood crêpes are favorites.

Key to Price Guide *see p298* **Key to Symbols** *see back cover flap*

WATERFRONT, GASTOWN, AND CHINATOWN Water Street Café

300 Water St., V6B 1B6 **Tel** *(604) 689-2832*

Map 3 B2

Across from the steam clock, this intimate, upscale dining room is a pleasant respite from the tourist-clogged streets of Gastown. High ceilings, dark woods, and white tablecloths add to the appeal. Highlights of the Italian-inspired menu include seared sesame-crusted ahi tuna, veal scaloppini, and classic pasta dishes like smoked salmon penne.

DOWNTOWN Diva at the Met

645 Howe St., V6C 2Y9 **Tel** *(604) 602-7788*

Map 3 A2

Part of the stylish Metropolitan Hotel, this well-lit, multi-tiered dining room surrounds an open kitchen where chefs turn organic, local ingredients into modern dishes such as the restaurant's signature smoked Alaskan black cod. Save room for the caramelized Stilton cheesecake. The lounge and patio menu offers a delicious Kobe beef burger.

DOWNTOWN Fleuri

845 Burrard St., V6Z 2K6 **Tel** *(604) 642-2900*

Map 2 F2

Tucked inside the Sutton Place Hotel *(see p291)*, Fleuri is the perfect restaurant for special occasions. Its menu stresses innovative French cooking; highlights include lobster and corn bisque as a starter and seared snapper with prosciutto-wrapped fennel for a main. The adjacent Gerard Lounge is a good place for a pre-dinner drink.

DOWNTOWN Yew Restaurant & Bar

791 W Georgia St., V6C 2T4 **Tel** *(604) 692-4939*

Map 2 F2

Walnut paneling and oak parquet floors provide a quietly dignified setting for fine dining. This restaurant, in the Four Seasons Hotel, offers urban West Coast cuisine with a strong show of seafood. The prix-fixe menu, which is offered between 5 and 10pm daily, is a good deal.

GRANVILLE SOUTH AND YALETOWN Elbow Room

560 Davie St., V6B 2G4 **Tel** *(604) 685-3628*

Map 2 E3

A Vancouver institution, the Elbow Room is known for its service, or, more accurately, the attitude, which you will either love or hate. Ask for coffee and you will be told to get it yourself. The abuse is all in good humor, and if you don't finish your meal, you make a donation to charity.

GRANVILLE SOUTH AND YALETOWN Stepho's

1124 Davie St., V6E 1N1 **Tel** *(604) 683-2555*

Map 2 E3

Both the quality and value of this lively restaurant are excellent. The setting is all Greek – terra-cotta floors, white stucco walls, arched doorways, blue-and-white tablecloths, and lots of colorful flowering plants. Traditional Greek fare, such as the ever-popular *souvlaki* (pork) and roast lamb, is served in generous portions. No reservations.

GRANVILLE SOUTH AND YALETOWN Urban Thai

1119 Hamilton St., V6B 5P6 **Tel** *(604) 408-7788*

Map 2 F4

The menu at this funky spot combines elements of Thai and other Asian spices with Western ingredients, resulting in notable dishes such as *osso bucco* Thai-style and mango and cashew nut stir-fry. More traditional offerings include chicken satay and curries. Lunch specials are a good deal and downtown delivery is free.

GRANVILLE SOUTH AND YALETOWN Blue Water Café

1095 Hamilton St., V6B 5T4 **Tel** *(604) 688-8078*

Map 2 F4

This restaurant, situated in a converted warehouse with exposed brickwork and wooden beams, offers a menu that emphasizes locally harvested wild seafood. The restaurant also features the city's largest selection of oysters, with a menu that explains the subtleties of each source. Save room for a delicious fruit crêpe.

GRANVILLE SOUTH AND YALETOWN C Restaurant

1600 Howe St., V6Z 2L9 **Tel** *(604) 681-1164*

Map 2 D4

One of the city's most innovative and upscale venues for seafood, C presents entrées such as crispy halibut with Quadra Island clams. The 6- or 14-course tasting menus can be paired with local wines for the ultimate seafood splurge and the dining experience is enhanced by the view of False Creek through floor-to-ceiling windows.

FARTHER AFIELD Granville Island Public Market

Johnston St., V6H 3S3 **Tel** *(604) 666-5784*

Map 2 D4

This harborside market is popular with both locals and tourists. Highlights include game such as venison and buffalo, locally harvested seafood, and seasonal fruit and vegetables from Vancouver Island and the Okanagan Valley. Many stalls serve hot food to go, including the Stock Market, renowned for its soups.

FARTHER AFIELD Naam

2724 W 4th Ave., Kitsilano, Vancouver, V6K 1R1 **Tel** *(604) 738-7151*

Road Map 1 A1

One of the only remaining hints of Kitsilano's days as a gathering point for alternative lifestylers in the early 1970s is Naam, the city's oldest vegetarian restaurant. Open 24 hours daily, it is known for large servings, easygoing service, and creative vegetarian dishes. No reservations on weekends.

FARTHER AFIELD Aphrodite's Organic Café and Pie Shop

3598 W 4th Ave., Vancouver, V6R 1N8 **Tel** *(604) 733-8308*

Road Map 1 A1

Featuring locally sourced organic meats, greens, and eggs, brunch is understandably the main attraction at this casual café on busy 4th Avenue, in the Kitsilano neighborhood. Also on the menu are fine pies, quiches, and sandwiches. The local art on the walls and the hip mismatched interior decor help brighten up Vancouver's rainiest day.

FARTHER AFIELD Bridges
1696 Duranleau St., Granville Island, V6H 3S4 **Tel** *(604) 687-4400*   **Map** *2 D4*

This big, bold, canary-yellow building on the edge of Granville Island is difficult to miss. Bridges offers a choice of three dining experiences: a fine dining room upstairs; a more casual bistro downstairs; and a lounge serving selections from local micro-breweries. Tables from the latter two spill onto the wharf.

FARTHER AFIELD Kirin Seafood Restaurant
200 Three West Centre, 7900 Westminster Hwy, Richmond, V6X 1A5 **Tel** *(604) 303-8833*   **Road Map** *1 A1*

Enjoy Cantonese, Shanghai, and Szechuan specialties and award-winning dim sum in this big restaurant filled with traditional decor. Kirin is popular with Chinese families and those on bus tours, and the service is excellent despite the large number of diners. Other city locations include downtown at 1172 Alberni St, (604) 682-8833.

FARTHER AFIELD Pacific Institute of Culinary Arts
1505 West 2nd Ave., V6H 3Y4 **Tel** *(604) 734-4488*   **Map** *2 D5*

Budding chefs studying at the Pacific Institute of Culinary Arts prepare meals for the general public. The quality of the food in relation to price is excellent, with fixed-price, three-course meals offered daily at lunch and dinner. There is a seafood buffet every Friday. Desserts and pastries made by the institute's bakery classes are sold at an adjacent bakery.

FARTHER AFIELD Pair Bistro
3763 W 10th Ave., West Point Grey, Vancouver, V6R 2G5 **Tel** *(604) 224-7211*   **Road Map** *1 A1*

Off the main tourist trail, this small, sophisticated bistro serves indigenous British Columbia cuisine. For a starter, the wild mushroom latte is a real treat. Main meal highlights include slow-braised bison ribs and rosemary-crusted elk medallions, and organic British Columbia ingredients are used where possible. The wine list highlights local wines.

FARTHER AFIELD Hart House Restaurant
6664 Deer Lake Ave., Burnaby, V5E 4H3 **Tel** *(604) 298-4278*   **Road Map** *1 A1*

An ideal venue for a special occasion, this traditional restaurant is within the walls of an old Tudor mansion overlooking a park and lake. Casual yet elegant, it presents a seasonal menu full of West Coast offerings, including halibut, salmon, and pork tenderloin. Reserve a patio table in warmer weather. Closed Monday.

FARTHER AFIELD Raincity Grill
1193 Denman St., Vancouver, V6G 2N1 **Tel** *(604) 685-7337*   **Road Map** *1 A1*

This popular West End fixture with views across to English Bay is known for its commitment to using local produce including seafood, meats, and organic vegetables. The Saltspring Island mussels are a favorite on the appetizer menu, while Fraser Valley pork is consistently good as a main. Try the honey and yogurt cheesecake for dessert.

FARTHER AFIELD The Salmon House
2229 Folkestone Way, West Vancouver V7S 2V6 **Tel** *(604) 926-3212*   **Road Map** *1 A1*

Well worth the effort to find, this restaurant combines traditional Pacific Northwest cuisine with sweeping views across the water from its mountainside location. The seafood chowder is a delicious way to start a meal, while the house specialty of salmon barbecued over an open-flame, alderwood-fired grill is a good choice for a main dish.

FARTHER AFIELD The Teahouse Restaurant
7501 Stanley Park Dr., Vancouver, V6G 3E2 **Tel** *(604) 669-3281*   **Road Map** *1 A1*

For the finest sunset views in the city, reserve an outdoor table at this restaurant overlooking Ferguson Point in Stanley Park. Inside and out, the experience is intimate and stylish, with professional service and a menu of healthy, contemporary cooking. All local game and seafood is represented, including delicious lamb and seasonal wild salmon.

FARTHER AFIELD Tojo's
1133 W Broadway, Vancouver, V6H 1G1 **Tel** *(604) 872-8050*   **Road Map** *1 A1*

Authentic Japanese cuisine and the ultimate in sushi is offered from the hands of owner and master sushi chef Hide-kazu Tojo. Try the fixed-price *omakase*, which literally translates to "chef in your hands" and you will be presented with an imaginative meal prepared especially for your dining party. Dinner only.

FARTHER AFIELD Vij's
1480 W 11th Ave., Vancouver, V6H 1L1 **Tel** *(604) 736-6664*   **Road Map** *1 A1*

Expect queues here, as no reservations are accepted and the food, a Pacific Northwest contemporary adaptation of various East Indian cooking styles, is fabulous. Order curry like no other, such as beef short ribs in cinnamon and red wine curry. Adding to the appeal is a welcoming and tranquil ambience. Dinner only; take-out next door.

FARTHER AFIELD Bishops
2183 W 4th Ave., Vancouver, V6K 1N7 **Tel** *(604) 738-2025*   **Road Map** *1 A1*

Consistently listed as one of the city's top restaurants, Bishops combines intimate dining and flawless service. Organic ingredients determine the West Coast-themed seasonal menu, which changes weekly. Local seafood is well represented, but meats such as duck, pork, and beef also feature. Dinner only. Dress is smart casual.

FARTHER AFIELD CinCin
1154 Robson St., Vancouver, V6E 1B5 **Tel** *(604) 688-7338*   **Road Map** *1 A1*

CinCin's imaginative menu emphasizes wood fire-grilled Italian specialties with other Mediterranean touches. Try the grilled sea bass stuffed with cherry tomatoes, olives, and fennel. The setting is suitably European, with rich-colored furniture and ambient light.

Key to Price Guide *see p298* **Key to Symbols** *see back cover flap*

FARTHER AFIELD West

2881 Granville St., Vancouver, V6H 3J4 **Tel** *(604) 738-8938* **Road Map** *1 A1*

Behind the unassuming doorway on South Granville lies a spacious interior with sleek, geometric decor and a menu featuring classic cooking with a modern twist. Regional fare includes bison, duck, and salmon. The two chef's tables are perfect for watching the kitchen at work. Near the Arts Club Theatre, it is ideal for pre- and post-theater dining.

BRITISH COLUMBIA

COWICHAN BAY The Masthead

1705 Cowichan Bay Rd., V0R 1R0 **Tel** *(250) 748-3714* **Road Map** *2 B5*

This restaurant, housed in the historic 1863 Columbia Hotel, prides itself on a menu built around local produce, seafood, and its selection of British Columbia wines. The rich seafood chowder is justifiably popular while halibut is a reliable main. Its location right on Cowichan Bay provides lovely harbor views.

CRANBROOK Ric's Lounge & Grill

209 Van Horne St. S, V1C 6R9 **Tel** *(250) 417-0444* **Road Map** *2 C4*

Situated inside the Prestige Rocky Mountain Resort and beside the railroad museum, this large restaurant offers a typically wide-ranging hotel menu of salads, steaks, and seafood. The lunchtime menu includes burgers and sandwiches. Adjacent to the restaurant is a pleasant bar with a menu of well-priced pub food.

FERNIE Curry Bowl

931 7th Ave., V0B 1M5 **Tel** *(250) 423-2695* **Road Map** *2 C4*

Ensconced in an unassuming converted bungalow along the main highway through town, the Curry Bowl dishes up delightfully inexpensive Thai, East Indian, and Indonesian cooking. Choices range from simple rice and noodle dishes like *nasi goreng* and pad thai to a mouthwatering mango and shrimp curry.

GALIANO ISLAND Galiano Grand Central Emporium

2740 Sturdies Bay Rd., V0N 1P0 **Tel** *(250) 539-9885* **Road Map** *2 B4*

Open at 7am, this restaurant filled with an eclectic collection of furniture – think bench seats from old school buses – typifies the island's laidback ambience. At breakfast, only free-range eggs are used in the omelets, while the rest of the day, healthy sandwiches made to order are the highlight. Dinner dishes are displayed on a blackboard menu.

GIBSONS Chasters

1532 Ocean Beach Esplanade, V0N 1V5 **Tel** *(604) 886-2887* **Road Map** *2 B4*

Views of the ocean, a beautiful landscaped garden, fresh West Coast cuisine, and a well-thought-out wine list are the main draws at this intimate, casual restaurant on the Sunshine Coast. Start with the pecan-crusted goat's cheese, and continue with the seafood trio. Chasters is located inside the Bonniebrook Lodge. Open for dinner Wed–Sun.

GOLDEN Eagle's Eye Restaurant

1500 Kicking Horse Trail, V0A 1H0 **Tel** *(250) 439-5424* **Road Map** *2 C4*

At an elevation of 2,347 m (7,700 ft), Eagle's Eye is Canada's highest restaurant. Reached by gondola, it is a beautiful timber and stone building with, as you would expect, stunning mountain views. Contemporary Canadian cooking is featured on the thoughtful menu, with the gondola ride included in some lunch and dinner dining packages.

KAMLOOPS Chapters Viewpoint

610 W Columbia St., V2C 1L1 **Tel** *(250) 374-3224* **Road Map** *2 B4*

This casual restaurant delivers on the views of the Kamloops landscape implied by its name. The menu features steaks, seafood, and dishes incorporating Navajo and Mexican flavors. The Macho Nachos are a popular starter to share while slow-roasted prime rib is a favorite main. Chapters is open for breakfast, lunch, and dinner.

KELOWNA Hanna's Waterfront Lounge & Grill

1352 Water St., V1Y 9P4 **Tel** *(250) 860-1266* **Road Map** *2 B4*

Hanna's offers standard, down-to-earth North American fare – pasta, pizza, steaks, and seafood – in a casual, family-friendly environment. The wine list leans heavily toward local producers. There are great views of Lake Okanagan from the elevated patio, making this a popular destination in summer.

KELOWNA Old Vines Restaurant

3303 Boucherie Rd., V1Z 2H3 **Tel** *(250) 769-2500* **Road Map** *2 B4*

At Quail's Gate Estate Winery, high above the sparkling water of Okanagan Lake, a small stone cottage with a large patio serves as a restaurant for vineyard visitors. The menu is filled with light, contemporary choices such as prawn fettuccine, and asparagus and wild mushroom risotto, all easily paired with wines by the glass.

NANAIMO Wesley Street Café

321 Wesley St., V9R 2T5 **Tel** *(250) 753-6057* **Road Map** *2 B4*

One of a cluster of historic buildings in the natural amphitheater sloping down to Nanaimo Harbour, this low-key yet intimate restaurant dishes up classic entrées with contemporary flavors, such as yam-crusted salmon filet. Local and organic ingredients are used whenever possible on a menu that changes weekly. Closed Sun and Mon.

NELSON Vienna Café
411 Kootenay St., V1L 1K7 **Tel** *(250) 354-4646*   **Road Map** *2 C4*

One of the best places to soak up Nelson's easy-going nature is the casual Vienna Café, where tables are surrounded by the used books within Packrat Annie's Bookstore. The menu is simple and inexpensive, with healthy drinks made to order, a delicious free-range chicken burger, and fresh soups created daily.

NELSON All Seasons Café
620 Herridge Lane, V1L 6A7 **Tel** *(250) 352-0101*   **Road Map** *2 C4*

This comfortable, busy restaurant featuring a tree-canopied patio with its own herb garden is found in a restored heritage cottage on a downtown back alley. Its diverse, West Coast menu changes seasonally, but may include caramelized butternut squash fettuccine or rack of venison grilled with a port demi-glaze. Dinner only.

PARKSVILLE Cedar Dining Room
1155 Resort Dr., V9P 2E5 **Tel** *(250) 248-2072*   **Road Map** *2 B4*

This beautiful dining room at beachfront Tigh-Na-Mara Resort is decorated in stylish earthy tones. Breakfast offers a better-than-average selection, including poached eggs on a crab and shrimp cake. The best way to try a selection of local seafood is with a mixed grill. Other choices include mint and garlic crusted rack of lamb.

PENTICTON Bogner's of Penticton
302 W Eckhardt Ave., V2A 2A9 **Tel** *(250) 493-2711*   **Road Map** *2 B4*

Located in a charming, wood-sided 1915 heritage house, this restaurant boasts crystal glassware and white linen on the table. The menu is mostly European, with dishes such as filet mignon, NY steak, and roasted duck breast. This romantic venue is good for a special occasion. Not wheelchair accessible. Dinner only. Closed Sun–Tue.

PRINCE GEORGE The Twisted Cork
1157 5th Ave., V2L 3L1 **Tel** *(250) 561-5550*   **Road Map** *2 B3*

A solid brick and stone exterior with a tastefully decorated interior is the setting for this popular restaurant. Fresh, locally sourced ingredients are used in delicious dishes such as bison and Guinness pie, wild British Columbia salmon, and halibut baked on a cedar plank.

PRINCE RUPERT Cow Bay Café
205 Cow Bay Rd., V8J 1A2 **Tel** *(250) 627-1212*   **Road Map** *2 A3*

Book ahead at this small 32-seat restaurant, where tables spill out onto the Prince Rupert Harbour dock. Enjoy a front-row view of the busy waterway and a menu that changes daily. The menu is mostly dependent on the seafood and produce available locally. Notables include crab cakes and various home-made desserts.

QUALICUM BEACH Beach House Café
2775 W Island Hwy., V9K 2C4 **Tel** *(250) 752-9626*   **Road Map** *2 B4*

This popular restaurant is well situated for viewing beautiful sunsets over the water, but unlike the name suggests, there is no beach. The varied menu features dishes touched with Asian and German flavors, all served in the bright, airy dining room or on the inviting patio. Seafood dominates the appetizer menu, while main meals cover all bases.

REVELSTOKE Woolsey Creek Bistro
604 2nd St. W., V0E 2S0 **Tel** *(250) 837-5500*   **Road Map** *2 C4*

A popular gathering spot for locals in a town renowned for its outdoor recreation opportunities. The menu reflects the attitude of its customers, with strong coffee concoctions, inexpensive breakfasts, and healthy cooking such as seafood paella. The prices are also attractive, with all entrées under $20. Make reservations for weekend evenings.

SALT SPRING ISLAND Hastings House
160 Upper Ganges Rd., V8K 2S2 **Tel** *(250) 537-2362*   **Road Map** *2 B4*

A daily-changing, three-course regional menu is offered for dinner in the formal, wood-beamed dining room of this manor overlooking Ganges Harbour. Salt Spring Island lamb is a house specialty; vegetables, herbs, and fruit are grown on the property. One of the feature wines is produced organically on the island. Closed mid-Nov–mid-Mar.

SOOKE Sooke Harbour House
1528 Whiffen Spit Rd. **Tel** *(250) 642-3421*   **Road Map** *2 B5*

If you are planning one splurge while in British Columbia, make reservations at Sooke Harbour House. The four-course set menu, based strictly on wild seafood, free-range meat, and organic produce, has made this restaurant a frequent award winner. Stunningly located at a hotel of the same name *(see p295)* with sweeping water views.

SUMMERLAND Cellar Door Bistro
17403 Hwy 97 N., V0H1Z0 **Tel** *(250) 494-0451*   **Road Map** *2 B4*

This bistro, located in the Sumac Ridge Estate Winery, expertly pairs Okanagan wines with regional cuisine, including a tasty split pea soup and a daily pasta special. Other highlights include locally produced cheeses and its pastas and ice creams, made in-house. Open for lunch and dinner Apr–Oct. Winery tours available.

TERRACE Don Diego's
3212 Kalum St., V8G 2M9 **Tel** *(250) 635-2307*   **Road Map** *2 A3*

In a northern town not known for its cuisine, Don Diego's is a pleasant surprise. It is a busy, brightly painted restaurant, with a patio perfectly situated to catch the evening sun. For lunch, try the shrimp crêpes. In the evening, stick to Mexican offerings that change daily, mostly dependent on what produce is available.

Key to Price Guide *see p298* **Key to Symbols** *see back cover flap*

TOFINO The Pointe

500 Osprey Lane, Chesterman's Beach, V0R 2Z1 **Tel** *(250) 725-3100*   **Road Map** *2 A4*

This upscale, atmospheric dining room in the Wickaninnish Inn *(see p295)* has a grand circular fireplace and is famed for panoramic ocean views. Dungeness crab is popular on a menu that also includes freshly shucked oysters, black cod, halibut, and seasonal venison. At breakfast, the citrus Belgian waffle will set you up for a day of beachcombing.

UCLUELET Matterson House Restaurant

1682 Peninsula Rd., V0R 3A0 **Tel** *(250) 726-2200*   **Road Map** *2 A4*

This small, charming restaurant is located in a historic house along the main road through town. Always busy, it serves a variety of breakfast, lunch, and dinner selections. Seafood dishes and in-house baked desserts and pastries are the specialties on offer, with the creamy seafood chowder a popular choice at lunch.

VERNON Blue Heron Waterfront Pub & Restaurant

7673 Okanagan Landing Rd., V1H 1G9 **Tel** *(250) 542-5550*   **Road Map** *2 C4*

Even though it is outside city limits, the short drive to the Blue Heron is worthwhile for the sweeping lake views and relaxed ambience of this waterfront eatery. Choices run from pub staples like shepherd's pie and fish and chips to an oversized New York steak. Patio tables are most popular, with heat lamps allowing outside dining in cooler weather.

VICTORIA Barb's Place

Fisherman's Wharf, Erie St., V8V 1Y4 **Tel** *(250) 384-6515*   **Road Map** *2 B5*

With open-air dining at picnic tables set along a dock and surrounded by floating homes, Barb's is a favorite for fish and chips. It is well worth paying extra for halibut rather than the standard cod. On occasion, seals wait for handouts from diners. An enjoyable way to reach Barb's is by ferry from the Inner Harbour. Open Mar–Oct.

VICTORIA The Flying Otter Grill

950 Wharf St., V8W 1T3 **Tel** *(250) 414-4220*   **Road Map** *2 B5*

Open for breakfast, lunch, and dinner, this floating pub-style restaurant offers superb views of Victoria's bustling Inner Harbour. The ambience is casual, and the menu has a West Coast flavor, with an emphasis on fish, seafood, and fresh salads. It also serves great mojitos and margaritas.

VICTORIA Camille's

45 Bastion Sq., V8W 1J1 **Tel** *(250) 381-3433*   **Road Map** *2 B5*

A historic brick building houses this charming, romantic two-room restaurant. The diverse, often changing menu could feature locally raised seafood like mussels and salmon, or game such as venison and elk. In winter, bison and wild boar are specialties. Much produce is sourced from Vancouver Island farms. Wines are extremely well priced.

VICTORIA Il Terrazzo

555 Johnson St., V8W 1M2 **Tel** *(250) 361-0028*   **Road Map** *2 B5*

Tucked away down a narrow alley, this well-known restaurant is set in an original 1890s building. It offers northern Italian cuisine such as veal marsala and grilled baby squid, as well as wood-fired-oven specialties. The slow-braised *osso buco* is a good choice for hearty appetites. Brick fireplaces warm the courtyard terrace.

VICTORIA Pescatore's Seafood & Grill

614 Humboldt St., V8W 1A4 **Tel** *(250) 385-4512*   **Road Map** *2 B5*

Located on Victoria's Inner Harbour, Pescatore's takes full advantage of the sea's bounty. It offers fresh seafood dishes including home-made seafood antipasti, cedar plank roasted salmon, crab cakes, and live lobster. The well-stocked oyster bar is where many diners look for their starters. Brunch is served from 11am on weekends.

VICTORIA Empress Room

721 Government St., V8W 1W5 **Tel** *(250) 389-2727*   **Road Map** *2 B5*

Enjoy the sumptuous interior and an impressive menu – a modern fusion of classic cuisine with Pacific Northwest influences – at this fine-dining venue in the Fairmont Empress *(see p295)*. In summer, the most sought-after tables are on the covered veranda. Breakfast is a casual affair, but jeans and t-shirts are not permitted at lunch or dinner.

WHISTLER Ciao-Thyme Bistro

2–4573 Chateau Blvd., V0N 1B4 **Tel** *(604) 932-7051*   **Road Map** *2 B4*

This bright café dedicated to fresh organic foods is best known as a breakfast spot, with regulars recommending the omelets made from free-range eggs. Pecan cinnamon buns are also popular. For the rest of the day, it's light, healthy eating, including lots of creative salads to choose from. Busy during the summer months.

WHISTLER Trattoria di Umberto Restaurant

4417 Sundial Pl., V0N 1B4 **Tel** *(604) 932-5858*   **Road Map** *2 B4*

The warmth of Tuscany is reflected in celebrity chef and Vancouver native Umberto Menghi's inviting decor. Delicious pasta choices such as the simple *spaghetti alla amatriciana* are well priced while other highlights include Tuscan bean minestrone, veal shanks, oven-roasted rack of lamb, and poached black cod.

YOHO NATIONAL PARK Truffle Pig's Bistro

318 Stephen St., Field, V0A 1G0 **Tel** *(250) 343-6303*   **Road Map** *2 C4*

Inside Yoho's only general store, behind racks of groceries and with tables spilling onto the sidewalk, is a friendly little restaurant with remarkably good food. Breakfast and lunch options, described on a blackboard, include sandwiches and quiche. Enticing dinner choices include Albertan-raised buffalo ribeye steak. Closed for dinner Oct–May.

SHOPPING IN
THE PACIFIC NORTHWEST

Shop sign in Bellingham's
Fairhaven District

Downtown districts in the Pacific Northwest provide everything from the luxury goods offered by exclusive stores to bargains that can be picked up in flea markets. Outdoor gear manufactured by world-renowned local companies is popular. Shoppers can also purchase footwear and clothing to suit every taste; many secondhand shops sell vintage clothing and accessories. Other items to shop for are antiques, books, and music from the chain stores and independents; fresh produce; smoked Pacific salmon; and first-class wines. Native American and First Nations jewelry, carvings, paintings, and other handicrafts and artwork are sold throughout the region in specialty shops, cultural centers, and galleries. Delicious Canadian maple syrup is widely available in British Columbia.

Store window filled with antiques in Portland's Sellwood District

SHOPPING HOURS

Stores are generally open seven days a week. Standard hours are from 9 or 10am to 6pm, though many stores and malls remain open until 9pm on certain nights. Sunday hours are usually noon to 5pm. Smaller stores often open at 10am, close at 6pm, and are closed on Sundays or Mondays. The busiest shopping days of the week are Fridays and weekends.

SALES

Local newspapers are a good source of information on upcoming sales. End-of-season sales can offer as much as 70 percent off the regular price. In the days – and in some cases, weeks – following Christmas, many stores offer huge discounts and specials.

PAYMENT

Most stores accept all major credit cards, with Visa and MasterCard being the most popular. "Direct payment" with bank debit cards at point-of-sale terminals are also widely used. Traveler's checks are readily accepted with proper identification, such as a valid passport or a driver's license.

Hat store at Vancouver's Granville Island, one of many specialty shops

In most US stores, foreign currency is not accepted, whereas many Canadian stores will accept both US and Canadian currencies. However, the exchange rate offered by stores is generally substantially lower than what a bank or currency exchange office will give so it is best to change any currency you have in advance. Personal checks are rarely accepted.

SALES TAX

Sales taxes vary depending on which state or province you are visiting, and in the US they can vary depending on where you are within a state. In Washington, taxes are in the 8 to 9 percent range (with Seattle's at 8.9 percent), though groceries are exempt. Out-of-state or foreign visitors to Seattle

Glasshouse, Seattle's oldest glassblowing studio, at Pioneer Square

who have no sales tax at home are exempt, provided they show ID such as a valid driver's license. In Oregon, there is no sales tax. In British Columbia, a 7 percent provincial sales tax (PST) and a 6 percent federal Goods and Service Tax (GST) apply to most goods; the major exception is basic food items. Taxes are usually added to the price at the time of purchase, so price tags rarely include taxes.

RETURNS

Be sure you understand the store's return policy before you pay. Each store sets its own return and exchange policies, which are generally to be found posted at the cash register. Some stores offer full refunds, while others maintain an all-sales-final policy or give an in-shop credit note rather than a refund.

Keep your receipt as a proof of purchase, should you decide to return the item or find that it is in some way defective. Sale items are usually not returnable.

Fruit stall at Granville Island's public market, Vancouver

MARKETS

Farmers' markets held in cities and rural communities across the Pacific Northwest sell locally grown fruits and vegetables. Apples, apricots, plums, cherries, berries, tomatoes, and zucchini are common offerings. Some markets also sell seafood, baked goods, flowers, crafts, and locally made souvenirs.

Markets range from large and sheltered, such as Granville Island Public Market (see

Wine shop at Chateau Ste. Michelle, one of Washington's top vineyards

p219) in Vancouver and Pike Place Market (see pp132–5) in Seattle, to medium-sized open-air markets, such as the Saturday Market in Portland's Old Town District (see pp52–3), to small markets consisting of a few trucks parked in a lot or field. Many of the seafood merchants at these markets, particularly larger ones, will ship fresh fish to your home.

Most of the larger markets are open year round, whereas many of the smaller markets may be seasonal, running from early spring to late fall.

OUTLET STORES

Shoppers can find great bargains at outlet malls, sometimes saving as much as 70 percent off the regular price.

Oregon is home to the Columbia Gorge Factory Stores, east of Portland in Troutdale. Tanger Factory Outlet Center, the largest in the Pacific Northwest, offers tax-free shopping. Washington's 50-store Premium Outlets at North Bend is located east of Seattle.

British Columbia's outlet centers include the Roots and Danier Leather factory outlets in Coquitlam and New Westminster, just east of Vancouver.

FINE WINES

The Pacific Northwest produces world-class rieslings, pinot noirs and chardonnays, as well as dessert wines, such as late harvest wines and flavorful icewines made from grapes that are picked and

crushed while frozen. Pinot gris and pinot blanc are also becoming increasingly important varieties.

Hundreds of wineries in Oregon's Willamette Valley (see pp98–9), Washington's Yakima Valley (see p191), the greater Puget Sound area, and British Columbia's Okanagan Valley (see pp258–9) offer guided tours and wine tastings. Most of the wineries also sell directly to the public.

Winegrowers' associations in Oregon, Washington, and British Columbia provide visitors with maps and guides to regional wineries, as well as information about special events, such as Washington Wine Month (March), the Oregon Wine and Art Auction, and the Okanagan Fall Wine Festival, in British Columbia.

Kite store to suit all tastes and winds, Lincoln City, Oregon

Outdoor Activities

The dramatically varied terrain and beautiful land-scapes of the Pacific Northwest make it an ideal region for a wide range of outdoor activities, from such peaceful pursuits as bird-watching, whale-watching, hiking, and fishing to more exhilarating sports such as skiing, snowboarding, scuba diving, and white-water rafting. For information about particular activities, equipment rentals, instruction, and guided tours, contact the state or provincial tourist offices.

Dune buggies on Oregon's sand dunes, near Florence

Kite-boarding on the Hood River, off the Columbia River Gorge

ADVENTURE SPORTS

The dramatic landscape of the Pacific Northwest offers countless possibilities for thrill-seekers, such as hang gliding, paragliding, kite-boarding, hot-air ballooning, and sky-diving, to name just a few.

In Oregon, both Lakeview, in the south, and Cape Kiwanda, in the north, provide ideal conditions for hang gliding and paragliding, as does **Lake Chelan** in Washington. In British Columbia, the most popular spot for these sports is Malahat, north of Victoria, offering spectacular views of the Saanich Peninsula and Strait of Georgia. For more information about hang gliding and paragliding in BC, contact the **Hang Gliding and Paragliding Association of Canada**.

Hot-air ballooning offers another exciting way to get a bird's-eye view of the region. To float over Oregon's wine country in a balloon, contact **Vista Balloon Adventures**. In Washington, you can take a balloon ride over the Methow Valley and enjoy a champagne brunch with **Morning Glory Balloon Tours**, or fly over the Woodinville area vineyards with **Over the Rainbow**.

BEACHES

The shorelines of the Pacific Northwest are among the most scenic in the world. Although the waters are generally cool, swimming offers refreshment during the summer months.

The **Oregon Dunes National Recreation Area**, between Florence and Coos Bay, comprises 32,000 acres (12,800 ha) of huge sand dunes, some more than 500 ft (150 m) tall. Higher than those of the Sahara Desert, these steep dunes are ideal for sandboarding. The Umpqua Scenic Dunes Trail, 30 miles (48 km) south of Florence and approximately 1 mile (1.6 km) long, skirts the tallest dunes in the area. Enjoy the breathtaking views from the boardwalk's over-look, located 24 miles (39 km) north of North Bend.

Oregon's top beaches include Bandon, **Oswald West State Park**, Cannon Beach, **Sunset Bay State Park** beaches, and the beaches of the **Samuel H. Boardman State Scenic Corridor**.

Deception Pass State Park beaches, in the Puget Sound area, are located in Washington's most popular state park. A 15-minute drive from downtown Seattle, **Alki Beach** (see p159) offers a panoramic view of the city's skyline and of Elliott Bay. Other particularly beautiful beaches in Washington include Dungeness Spit, the longest saltwater sand spit in North America, and the sandy and cliff-lined beaches in **Olympic National Park**.

In British Columbia, among the beaches that dot Vancouver's shoreline the most popular are English Bay, Sunset (see p220), Kitsilano, Jericho, Locarno, Spanish Banks, and the Second and Third Beaches in Stanley Park (see pp226–7). Visitors are also drawn to the tranquil and beautiful shores of the Gulf Islands (see p255).

Sunbathers at Kitsilano Beach on English Bay, Vancouver

Sandboarding at Oregon Dunes National Recreation Area

BIRD-WATCHING

Throughout the year, bird-watchers are able to sight gulls, sandpipers, plovers, and ducks along the coasts of Oregon and Washington, while British Columbia boasts important migration habitats for water-fowl, shorebirds, and hawks. Contact the local **Audubon Society** chapter for more information about birds and the many superb birding spots in the Pacific Northwest, such as Oregon's **Malheur National Wildlife Refuge** and **Ten Mile Creek Sanctuary**, Washington's Skagit River, and the **George C. Reifel Migratory Bird Sanctuary** in British Columbia.

CAMPING

There are numerous campsites tucked away in wilderness areas, close to cities, and near beaches. All of the region's national parks and most state and provincial parks offer excellent campgrounds.

In the high country, camp-grounds are usually open from mid-June through August, and in lower elevations year-round. Space in most parks is available on a first-come, first-served basis. To reserve a spot in a state park in Oregon, call **Reservations Northwest**; in Washington, call **Washington State Parks**. In Canada, call **Parks Canada**, or to book a place in one of British Columbia's provincial parks, contact the reservation service that is run by **Discover Camping**.

CANOEING AND KAYAKING

Canoeing and kayaking are both easy and environmentally friendly ways of seeing the Pacific Northwest's beautiful waters along with its abundant marine life.

Washington's Puget Sound and San Juan Islands are the most popular destinations for sea kayakers in the Pacific Northwest. White-water kayakers flock to the state's many rivers, and Lake Ozette in **Olympic National Park** is a hot spot for canoeists.

Off Oregon, the ocean's waters are generally too rough for kayaking, but the bays along the coast and the Lewis and Clark National Wildlife Refuge, on the Columbia River, provide calmer waters for paddlers. For listings of canoe and kayak outfitters in the US, visit the **Arcadian Outdoor Guide** website.

For information about many canoeing and kayaking destinations in British Columbia, contact the **Recreational Canoeing Association of BC**.

White-water kayaking on the fast-moving McKenzie River in Oregon

CAVING

Whether you are an experienced caver or simply interested in venturing into tubes of lava and limestone, there are thousands of caving possibilities in the region. Among the most popular are the Oregon Caves National Monument, Lava River Caves, and Sea Lion Caves in Oregon; Washington's Gardner Cave; and British Columbia's Cody and Horne Lake Caves.

Caves are largely unaffected by the climate outdoors, so although it may be warm outside, temperatures inside average 50°F (10°C) year-round. Be sure to wear warm clothing and comfortable footwear. For new information about exploring the caves of the Pacific Northwest, contact the **Cave Guiding Association of BC** or the **National Caves Association**.

Mountain biking near Kamloops, in British Columbia's Interior

CYCLING AND ROLLERBLADING

Cycling is an inexpensive and healthy way of traveling around the cities and country-side of the Pacific Northwest. Most of the parks in the region have designated cycling trails as well as rental outlets for equipment; Portland, Seattle, Vancouver, and many other large cities have cycling paths.

Several companies offer long-distance cycling tours in the region. **Bicycle Adventures** offers tours through Oregon, Washington, and Western Canada. Contact state and provincial tourist offices for details on tour

Rollerbladers, cyclists, and walkers at Green Lake, Seattle

operators. For maps of cycling trails in Washington, contact the **Bicycle Hot Line** and for maps and general information about cycling in British Columbia, contact **Cycling BC**. Most local tourist offices and bike rental shops will also have information about cycling and rollerblading.

Bicycles for rent at Friday Harbor, on Washington's San Juan Island

ECOTOURISM

Several companies organize eco-tours, allowing travelers to enjoy the natural beauty of the Pacific Northwest's landscape while respecting local communities and the environment. Guided wilderness cruises, kayak tours around Washington's San Juan Islands, and llama treks through Silver Falls State Park in Salem, Oregon are among some of the ecotours available. Eco-friendly tours are increasingly popular with visitors and if you want to learn about the impact of

tourism, or obtain information about ecologically and socially responsible travel options, contact the **International Ecotourism Society**.

FISHING

The Pacific Northwest is a paradise for fishing enthusiasts. Pacific salmon, steel-head, perch, bass, trout, halibut, and sturgeon are among the region's catches.

For information on freshwater fishing in the US, contact the **Washington Department of Fish and Wildlife** or the **Oregon Department of Fish and Wildlife**. Most visitors' centers and fishing shops also provide details of local regulations.

In Canada, contact the **Sport Fishing Institute** for information about sport-fishing, and **Fisheries and Oceans Canada** for information on saltwater fishing licenses.

Fishing for trout in Oregon's peaceful McKenzie River Valley

GOLFING

Within the Pacific Northwest, golfers can choose from golf courses with scenic back-drops of mountain vistas, coastal views, or cityscapes. Because of the mild climate, you can golf all year-round in many areas of the region.

Most of Oregon's golf courses are clustered in the areas around Portland and Bend-Redmond; there are also several along the coast. While a few of Washington's resorts maintain private courses, most of its cities offer public ones. British Columbia has more than 200 golf courses, from par 3s to 18-hole championship courses. To obtain listings of both private and public courses, contact state, provincial, or local tourism offices.

Golfers on one of the many courses in the Pacific Northwest

HIKING

Hiking trails leading over mountains, through meadows and forests, and along seashores offer nature-lovers everything from strenuous climbs to leisurely strolls. All the national, state, and provincial parks have well-marked trails of varying levels of difficulty. Visitors' centers and the **American Hiking Society** are good sources of information about hiking. The **Pacific Northwest Trail Association** offers information about the scenic 1,200-mile (1,931-km) trail, which runs from the Continental Divide to the Pacific Ocean.

Most of the more popular hikes in the Pacific Northwest require minimal preparation, but if you intend to venture into little-known territory, plan to travel with a trained guide.

ROCK CLIMBING AND MOUNTAINEERING

The Pacific Northwest's Cascade, Coast, and Rocky Mountain systems offer innumerable possibilities for rock climbing and mountaineering.

In Oregon, **Timberline Mountain Guides** offer instruction and guided climbs on rock, snow, and ice. Rock climbers will want to visit the world-renowned Smith Rocks State Park, near Redmond, to check out its 1,300 climbing routes, some of which are the toughest in the world.

Visitors to Washington can hire a guide or take lessons from outfits such as **North Cascades Mountain Guides** and **Rainier Mountaineering**. The **Peshastin Pinnacles State Park** was created especially for rock climbers.

For information about climbing and mountaineering in British Columbia, contact the **Federation of Mountain Clubs of BC** or **BC Parks**.

Sailboats on Burrard Inlet, with West Vancouver in the background

WATERSPORTS

The Pacific coastline and the rivers and lakes of the Pacific Northwest attract enthusiasts of white-water rafting, scuba diving, swimming, boating, surfing, and windsurfing.

White-water rafting is one of the region's most popular sports, especially in the waters of the Cascades range. Destinations in Oregon include the Deschutes, Snake, and John Day Rivers; in Washington, the Wenatchee, Skykomish, and Methow Rivers; and in British Columbia, the Mackenzie River system. Basic training courses

Windsurfers on Hood River, near Oregon's Columbia River Gorge

are usually available for inexperienced rafters. To book a rafting trip in the US, contact **River Riders** or **Wildwater River Tours** in Washington. To find out about BC's outfitters, contact **BC Parks**. **Wedge Rafting** offers rafting as well as jet-boating tours that whisk passengers close to waterfalls.

The coasts of the Pacific Northwest, and of Puget Sound and the San Juan Islands in particular, offer scuba divers thousands of miles of ocean flora and fauna. Visit **3 Routes** on the Internet to access comprehensive scuba diving directories for Oregon, Washington, and British Columbia. There are also many prime surfing spots along the Pacific coast, through the Strait of Juan de Fuca, and around the San Juan Islands.

For windsurfers, the Columbia River Gorge, a stretch of the Columbia River which forms a natural divide between Oregon and Washington, offers ideal conditions and beautiful scenery. The popular Columbia Gorge Sailpark in Oregon has a large shallow area for beginners. British Columbia's best windsurfing is near the town of Squamish, a Coast Salish

word meaning "strong wind." The sport is also popular on the Sunshine Coast, in White Rock, and at Jericho Beach in Vancouver.

WHALE-WATCHING

Whale-watching is one of the most popular outdoor activities in the Pacific Northwest, particularly during the spring and summer. An offshore show, courtesy of more than 20,000 gray whales that migrate every year from Alaska to California and Mexico, can be seen from boats or from the shores of the Pacific Ocean in Oregon, Washington, and British Columbia. A number of charter companies run whale-watching cruises.

The best vantage points in Oregon include Cape Meares, Cape Lookout, Cape Kiwanda, Devil's Punchbowl, Cape Perpetua, Sea Lion Caves, Shore Acres State Park, Face Rock Wayside, Cape Blanco, Cape Sebastian, and Harris Beach State Park.

In Washington, orcas swim around the San Juan Islands and in the waters off Puget Sound; San Juan Island's **Lime Kiln Point State Park** is the only park in the US dedicated to whale-watching.

In British Columbia, of the dozens of companies that organize boat tours, most are Victoria-based. Both **Seacoast Expeditions** and **Five-Star Whale Watching** aim to minimize the negative impact of tourism on the whale populations. The shores of Vancouver Island's **Pacific Rim National Park Reserve** are world-famous for whale-watching.

White-water rafting the Nahatlatch River in southwestern British Columbia

WINTER SPORTS

The Pacific Northwest boasts some of the world's best snowboarding and downhill and cross-country skiing. Oregon's Mount Bachelor offers some of the best skiing in the US, and in the summer, you can snow ski down Mount Hood at Timberline Lodge, where the US Olympic Team practices. Most of Washington's 16 ski areas are in the Cascade Mountains, at locations such as Mount Baker, Stevens Pass, and Crystal Mountain *(see p186)*, though there are also a number of smaller ski areas in the eastern part of the state. In British Columbia, Whistler *(see pp256–7)* delights skiers with North America's longest vertical run, 7,000 acres (2,800 ha) of ski and snowboard terrain, more than 200 trails, and 12 alpine bowls. For details, contact **Tourism Whistler**.

In addition to snowboarding and skiing, other popular winter sports include ice skating, dogsledding, snowshoeing, snowmobiling, and heli-skiing (being lifted by helicopter to backcountry peaks for skiing or boarding off the beaten track).

SAFETY MEASURES

Both grizzly and black bears live in the national parks of the BC Rockies. Although bear sightings are rare, visitors

Snowboarding the challenging Mount Hood Meadows, in Oregon

DIRECTORY

ADVENTURE SPORTS

Hang Gliding and Paragliding Association of Canada
Tel *(877) 370-2078.*
www.hpac.ca

Lake Chelan
www.chelanflyers.com

Morning Glory Balloon Tours
Tel *(509) 997-1700.*
www.balloon
winthrop.com

Over the Rainbow
Tel *(425) 861-8611.*
www.letsgo
ballooning.com

Vista Balloon Adventures
Tel *(503) 625-7385.*
www.vistaballoon.com

BEACHES

Alki Beach
Tel *(206) 684-4075.*
www.seattle.gov

Cannon Beach
Tel *(503) 436-2623.*
www.cannonbeach.org

Deception Pass State Park
Tel *(360) 902-8844.*
www.parks.wa.gov

Olympic National Park
Tel *(360) 565-3130.*
www.nps.gov

Oregon Dunes National Recreation Area
Tel *(541) 750-7000.*
www.fs.fed.us

Oswald West State Park
Tel *(800) 551-6949.*
www.oregon.gov

Samuel H. Boardman State Scenic Corridor
Tel *(800) 551-6949.*
www.oregon.gov

Sunset Bay State Park
Tel *(800) 551-6949.*
www.oregon.gov

BIRD-WATCHING

Audubon Society
Tel *(800) 542-2748.*
www.audubon.org

George C. Reifel Migratory Bird Sanctuary
Tel *(604) 946-6980.*
www.reifelbird
sanctuary.com

Malheur National Wildlife Refuge
Tel *(541) 493-2612.*
www.fws.gov

Ten Mile Creek Sanctuary
Tel *(541) 547-4227.*

CAMPING

Discover Camping
Tel *(519) 826-6850*
or *(800) 689-9025.*
www.discovercamping.ca

Parks Canada
Tel *(888) 773-8888.*
www.pc.gc.ca

Reservations Northwest
Tel *(800) 452-5687.*
www.oregon.gov

Washington State Parks
Tel *Reservations:*
(888) 226-7688.
www.parks.wa.gov

CANOEING AND KAYAKING

Arcadian Outdoor Guide
www.thetent.com

Olympic National Park
See *Beaches.*

Recreational Canoeing Association of BC
Tel *(250) 592-4170.*
www.bccanoe.com

CAVING

Cave Guiding Association of BC
Tel *(250) 283-7144.*

National Caves Association
Tel *(573) 836-2256.*
www.cavern.com

CYCLING

Bicycle Adventures
Tel *(425) 250-5540.*
www.bicycleadventures.com

Bicycle Hot Line
(Washington)
Tel *(360) 705-7277.*

Cycling BC
Tel *(604) 988-7783.*
www.ccnbikes.com

should observe the rules posted at campgrounds. A leaflet published by Parks Canada, entitled "You are in Bear Country," gives safety tips for encounters with bears. The fundamental rules are: do not approach the animals, never feed them, and do not run. Bears have an excellent sense of smell, so when camping, be sure to store food or trash properly, inside a car or in the bear-proof boxes provided.

While less alarming, insects can be irritating. Take all possible measures to repel black-flies and mosquitos. Do not drink stream or river water without thoroughly boiling it first, as it may contain parasites.

When camping and hiking, be sure to bring a map, compass, flashlight, or headlamp with spare bulbs and batteries; sunglasses and sunscreen; a first-aid kit, including anti-histamines and bug repel-lent; a pocketknife; matches kept in a waterproof container, and a fire starter.

Sailing gear with flashlight, pocketknife, and other safety accessories

DIRECTORY

ECOTOURISM

International Ecotourism Society
Tel (202) 506-5033.
www.ecotourism.org

FISHING

Fisheries and Oceans Canada
Tel (613) 993-0999.
www.dfo-mpo.gc.ca

Oregon Department of Fish and Wildlife
Tel (503) 947-6000.
www.dfw.state.or.us

Sport Fishing Institute
Tel (604) 270-3439.
www.sportfishing.bc.ca

Washington Department of Fish and Wildlife
Tel (360) 902-2200.
www.wdfw.wa.gov

HIKING

American Hiking Society
Tel (301) 565-6704.
www.americanhiking.org

Pacific Northwest Trail Association
Tel (877) 854-9415.
www.pnt.org

ROCK CLIMBING AND MOUNTAINEERING

BC Parks
www.env.gov.bc.ca

Federation of Mountain Clubs of BC
Tel (604) 873-6096.
www.mountainclubs.bc.ca

North Cascades Mountain Guides
Tel (509) 996-3194.
www.ncmountainguides.com

Peshastin Pinnacles State Park
www.parks.wa.gov

Rainier Mountaineering
Tel (888) 892-5462.
www.rmiguides.com

Timberline Mountain Guides
Tel (541) 312-9242.
www.timberlinemtguides.com

WATERSPORTS

3 Routes
www.3routes.com

BC Parks
www.env.gov.bc.ca

River Riders
Tel (800) 448-7238.
www.riverrider.com

Wedge Rafting
Tel (604) 932-7171.
www.wedgerafting.com

Wildwater River Tours
Tel (800) 522-9453.
www.wildwater-river.com

WHALE-WATCHING

Five-Star Whale Watching
Tel (250) 388-7223.
www.5starwhales.com

Lime Kiln Point State Park
Tel (360) 902-8844.
www.parks.wa.gov

Pacific Rim National Park Reserve
Tel (250) 726-3500.
www.pc.gc.ca

Seacoast Expeditions
Tel (250) 383-2254.
www.seacoastexpeditions.com

WINTER SPORTS

Tourism Whistler
Tel (800) 944-7853.
www.whistler.com

NATIONAL PARKS

Crater Lake National Park
Tel (541) 594-3000.
www.nps.gov

Kootenay National Park
Tel (250) 347-9505.
www.pc.gc.ca

National Park Service
Tel (510) 817-1300.
www.nps.gov

North Cascades National Park
Tel (360) 854-7200.
www.nps.gov

US Forest Service
Tel (800) 832-1355.
www.fs.fed.us

STATE AND PROVINCIAL PARKS

Oregon State Parks
Tel (800) 551-6949.
www.oregon.gov

Smith Rock State Park
Tel (800) 551-6949.
www.oregon.gov

Washington State Parks
Tel (360) 902-8844.
www.parks.wa.gov

SURVIVAL
GUIDE

PRACTICAL INFORMATION

The Pacific Northwest's stunning scenery attracts visitors from around the world. Booming tourism – and in more recent years, ecotourism – has spawned an extensive network of facilities and services for visitors: internationally acclaimed accommodations and restaurants abound, while efficient transportation by air, land, and water takes travelers virtually anywhere

Historic Columbia River Highway sign

they want to go. The following pages provide useful information for all travelers planning a trip to this region. Personal Health and Security *(see pp328–9)* recommends a number of precautions; Banking and Communications *(see pp330–31)* answers financial and media queries. There is also information on traveling to the region *(see pp332–3)* and driving once there *(see pp334–5)*.

TOURIST INFORMATION

Maps and information about sights, events, accommodations, and tours are available free of charge from the **Travel Oregon**, **Washington State Tourism**, and **Tourism British Columbia**. These agencies also provide either free reservation services for a wide range of accommodation or referrals to such services. Most communities in the Pacific Northwest also operate visitors' information centers or seasonal tourism booths, which offer information about local activities, lodgings, and restaurants.

ENTRY REQUIREMENTS

Due to changing US immigration laws, visitors to Washington and Oregon who are traveling from outside the US should check current entry requirements with a US embassy or consulate before leaving. All visitors must have a valid passport, and visitors from most countries must have a non-immigrant visitor's visa. Citizens of Australia, New Zealand, South Africa, the UK, and many other European countries can visit the US without a visa if they plan to stay for fewer than 90 days. All travelers under the Visa Waiver Program must pre-register with the Department of Homeland Security's Electronic System for Travel Authorization (ESTA) at www.cbp.gov well in advance of their departure.

Visitors to Canada (including US citizens) must carry a valid passport (for US visitors,

a US passport card or enhanced driver's license is acceptable when crossing the border by land or sea, but not by air). A visa is not necessary for visitors from the US, EU, UK, and British Commonwealth countries. In your home country, the nearest Canadian consulate, embassy, or high commission will have current information on visa regulations. Visitors who are under the age of 18 and traveling alone must carry a letter from a parent or

guardian giving them permission to do so.

All travelers who plan to stay in Canada or the US for 90 days or longer must have visas. If crossing the border by car, be prepared for customs personnel to do a search.

Canadian landed immigrants should check the regulations before traveling to the US – citizens of some Commonwealth countries that were formerly exempt from the visa requirement are now required to have a visa.

Crystal Mountain, Washington, a perfect winter ski destination

◁ **Hikers on the lower slopes of Mount Rainier, Washington**

WHEN TO GO

Visitors should first determine what they would like to do. The region's winter weather is ideal for skiing and other snow sports, while warmer weather suits hiking, cycling, fishing, and watersports. (See also pp30–33 for details on seasonal events and weather in the Pacific Northwest.)

The peak tourist season extends from mid-May through September. In the metropolitan areas of Portland, Seattle, and Vancouver, spring is often quite rainy, with temperatures in the 60 to 69°F (16 to 21°C) range. Along the coast, mild summer temperatures average 77°F (25°C) and occasionally go as high as 85°F (29°C), which makes walking around these cities comfortable. Central and eastern regions can be significantly hotter than the coast.

In early September, trees at the higher elevations begin to change color, making excursions out of the cities even more scenic. In September and early October, the weather in the three major cities, particularly in Seattle, can be quite dry and sunny.

Although the weather is generally clement along the coast, rain is not uncommon in other areas. It starts to get chilly again in the fall, toward the end of October.

Except in areas catering to skiers and other snow sports enthusiasts, winter is the least popular season to visit. This makes it an ideal time of year for visitors who are looking for fewer crowds and more affordable hotel rates. Though snowfalls in the three main coastal cities are relatively rare, in the interior and eastern regions they can be frequent and heavy. If you plan to cross from west to east between late fall and early spring, inquire first about road conditions.

TIME ZONES

There are two time zones in the Pacific Northwest: Pacific Standard Time (PST) and Mountain Standard Time (MST). Washington and most of British Columbia and Oregon lie within the Pacific time

Bikes and windsurfing gear in Hood River, Oregon

zone. Parts of Oregon, along the Idaho border, and parts of British Columbia, along the Alberta border, lie within the mountain time zone. The clocks are turned back one hour in October; in April they are turned forward one hour to Daylight Savings Time.

CUSTOMS ALLOWANCES

Visitors 21 years of age and over are permitted to enter the US with two pints (1 liter) of alcohol, 200 cigarettes, 50 cigars or 4 pounds (1.8 kg) of smoking tobacco, and gifts worth up to $100. Visitors to British Columbia who are 19 years of age or older are allowed up to 3.15 pints (1.5 liters) of wine or 2.4 pints (1.14 liters) of liquor, 200 cigarettes, 50 cigars, or 0.44 pounds (200 grams) of tobacco, and gifts worth up to $60.

Restricted items include meats, dairy products, and fresh fruits and vegetables. Travelers entering either

"Pioneers" at the National Historic Oregon Trail Interpretive Center

country with more than $10,000 in cash or traveler's checks must declare it.

OPENING HOURS AND ADMISSION PRICES

Most businesses are open weekdays from 9am to 5pm, but many in Seattle's, Portland's, and Vancouver's downtown districts stay open later. Many businesses are also open on weekends. Banks open from 9 or 9:30am to 4:30 or 5pm, and some offer limited hours on Saturdays. Most attractions are open daily, except perhaps on public holidays (see p33). Opening hours can be shorter outside the summer season.

Most attractions charge an admission fee, but discounts are widely available for families, children, students, and seniors. Check tourist brochures and local papers for discount coupons.

TAXES

In Oregon, hotel tax is 8–12.5 percent and there is no sales tax. Hotel tax in Seattle is 15.6 percent but varies throughout the rest of the state; and Washington's sales taxes are in the 8 to 9 percent range but do not apply to groceries.

In British Columbia, a 7 percent provincial sales tax (PST) and a 5 percent federal Goods and Service Tax (GST) apply to most goods and services. Hotel rooms are subject to GST, PST, and an additional 3 percent hotel tax.

A restaurant and wine bar in Portland's South Park Blocks

ETIQUETTE

Pacific Northwesterners' dress tends to be casual, practical, and dependent on the weather. Stricter clothing requirements apply in theaters, high-end restaurants, and other more formal places. Designated beaches allow topless and nude sunbathing.

ALCOHOL AND CIGARETTES

Alcohol is available only in government liquor stores, beer and wine stores, and licensed restaurants, bars, and clubs. Drinking alcohol in non-licensed public places is illegal, as is driving with an open bottle of alcohol. There are also strict laws against drinking and driving.

The minimum legal drinking age in Oregon and Washington is 21; in British Columbia, 19. Younger travelers are advised to carry photo identification, such as a passport or driver's license, should they need to prove they are of legal age to enter bars or clubs or to order alcohol in restaurants.

In Oregon and Washington, cigarettes can be sold only to people 18 or older; in British Columbia, 19 or older. It is illegal to smoke in public buildings and on public transportation. Smoking in restaurants, pubs, bars, and shopping centers is prohibited.

TIPPING

Tips and service charges are not usually added to restaurant bills. For service at restaurants, cafés, bars, and clubs, and for tour guides, a standard tip is 15 to 20 percent of the amount before taxes. Porters and bellhops should be tipped at least $1 per bag or suitcase; cloakroom attendants, $1 per garment; and chambermaids, a minimum of $1 to $2 per day.

TRAVELERS WITH DISABILITIES

The Pacific Northwest has some of the world's best facilities and recreational opportunities for travelers with physical disabilities. Most public buildings, hotels (see p280), public transit, and entertainment venues are wheelchair accessible. However, some older buildings and smaller venues may not be. Taxi service is available for people with wheelchairs, and parking spaces closest to the entrance of most buildings are reserved for persons with disabilities (note that permits may be required).

The **Society for Accessible Travel and Hospitality** is an excellent source of information. To find out about barrier-free sports and recreation opportunities in British Columbia, contact **BC Disability Games**.

SENIOR TRAVELERS

Reduced rates for attractions, hotels, transportation, and services are often available for seniors. Photo identification proving one's age may be required. Seniors are eligible for discounts with Amtrak and VIA rail services and with Greyhound bus services (see p333). If discounts are not advertised, inquire when purchasing tickets. Also inquire about discounts for seniors' traveling companions.

For discounts and more information about traveling as a senior, contact the **American Association of Retired Persons**, in the US or Canada. For information about learning programs for people 55 years of age and older, contact **Elderhostel**.

WOMEN TRAVELERS

The Pacific Northwest is generally safe for women travelers. However, caution is advisable in deserted places and walking around alone after dark is not advisable, especially if you do not know the district very well. Keep a confident attitude, avoid telling anyone you are traveling alone, and do not hitchhike.

TRAVELING WITH CHILDREN

The Pacific Northwest is extremely child-friendly, with many attractions suited to children, including zoos and a multitude of festivals, events, and programs. The region's beaches and popular

Petting zoo at Port Townsend's farmers' market, Washington

Oregon Museum of Science and Industry, in Portland

outdoor activities can entertain children year-round. Admission to attractions is often free for children under five who are accompanied by a parent. In most cities in the Pacific Northwest, children under five can also travel for free on public transportation when they are accompanied by a parent; there are often concession fares for older children.

Many hotels offer cribs, high chairs, even baby-sitting services, and restaurants generally welcome children. With more upscale establishments, you may wish to inquire in advance whether children are welcome.

When renting a car, be sure to reserve a child's car seat in advance.

STUDENT TRAVELERS

An international student identity card (ISIC), administered by the **International Student Travel Confederation**, entitles full-time students to discounts on travel as well as admission to movies, galleries, museums, theaters, and many other tourist attractions. The ISIC should be purchased in the student's home country; they are available at **STA Travel** and **Travel CUTS** (in the US and Canada only).

A wide range of bus and rail (see p333) discounts are available to students. Ask for a copy of the *ISIC Student Handbook*, for listings of places that offer discounts to cardholders, as well as travel tips.

Members of **Hostelling International** (HI) can stay at HI locations throughout the Pacific Northwest (see p279). Ask about free shuttles and other amenities at HI's regional offices.

CONVERSION CHART

Imperial to Metric
1 inch = 2.5 centimeters
1 foot = 30 centimeters
1 mile = 1.6 kilometers
1 ounce = 28 grams
1 pound = 454 grams
1 pint = 0.6 liter
1 US pint = 0.5 liter
1 US quart = 0.9 liter
1 gallon = 4.6 liters
1 US gallon = 3.8 liters

Metric to Imperial
1 centimeter = 0.4 inch
1 meter = 3 feet 3 inches
1 kilometer = 0.6 mile
1 gram = 0.04 ounce
1 kilogram = 2.2 pounds
1 liter = 1.8 pints/1.1 US quarts

Bear in mind that 1 US pint (0.5 liter) is a smaller measure than 1 UK pint (0.6 liter).

ELECTRICITY

Electrical sockets accept two- or three-prong plugs and operate at 110 volts. You will need a plug adapter and voltage converter to operate 220-volt appliances such as hairdryers and rechargers. Batteries are universal and are readily available.

Standard North American plug

DIRECTORY

TOURIST INFORMATION

Tourism BC
Tel (800) 435-5622.
www.hellobc.com

Travel Oregon
Tel (800) 547-7842.
www.traveloregon.com

Washington State Tourism
Tel (800) 544-1800.
www.experiencewa.com

TRAVELERS WITH DISABILITIES

BC Disability Games
PO Box 56037,
RPO Valley Center,
Langley, BC, V3A 8B3.
Tel (604) 530-7738.
www.bcdisability
games.org

Society for Accessible Travel and Hospitality
347 5th Ave, Suite 605,
New York, NY 10016.
Tel (212) 447-7284.
www.sath.org

SENIOR TRAVELERS

American Association of Retired Persons
601 E Street NW,
Washington, DC
20049.
Tel (888) 687-2277.
www.aarp.org

Elderhostel
11 Avenue de Lafayette,
Boston, MA 02111-1746.
Tel (800) 454-5768.
www.roadscholar.org

STUDENT TRAVELERS

Hostelling International
National Administrative
Office,
8401 Colesville Rd.,
Suite 600, Silver Spring,
MD 20910.
Tel (301) 495-1240.
www.hiusa.org
www.hihostels.ca

International Student Travel Confederation
www.istc.org

STA Travel
Tel In US:
(800) 781-4040.
www.statravel.com

Travel CUTS
Tel In US:
(800) 592-2887.
In Canada:
(800) 667-2887.
www.travelcuts.com

USEFUL NUMBERS

Canada Border Services Agency
www.cbsa.gc.ca

Canada Revenue Agency
www.cra-arc.gc

Personal Health and Security

Hospital sign

The Pacific Northwest prides itself on the safety of its towns and cities and on its welcoming attitude toward visitors. Street crime is rare, and police are a visible presence as they patrol the major cities on horseback, motorcycle, and foot. However, it is still wise to be vigilant and to find out from your hotel or a tourist information center which parts of town should be avoided. In the open countryside, bear in mind natural dangers, such as unexpectedly inclement weather and wild animals. Always heed local warnings.

GUIDELINES ON SAFETY

While traveling, it is always advisable to take a few basic precautions and at all times to remain aware of your surroundings.

Carry traveler's checks and small amounts of cash in a secure bag, purse, or pocket, and do not carry your wallet in a back pocket. Pickpockets and thieves, who are often well dressed and tend to work in pairs, target their victims in airports, malls, and other crowded areas.

Always watch your luggage carefully at airports and while checking in and out of your hotel. Although theft is rare in hotel rooms, ask at your hotel if you can store valuable items, such as jewelry, credit cards, or extra cash, in the hotel safe.

When you use an automated teller machine (ATM), choose one that is located in a well-lit, busy area and never let a stranger look over your shoulder or assist you in using your bank card.

Travelers with cars should park in well-lit garages or use valet parking if offered by the hotel, and avoid leaving valuable items in the car. Always lock the doors when you

park the car and leave the glove compartment empty and open. It is also advisable to keep the car doors locked while driving.

MEDICAL MATTERS

Most major cities in the Pacific Northwest have walk-in medical clinics, which are usually sufficient for minor injuries and ailments. Clinics and hospitals are listed in the Yellow Pages of the telephone directory. Without insurance, medical services can be expensive. Even with insurance, you may have to pay upfront for the medical treatment and seek reimbursement from your insurance company later.

Nonprescription painkillers and other medicines can be obtained from drugstores, many of which are open 24 hours a day. Prescription drugs can be dispensed only from a pharmacy. If you take a prescription drug, pack an extra supply, as well as a copy of the prescription. A first-aid kit is also recommended when camping or trekking into remote areas.

If you have HIV or AIDS, call the embassy or consulate of the country to which you are traveling to find out about regulations regarding travelers with either of these conditions. The entry requirements can change at short notice.

Compact first-aid kit, an essential item for travelers

EMERGENCIES

Dial 911 if the emergency requires the fire department, police, or an ambulance; if you are not in a major city, dial 0. The call can be made free of charge from any telephone. Most hospitals have a 24-hour emergency room; be prepared for a long wait. Although they may be busy, public hospitals can be much less expensive than private ones. Hospitals in British Columbia will provide treatment to anyone, regardless of health care coverage; in the US, visitors must provide payment or proof of insurance coverage before receiving treatment.

NATURAL HAZARDS

Before setting off to hike or camp, check with the appropriate state, provincial, or federal forest service for information on the conditions in the area and recommended safety precautions. Skiers and snowboarders should heed warning signs and stay on groomed runs and trails. It is always best to be accompanied when engaging in any such outdoor activity. Insects are another hazard. While black flies, which are common in the spring, are

Moose warning sign

Avalanche warning sign

annoying, they are relatively harmless. Mosquitoes, however, which are prevalent in the summer, can be carriers of the potentially fatal West Nile virus. Ticks, which can be carriers of Lyme disease, are found in dry, wooded areas. To protect yourself, use insect repellent and wear long sleeves, long trousers, and socks. If you are bitten and develop a rash or flu-like symptoms, seek medical attention immediately.

Heed the red-tide warnings that alert shellfish collectors to contamination. When camping, beware of cougars, wolves, coyotes, and bears *(see p318)*. Leaving food out

Vancouver police officers on duty

can attract dangerous wildlife and is illegal in many areas, as is feeding wild animals.

LAW ENFORCEMENT

The Portland and Seattle police departments are present in these cities on foot, on horseback, motorcycle, and in cars. Neighborhood security teams, made up of citizen volunteers, also patrol on foot in some areas. Outside metropolitan areas, there are county police and sheriff's offices to assist you. British Columbia is policed by the Royal Canadian Mounted Police (RCMP); some municipalities also have their own police forces. In addition, you are likely to see security officers from private security companies in airports and public places, and on Vancouver's downtown streets.

It is illegal to comment on or joke about bombs, guns, and terrorism in places such as airports, where it is possible to be arrested for an off-the-cuff remark.

Drinking and driving is taken very seriously in the Pacific Northwest, and it is illegal to carry open alcohol containers in a vehicle. Police checks for impaired drivers are increasingly common. Narcotics users can face criminal charges, followed

by moves for deportation; penalties are especially severe in the US.

LOST OR STOLEN PROPERTY

Although the chances of retrieving lost or stolen items are slim, it is nevertheless important to report missing items to the police as soon as possible. Be sure to obtain a copy of the police record in case you need it for an insurance claim.

Before leaving home, make photocopies of important documents such as your passport, driver's license, credit cards, and identification cards; keep one set of photocopies at home, another set with you.

Should you lose your passport, contact your nearest embassy or consulate. Visitors do not generally need a new passport if they are returning directly to their home country and so may be issued a temporary one. However, if you are traveling on to another destination, you will need to replace your permanent passport. Report lost credit cards and traveler's checks as soon as you notice them missing; American Express, MasterCard, Visa, and Thomas Cook all have toll-free call centers open 24 hours a day, seven days a week. If you have a record of the traveler's checks' numbers, replacing them should be fairly straightforward and new ones are often issued within 24 hours. For items lost on public transit or in a taxi, contact the lost-and-found departments of the appropriate transit system or taxi company.

A park ranger

TRAVEL INSURANCE

Travel insurance is essential when traveling. Consider purchasing insurance for health and medical emergencies, trip cancellation and interruption, theft, and loss of valuable

possessions. A minimum of $1 million medical coverage is recommended, especially if you are traveling to the US. Insurance for luggage and travel documents can be arranged through a travel agent or the airline. Emergency dental, out-of-pocket, and loss-of-vacation expenses are generally covered by separate policies. Ask your travel agent or insurance company to recommend suitable insurance; also check with your credit card company (see p330).

DIRECTORY

EMERGENCIES

Police, Fire, Ambulance
Tel In major cities call 911; elsewhere, dial 0.

Hospitals
Tel Call 411 for directory assistance.

EMBASSIES AND CONSULATES

Links to US Embassies and Consulates Worldwide
www.usembassy.gov

Links to Canadian Embassies, Consulates, and High Commissions Worldwide
www.international.gc.ca

LOST OR STOLEN CREDIT CARDS AND TRAVELER'S CHECKS

American Express
Tel (800) 869-3016 for credit cards, (800) 528-4800 for traveler's checks.

MasterCard
Tel (800) 627-8372.

Thomas Cook
Tel (800) 223-7373

Visa
Tel (800) 847-2911 for credit cards, (800) 227-6811 for traveler's checks.

Banking, Local Currency, and Communications

Both in the US and Canada the unit of currency is the dollar, which is divided into 100 cents. Coins include denominations of 1 cent (penny), 5 cents (nickel), 10 cents (dime), 25 cents (quarter), and $1 (buck; in Canada it is often called a "loonie"). In Canada, there is also a $2 coin, a "toonie." Bank notes, or bills, are printed in denominations of $5, $10, $20, $50, and $100 in both countries, and in $500 and $1,000 in Canada, though these larger denominations are less common. In the US, a $2 bill is also in circulation, but it is uncommon. Plan to arrive with $50 to $100 in local currency and get small change as soon as possible for tipping and transportation.

Credit cards, a convenient method of payment for travelers

BANKS AND FOREIGN CURRENCY EXCHANGE

Most banks are open from 9 or 9:30am to 4:30 or 5pm, with many in downtown locations offering extended hours, especially on Fridays. Many banks are closed Saturdays, and all are closed Sundays and statutory holidays.

Exchange rates for foreign currency are posted in banks where exchange services are offered (usually the main branches of large banks) as well as at foreign exchange brokers, **American Express** and **Travelex** being the most popular ones.

AUTOMATED TELLER MACHINES (ATMS)

Automated Teller Machines (ATMs) can be found in bank branches, shopping centers, gas stations, grocery stores, mini-marts, transit terminals, and airports. They offer one of the most convenient ways of obtaining local currency

An ATM, common throughout the Pacific Northwest

since you can, in most cases, use your debit card or a major credit card to withdraw cash. Consult with your bank, credit union, or credit card company before leaving home about which ATM systems will accept your bank card, and what fees and commissions will be charged on each transaction made outside your home country.

TRAVELER'S CHECKS

Traveler's checks provide one of the safest ways to carry money on a vacation. They are widely accepted at stores, hotels, and restaurants in major cities, but may be difficult to use in rural areas or areas less geared to tourism.

Foreign currency checks can be exchanged at any bank and at some major hotels, but it is advisable to purchase checks in US or Canadian currency, depending on your destination. Choose small denominations, such as $10 or $20, as most retailers prefer not to part with large amounts of change. A passport or other photo identification is required to cash traveler's checks at a bank. Checks issued by American Express and Thomas Cook are the most popular and, as such, the most readily accepted. Rarely will a personal check be accepted.

CREDIT CARDS

Credit cards such as Visa, MasterCard, American Express, Discover, and Diners Club are widely accepted and can be used to pay for just about anything, from a cup of coffee to a hotel room.

Not only do credit cards allow you to carry a minimal amount of cash but they are often required when checking into a hotel or renting a car – many such businesses will insist on taking a credit card imprint as a form of deposit. Credit cards can be used to obtain cash advances at banks and ATMs, and can also be handy in emergency situations.

If your credit card company offers travel insurance, keep a copy of the statement of conditions and coverage with your travel documents. Before leaving home, be sure to note all emergency contact numbers connected with your credit card in case of loss or theft.

WIRING MONEY

In an emergency, visitors can have cash wired from home by way of electronic money transfer services offered by American Express, Thomas Cook, and **Western Union**.

POSTAL SERVICES

Post Offices generally open weekdays from 9am to 5pm. Stamped, addressed mail can be dropped into roadside mailboxes, which are blue in the US and red in Canada. Pick-up times are listed on the boxes. Most hotels will also accept letters and postcards at the front desk.

Mail sent within the US or Canada takes from one to five business days for delivery (longer if no zip or postal code is given); overseas mail up to seven business days. Courier companies and the priority services of the

US Postal Service and Canada Post offer speedier delivery. Priority mail costs more than regular mail but usually less than courier services.

TELEPHONES

Public pay phones are virtually everywhere, including bars, restaurants, public buildings, gas stations, and street corners, and at rest stops outside urban areas. Local calls made from pay phones in the US cost 35 cents; in Canada, 25 cents. Most pay phones are operated by coins, though increasingly more accept phone cards and credit cards too. Any combination of coins, excluding pennies, can be used. Keep in mind that making phone calls from hotel rooms can be expensive; inquire about rates first. It is usually cheaper to use the pay phone in the lobby.

For local calls, dial the area code followed by the seven-digit number. For long-distance calls within North America, dial 1, followed by the area code and the local number. For calls outside North America, dial 011, followed by the country code (Australia: 61; New Zealand: 64; South Africa: 27; UK: 44), then the city or area code, then the local telephone number; or dial 0 for operator assistance.

Coin-operated pay phone

Vending machines in Seattle, dispensing a range of newspapers

CELL PHONES, INTERNET, AND E-MAIL

Cell phones can be rented in many cities, or visitors can have their own mobiles tuned to local networks. Check with your cell phone service provider before leaving home. Alternatively, cell phones can be purchased in many places, from kiosks in shopping malls to stores and the Internet.

The Pacific Northwest is ahead of many places in terms of computer and Internet use. E-mail and the Internet can be accessed from most hotels and public libraries, or from the ubiquitous local Internet café or coffee shop. Rates for computer use vary but are generally reasonable.

FAXES AND MONEY ORDERS

Faxes can be sent from most hotels and many business facilities. The most common service for sending money is operated by Western Union.

COMMUNICATIONS AND MEDIA

Newsstands in the US carry most major international and national papers, including the *New York Times*, the *Wall Street Journal*, and *USA Today*. Local papers are available at sidewalk boxes, coffee shops, and convenience stores. The most widely read newspapers in Seattle are the *Seattle Times*, *The Seattle Weekly*, and *The Stranger*. In Portland, it is the *Oregonian* and *Willamette Week*.

The US is famous for having a multitude of TV channels, provided by the four networks – ABC, CBS, FOX, and NBC – as well as by cable channels. CNN is a national 24-hour headline news station.

Various radio stations in the US offer local news bulletins and weather forecasts. National Public Radio is a good source of commercial-free news and entertainment; it is usually located along the FM band.

The *Globe and Mail* and the *National Post* are the national newspapers in Canada and are readily available at newsstands, as are international papers. Vancouver's two dailies are the *Vancouver Sun* and *The Province*, and most smaller BC cities have a local paper.

The CBC, Canada's public broadcasting corporation, has local, national, and international television and radio programming. VTV, the Vancouver affiliate of CTV, Canada's largest private television broadcaster, airs news and other programs daily.

AREA CODES

Oregon

Portland, Salem & Astoria	**503/971**
Oregon, elsewhere	**541**

Washington

Western Washington

• Seattle	**206/564**
• Eastside	**425/564**
• Southside, including Tacoma	**253/564**
• Elsewhere	**360/564**
Eastern Washington	**509**

British Columbia

Vancouver/Lower Mainland	**604/778**
BC, elsewhere	**250/778**

DIRECTORY

American Express
www.americanexpress.com

Travelex
www.travelex.com

Western Union
Tel In US & Canada:
(800) 225-5227.
www.westernunion.ca

TRAVEL INFORMATION

Passenger jet at takeoff

The three major airports in the Pacific Northwest are conveniently located to serve the metropolitan areas of Portland, Oregon; Seattle, Washington; and Vancouver, British Columbia. But these urban centers can also be easily accessed by train, car, or bus on the region's excellent network of well-maintained highways. Train travel is ideal for enjoying the picturesque landscape; buses are relatively inexpensive; and driving is particularly popular, as it enables travelers to visit many locations that would otherwise be difficult to reach. Once you have arrived in the Pacific Northwest, ferries and cruises provide a scenic way of traveling between coastal communities.

ARRIVING BY AIR

Washington's major airport is **Sea-Tac International Airport** (SEA), located between Seattle and Tacoma. In Oregon, **Portland International Airport** (PDX) is just a few miles outside the city proper. Most major carriers fly into these airports, though international passengers may need to stop in Seattle and transfer to another plane to fly into Portland.

United Airlines offers flights to the major cities of the Pacific Northwest, while **Alaska Airlines** and **Horizon Airlines** fly to these as well as to regional destinations. **San Juan Airlines** and **Kenmore Air** fly between Seattle and the San Juan Islands.

The point of arrival for most international visitors to British Columbia is **Vancouver International Airport** (YVR), which is served by Canada's major carrier, **Air Canada**, as well as other national airlines from around the world. **WestJet** is a low-cost national alternative that links up with other major airlines. Air Canada's regional division flies to most major BC destinations; smaller airlines, such as **Harbour Air**, serving the Gulf Islands, and **Hawkair**, serving northern BC, connect the province's smaller communities.

TRANSPORTATION FROM THE AIRPORT

Taxis and the less expensive shuttle buses are readily available at all of the three major international airports in the Pacific Northwest. Some hotels provide shuttle service;

ask when booking your room. The least expensive way to get into the cities from the airports is by public transit. The **MAX** light rail system is ideal for getting into Portland; **Gray Line** also offers an airport service. Seattle's **Metro Transit** buses run regularly from Sea-Tac Airport, and several share-ride shuttles are available. **TransLink** buses run regularly from the Vancouver airport, as does the **Vancouver Airporter** bus, traveling between the airport and downtown hotels.

TRAVELING BY BUS

Although the bus may be the slowest way of getting to the Pacific Northwest, it may also be the most economical way. **Greyhound** has bus routes throughout the region; **Gray Line** and **Pacific Coach Lines** offer sightseeing tours. Discounts are often available for children, students, and senior citizens.

A Greyhound bus, an economical way to travel long distances

TRAVELING BY TRAIN

If you are traveling from within the US or Canada, the train is a good way to get to the Pacific Northwest and to travel within it. **Amtrak** offers daily services to Washington and Oregon from the Midwest and California and has daily runs between Vancouver, Seattle, Portland, and Eugene, Oregon.

In British Columbia, **VIA Rail**, Canada's national rail service, links Vancouver to Alberta and the rest of Canada. **Rocky Mountaineer Vacations** takes a scenic route to Kamloops, continuing on to Jasper, Banff, or Calgary, in Alberta. Reserve seats

Union Station, Portland's Italian Renaissance-style train depot, opened 1896

through a travel agent or
VIA Rail directly.

TRAVELING BY CAR

Oregon, Washington, and
British Columbia maintain
an extensive network of
highways. The major interstate through Oregon and
Washington is I-5, running
north to British Columbia and
south to California. The best
route to eastern Washington
from Seattle is I-90; the most
accessible route to eastern
Oregon from Portland is I-84.
The Trans-Canada Highway
traverses British Columbia,
linking it to the rest of the
country. There are no tolls on
roads leading into Portland
and Seattle, and all US

Washington State Ferries terminal, Port Townsend

interstate highways are free.
Speed limits and seatbelt
laws are strictly enforced.
Travelers driving across
the Canada–US border can
choose from 16 crossings.
Bring your passport and a
current driver's license. In
some cases, an International
Driving Permit will be
required. Rules governing
border crossings are subject
to change; check with the
authorities before traveling.

TRAVELING BY FERRY

Ferries are an important,
and scenic, mode of transportation in the Pacific
Northwest. **Washington
State Ferries** *(see p162)*
travel regularly between
Washington's mainland and
the Puget Sound and San

Juan Islands, as well as to
Sidney, British Columbia,
17 miles (27 km) north
of Victoria.
In British Columbia, **BC
Ferries** travels 40 routes
along the Sunshine Coast,
in the Gulf Islands, the
Queen Charlotte Islands,
the Discovery Coast Passage,
and between the mainland
and Vancouver Island. It
has two terminals in the
Vancouver area: one in
Tsawwassen, the other
in Horseshoe Bay. Unlike
BC Ferries, the **Victoria
Clipper** provides a route to
Washington. It also travels
from Victoria and Seattle to
the San Juan Islands.
BC and Washington ferries
carry both foot passengers and
vehicles, and offer discounts
to students and seniors.

**Amtrak train, offering convenient
travel and sightseeing at once**

DIRECTORY

AIRPORTS

**Portland
International
Airport**
Tel (877) 739-4636.
www.pdx.com

**Sea-Tac International
Airport**
Tel (800) 544-1965.
www.portseattle.org

**Vancouver
International
Airport**
Tel (604) 207-7077.
www.yvr.ca

AIRLINES

Air Canada
Tel (888) 247-2262.
www.aircanada.com

Alaska Airlines
Tel (800) 252-7522.
www.alaskaair.com

Harbour Air
Tel (800) 665-0212.
www.harbour-air.com

Hawkair
Tel (800) 487-1216.
www.hawkair.ca

Horizon Airlines
Tel (800) 252-7522.
www.alaskaair.com

Kenmore Air
Tel (866) 435-9524.
www.kenmoreair.com

San Juan Airlines
Tel (800) 874-4434.
www.sanjuanairlines.com

United Airlines
Tel (800) 864-8331.
www.united.com

WestJet
Tel (888) 937-8538.
www.westjet.com

TRANSPORTATION
FROM THE AIRPORT

MAX (TriMet)
Tel (503) 238-7433.
www.trimet.org

Metro Transit
Tel (206) 553-3000.
www.metro.
kingcounty.gov

TransLink
Tel (604) 953-3333.
www.translink.ca

**Vancouver
Airporter**
Tel (604) 946-8866.

BUS COMPANIES

Gray Line
*Tel In Portland & Seattle:
(800) 472-9546.
In Victoria:
(800) 667-0882.*
www.grayline.com

Greyhound
*Tel In US: (800) 231-2222.
In Canada: (800) 661-8747.*
www.greyhound.com (US);
www.greyhound.ca (Can)

Pacific Coach Lines
Tel (800) 661-1725.
www.pacificcoach.com

RAIL COMPANIES

Amtrak
Tel (800) 872-7245.
www.amtrak.com

**Rocky Mountaineer
Vacations**
Tel (877) 460-3200.
www.rockymountaineer.
com

VIA Rail
Tel (888) 842-7245.
www.viarail.ca

FERRY COMPANIES

BC Ferries
Tel (888) 223-3779.
www.bcferries.com

Victoria Clipper
Tel (800) 888-2535.
www.clippervacations.
com

**Washington
State Ferries**
*Tel (800) 843-3779 or
(206) 464-6400 (Seattle).*
www.wsdot.wa.gov

Traveling by Car in the Pacific Northwest

Driving is the best way to explore the Pacific Northwest, especially if you want to enjoy the spectacular beauty of more remote areas, such as Oregon's Hells Canyon, the mountains of Washington's Olympic Peninsula, or British Columbia's Okanagan Valley. In major cities, parking may be hard to find and traffic heavy during rush hours; tune into local TV or radio news for reports on traffic and road conditions, particularly if you visit in the winter. Rental cars are widely available at airports and in the cities and towns.

DRIVER'S LICENSE AND INSURANCE

In the US, you do not need an International Driving Permit if you are carrying a valid driver's license from the country in which you live. You must, however, carry proof of auto insurance, vehicle registration, and, if renting a car, the rental contract.

A valid driver's license from your own country entitles you to drive for up to six months in British Columbia. It is advisable to carry an International Driving Permit as well, in case you run into problems.

Insurance coverage for drivers is compulsory. Before leaving home, check your own policy to see if you are covered in a rental car. Most rental agencies offer damage and liability insurance; it is a good idea to have both. Insurance can be purchased on arrival through the **British Columbia Automobile Association (BCAA)**; in the US, contact the **American Automobile Association (AAA)**.

RULES OF THE ROAD

Vehicles are driven on the right-hand side of the road in both the US and Canada. Right-hand turns on a red light are permitted after coming to a complete stop unless otherwise indicated.

Distances and speed limits are posted in miles in the US, and in kilometers in Canada. Speed limits vary from 25 mph (40 km/h) on neighborhood streets to a maximum of 65 mph (105 km/h) on major highways. Speed limits are strictly enforced. On most major highways in the Pacific Northwest, carpool lanes are available for vehicles with two or more passengers, to reduce pollution and traffic.

Four-way stops are common in the Pacific Northwest. The first car to reach the intersection has the right of way. At intersections with no stop signs, drivers must yield to the car on their right.

Coin-operated parking meter

Because traffic in and around Portland, Seattle, and Vancouver can be heavy, it is wise to avoid rush hours in these cities, generally between 7:30 and 9:30am and from 3:30 to 6pm on weekdays. On city streets, parking meters offer between 15 minutes and two hours of parking. Be sure to put money into the meter and to read all signs since parking enforcement officers are especially active within city limits.

Seat belts are compulsory throughout the Pacific Northwest for both drivers and passengers, and children weighing less than 40 lbs (18 kg) must be in the appropriate child seats. Cyclists and motorcyclists are required to wear helmets. Driving while intoxicated (which is defined as having a blood alcohol content of more than 0.08 percent) is a criminal offense. If you are involved in an accident, contact the local police. (In Canada, local policing may be done by the Royal Canadian Mounted Police, or RCMP, depending where you are.)

SAFETY ON THE ROAD

Potential safety hazards for drivers include gravel roads, which can become very slippery when wet, heavy snowfalls, black ice, and fog, which can be particularly thick along the coast. To be safe, always carry a spare tire, and salt or sand in winter, a flashlight, jumper cables, blankets, water, some emergency food, and a shovel. Before venturing out onto back roads, be sure to inquire about road conditions and weather forecasts and to have a full tank of gas. Refill the tank fairly often along the way as an extra precaution. If you know you will be driving on dirt roads or in treacherous conditions, you may want to rent a vehicle with four-wheel drive.

During the spring and summer, wildlife such as deer, bears, and moose have been known to rush out of the woods onto the roads.

The spectacular Columbia River Historic Highway, near Rowena, Oregon

Speed limit

Gas pump

Road conditions

Rest area

Wildlife

Signs will indicate where wildlife is most likely to appear; take extra care in these areas.

CAR RENTALS

Car rental agencies such as **Alamo**, **Avis**, **Budget**, **Enterprise**, **Hertz**, **National**, and **Thrifty** are located within the cities and towns as well as at airports. To rent a vehicle in the US or Canada, you must be 21 years of age and have a valid driver's license. If you are younger than 25, you will likely have to pay a higher insurance premium. A major credit card is usually required, even when you are prepared to make a hefty cash deposit.

Sign for a rental car agency

Rent a car that suits your destination: a small car or sedan is appropriate for city sightseeing, but if you plan to cross mountain ranges, especially between October and April, you may want to request a sturdier, high-traction vehicle. Recreational vehicles (RVs) can also be rented but are more expensive and usually need to be reserved well in advance. Many outlets are reluctant to rent their cars if they know there is a risk of gravel roads chipping the paintwork, so if you plan to drive along back roads, you may be best off renting from an outlet in the backcountry.

FUEL

Most vehicles in the US and Canada run on unleaded fuel, sold by the gallon in the US and by the liter in Canada. Fuel prices fluctuate, and are generally higher in Canada than in the US, although Canadian prices are still significantly lower than they are in Europe.

Service stations are usually self-serve (except in Oregon, where law prohibits self-serve), and many are closed at night. At full-serve stations, you remain in your car while an attendant fills up your gas tank and usually washes the windshield, making full-serve slightly more expensive. Be sure to keep your gas tank full when traveling through the mountains or in more remote areas.

ROADSIDE ASSISTANCE

Emergency road service is available 24 hours a day, 365 days a year, anywhere in the US or Canada. Members of the **American Automobile Association** and **Canadian** or **British Columbia Automobile Association** can call 1-800-222-4357. Be prepared to give your name, membership number and expiry date, phone number, vehicle type, license plate number, exact location, and tow destination.

DIRECTORY

REPORTS ON ROAD CONDITIONS

in British Columbia
www.drivebc.ca

in Oregon
Tel (800) 977-6368.
www.tripcheck.com

in Washington
Tel (206) 368-4499 or (800) 695-7623. **www**.wsdot.wa.gov

CAR RENTALS

Alamo
Tel (877) 222-9075.
www.alamo.com

Avis
Tel (800) 230-4898.
www.avis.com

Budget
Tel (800) 527-0700.
www.budget.com

Enterprise
Tel (800) 261-7331.
www.enterprise.com

Hertz
Tel (800) 654-3131.
www.hertz.com

National
Tel (877) 222-9058.
www.nationalcar.com

Thrifty
Tel (800) 847-4389.
www.thrifty.com

ROADSIDE ASSISTANCE

American Automobile Association
Tel (800) 222-4357.
www.aaa.com

British Columbia Automobile Association
Tel In Lower Mainland, BC: (604) 293-2222 or cell users: *222. In other areas of Canada & US: (800) 222-4357. **www**.bcaa.bc.ca

Canadian Automobile Association
Tel (800) 222-4357 (24-hr emergency service). **www**.caa.ca

A gas station, one of many on major highways and in towns and cities

General Index

Acknowledgments

Dorling Kindersley and International Book Productions would like to thank the following people whose contributions and assistance have made the preparation of this book possible.

Main Contributors
Stephen Brewer, a New York-based travel writer, is proud to have been born in Oregon, where he spends as much time as he can.

Constance Brissenden has explored beautiful British Columbia for more than 25 years. A freelance writer living in Vancouver, she has written 12 books on travel and history.

Anita Carmin, a Seattle native, specializes in travel writing. Her assignments have taken her from the ballrooms of Europe to a remote jungle lagoon on the Yucatan Peninsula.

Additional Contributors
Allison Austin, Cora Lee

Additional Picture Research
Rachel Barber, Rhiannon Furbear, Ellen Root

Additional Photography
William Carleton, Frank Jenkins, Helen Townsend, Lisa Voormeij, Peter Wilson

Cartography
VISU*TronX*, Ajax, Ontario, Canada

Proofreader
Garry Bowers

Indexer
Barbara Sale Schon

For Dorling Kindersley
Publishing Manager Helen Townsend

Art Editor Ian Midson

Cartographers Casper Morris

DTP Designers Jason Little, Conrad Van Dyk

Picture Researcher Claire Bowers

Proofreader Lucilla Watson

Additional Editorial and Design Assistance
Claire Baranowski, Uma Bhattacharya, Jo Cowen, Gadi Farfour, Lydia Halliday, Vinod Harish, Mohammad Hassan, Andrew Hempstead, Rose Hudson, Jacky Jackson, Jasneet Kaur, Priya Kukadia, Vincent Kurien, Maite Lantaron, Hayley Maher, Alison McGill, James McQuillen, Kate Molan, Catherine Palmi, Marianne Petrou, Pete Quinlan, Rada Radojicic, Marisa Renzullo, Sands Publishing Solutions, Azeem Siddiqui, Sadie Smith, Helen Townsend, Hugo Wilkinson, Karen Villabona, Lisa Voormeij.

Special Assistance
The publisher would also like to thank the following for their assistance: Amy Buranski, Experience Music Project; Cindy Bjorklund and Tim Manns, National Park Service; Perry Cooper, Seattle Center; Ardie Davis, Domaine Serene; Courtney Hallam; Angelika Harris; Leslie Lambert, Nathalie Levesque, and Natalie Stone, National Archives of Canada; Donald Olson; Jeffrey Richstone; Dana Selover; Tammy Walker, Walla Walla Chamber of Commerce.

Photography Permissions
The publisher would also like to thank the following for their assistance and kind permission to photograph at their establishments: American Advertising Museum; Capilano Suspension Bridge and Park; Catch the Wind Kite Shop; Christ Church Cathedral; End of Oregon Trail; Evergreen Aviation Museum; Experience Music Project; Fraser – Fort George Regional Museum; Governor Hotel; Granville Island Public Market; Helmcken House; Klondike Gold Rush National Historic Park; Multnomah County Library; Museum of Flight; National Historic Oregon Trail Interpretive Center; Oregon Maritime Center; Oregon Museum of Science and Industry; Pacific Place; Pioneer Place; Port Townsend Farmers Market; Portland Art Museum; Powell's City of Books; Seattle Aquarium; Seattle Children's Museum; Tillamook County Creamery Association; Victoria Bay Centre; Victoria Parliament Buildings.

Picture Credits

Key: a-above; b-below/bottom; c-centre; f-far; l-left; r-right; t-top.

Works of art have been reproduced with the permission of the following copyright holders: Steve Badanes, Will Martin, Donna Walter, and Ross Whitehead *Fremont Troll*, 1990 158bl; Jonathan Barofsky *Hammering Man* 120, 128tr; Richard Beyer *People Waiting for the Interurban* 158t; Neototems Children's Garden, an artwork by Gloria Bornstein © 2002 142t; Dale Chihuly *Benaroya Hall Silver Chandelier* 1998 129t; CITY OF VANCOUVER: *Percy Williams* by Ann McLaren 1996 213c; *Captain John Deighton (Gassy Jack)* by Vern Simpson 1970 201c, 204tl; *The Crab* by George Norris 1968 221t; *Girl in a Wetsuit* by Elek Imredy 1972 226t; *Gate to the Northwest Passage* by Alan Chung Hung 1980 220c; *Inukshuk* by Alvin Kanak 1906 26t, 196tl; *Chinatown Millennium Gate* by Joe Y. Wai Architect, Inc. 2002. 204b; EXPERIENCE MUSIC PROJECT: gold record belonging to Jimi Hendrix 141t; Georgia Gerber, *Rachel the market pig* 133bl; Themis Goddess of Justice Jack Harman 1982 208tl; *Allow Me* by J. Seward Johnson, Jr. Life-size, bronze sculpture. Image release courtesy of The Sculpture Foundation info@tsfmail.com 1981 57t; © Raymond Kaskey 1985 *Portlandia* 63c; Eric Metcalfe *Attic Project* 218b; Jack Mackie *Dance Steps on Broadway* 1981 153bl; PORTLAND ART MUSEUM: courtyard artwork 58tr; Seattle Public Utilities decorative manhole cover 118tl, 122tl; Alan Storey Broken Column 211c; *Logger's Culls*, c.1935, oil on canvas, Vancouver Art Gallery, VAG 39.1, photo: Trevor Mills 211t; Hai Ying Wu *The Fallen Firefighters' Memorial* 1998 122cl.

The publisher would like to thank the following individuals, companies, and picture libraries for permission to reproduce their photographs:

4CORNERS IMAGES: SIME/Hans-Peter Huber 11cra; ALAMY IMAGES: Pat Canova 122cl; Danita Delimont/Janis Miglavs 10cla; Mike Finn-Kelcey 212ca; ImageState/Randa Bishop 221tl; Dennis MacDonald 10c; Brad Mitchell 181tc; Bernard O'Kane *Perre's Ventaglio III* by Beverly Pepper, 1967 144tl. © ALASKA DIVISION OF TOURISM: 274b; © Joel Bennett 274cl; © Harold Wilson ADF & G 274cr; © White Pass & Yukon Railroad 275t; © Mark Wayne 275ca; 275cb; 275b. AMAZON.COM, INC: 41B. BC ARCHIVES: PDP00289 34; PDP04222 35c; PDP03716 38c. BC PLACE: 213tc. BELLINGHAM/WHATCOM COUNTY CONVENTION AND VISITORS BUREAU: Jim Poth 18t; Island Mariner Cruises 23t; Keith Lazelle 23ca; Island Mariner Cruises 95br. THE BOEING COMPANY: 41c. BROUSSARD COMMUNICATIONS: John Valls 297bl. PEARL BUCKNALL: photgraphersdirect.com 217br.

CHATEAU BENOIT: Ashley Smith 98b. CHATEAU STE. MICHELLE: 45b, 181b, 315t. THE CHILDREN'S MUSEUM, SEATTLE: 148tc; CITY OF VANCOUVER ARCHIVES: Stuart Thomson photo CVA 99-2507 27br; C. Bradbury photo SGN 1551 36c; Harry T. Devine photo LGN 1045 203b; W. Chapman photo CVA 677-441 221b. CN IMAX THEATRE AT CANADA PLACE: 202t. COLUMBIA HOSPITALITY: 136br; CONVENTION & VISITORS ASSOCIATION OF LANE COUNTY OREGON: front endpaper b, Sea Lion Caves 22t; Sally McAleer 28cl; Darrel Lindblad 27cr; Norm Coyer 29tl; 86; 96l; Sally McAleer 96b; Sandland Adventures 96c; Michael Chafron 99c; Dianne Dietrick Leis 101t; Sandland Adventures 316t; Lon Beale 317t; Sally McAleer 317b; Randy Siner 318cr; Dick Dietrich 318b. CORBIS: Christophe Boisvieux 11bc; © Museum of History and Industry/Wilse 123br; COURTESY OF COLORADO HISTORICAL SOCIETY: CHS.J1449,

William Henry Jackson 39c. CRYSTAL MOUNTAIN: Jeremy Martinson www.cascaonline.com 186t, 186b, 324b. CRYSTAL SPRINGS RHODODENDRON GARDEN: Barbara L. Darval 74tr.

DENVER PUBLIC LIBRARY, WESTERN HISTORY COLLECTION: X-31120 27bl, X-31012 27bc, Z-244 37c. DOMAINE SERENE: 98c. DORST, ADRIAN: 255c. DREAMSTIME.COM: Steve Rosset 194–5.

EXPERIENCE MUSIC PROJECT: 147bc, 147tc; Stanley Smith 146t; Lara Swimmer 146b.

FAIRMONT HOTEL VANCOUVER: 210tr. FERNIE ALPINE RESORT: 261t, 262c. FOUR SEASONS OLYMPIC HOTEL: Photos by Robb Gordon 119tr, 128b.

GETTY IMAGES: altrendo nature 10br; Stone/Chuck Pefley 11tl; GOVERNOR HOTEL: 48clb. GRANVILLE ISLAND: 214. GRANVILLE ISLAND BREWING: 216tl GRANVILLE ISLAND MUSEUMS: 219bl. GUNTER MARX – STOCK PHOTOS: 2-3, 22cl, 24c–25c, 25b, 31t, 32t, 33b, 175t, 188t, 222, 254c, 254b, 255b, 256c, 267c, 268t, 270b, 273b, 319b.

HELLS CANYON ADVENTURES: Ed Riche 115b, 115c; HEMISPHERES IMAGES: Camille Moirenc 244bl; Phillipe Renault 328cla.

IMES, CHUCK: Medford, OR 58tl.

JOHN DAY FOSSIL BEDS NATIONAL MONUMENT: Courtesy of National Park Service and NWIA 111c.

KAMLOOPS TOURISM: 317c. KOOCANUSA PUBLICATIONS: 261b.

COURTESY OF LEAVENWORTH CHAMBER OF COMMERCE: 33t. L'ECOLE NO. 41 WINERY: Brent Bergherm 192tr; LEONARDO MEDIA LTD.: 60br.

H.R. MACMILLAN SPACE CENTRE: 221cra; MEDICINE WHEEL WEBSITE DESIGN: 190tl. MICROSOFT: 159bc. MOUNT ST. HELENS NATIONAL VOLCANIC MONUMENT: 20b, 41t, 193cl. MSCUA, UNIVERSITY OF WASHINGTON LIBRARIES: UW4215 117c, UW6991 124br, A. Curtis 63021 37c, UW10921 39t. THE MUSEUM OF FLIGHT: 159cr.

NATIONAL ARCHIVES OF CANADA: E. Sandys C-011040 8; Thomas Mower Martin C-114455 9c; Theodore J. Richardson C-102057 26c–27c; William George Richardson Hind C-13978 26b; John B. Wilkinson C-150276 27t; Robert Petley C-103533 35b; Peter Rindisbacher C-001904 36cb; Alfred Jacob Miller C-000411 36t; Henry James Warre C-001621 37b, C-001623 38br; Charles William Jefferys C-70270 37t; Robert William Rutherford C-09870 38bl; Lady Frances Musgrave C-35986 40t; Edward Roper C-011035 195c, R9266-350 277c; 211br; Edward D. Panter-Downes C-009561 42; Washington F. Friend C-129778 43c; Capt. Francis G. Coleridge C-102427 323c. NATIONAL PARK SERVICE: 21t, 25ca, 108t, 188b, 188c, 189bl, 189br, 189c. NEW-SMALL AND STERLING STUDIO GLASS LTD: © David New-Small 215t; Photo: Erica Henderson 217c;

© David New-Small, photo: Kenji Nagai 218c. NORTHERN BC TOURISM ASSOCIATION: 269br. NORTHERN ROCKIES REGIONAL DISTRICT & TOWN OF FORT NELSON: Hank Schut 269tr.

ODYSSEY MARITIME DISCOVERY CENTER: 118cb; OREGON COAST AQUARIUM: 95bl; ORPHEUM THEATRE: Photo: David Blue 233t.

PIKE PLACE MARKET PRESERVATION & DEVELOPMENT AUTHORITY: 40br, 134bl; PHOTOLIBRARY: Jtb Photo Communications 209br.

ROYAL BRITISH COLUMBIA MUSEUM: 252b, 252cb, 252ca, 252t, 253c, 253b, 253t.

SEATTLE AQUARIUM: 138br, 138tr, 139bl, 139cr, 139tl; Bryce Mohan Photography 138cl, 139crb. SEATTLE CENTER: Photo by Carson Jones 142t; 145br. SEATTLE CHILDREN'S THEATRE: Chris Bennion 161b. SEATTLE'S CONVENTION AND VISITORS BUREAU: 123b, 138t. SOUTHWEST WASHINGTON CONVENTION & VISITORS BUREAU: 193c.

TERRA GALLERIA PHOTOGRAPHY: 189t; TILLICUM VILLAGE: 181cr; TIPS IMAGES: Andreas Pistolesi 214.

UNIVERSITY OF BRITISH COLUMBIA MUSEUM OF ANTHROPOLOGY: 230b, 230cb, 231b, 231c.

Logger's Culls, c.1935, oil on canvas, VANCOUVER ART GALLERY, VAG 39.1, photo: Trevor Mills 211t. VANCOUVER OPERA: Tim Matheson 233b. VIEWFINDERS: 30b, 31b, 66, 87b, 92r, 97b, 97t, 103b, 105b, 106b, 106c, 107b, 107t, 108b, 108c, 109b, 109c, 110tl, 111b, 114b, 114c, 115t, 174b, 174tr, 175b, 175t, 178tr, 179c, 179t, 183b, 191t, 192b, 320t.

WALLA WALLA CHAMBER OF COMMERCE: 30t, 191b. WOODLAND PARK ZOO: Rice Brewer 157cra; Dennis Conner 156tl/ca/cb, 157t; Agnes Overbaugh 157bc. WORLD PICTURES: 270t.

Elevation relief art modified by VISU*TronX* from: Mountain High Maps® Copyright © 1993 Digital Wisdom Inc.

Front Endpaper: DREAMSTIME.COM: Steve Rosset tl.

JACKET: Front - SUPERSTOCK: Carmel Studios; Back - CORBIS: All Canada Photos/Chris Cheadle bl; DORLING KINDERSLEY: Tim Draper clb, Bruce Forster cla, Scott Pitts tl. Spine - SUPERSTOCK: Carmel Studios t.

All other images © Dorling Kindersley
For further information see:
www.dkimages.com

SPECIAL EDITIONS OF DK TRAVEL GUIDES

DK Travel Guides can be purchased in bulk quantities at discounted prices for use in promotions or as premiums. We are also able to offer special editions and personalized jackets, corporate imprints, and excerpts from all of our books, tailored specifically to meet your own needs.

To find out more, please contact:
(in the United States) **SpecialSales@dk.com**
(in the UK) **TravelSpecialSales@uk.dk.com**
(in Canada) DK Special Sales at
general@tourmaline.ca
(in Australia)
business.development@pearson.com.au

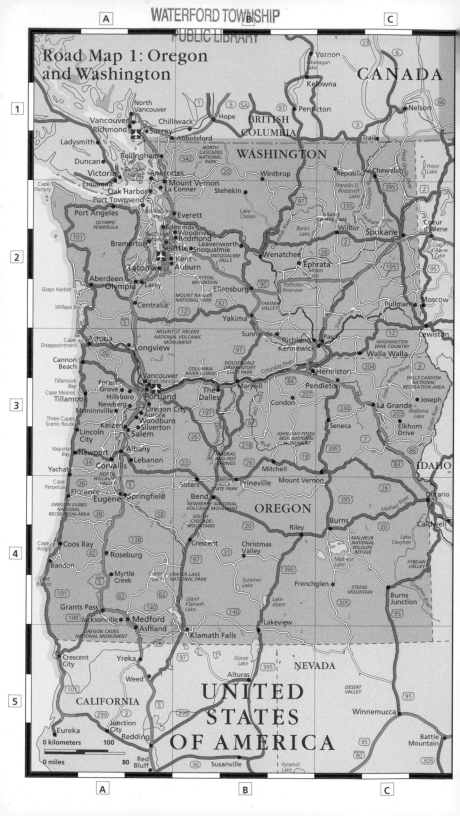